'*Intact* shocks and startles v
compassionate and challenging   ... ...y rigorous.
It left me questioning so many assumptions – what is natural,
or normal? Who should decide what's best for other people's bodies,
and how? I am now thinking afresh about how I live in my own
body, in a world where, as Clare Chambers argues, nobody's
body is ever allowed to be good enough, just as it is'
Timandra Harkness, author of *Big Data*

'Women's bodies . . . will always be a problem to solve. They will
never be acceptable. That's what makes Chambers's position in
Intact so appealingly radical: she argues that bodies do not
need to be modified. Your body is valuable just as it is,
because it is you' Sarah Ditum, *Unherd*

'As an even-handed, thoughtful overview of some of these very
difficult and now political issues, *Intact* stands alone . . . As a
way of working, it's exemplary – as well as in its content'
Richard Reeves

'A bold and brilliant book. Clare Chambers lucidly challenges the
unquestioned assumptions of our visual culture. Intact is unique in
its breadth, considering body modifications from make-up, to body
building, to surgery and tattooing. She does not question the
individual's right to change their body, but does question the
social positioning of such choices. For the naming of
"shametenance" alone this book should be a bestseller'
Heather Widdows, author of *Perfect Me*

'Clare Chambers's rich and spirited new book' Louise Perry, *The Times*

'In this cogently argued and insightful book, Clare Chambers calls for
us all to reject the pervasive messages that our bodies aren't good
enough and instead to accept and value the bodies we have. Intact
is an essential read for all educators, policy makers, researchers
and all those ready to call time on the beauty myths'
Professor Nichola Rumsey OBE, UWE Bristol

'A wonderfully rich book. It's not easy to combine complex, rigorous philosophy with clear and engaging prose. But Clare Chambers pulls this off brilliantly here' David Edmonds, author of *Wittgenstein's Poker*

'Essential reading for anyone with a body – whether you love your body, hate your body, or fall somewhere in between, Clare Chambers will reshape how you think about it. Timely and trenchant, *Intact* recovers a seemingly lost principle: bodies matter. The significance of the material body for social and political justice, especially for historically oppressed groups, finds a stunning defence in these pages. You, your body, however it is, is good just as it is: a simple, but powerful statement of the fundamental equality of all persons' Lori Watson, Professor of Philosophy, University of Washington at St Louis

'A pleasure to read because it's packed with new (to me) information and ideas and so absorbingly readable. A must-read for psychotherapists, doctors and everyone else who enjoys connecting ideas' Philippa Perry (Twitter)

'*Intact* is humane, generous, thought-provoking and sensible (great to see a mainstream philosopher discussing disability and deafness too)' Tom Shakespeare (Twitter)

ABOUT THE AUTHOR

Clare Chambers is Professor of Political Philosophy and a Fellow of Jesus College, University of Cambridge. The author of the acclaimed *Against Marriage*, she specializes in feminism, bioethics, contemporary liberalism and theories of social justice.

CLARE CHAMBERS

Intact

A Defence of the Unmodified Body

PENGUIN BOOKS

PENGUIN BOOKS

UK | USA | Canada | Ireland | Australia
India | New Zealand | South Africa

Penguin Books is part of the Penguin Random House group of companies
whose addresses can be found at global.penguinrandomhouse.com

First published by Allen Lane 2022
Published in Penguin Books 2023
001

Grateful acknowledgement is given for permission to use the following images:
p. 65, copyright © British Natural Bodybuilding Federation; p. 75, courtesy of Madame
Gandhi; p. 82, courtesy of GREEN BEAUTY on Youtube; p. 140, copyright © Alamy;
p. 220, courtesy of Gemma Cockrell/Abi Moore photography; p. 240,
courtesy of Caroline Partridge and Face Equality International.

Typeset by Jouve (UK), Milton Keynes
Printed and bound in Great Britain by Clays Ltd, Elcograf S.p.A.

The authorized representative in the EEA is Penguin Random House Ireland,
Morrison Chambers, 32 Nassau Street, Dublin D02 YH68

A CIP catalogue record for this book is available from the British Library

ISBN: 978-0-141-99250-1

www.greenpenguin.co.uk

Contents

Introduction

Your Body is Never Good Enough

'I used to be very talkative when I was a little kid, and now I'm just shy. I'm anti-social.'

Nadia, a fourteen-year-old American girl, sits on a sofa in her home. She is articulate and calm as she explains to a CNN reporter that she has been bullied about her appearance since she was in first grade.[1] Watching her on screen it is difficult to see what's wrong with her. Nadia looks like a perfectly normal, attractive, teenage girl. Then she explains. When Nadia was seven years old a girl told her that she had the largest ears the girl had ever seen.

'I was speechless,' Nadia says. 'I didn't think about it until she said that.'

Nadia slightly tilts her head. Now we can see the problem.

Well, we can see her ears. And we've been told what the problem is. It's her ears. Her ears are too big. And people aren't afraid to tell her so.

Your body is never good enough.

Sometimes you know this because you're told so. 'You need to lose weight,' says your mother, your doctor, a public health campaign. 'Is your body beach ready?' a billboard demands. The question is rhetorical: the only answer it will accept is 'no'.

Sometimes you know this by osmosis. Streamed selfies seep into your subconscious. Appearance anxiety hangs in the air. Everyone is judging, critiquing, shaming. It doesn't seem to matter if the target is another body or your own; the process is the same. Every body is wrong; no body feels right.

Sometimes you receive a compliment. 'I like your hair!' 'Have you lost weight?' 'Nice ass!' It's good to be appreciated – but are these compliments all they seem to be? Why do they leave you feeling worse? Why don't they dispel the feeling that *something about you needs to change*?

Distress about our bodies has reached epidemic levels, exacerbated by social media and selfie culture. Our bodies are always under surveillance, must always be camera-ready – only now the camera *always* lies. No image is left unfiltered; no photo is left unshopped; the ultimate act of courage is to post with no make-up.

Sometimes we change the image. Sometimes we change the body itself. Body modifications once thought extreme are now mainstream: cosmetic surgery reaches many people and sculpts almost every body part. Members of the British Association of Aesthetic Plastic Surgeons (BAAPS) performed 28,347 surgical procedures in 2018, including a 'sharp rise' in liposuction for both women and men. According to BAAPS, that rise was driven by 'the popularity of TV shows such as *Love Island*' and 'the fashion for women's athleisure clothing'.[2]

Body modifications once thought counter-cultural are now simply cultural: piercings and tattoos are no longer just for goths, punks and sailors. 'Last week my MOM got an actual TATTOO,' tweeted @JoMoore in 2019. 'I'm still in shock. Important deets – 1. She's been drunk twice, ever 2. She thinks "crap" is quite a bad swear word 3. She got the tattoo on a Women's Institute coach trip to Chester 4. It's of a ball of wool and knitting needles.'[3] The tweet has been liked 32,000 times.

Even body modifications once thought outlandish no longer cause the bat of a Westernized eyelid: they seem unremarkable, even inevitable. There is a brisk market in injecting Botulinum toxin, an actual poison, into the face. Or you could have a so-called 'Vampire Facial', which also involves injecting things into your face – this time it's platelets extracted from your own blood.

Surgeries that were unheard of relatively recently are now familiar: labiaplasty, buttock enlargements. In the late twentieth century you wanted small buttocks and no one would mention your labia; in the early twenty-first century you want large buttocks and small labia, and everybody's talking.

Many women will try any diet, exercise, or device that promises to help them 'get their body back' after pregnancy. I googled 'get your body back' and found over 5 billion results. The first was a personal trainer offering thirteen ways to get your body back into shape after giving birth.[4] Here they are:

1. Cut out sugar.
2. Drink lots of water with fresh lemon.
3. Use a smaller plate.
4. Slow down.

Not by sitting on the sofa and having a rest with your baby, you understand, but during mealtimes. 'Eat with chopsticks or scale down the size of your utensils. Use a small fork and a teaspoon, for example.'

5. No white bread, rice, flour, or pasta.
6. Eat soup for dinner . . . for at least three nights in a row.

With a teaspoon, presumably, although the chopsticks would make it even slower.

7. Avoid red meat.
8. Eat the rainbow.

Every plate should resemble a Pride flag.

9. Prepare for eating carrots, celery, peppers, etc. in advance.

We're not talking mental preparation here: you don't have to psych yourself up to crudités. We're talking chopping and bagging.

10. Eat a cup of Cheerios or Chex if you need a snack.

Surprising, this one. It's something to do with gluten.

11. Do NOT sit and eat while watching TV.
12. Get off your butt, get moving and CHALLENGE yourself to break a serious sweat at least 5 days a week for an hour.

And then the final one – and here the irony is almost overpowering:

13. BREATHE. Relax and let go.

It's not just personal trainers offering advice, either: the third result for 'get your body back' was the mainstream medical advice website

WebMD. 'Dedication and patience are key to losing postpartum baby weight and looking like your pre-baby self again,' it instructs.[5]

Another first-page result is the website of personal trainer Sia Cooper, who states: 'My sole mission is to shape and create fit mommies by providing workouts, recipes, and fitness tips.'[6] Sia is scathing about failure. 'I constantly get asked how I snapped back into shape within two weeks after giving birth to my second baby,' she writes.

> For starters, it was not easy by ANY means. I credit staying active throughout my entire pregnancy for allowing me to bounce back so easily. People can say that it's genes, age, how many babies I've had, or whatever, but to me that is all complete bullshit. Hard work did the trick and the thing about it is that many women are not willing to put in the time and effort that it takes and then there are some that can't due to health reasons, high risk pregnancy, etc. However, if you are physically able to do it, **why not?**

Why not indeed – or, alternatively, why?

In the quest to 'get your body back', which body should you be aiming for? Where along the journey to old age should your body be suspended? Which body should be reclaimed? The very idea of *getting your body back* suggests that there was one moment when you had the body that was really, authentically, naturally *yours*. On this understanding our real bodies are not the saggy, stretchy, lumpy, wrinkly ones that, somehow, we find ourselves in. When women try to get their bodies back they are usually aiming for the post-pubescent, pre-pregnancy body, a body that exists for perhaps ten or twenty years of the average woman's eighty-three years of life. Somehow, that minority body becomes not just the *ideal* body but the *authentic* body: the one that most accurately characterizes who you really are, inside.

In this narrative, the body must be constantly modified to remain true to itself. But why on earth should that particular body, the one that has done so much less than you have, be the 'real' you?

This book reclaims the value of the unmodified body. We must insist: our bodies are good enough just as they are.

My argument throughout is that the unmodified body is a political concept. By this I mean that the unmodified body is not only something that exists in the world as a real, material object. It is also an idea that is constructed by political processes: relations of choice and power, structures of hierarchy and equality, norms of behaviour and understanding. What the body *is*, and what modification *means*, are matters of political significance.

This is not to say that there is no such thing as biology, or that the body has no reality of its own. The body is a real thing, one that opens possibilities and imposes constraints. We do things through our bodies, and we do things to our bodies. We live in and with them. Fundamentally, we *are* them. Asserting the significance of our bodies is central to my argument.

But the body is also the site of political meaning. It's the surface on which we're expected to inscribe our identities. Its appearance gives or denies access to various positions of privilege, membership of social groups, indicators of esteem. What we look like, who we are, and how we should be treated are closely related. And the dominant message of many contemporary cultures, especially Westernized, capitalist cultures, is: *your body is not good enough. It needs to be changed so that it truly represents who you are, and so that it meets standards of who you should be.*

Against the pressure to modify, I defend the unmodified body as a political principle. It is *politically significant* to resist pressures to change our bodies.

Each of us has to operate within the norms and demands of our society. In the face of constant social pressure, we must repeatedly choose whether to comply or resist. If no one modified their bodies then the norm of modification would collapse. Body modification is a social practice, one that exists as the result of many individual acts of compliance. Individual acts of resistance matter. Refusing to modify our bodies can be an act of rebellion, an assertion of autonomy.

But this is not a self-help book. Individual acts of resistance are not enough to overcome overwhelming social norms, bolstered by commercial interests and entrenched inequalities. The costs of resistance are distributed unequally, and not everyone is able to bear them. Body modification can be a coping strategy, a way of dealing with the fact that your body does not meet the standards set for it. Sometimes people modify their bodies, whether by dieting, make-up, or surgery, so they don't have to think about them any more. Modification can be a route to enhancement, but it can also be a route to invisibility. We cannot always expect individuals to challenge or change the structures that oppress them.

What we ultimately need is collective action to disrupt the social norms and structures that denigrate our bodies. There are many sorts of collective action: grassroots activism, consciousness-raising, public campaigns, commercial initiatives, legal measures. I'll discuss some of these measures throughout the book. But the first step for collective action is to understand the problem: to look at things a different way. This book is part of that process.

The most obvious objection to my argument will be that body modification is a matter of individual choice. In one sense, I agree. What we do with our bodies should generally be up to us. But I strongly resist the idea that what we do to our bodies is characteristically the result of our choices. Or rather, I'll show how the choices we make about our bodies are inevitably shaped by our social context, and the norms we find there. Our choices must react to the social structures we navigate. These are structures of social power. They are political.

My argument ultimately is not that individuals have a *duty* to resist modification, or that we do anything morally wrong if we decide to modify our bodies. My argument is much more modest, yet still radical. It is that the unmodified body, understood in the political sense that I lay out throughout the book, should be *presumed to have value*.

The unmodified body is not an ultimate goal. It is not a mark of perfection. It is not a standard to be measured against, not a purity to be preserved, not a badge to be earned. Whether you are permitted to remain unmodified, and the stakes of doing so, depends on where your body stands in various hierarchies: your sex and gender, your class and profession, your race and skin colour, your age and weight, your difference and disability. Prizes for remaining unmodified would be prizes for the privileged.

Instead, the unmodified body is a premise. It is a foundation. The unmodified body should be defended as a default. It does not have overriding value. Individual bodies should not be judged for their levels of non-modification. But the *principle* of the unmodified body does have value, and we are in a position where that value needs defending.

The second obvious objection to my claim that we should value the unmodified body is that some bodies *need* changing. Some bodies, this objection says, are deficient in some way. They are left unhealthy by poor diet or inadequate exercise. They suffer from disease or disability. They fail to meet standards of normal functioning. In these cases, so the objection goes, body modification is to be recommended: it is an entitlement, or even a duty.

In response to this challenge, I'll show how even notions of health and disability are strongly shaped by politics: by social norms, by cultural context, by structures of power and oppression. It's true that some bodies – all bodies, in fact – have limitations, impose constraints, fail to flourish. It makes sense to pursue modifications that might make our bodies work better for us. But the pressures to modify wildly outweigh the potential for success. The standards imposed on our bodies cannot be met because inadequacy is built in. Asserting the value of the unmodified body is a necessary corrective. The real culprit is not the act of body modification itself, but the virtually overwhelming *pressure to* modify.

The unmodified body must be understood as something *real* and something *valuable*. In some ways, this is an intuitive position. Leaving our bodies as they are, being content with them as they are, even being grateful for them and positive about them – all these dispositions seem attractive and virtuous. We have many ways of expressing this idea that we should value our unmodified bodies. We should treat our bodies as temples. We should be as nature made us. We should embrace body positivity.

This intuition will resonate more with some people than with others. Some people won't see the appeal: they see their body as a blank canvas, as something to be worked on, shaped and sculpted to their own desires. And it is certainly true that not all modifications are suspect. Body modification can be a sort of creativity, a rebellion, an expression of individuality. Body modification can also be pursued in search of other goods: health, wealth, happiness. It can be an act of virtue: of caring for ourselves, of making an effort. And it can simply be an expression of freedom. In general, we should allow people to make their own choices about things that primarily affect them – like their bodies – even while we try to change the oppressive political conditions that shape those choices.

But a large amount of modification is not unfettered creativity, nor is it health- and happiness-affirming. It is undertaken from shame, or to fit in, or to escape discrimination. It is never-ending, can never be complete, will never allow satisfaction. It requires conformity, docility, self-harm. And we do not choose it in a vacuum. We choose it because it makes sense in our cultural context. We are encouraged to do it to feel good, required to do it to fit in; subtly and not-so-subtly the conditions that shape our choices are laid down by others.

How do we tell the difference? What sorts of body modification are to be celebrated and which are to be criticized? I answer these questions by developing an account that can explain and preserve the value of leaving our bodies just as they are, without fetishizing some fictional pure body that never existed.

Defending the unmodified body is a matter of public health and a matter of equality. The culture of body modification has reached a point where it threatens our health, both physical and mental. Many of the modification practices that have become standard are detrimental to physical health, bringing risks and side-effects. Anxiety about appearance is ubiquitous and has devastating consequences for public health. Asserting the value of the unmodified body is one way to resist.

The culture of body modification also has serious implications for equality. Increasingly, everyone is affected by body-image anxiety, but pressures to modify impact unequally on various social groups. Women and girls, transgender people, adolescents, sexual minority groups, and people with larger or heavier bodies are more vulnerable to poor body image than are people not in these groups, and body image has a more nuanced but unequal impact on people depending on their racial identity and whether they have a disability or visible difference.[7] Some people are subjected to greater scrutiny and judgement of their appearance than others.

Moreover, a key part of many modification norms is their connection to shame. On the one hand all of us face pressures to modify, but, on the other hand, modification is individualized. We don't view our bodies as being just like everyone else's. We're trained to view them as uniquely deficient, specifically shameful. In this way, a norm that affects nearly everyone creates an experience of inequality.

The content of appearance norms is discriminatory, too. The ideal body is not normatively neutral. It plugs into hierarchies of race, sex, disability, class, age, gender and sexuality. It reinforces structures of discrimination. Throughout the book I'll show the complex interactions between norms of modification and hierarchical social structures.

The very idea that some sorts of bodies *need* to be changed is a denial of basic equal moral worth of the people themselves. If you need to change to be socially acceptable then you are deficient as you are. That position is at odds with awarding equal status to everyone. Body modification very often invokes identity in a way that gets to the core of individuals' worth and status, and its requirements and standards are not egalitarian.

My argument is *not* that being equal means being unmodified. My argument is that equality requires having equal access to the possibility of an unmodified body. This possibility, in turn, depends on the body one starts with, and on the socio-economic implications of leaving it that way.

I've deliberately chosen the rather unfamiliar idea of the unmodified body to make clear that what I'm defending is a complex political concept, not a simple material thing. If we try to define the idea literally, we quickly become tangled in contradiction, vagueness and counterintuitive implications. Everything we do, or don't do, has an effect on our bodies. What we eat, how active we are, how much time we spend in the sun – all these everyday choices shape our bodies. Your body will be subtly different if you read this book rather than going for a run. Does that mean that reading a book is body modification? I certainly don't want to discourage reading!

Consider food. Everyone has to eat to stay alive, and what we eat can have a huge impact on our bodies. So, if eating is a practice of body modification, then the unmodified body is both impossible and undesirable.

It might be tempting to say that eating is a body modification practice only if the *intention* is to create a certain body shape and size.

Sometimes, we eat purely for sustenance or taste, regardless of the effect that the food will have on our appearance. Other times, we attempt to manipulate our bodies by using food and eating practices that we hope will make us slimmer, fatter, or more muscled. I discuss the use of food to build muscle in the next chapter. The practice of eating to lose weight is so familiar that it has its own name – dieting – and sustains a vast global industry. Using food deliberately to create a larger body occurs in the feederism community, a group united by a sexual preference for bodies that are already large or are in the process of becoming larger.[8] Some people in this community, known as 'fat admirers', find large bodies attractive and don't care how they got that way; they may pair up with people who are large by accident or genetics. Others, known as 'feeders', get their kicks from encouraging others to put on weight. They seek out partnerships with 'feedees', people who find it appealing or sexually exciting to grow larger. For feeders and feedees, for dieters and bodybuilders, food clearly becomes a body modification practice.

Other cases are not so simple. We cannot always tell whether eating is an intentional act of body modification because most eating is explained by a complex mix of factors, including cost, culture, social expectations, circumstance, convenience, taste, habit, emotions, ceremony, energy levels, duty, shame, and greed. Clearly the principle of the unmodified body cannot demand an end to eating; but nor can it ignore the complex interaction between food and the socially constructed permanent inadequacy of the body. Body modification and the unmodified body cannot be unambiguously defined at the outset: they are ideas that will reveal themselves as we go.

Perplexing as it is, if we jettison the idea of the unmodified body we lose the ability to critique the normalization of modification. We need to engage with the philosophical problem – what *is* the unmodified body? – so that we can tackle the political one – asserting the *value* of the unmodified body. How else can we assert that we are, at least sometimes, good enough *just as we are*?

The principle of the unmodified body is based on equality between persons. It respects diversity and freedom. One of the ways we create and maintain oppressive inequality is by devaluing the unmodified body. When we say that some bodies are deficient and must be changed to meet the standard set by the others, we are saying that some bodies, and the people whose bodies they are, are inferior to others.

Instead, I say: *your body is good enough just as it is* because your body is *you*, and it is *yours*, and *you* have an inalienable value that all others must recognize and respect. Treating people equally means asserting the political principle of the value of the unmodified body.

REASONS TO MODIFY

The principle of the unmodified body implies that modification practices are suspect. But other ideals push us in a different direction.

Three values often motivate body modification. These are health and hygiene, appearance, and identity. Each of these values has its own logic of modification, its own way of countering the claim that *your body is good enough just as it is*. These values express the logic *your body can be better*. Sometimes they go so far as to assert *your body should be better*.

1. Health and hygiene

> *Among the other virtues, we may also give Cleanliness a place; since it naturally renders us agreeable to others, and is no inconsiderable source of love and affection. No one will deny, that a negligence in this particular is a fault.*
>
> David Hume, *An Enquiry Concerning the Principles of Morals* (1777)[9]

Let's take health to mean something broad and intuitive, concerning the body's survival and function. Securing health requires doing many things to the body: nourishing it with food and drink, exercising it, treating it when it is sick, cleaning it and maintaining good standards of hygiene. These things are body modification practices in the literal sense because they change the body, often quite considerably; certainly, the body would be different if they were not done. But it would be highly counter-intuitive to think that respecting equality requires refraining from modifications that aim at health, such as maintenance, hygiene and medical treatments.

Still, these concepts hide some complexity. Consider *maintenance*. It seems a simple enough concept: it's what you need to do just to keep things going roughly as they are, to meet basic standards of acceptable functioning. But what maintenance means varies from body to body.

How often do you need to wash your hair? If you are white or Asian with straight hair, you will most probably feel the need to wash your hair several times a week, possibly even every day. Straight hair tends towards greasiness. If you are Black with Afro hair, you will probably wash your hair much less often – every two weeks is ideal, according to some natural hair experts.[10] Afro hair tends towards dryness.

How long does it take to style your hair? According to one survey, the average American woman spends six full days per year on her hair.[11] But this statistic hides a lot of variation, and not all of it is basic maintenance. If you have short hair you may be fine doing no styling at all. What about longer hair? If you have straight or wavy hair you may have the option of doing nothing more than brushing it, and you can probably go to bed with no special preparation. If you have Afro hair you will probably prepare your hair before bed by twisting it, tying it, or wrapping it in a silk scarf, and you will have to allocate more time to maintenance-level styling.[12] 'While white women can quite reasonably rock the tousled, just-got-out-of-bed, shabby chic effect, the hair that grows from my head does not accommodate such a laissez-faire approach to grooming,' writes natural hair advocate Emma Dabiri. 'Can you imagine running a brush through your hair and done? As I write this, I'm feverishly making impossible calculations about how I'm going to get my hair done tonight, in preparation for tomorrow morning.'[13]

It's not just hair that requires different levels of maintenance from person to person. Disability and illness produce bodies with different basic needs. If you have cystic fibrosis, you will probably have to engage in daily physiotherapy to clear your airways, whether alone, with assistive equipment, or with another person. This maintenance requirement is vital but also demanding: the Cystic Fibrosis Trust advises that most people with the condition need two sessions of airway clearance of between 10 and 45 minutes each day.[14] If you have diabetes, your daily routine will involve regular blood-sugar checks, medication, monitoring your food intake, and eating regardless of appetite. This is an arduous and stressful regime: one website for people with diabetes and their families is called Diabetes Daily Grind.[15]

So, maintenance varies from body to body. But it also varies in time and place. What counts as maintenance in the beauty context has become ever more demanding. Practices that were once seen as exceptional are now seen as routine. Consider body hair. The norm now is that women should remove hair not only from their legs, face and armpits but also from their arms and pubic area. As philosopher of beauty Heather Widdows puts it:

> it is now the case that leg hair and underarm hair are regarded as unacceptable in nearly all contexts. This is a very clear change over a short period of time. Only a generation ago, it was far more acceptable to leave visible leg and underarm hair; indeed underarm hair in some contexts was regarded as a sign of sexual liberation and sexiness. Younger women are increasingly removing at least some pubic hair, and nearly complete removal is becoming more common and associated with cleanliness and respect for sexual partners.[16]

This trend has developed in the last twenty years, as can be seen in an episode of the TV series *Sex and the City* from the year 2000. Lead character Carrie Bradshaw, a New York fashion icon and sex journalist, goes to get a bikini wax while in Los Angeles. She is expecting just to have the outer edges of her pubic hair removed. Instead, the beauty therapist does something Carrie has never heard of: a Brazilian wax, or complete pubic hair removal. 'I got mugged!' Carrie tells her friends over brunch. 'She took everything I got! . . . I feel like one of those freaking hairless dogs.' Only Samantha, the character distinguished by her adventurous sexual promiscuity, has ever heard of the procedure.[17] The episode was widely credited with introducing the Brazilian wax to the viewing public.[18] Nowadays complete pubic hair removal is a mainstream practice for women under thirty-five.[19] It's routine maintenance for this millennium.

On the one hand, increasing standards of bodily maintenance are to be celebrated. Who would want to return to the Tudor era, when linen underwear substituted for showers,[20] or the Victorian era, when bath-water was shared by the whole family? (The phrase 'don't throw the baby out with the bathwater' refers to the practice of a family bathing in the same water, one after another, starting with the most senior members and ending with the baby.) On the other hand, decreasing standards of appearance are preferable. The modern woman's licence to sling on jeans and a T-shirt is surely preferable to previous centuries' requirements of a corset and elaborate layers of petticoats and skirts.[21] But simpler dress is paid for with closer scrutiny of the body underneath.

We can see that maintenance and hygiene are not clear-cut categories. At the same time, there is no plausible shared intuition that there is anything valuable about leaving the body unmodified in these respects. When I say *your body is good enough just as it is* I am not aiming to excuse being unwashed or to condemn medical treatment. So, there is a puzzle. In Part Two I'll address it directly. I'll show that even the concept of health often conceals political and ethical judgements, so that a demand to modify for health or hygiene often conceals a political judgement about status and hierarchy. Moreover, there is real doubt that pressures to modify for health reasons are effective. Many public health campaigns end up having no effect, or even making things worse. For example, there is no evidence that campaigns that aim to reduce obesity levels succeed, and there *is* evidence that some well-intentioned measures, such as including calorie information on restaurant menus, encourage eating disorders such as anorexia and bulimia.[22]

At the same time, there is a materiality to the body, facts about how it works, what it can do and how it feels that make a genuine difference. Part of my argument is that pressures to modify lead us to both over- and under-emphasize our bodies. We over-emphasize how they appear from the outside – how they look, how they compare, where they rank – and we under-emphasize how they feel from the inside, what it is to live *in* and *through* and *as* our bodies.

2. Appearance

*Since women are taught to see themselves from the outside as
candidates for men, they become prey to the huge fashion and
diet industries that first set up the ideal images and then exhort
women to meet them. The message is loud and clear – the
woman's body is not her own. The woman's body is not satis-
factory as it is.*

Susie Orbach, *Fat Is A Feminist Issue* (1978)[23]

We care about how our bodies look. This concern for our body's
appearance may be cross-cultural and timeless, although the form it
takes is not. What is considered beautiful varies across time and place,
as does the importance of beauty. Typically, how important it is for a
person to be beautiful also depends on other social facts about them:
their sex, race, class and age.

Within current beauty norms in capitalist societies, the logic of the
value of appearance pushes us *towards* body modification, not away
from it. A huge amount of body modification is motivated by the
desire to look better: to comply with whichever appearance norms
motivate us or dominate our social circle.

There are many classic feminist works that analyse and critique the
demand that women be beautiful. Notable feminist texts on beauty
over the last fifty years or so include, by date of first publication, Germaine Greer's *The Female Eunuch* (1970), Andrea Dworkin's *Woman
Hating* (1974), Susie Orbach's *Fat Is A Feminist Issue* (1978), Naomi
Wolf's *The Beauty Myth* (1990), Sandra Lee Bartky's *Femininity and
Domination* (1990), Iris Marion Young's *On Female Body Experience* (1990), Susan Bordo's *Unbearable Weight* (1993) and Heather
Widdows's *Perfect Me* (2018). This is by no means an exhaustive list.

Without wishing to give a false sense of homogeneity, what feminist
work like this has shown is that beauty norms are a key part of the
patriarchal system. The demand that women be beautiful plays a crucial and significant role in maintaining gender inequality.

The demands of beauty keep women and girls down in a surprisingly diverse range of ways. Perhaps the most obvious is that a cultural
expectation that women and girls focus on beautifying themselves

means that they must divert their energy, attention and resources away from other pursuits that might better serve their interests or increase their power, such as becoming fit, strong, skilled, highly qualified, career-driven, or politically active.

The culturally demanded focus on beauty further disadvantages women because they are expected to work to be beautiful but are not generally rewarded for that work. While some women gain success and esteem from their looks, it is also common for a woman's beauty to be used against her – she is deemed stupid, an airhead, a dumb blonde, asking for it – and for her beauty work to be dismissed as evidence of her incompetence, irrationality, unseriousness and lack of commitment to loftier pursuits.

Perhaps the most significant concept in feminist critical analysis of beauty and patriarchy is *objectification*. This term denotes the ways that women are made into objects: for display, for use by men, for judgement, for the satisfaction of others. Beauty is not the only mechanism for objectification. Sexual objectification practices such as pornography and prostitution, property objectification practices such as arranged marriage and slavery, and service objectification practices such as treating women as facilitators of others' happiness have all been key sites of feminist critique. Beauty is part of a generalized system by which women and girls are treated more as objects than as full human agents with desires and projects of their own.

At another level of critique, feminists have shown how beauty demands serve to divide and separate women, creating hierarchies between women deemed beautiful, plain, or ugly, and inciting competitiveness or resentment. Beauty thus acts as a way of disrupting solidarity between women, which might develop into consciousness-raising and resistance. It keeps women focused on looking attractive to others, including (but not only) men, and provides a way of disempowering women as they age – a process that might otherwise increase their power and status. And, as Black feminists such as Patricia Hill Collins, Audre Lorde and Toni Morrison have shown, beauty standards are racialized in ways that also maintain white supremacy.[24] In order to be beautiful, women must have facial features, hair and skin tone that reflect whiteness, making beauty norms a powerful part of the intersection of sexism and racism.

Next, feminists have argued that beauty norms damage women's psychological well-being. Beauty is not inevitably pernicious, but what is so harmful is the combination of a universal ideal with an unattainable standard. The current beauty norm in most parts of the world is that all women should try to be beautiful, but no woman is ever beautiful enough. This combination makes shame and guilt a permanent feminine condition, something I explore in more detail in Chapter 2.

Body image anxiety has now reached epidemic proportions and is increasingly affecting men, too. 'There has been interest in appearance since records began,' write psychologists Nichola Rumsey and Diana Harcourt, 'but never have "looks" demanded as much attention, particularly in resource-rich countries, as now.'[25] They report that:

> in a recent survey of 77,000 adults . . . only 16% of women and 27% of men reported liking what they see when they look in the mirror, whilst 46% of women and 62% of men reported feeling ashamed of how they look. More than two-thirds of women (70%) and almost half of men (41%) felt pressure from the media to have a perfect body.[26]

Other researchers agree. A recent survey by Girlguiding UK found that the top three pressures faced online by British girls aged eleven to sixteen were 'to look pretty all the time', 'to get more likes', and 'to have a picture-perfect life'.[27] The causes of this widespread distress are multiple, but there is a general agreement that social media and the visual culture it feeds plays a huge part.

Intact draws on and repeats many of the classic feminist critiques of beauty. They are the giants on whose shoulders I stand. What I hope to add is breadth: a widening beyond beauty and appearance norms to the more generalized pressure to modify our bodies in pursuit of acceptability. The imperative that all women must be beautiful, and the impact this has on the lives and well-being of women and girls, is stronger than ever. Feminine beauty norms remain an urgent political issue in their own right, but they operate within a broader context that demands constant body modification. All women *have* to be beautiful. All people *have* to look good. And modification is prescribed not just for beauty but for identity and health, making the task of asserting the political principle of the unmodified body much more complex.

It's not an effective feminist strategy simply to urge women and girls to reject beauty ideals. That project is intensely demanding for those who undertake it, making it unrealistic for virtually everyone. Feminists who practised this mode of resistance have always been vilified for doing so, and the smartphone and social media era has intensified the focus on sharing and ranking the visual. Moreover, even if someone does manage to reject beauty ideals, the more generalized pressure to modify is left intact. So, while the feminist critique of beauty norms remains as urgent as ever, we must widen our lens.

3. Identity

The Mirror Of Erised . . . struck me as a really heart-breaking image for my own condition. If I looked in the magical mirror, and saw myself exactly as I most long to be, what would I see? It was a key moment for me when I first read that passage in The Philosopher's Stone, *and realised more clearly than I ever had before that my own answer to that question was, unavoidably, 'Myself as a woman, of course.'*

Sophie-Grace Chappell,
open letter to JK Rowling (2020)[28]

Identity, in the sense I mean it, is more about what we *represent* than who we are. Who we are, at base, persists regardless of any modification: you are you, and you still will be no matter how your body changes. There is simply no one else you could be. Modification for identity is not fundamentally about changing *you*, but rather about changing who or what you *represent*: yourself 'as a' what? What is your image, your membership, your belonging?

As the quote from philosopher Sophie-Grace Chappell above shows, a significant part of our identity is about how we *look*. Chappell, a trans woman, found key insight into her own gender identity before her transition when visualizing herself in the mirror: gazing on her image from the outside, as she hoped to be seen by others. Womanhood as identity, on this analysis, is a matter of appearance: how others see and relate to you. It is something that is reflected back at oneself.

Our identities are only partially within our control. A great deal about them is determined externally, by the identities of our parents and peers, by the standards and categories of our societies, by our encounters and opportunities. Our parents typically raise us to have a certain identity: to hold certain values, to participate in certain practices, to belong here rather than there, to represent this rather than that. Most of what they do to shape our identity is not body modification, but some of it is: how they style our hair, whether they modify our genitals, put us in braces or give us cosmetic surgery, how they raise us to relate to food and exercise.

Other aspects of our identities are imposed on us from outside our families. You are placed within a category or a community according to the standards of your society. What your race is, for example, depends not (only) on your genetic heritage but on the categories of race that exist in your society and the way your body fits, or appears to fit, within them. To take another example, a religious identity is not entirely within your control: whether you count as a member of any given religion depends on the standards set by that religion, and whether its members recognize you as one of their own. Identity claims are typically contested and may be very controversial: whether you truly count as a member of some group may be a matter of dispute between you and them, and they may disagree among themselves.

So, identity is a social category, and as such it is not entirely within our control. However, we can attempt to shape our own identities, and a lot of what we do on a daily basis is oriented towards expressing or affirming our identity. We seek to express our identity as a way of showing that we have control over it. We seek affirmation of our identity from others as a way of asserting our right to exist. That we feel our right to exist is under threat is, of course, part of the problem. Its origins are multiple, and they include attacks on job security, on welfare, on health care, on rights of citizenship and migration, as well as attacks on the body-as-identity.

One way we assert ourselves is with body modification. We change the way we look, the way we are embodied, to fit more closely with the identity we wish to represent, or feel we must represent, or predict will offer us the best protection. As sociologist Debra Gimlin puts it, 'individuals negotiate the relationship between body and self in the context of a social structure and culture that simultaneously provide resources for the creation of identities and place limits on those identities.'[29] Social norms give us scope to be creative and self-determining, but there are also rules to follow. 'Women value hair that coincides with identity,' Gimlin concludes from her observations in a hair salon in Long Island. 'If their hairstyle misidentifies their age, income, occupation, or education, they feel unsettled and self-conscious.'[30]

Some identities are very amenable to being achieved through body modification since they are significantly based on embodiment or appearance. Femininity (as opposed to femaleness or womanhood) may be one example, although successfully inhabiting a feminine identity requires significant behavioural compliance as well. Some identities require body modification as a minor yet important part, for example circumcision in Judaism and Islam. Other identities are based only superficially on our bodies and so body modification is irrelevant to achieving them or is only instrumentally useful. But almost all identities require some conformity to norms of appearance.

A related aspect of identity is less about group membership and more about personal attributes. We might identify as someone who is put together, capable, popular, relaxed, bohemian, sexy, or quirky. These identity characteristics may have bodily attributes and may require body modification. For example, we might associate being thin (for women) or being muscly (for men) with being in control, or we might associate a woman's flawless skin and a certain style of make-up with professional competence. These associations work on ourselves, too: we may seek to make physical changes on our own bodies to more perfectly realize what Widdows calls our 'imagined self'.[31] In her interviews with women who had undergone cosmetic surgery, Gimlin finds that identity played a key role. 'Invariably, the women's accounts involve bodies that were flawed in some way for which the individual claimed not to be responsible,' she writes. 'Their flawed bodies are inaccurate indicators of character, and so they effectively lie about who the women are ... Plastic surgery becomes for them not an act of deception but an attempt to align body with self.'[32]

The principle of the unmodified body is that your worth should not depend on what your body is like. Who you are, in the sense of your status and political entitlements, should not depend on your body fitting some ideal. Identities certainly form around bodies, of that there is no doubt. The question then is how any given identity relates to equality and difference. Is the unmodified body viewed as simply a site of difference, or is it also understood as deficient?

NATURAL, NORMAL, WHOLE

Let's take stock. Our bodies have a basic, intrinsic value that derives from the equality and respect we are owed as persons. That basic value inclines against modification: it tells us that body modification is unnecessary because our bodies have value just as they are, as a pre-requisite of equality.

The unmodified body is a political principle, and it is a premise not a conclusion. The unmodified body is subjected to three logics of modification: health, appearance, and identity. We may want to change our bodies to make them healthier or function better, to make them look more attractive, or to make them more fully represent a given identity. This modification can be compatible with the political principle of the unmodified body but, often, it's not.

In the following chapters I'll show how the pressures to modify our bodies are overwhelming; how they reflect and reinforce structures of domination and oppression; how they undermine the basic equality that we all should share. My aim is not to demonize modification. All of us have little choice but to modify our bodies in some way or other, and the pressures to modify are greater the more our bodies are deemed inferior. There is no basis for ranking bodies on how unmodified they manage to be. Instead, I'll show the political role of the pressure to modify, and the urgent need for collective action to resist it.

The unmodified body is not a shape that can be objectively described, not a body that looks like this or that, not a fixed point in time. It is a political principle. It consists of two claims: that the body is a real, material thing, with significance and value of its own; and that the body is at the same time an inexorably political concept, subject to the vagaries of interpretation, manipulated by social norms and structures.

I'll develop this principle of the unmodified body by considering a series of more familiar proxy concepts. None of them capture it exactly, but each skim its surface.

The first proxy for the unmodified body is the idea of the *natural* body. The natural body is a promising proxy for the unmodified body because it, too, claims to stand in contrast to social ideals. But, in fact, configurations of naturalness exist only in the context of some social or cultural creation. Nature seems paradigmatically to *contrast* with culture, but it cannot escape it.

I explain in Part One how concepts of nature and naturalness have often been used to constrain or confine: to assert a fixed, unchanging state that humans of this kind or that have, and must morally maintain. Nature has been particularly used to maintain the gender binary as an oppressive and hierarchical structure. But we will see how recourse to nature can help us resist oppression, by helping us to reclaim a way of being that is not what our society demands of us. Nature, I argue, is a frenemy – sometimes friend, sometimes enemy. In the current political and ecological moment we should be willing to treat it more as a friend, for it acts as a corrective against the intense pressures to use our bodies in the service of culture.

In Part Two I defend the principle of the unmodified body against the claim that what counts is *normality*, even normality understood in terms of health and functioning. Whether a body is normal depends entirely on what it's being compared with. Standards of normality always invoke hierarchies, most obviously those of sex, race, disability and age. Ambiguities of normality are everywhere, even within the discipline of medicine. Medicine presents itself as the neutral protector and restorer of normality, but its views about normality shift radically between time and place, demonstrating that clinical normality is context dependent.

This context dependence should not be understood as undermining the reality of the material body. The body exists, with its functions and dysfunctions, as both enabler and limit at one and the same time. What emerges from this analysis is that normality can be viewed both from the outside, as a comparison with others, or from the inside, as an experience. Once normality is recognized as an experience, it becomes possible – though not easy – to make it into a choice. That is to say, it is possible to create a normal body either by changing the body or by changing our perspective on it. This opens the intriguing possibility of choosing to be normal *just as we already are*.

The third proxy concept for the unmodified body is the idea of the *whole body*. In Part Three I explore the idea that body modification might be an act of virtuous self-improvement, that it might be the only bearable response to dysphoria, and that it might be an act of creativity in itself. In each case, I analyse the political conditions that make those strategies coherent and show how they interact with the principle of the unmodified body. I argue that the idea of bodily integrity is one way of understanding the unmodified body, and that its role is to act as a defence against unconsented-to modifications. We need to be able to make choices about our lives, and to have our bodies left intact so that we can do that.

The unmodified body is a political idea as well as a material reality; a philosophical construct and a real, living thing. As a political–philosophical construct the unmodified body is the body without oppressive social construction. It is the body that is allowed to be equal. As a material reality the unmodified body is the body that has not been shaped or altered in pursuit of a social ideal; it is the experience of embodiment. Taken together, the unmodified body is not an image of perfection, or a goal to be attained. It is a premise, a baseline, something that should be treated as a *default*.

NOTES ON METHOD

One challenge is to develop an account that values the unmodified body without fetishizing it, or without simply reflecting my own experience and prejudice. In writing I have asked myself a series of challenging questions. Am I simply resistant to practices that I, or people like me, don't do? Does my position on body modification reflect anything more than my own identity: my class, race, culture, sex, gender, sexuality, profession? As an academic philosopher, am I predisposed to value modification of the mind above modification of the body? Am I suffering from the delusion that I know the meaning and purpose of body modification practices even when I am not a member of the group that typically engages in them? Does my account simply reflect my perspective as someone who has suffered from certain kinds of dissatisfaction, dysfunction, or dysphoria but not others?

These are difficult questions. And they are questions that no one can escape. There is no one whose perspective is unsullied by their own experience. Each one of us is situated within a particular social context and body. Each one of us has first-person access to some experiences and not others. Each one of us gains both insight and bias from our own subject position. So, I am not uniquely qualified to write this book by virtue of my personal identity and characteristics, but I am not uniquely disqualified either.

Intact discusses some bodily experiences that I have had, and many others that I haven't. I've tried to understand unfamiliar ways of being in a body by reading others' accounts and by talking to people who've had those experiences. As a philosopher rather than a sociologist, psychologist, or journalist, my research focuses more on written accounts than on direct interviews. My understanding is necessarily partial, permanently incomplete. I don't think this can be avoided.

Our perspectives are limited not only because of differences between individuals, but also because different social categories, different positions in a hierarchy, intersect in complex ways. This is the principle of intersectionality.[33] We cannot separate out parts of our identity and social position because each has to be read through the lens of the others. For example, the experience and meaning of womanhood differs by race, class, disability status, gender identity and sexuality. Intersectionality forces us to acknowledge the partiality of any perspective, and to recognize that many perspectives have been systematically silenced.

Some scholars respond to the fact of intersectionality by focusing on those suppressed perspectives. In Western colonial societies such as Europe and North America, that means giving particular attention to the thought and traditions of indigenous and First Nations people, to Black and minority ethnic people, as well as to identities that are marginalized in other ways. That work is extremely valuable, and I have engaged with a variety of perspectives here – although limitations of time, space and my own scholarly expertise mean that there are inevitable omissions.[34] But my focus is on the dominant narratives and power structures of Western, capitalist societies, those built on white and male supremacy. I show how mainstream social norms affect people who live in those societies, including members of majority and minority groups, and how marginalization and subordination are maintained by pressures to modify.

My method is the method of philosophy and of feminism. *Philosophy* tells us that we can develop a perspective with rigour and justification by focusing on reasons, arguments and implications. The philosophical method also aims for clarity and precision, which hopefully guide us towards truth even as they add complexity.

Philosophers like to make simple things complicated and complicated things simple. We try to make complicated things simple through careful definition and precise analysis of concepts. At the same time, we make simple things complicated by questioning things: by taking obvious truths and showing why they are doubtful. So philosophers question everything, including whether tables are really there, whether $2+2=4$, how we can be equal when we're all different, and how you know you exist. With philosophy we attempt to step outside our own experience, while recognizing that complete objectivity is impossible; certainly, we step away from received wisdom. *Because everyone else thinks it* is never a good reason to agree, for a philosopher. In fact, it's a reason for suspicion.

One crucial part of doing philosophy is that we must always try to make things as difficult for ourselves as possible. In philosophy (as with most intellectual disciplines) it is never enough to state a claim or assert an argument; we must always consider objections. If the objections we encounter are weak, we should make them stronger: this is the philosophical principle of charity. If we don't encounter any objections from real-life others, because we are making new claims that haven't yet been tested, we must invent those objections to test ourselves. The philosopher must always be thinking, *what's the strongest objection to the argument I am making?* And only then, *how can I respond?*

You'll see this feature of philosophy in the parts of *Intact* that are hesitant, tentative, constructing confusion and ambiguity and doubt. I'm trying to make things as difficult for myself as I can. But you'll also see it, or so I hope, in the parts of *Intact* that are bold, assured and provocative. Once you've given your real or imagined opponent the best possible odds, your own argument becomes stronger.

Feminism tells us that the philosophical project is necessarily limited, and that its claims to purity and abstraction are suspect. It tells us that we can learn a great deal about politics and power from our own personal experiences and the experiences of others. It tells us that our actions, beliefs and preferences are not entirely our own: that we are socially constructed, and that this social construction explains the status and many of the beliefs of women, men and children.

As a political movement, feminism insists that women be allowed to act freely and be treated equally. Its analysis shows that these twin demands, lofty and lowly as they are, are seldom met. Feminism demands an arduous but enriching process of *critical engagement* with ourselves and each other. It shows us to seek the commonalities and the differences in women's experiences, and to develop a political perspective aimed at liberation. Feminism agrees with philosophy that what seems obvious from a dominant perspective seldom is.

The CNN report on Nadia, the fourteen-year-old girl bullied for the size of her ears, is presented as a piece of good news: a heart-warming tale of philanthropic rescue. The reporter is Dr Sanjay Gupta, CNN Chief Medical Correspondent, who describes what happened next:

> Her mom, desperate to help, turned to the internet, and stumbled across the Little Baby Face Foundation. The non-profit organization offers free plastic surgery to children, like Nadia, who are bullied because of their physical appearance and can't afford an operation.
>
> **Dr Gupta**: 'There may be people, Nadia, who say, "Look, you don't need to do this. This, this is just who you are. It's the way you were born. You know, people should love people for who they are." What do you say to those folks?'
>
> **Nadia**: 'I say that they're right . . . but they'll never stop. It'll just keep going. Get worse and worse.'

Dr Gupta describes how Nadia applied to the Little Baby Face Foundation for an otoplasty, an operation to pin back her ears. She was accepted and the Foundation flew her to New York, where she saw plastic surgeon Dr Thomas Romo III. He agreed to do the otoplasty. But he wasn't going to stop there.

On the film, Nadia lies on a medical couch in a hospital gown.

Dr Romo points at various parts of her face with the pen he has just used to draw incision marks on her ears. 'I love thin chins,' he says, with a grin. He pauses. 'But I don't want them as pointy as that chin.' Dr Romo is a man who knows what he wants in a chin. 'We talked about that, didn't we?'

Nadia nods. They did talk about that. 'Mm hm,' she agrees. Dr Romo doesn't wait to hear her answer. He knows what they talked about. (He probably did the talking.) 'We looked at some pictures of some people, and their chins come off just a liiiiiiitttttle bit more square.' He puts his finger and thumb each side of Nadia's chin and draws them apart to indicate the sort of chin he does like. 'So that's exactly what we're gonna do too.' He uncaps his pen.

The reporter voices over. 'And, there was more,' he says. Dr Romo wants to operate on Nadia's septum. Apparently, it's not straight. He holds his nice straight pen up against Nadia's nose to show what it should be like. 'As the septum goes, so goes the nose,' Dr Romo explains.

Nadia is still lying on the couch in a hospital gown. She looks tiny between the two men, both of whom are wearing scrubs. The surgeon sits on Nadia's right, the reporter, Dr Gupta, sits on her left. Dr Gupta intervenes. 'She never talked about the nose or the chin before, right?'

Dr Romo knows where this is going, and he doesn't wait for Dr Gupta to finish. 'She did not,' he says, leaning back in his chair and adjusting his glasses, 'because she didn't recognize it.'

Sound familiar? Nadia 'didn't recognize' that her ears were too big, either – not until a seven-year-old girl told her so. But that girl was a mean bully. Dr Romo is a heroic saviour.

Back to voiceover. 'Dr Romo said all three surgeries combined are necessary, to balance out Nadia's features.' The surgeries are *necessary*. Nadia didn't ask for them, but Dr Romo is going to do them. Otherwise she would have a chin that he doesn't like, which wouldn't be good. And she'd have unbalanced features. Presumably Dr Romo doesn't like those, either.

Later Nadia walks to the operating room. Dr Gupta asks her how she feels. 'Nervous,' she says. 'Excited.'

Nadia has all three procedures, in a four-hour operation that we are told would cost her $40,000 if the Foundation were not paying. We're not told whether Dr Romo forgoes his fee, or whether he benefits financially for managing to upsell his vulnerable patient from one surgery to three. We are told that no one thinks the surgery will be enough to undo the emotional trauma Nadia has suffered: she'll need counselling, too.

Or, at least, she'll need both surgery and counselling to deal with the trauma caused by other children telling her that her ears are wrong. It seems that the effects of Dr Romo telling her that her nose and chin are wrong can be fixed by surgery alone. It's not clear what the difference is. Were the bullies wrong about Nadia's ears, whereas Dr Romo is right about her nose and chin? After all, Dr Romo is an expert and bullies are just kids. What do they know?

But if the bullies were wrong about Nadia's ears, then presumably Dr Romo wouldn't be operating on her ears. He'd take one look at Nadia and say, 'Your ears are fine! Leave them be! You look great! Just … let me fix your unpleasantly thin chin and imperceptibly unbalanced nose.'

He didn't say that, so, the bullies must have been right after all. The bullies and Dr Romo are both right. Nadia's ears are too large, and her chin is too thin, and her nose is too bendy. This fourteen-year-old girl needs some serious modification. The difference between the bullies and Dr Romo must be this: *the bullies could only tell Nadia what was wrong with her face. Dr Romo can tell her what is wrong with her face AND he can fix it.*

He'd better fix it soon, too. We can't wait and see how Nadia feels about her appearance once her ears are changed. We can't wait until Nadia is an adult. We can't wait and see how her face will change as she grows, or how her self-esteem strengthens as she matures. If we wait, maybe she'll need counselling to deal with the trauma of knowing Dr Romo's truths as well as the bullies' truths.

Three days after the operation, Nadia is still swollen and bandaged on ears, nose and chin. On camera, Dr Romo cuts the ear bandages off and hands her a mirror so that she can see her new face for the first time.

Nadia lifts the mirror while the surgeon, her mother and the camera crew watch.

'I look beautiful,' she says. 'This is exactly what I wanted.'

Nadia shakes her head from side to side in the motion that usually means 'no'.

'I love it,' she says.

Nadia gives a small smile. It's hard to tell whether she would smile more if she weren't swollen around her nose and chin.

Uplifting music plays. Dr Gupta signs off the report. His work, at least, is done.

PART ONE

Natural

The unmodified body is a political principle. It's a deliberately unfamiliar way of trying to capture the significance of refusing various social pressures to work on one's body. *Naturalness* is a much more familiar way of describing a body without certain sorts of modification.

The idea of the natural body is initially very appealing. After all, nature is the source of our bodies. It is our embodiment, the fact of having bodies, that makes us like other parts of the natural world; specifically, like (other) animals. We humans think of ourselves as *unlike* animals in things to do with our minds: our intellect, our morals; and in things to do with our creations, our artifices. We think of ourselves as *like* animals in things to do with our bodies: our hunger and thirst, our vulnerability to pain and disease, our need for shelter and habitat, our sexual urges and our instinct to procreate.

The very concept of 'nature' is most easily – one might say naturally – contrasted with a variety of concepts to do with human interference. 'Nature or nurture?' we ask, meaning something like 'Is this just how things are, or is it caused by humans?' The very concept of 'the natural world' is usually taken as synonymous with the non-human: it's about wildlife, animals and plants, the geological structures of our planet. It's not, somehow, about *us*.

If human interference is what makes things unnatural, then the natural body is the body that we have if we *leave things as they are*. It's the body that results from letting nature do its work. It's the body we have when we stay out of the way. All these ways of thinking imply that the natural body is the default. It's the body we have first. Subsequent bodies – the bodies we have later in life – will be natural only insofar as we *don't* do certain things to them. The natural body is the body *without*.

But what is the natural body without? If *nature* is contrasted with *human*, and if nature is always disrupted by human action, it would be impossible for the human body to stay natural – or even to be natural in the first place. The moment we do something to a body we would transform it into a product of human interference. But this way of thinking would mean that the body stopped being natural the moment we consciously did anything to it, including feeding it, or clothing it, or moving it. To think in this way would be to lose the concept of the natural body altogether.

Even the newborn body is created by human action, although Western philosophy has traditionally obscured this fact. Thomas Hobbes famously instructed his readers to assume that human beings spring up from nowhere like mushrooms from the ground, as assuming otherwise would cause problems for his theory. Which means, of course, that there are problems with his theory.[1]

Every human being relies on its mother's gestational labour. It must be birthed by its mother, often with the assistance of other humans. It then requires many years of effortful care and nurturing, all from humans. If being natural means being without human interference, then no human and no human body can ever be natural.

The concept of nature and the natural body is closely intertwined with issues of sex and gender. Sex in the sense of reproduction is the basic requirement of us existing at all, as a species and individually. Sex in the sense of male and female are necessary categories and bodies for reproduction to occur. Sex is a fundamental issue in the chapters in Part One, then, along with the question of whether and how sex explains gender.

The very concept of the natural body already needs distinctions between different kinds of human acts. We can't say that a natural body is a body without interference. We must say that some human acts disrupt the body's naturalness and some do not. And so the concept of nature is necessarily constructed. There is no pre-political natural body. What counts as nature is always up for debate.

If the concept of the natural body is to make sense at all it must be compatible with being gestated and birthed by its mother. It must also allow being fed, being exercised, being clothed and sheltered, being cleaned and maintained, interacting with others – generally being used to live a normal, full life. 'Normal' – there's a problematic term, and one that will occupy us in the second part of the book, but let it go for now.

Perhaps we might try to restrict the idea of a natural body to one that has been altered only to maintain the body's basic health and hygiene. However, that definition would still be too restrictive. Very few acts are *necessary* to maintain the body's basic health and hygiene, and almost everybody will go above and beyond those acts. We could survive on very minimal rations, but no one who has a choice eats only the bare minimum for survival. Our hygiene and clothing needs for survival are similarly minimal; again, anyone who can will exceed them. If the natural body is destroyed by any unnecessary action, then having a natural body is something to be pitied rather than respected, because it is a situation that anyone with a choice would avoid.

There's no reason to celebrate doing only the bare minimum to our bodies. We might even say it's not natural for humans to give their bodies and themselves only the most rudimentary care. We want to look after ourselves: to preserve our bodies' good health, to improve our bodies' functioning, to take pleasure from our bodies, to create bodies that other people can enjoy looking at, being close to, or touching. A body that is maintained as a fully flourishing body is surely what we should want for ourselves, and something that is compatible with our understanding of our nature.

But then, what really makes a body natural? As we can already see, this is not a straightforward factual question. The concept of the natural body is immensely useful, but it is slippery. When we call something natural, we need to be clear what we mean, and we need to be aware of the assumptions that are hiding in plain sight. Why is it more natural to shower than to wear a corset? Is it unnatural to have a haircut or a bikini wax? If your body is still natural after you've brushed your teeth, is it still natural after you've put on lipstick? What is the value of a natural body?

Inconsistency in our use of the concept of nature is built into our practices. We often use the adjective 'natural' to describe particular body parts. But when we use it in that way, we are not consistent about what has to happen – or not happen – to the body part for it to count as natural. Over the next few chapters I'll chart those differences and their political significance.

The simplest way of using the term 'natural' to describe our bodies is in a contrast with something that is artificial. 'Natural nails' is a great example. It's a term used by nail salons and it means, very simply, the nails that grow out of your fingers. It's contrasted with nail extensions and artificial nails: nails that are not grown by the body but are made of plastic and attached with adhesive. When you go to a nail salon you can have acrylics and nail extensions, or you can have a manicure on your natural nails.

This is the simplest and most intuitive way to understand the concept of naturalness: as a contrast with artificiality. Notice, though, that there are some puzzles surrounding this idea of naturalness too. Natural nails are contrasted with artificial nails and nail extensions, but natural nails may be manicured and polished. Why does nail varnish not make our nails unnatural? That's sticking something onto our nails, just as with artificial nails. Artifice does seem to contrast with nature, but not in a straightforward way.

Another example that uses the same logic is natural breasts. This term refers to breasts that are wholly grown by the body, in contrast with artificial breasts, which are created or augmented by implants.

There's a Guinness World Record for the largest natural breasts. The title belongs to Annie Hawkins-Turner, and she'd wear a 48V bra if that size were even made. Hawkins-Turner finds it almost impossible to get a bra that fits. Her breasts measure 177.8 cm around their fullest part; each one weighs more than the average four-year-old. Hawkins-Turner has to move carefully to avoid pain. But she does not want to change her body. According to the Guinness World Records website, 'Annie was advised by doctors to have a breast reduction, but she refused, explaining: "I don't want to mess with nature." '[2] She now poses for glamour shots on her 'very lucrative' adult website.[3]

Natural nails and natural breasts use *nature* as a contrast with *artifice*. The contrast often implies that nature is superior. Sometimes, though, nature and artifice go hand-in-hand.

Not convinced?

Let's go to the theatre.

Bring your protein shake.

I

Keeping Things Natural

Bodybuilding and Masculinity

I'm in a provincial theatre at one o'clock in the afternoon, watching men in satin posing pouches and women in sparkly bikinis. Although the weather is cool and they're virtually naked, the performers on stage are dripping with sweat. Their sweat is laced with oil and fake tan, running down their faces and bodies in brown Bisto streaks. The stage is a spectacle of biceps, triceps, lats and deltoids, all under intense pressure, even though they're not lifting anything. Just displaying their bodies to their full advantage takes every ounce of strength the competitors have.

I'm at a regional heat for the British Natural Bodybuilding Federation annual awards. It's being held in Essex, the county of England stereotyped as focusing on cosmetic surgery, fake tans, casual sex and binge drinking. Some of the competitors may have had cosmetic surgery (there are a few who seem to have breast implants), but most don't look like they have. All the white contestants are wearing fake tan. I have no idea about their sex lives, but there's no way they can binge drink and keep these bodies.

This is a competition for 'natural bodybuilders', and yet these competitors don't look natural. The fake tan in particular is *obviously* fake. In the foyer of the theatre there's an advert for the brand of choice. It depicts two female bodybuilders in bikinis posing and standing on a montage of bottles of tan. The name of the brand is 'Dark As . . .' How to fill in the ellipsis? It's dark as blackface.

The performers are not wearing Dark As . . . as a racist parody. For the white competitors it's a necessity of the sport. In this respect, the black- and brown-skinned competitors have an advantage: they don't need artificial tan, avoiding both faff and fakery. Still, the sheer amount of fake tan used by the bodybuilders puzzles me at first. Why don't they just apply a healthy, subtle bronze glow?

But then I realize. It's like Warhammer.

Warhammer is a hobby beloved by many children – as well as adults who find they can finally afford the models of their dreams. 'Imagine if Disney were founded by a bunch of people who had been primarily inspired by heavy metal album covers.'[1] It involves collecting and painting miniature fantasy warriors, and then battling them against each other in an elaborate tabletop wargame. Painting a Warhammer miniature involves multiple steps with different painting techniques: basecoating, layering, drybrushing. It also involves multiple colours with names like Armageddon Dust, Runefang Steel and Tyrant Skull. It's fastidious work: the figures are tiny. Once the various colours have been applied the final layer is an all-over wash of thin watery dark paint, perhaps Nuln Oil or Reikland Fleshshade. It seems wrong: why cover the meticulous colour work with a murky monochrome? But the wash is vital. It settles in the model's crevices and highlights the fine detail. Only once the wash is applied can you see the intricacy of the figure.

Dark As … is the Nuln Oil of bodybuilding. Nuln Oil highlights armour, weapons and cloth; Dark As … emphasizes vascularity and muscle striation. When it's supplemented with body oil the tan emphasizes the muscles and makes them shine under the stage lights.

So natural bodybuilding involves obvious fakery. And the bodies on display are certainly not the result of leaving the body alone, nor are they a side-effect of normal activity. Even heavy manual work will not get you a body like these. Getting a bodybuilder's body takes hours in the gym and requires painstaking exercises that precisely target each individual muscle group. It's no good only working your pecs, or pectoralis major (the large muscles of the chest) – you also need to isolate your serratus anterior, the small finger-like muscles that run just underneath. Nice biceps, but where's your subscapularis? And, like Batman, a bodybuilder never skips leg day.[2]

What, then, makes the natural bodybuilders *natural*? The answer to this question will tell us about bodybuilding, but it will also show us something vital about the politics and philosophy of the concept of naturalness.

Bodybuilders are the monarchs of body modification. There are both male and female bodybuilders, but I'm going to focus on the men's competitions because they offer an insight into the male body and, ultimately, masculinity itself. At the end of the chapter, I'll consider what we can learn from women's bodybuilding.

Women's bodies are routinely displayed and judged, in formal competitions but also in the pages of gossip magazines, on social media, and generally in our cultural discourse. The female bodybuilder is neither a unique nor a typical instance of the scrutinized female body. The male body, in contrast, is less commonly the subject of aesthetic display. The history of male bodybuilding gives us a glimpse into the ideal of the male body – and indeed, of manhood itself – as it shifts through the twentieth and twenty-first centuries. Along the way we'll also see how the concept of a 'natural' body is constructed, and how the concept can be put to use.

PHYSICAL CULTURE AND
THE GREAT COMPETITION

Bodybuilding is the quest to create – to build – the ideal body. But what counts as an 'ideal' body depends on the time and place.

Bodybuilding as a competitive practice began in the late nineteenth century, when it was known as 'physical culture'. It emerged alongside strongman competitions, often associated with circuses and carnivals, in which men would impress audiences with feats of great strength while wearing leopard-skin loincloths. The leopard skin symbolized a primitive, caveman strength: an affinity with nature.[3] Physical culture was different, though the leopard skin remained a theme. Physical culture emphasized the *appearance* of the body. It had to be strong, but it also had to look good. The strength should be visible even in repose; the muscles should be aesthetically pleasing.

The first national bodybuilding contest in the UK was the 'Great Competition' held in the Royal Albert Hall in London in 1901. The show was sold out, remarkable for a venue with 15,000 seats. One of the judges was Arthur Conan Doyle, physician and creator of Sherlock Holmes. Doyle had for several years been following an exercise regime devised by his fellow judge and the Competition's organizer, strongman Eugen Sandow. The third judge was Charles Lawes, who, as an athlete and sculptor, had a fine appreciation of the human body's form and function.[4] The victor was a man from Lancashire named William Murray. His prize was a large golden statue and the title of 'Best Developed Man in Great Britain and Ireland'.[5]

Reporters at the time noted that there were many Americans in the audience, and perhaps the Great Competition was an impetus for the emergence of American bodybuilding in the early part of the twentieth century. The first American bodybuilding competitions took place in the 1920s. Those early competitions morphed into the Mr. America contest, first held under that name in 1939. In 1948 the first Mr. Universe competition was held in the UK, quickly drawing competitors from around the world.

In its first incarnations bodybuilding tested for 'symmetry, harmony, shape, and beauty'.[6] The aim was to create an all-round image of manhood, and the inspiration was Ancient Greek statues of gods and athletes. So, if you wanted to be the ideal man in early twentieth-century America or Britain, you wanted to be like an Ancient Greek – though, crucially, without the homosexuality. Efforts to distinguish bodybuilding from homoeroticism have preoccupied many of its practitioners.

THE GREEK IDEAL

The Cambridge Museum of Classical Archaeology holds about 600 plaster-cast reproductions of statues from Ancient Greece and Rome. As the museum says, 'Every cast is a copy, a replica, a fake even.'[7] The museum collects and displays them partly so that visitors can see and compare a wide range of ancient sculptures, the originals of which are scattered around the world. But the casts are also displayed as historical objects in their own right. Most of them date from the late nineteenth century, the era of the strongman and just before the birth of competitive bodybuilding. At that time, British stately homes were filled with such casts, a style of interior design intended to display the owner's 'cultural capital acquired by studying the Classics and going on a Grand Tour around Italy (and, later, Greece)'.[8] These statues also demonstrated the aesthetic ideal of the time. They show the bodies that the era found beautiful, and they also indicate that the naked or near-naked human form was deemed appropriate for display in polite society, if it conformed to a certain ideal.

Early bodybuilders would often pose in stances inspired by Greek statues. Steve Reeves (Mr. America 1947) poses as the Discobolus (the Discus Thrower) on the front of John D. Fair's history *Mr. America: The Tragic History of a Bodybuilding Icon*. Reeves holds a discus low down by his hips and holds his other hand aloft. His pose displays his biceps without him clenching his fist. There is no visible tension in his stance. He looks posed yet comfortable. In another image celebrating his 1950 Mr. Universe title, Reeves poses on a plinth, as if in a museum.

Reeves also looks *real*: non-artificial, *natural*. He is muscled and defined, but entirely plausible-looking. He looks sculpted, as befits the

STEVE REEVES : *1950 Mr Universe*

Steve Reeves as Mr. Universe 1950

statuesque ideal, but he looks sculpted out of human flesh, using human tools. You can imagine meeting him. You can imagine *being* him.

The Greek gods were beautiful, but they were also powerful and virtuous. And the early bodybuilders were also expected to display all the qualities of masculine perfection. At its inception the Mr. America contest celebrated the perfect mix of form and function. Weightlifting contests measured only function. Beauty pageants measured only appearance. Bodybuilding measured both.

Vanity was not a manly trait in the first half of the twentieth century, and so the idea of training just for appearance was suspect. Training for these early bodybuilders focused on function – on what the body could *do*. If the body could perform well, it would look good. There's a sense, then, in which these early bodybuilders were not engaging in intentional body modification at all. They wanted to look good, but looking good was not supposed to be the primary intention of the exercising they did. Looking good could be construed as a side-effect, almost an afterthought.

Consider John Grimek, who dominated bodybuilding in the sport's early years. He won Mr. America in 1940 and 1941 and was considered the ideal bodybuilder – so much so that it seemed he could never lose. The Mr. America organizers feared that the perfection of Grimek's physique meant that he would just keep winning, a result which would have discouraged new entrants and killed the competition. So they changed the rules to forbid bodybuilders from re-entering the contest after they had won it once.

Grimek had an unbeatable physique. But he was not a deliberate bodybuilder. He 'considered himself chiefly a weightlifter' and had to be talked into entering the world of bodybuilding.[9] His perfect physique just *was*. It was, in a sense, natural.

The Mr. America contest had started just one year before Grimek's first victory, in 1939. That initial competition was held in the Junior High School Auditorium in Amsterdam, NY. The poster advertising the contest had no pictures, no models, no ideals to aim at. It was filled instead with small print. The aim of the contest, the poster instructed, was 'To select the Finest Physique in the United States as representing "Mr. America."' Proceeds, the poster announced prominently, would be given to 'the Knothole League, an organization doing fine work among under-privileged boys, especially giving guidance and material help in baseball and athletics. Remember,' the poster continued, 'that "BUILDING BOYS IS BETTER THAN MENDING MEN."'[10]

This first competition proudly advertised its connections to masculine virtue in all its forms. Mr. America would showcase perfect men, and it would also fund the creation of the perfect men of the future.

The 1939 competition divided contestants into three classes based on height, with a winner to be selected from each. In addition, separate awards were given for 'Finest Chest' and 'Finest Abdomen'. Bob Hoffman, judge and the editor of *Strength & Health* magazine (strapline: 'Devoted to the Culture of Mind and Body'), waxed lyrical about the competitors. 'I was simply overwhelmed by the many beautiful examples of male physique,' he gushed. 'There are 450,000 words in our language ... but words simply cannot describe the magnificent display we saw at Amsterdam.'[11] The winner was Bob Goodrich, who had developed his physique through running, gymnastics and acrobatics. Like Grimek after him, Goodrich 'really didn't train per se for the Mr. America contest: he just walked in, showed off his body, and won'.[12]

Judge Bob Hoffman was adamant that having muscular body parts would not be enough to win. Mr. America had to have *everything*. He had to be the ideal man. Hoffman described Steve Sanko, winner of the 1944 Junior Mr. America contest, in the following way: he 'has fine posture, an engaging smile, is handsome in a manly sort of way, with thick black hair and fine teeth, is modest to the extreme, one of our world famous weightlifters, a fitting example of America's best young manhood'.[13]

The Greek ideal distinguished muscles that *looked big* from muscles that *did things*, favouring the latter. Jimmy Payne, Mr. America 1950, set out this view clearly. 'I believe that it is the quality of muscle that counts and not size,' he argued. A big bicep 'sure looks good, but what can you do with it?'[14] Views like Payne's kept the Greek ideal going into the 1950s, with competitors expected to demonstrate all-round virtue. The 1955 Mr. America contest included questions on entrants' 'hobbies, athletic background, what work they did, and other details designed to determine good character'.[15]

In these years of the Greek ideal, years in which Mr. America had to show the full range of manly virtues, we see a picture of masculinity that is well-rounded and balanced. The ideal man has beauty without vanity. He has form as a side-effect of function. He has interests beyond himself: hobbies, opinions. He has a steady job. He is, first and foremost, someone for men to look up to. Women might swoon over him, too, but that's really not what he's there for. Mr. America at this time was also notably white and avowedly straight. It would not be until the Civil Rights era that black bodybuilders were properly rewarded in competitions, and not until the 1970s that the homoerotic elements of bodybuilding could be more openly acknowledged.[16]

The Greek ideal of masculinity eventually fell out of fashion. In bodybuilding, West Coast Muscle Beach culture started to shift the focus towards size in the late 1940s. By the late 1950s and 1960s bodybuilding competitions no longer emphasized the concept of all-round virtue. At the same time that the Greek ideal was losing favour in bodybuilding it was going out of fashion in stately homes. 'Plaster casts were once a primary vehicle for an art education, but when the classical ideals they represent fell out of fashion, so too did casts,' reports the Museum of Classical Archaeology. 'Many cast collections were broken up, destroyed or, at best, relegated to basements in the course of the 1960s and 1970s; many museums could no longer see a use for them.'[17]

So, the demise of Ancient Greek ideals of masculinity was not unique to bodybuilding. But in the bodybuilding world the ideal stood no chance against two distinct phenomena: Schwarzenegger and steroids.

THE GREATEST
BODYBUILDER OF ALL TIME

Arnold Schwarzenegger, five-times Mr. Universe and seven-times Mr. Olympia, is the paradigmatic 1970s' bodybuilder. Actually, he's probably the paradigmatic bodybuilder full stop. In the context of his movie career, he's commonly referred to as 'Arnie'. Bodybuilders retain his full forename, however, immortalized in bodybuilding standards like the Arnold Classic competition and the Arnold Press, a deltoid exercise he invented.

Schwarzenegger smashed the Greek ideal of all-round masculine virtue and replaced it with *size*. In the Arnold era and beyond, the perfect male body would be BIG.

Anyone looking at images of Schwarzenegger in his prime can see his size. But it's worth emphasizing just what a shift in the bodybuilding ideal he was by comparing Arnold to Steve Reeves, the Schwarzenegger of the 1940s and 1950s. Both Schwarzenegger and Reeves remain iconic bodybuilders to this day; both made the leap from bodybuilder to film star. Reeves, 6'1" tall, had 18½" arms, a 52" chest, a 29" waist, 26" thighs and 18½" calves.[18] Schwarzenegger, at 6'2", was only one inch taller than Reeves, but his muscles were gargantuan in comparison. Official figures, though these are sometimes disputed, give Schwarzenegger 22" arms, a 57" chest, a 34" waist, 28½" thighs and 20" calves.[19] Reeves famously said, 'When your arms are bigger than your head, something's wrong.' Arnie made it right.

Schwarzenegger's body was a step change away from the Greek ideal, and yet he was competing in an era that was still influenced by that ideal. In the 1977 documentary *Pumping Iron*, he describes his process in terms reminiscent of the origins of the sport. 'Do you visualize yourself as a piece of sculpture?' the interviewer asks. 'Yeah, definitely,' Schwarzenegger replies.

> Good bodybuilders have the same mind when it comes to sculpting [that] a sculptor has. And if you analyze it, you look in the mirror and you say, okay, I need a little bit more deltoids, a little bit more shoulders, so that the proportion's right. So what you do is you exercise and put those deltoids on, whereas an artist would just slap on some clay on each side, you know, and this may be the easier way. We go through the harder way, because you have to do it on the human body.[20]

So Schwarzenegger was still aware of the masculine ideal that prevailed at the start of the sport. Unlike the early bodybuilders, though, Schwarzenegger and his peers are very definitely engaging in body modification. Their physiques are not the side-effect of functional labour or exercise. They are deliberately formed, via exercises chosen specifically for the aesthetic results they will have. And while symmetry and beauty were still important in elite bodybuilding in the 1970s, they were nothing without *size*.

BRUTALLY HUGE:
THE USE OF STEROIDS

Steroid use among bodybuilders became widespread in the 1960s. By the 1975 Mr. America contest, according to the winner Dale Adrian, everybody was on them.[21]

We might date the full transformation of the bodybuilding ideal from sculpture to size to the 1981 Mr. America competition, because that was the year that the Most Muscular Man title stopped being awarded. Until 1981, Most Muscular Man had been awarded as a separate, inferior title to Mr. America – a sort of runner-up prize. It had always been possible to win the overall title *without* being the most muscular, because other qualities such as symmetry and all-round appearance mattered just as much as bulk. But by 1981 only size mattered, and so the Most Muscular Man title was obsolete.

That year, Mr. America was a bodybuilder named Tim Belknap. His thighs, at 29",[22] were 'so large that squats were counterproductive'.[23] Belknap does not look natural. He looks like a diagram of the muscular system in a biology textbook.

Modern-day bodybuilders have gone even further. Since the 1980s bodybuilders have trained for enormous bulk combined with incredibly low body fat. This combination gives the 'ripped' look: each muscle stands out distinctly and prominently. Contemporary bodybuilding also prizes extreme 'vascularity', where the veins bulge and stand out from the skin. The result is a physique that looks almost as though it has been dissected. It's proudly freakish.

The average person who looks at a modern-day elite bodybuilder won't swoon with lust or envy; they're more likely to recoil in disgust. Even Schwarzenegger isn't keen on the modern aesthetic. Speaking in 2015 to an audience of bodybuilding fans he said:

> So if I would be like a judge, I ask myself always the question, as a judge – forget it now, that I have been Mr. Olympia and all this – but let's say I am a judge. And I sit there. The question is, 'Whose body do I want to have?' That's what it comes down to. And I think that Cedric [McMillan] had such a beautiful body. He was so well-proportioned,

Dexter 'The Blade' Jackson, winner of the Arnold Classic 2015 competition

that I thought he should have placed higher than he did [in the Arnold Classic 2015 competition]. And unless we change the judging procedure, and unless we do something about where they stop just using guys with the thickest neck, and the biggest muscle, but not look as pleasing . . . Because look at the old days, when Steve Reeves won. When Steve Reeves won, and you saw him on the beach, you say to yourself 'I would love to have this guy's body. Wow! Look at how beautiful this man looks!' But that's not what you can say about those guys today that win those competitions. And so what I'm trying to tell the judges is that you got to go, and consider, look at everything. Like for instance, so many of those guys have their stomachs sticking out. You know, what is, what are we talking about here? It used to be that we should have a V-shaped body. Now . . . it's like . . . I dunno, it's kind of like a bottle-shaped body or something like that. It's a weird thing that's happening on stage that no-one can pull in their stomach any more for a long period of time, and stand on stage, with a vacuum and pulled-in

stomach, shoulders out, and to look athletic. So it's all of this, you
know, kind of, you know, stomach sticking out, and all this, kind of – it
doesn't *look right* any more.[24]

When Schwarzenegger talks about bodybuilders' stomachs sticking
out, he's talking about 'Roid Gut', where 'roid' means steroid, or
palumboism in medical parlance. The bodybuilders with distended
stomachs don't have *fat* bellies. To be a top bodybuilder you have to
have a great deal of muscle, but you also have to have extremely low
body fat. It's the combination that gives the ripped look. Sumo wres-
tlers are immensely muscular, but they are also very fat and so you
can't see their muscles. People who are starving as the result of famine
or disease have extremely low body fat, but their malnutrition depletes
their muscles as well, so they look emaciated.

Managing to grow muscles while shrinking body fat is the skill of
bodybuilding. Most training regimes require alternating 'bulking
phases' with 'cutting phases'. A bulking phase is when the bodybuilder
eats large amounts of protein and aims to build muscle and put on
weight. A cutting phase is when the bodybuilder restricts his diet, aiming to lose fat without losing muscle.

Cycling between bulking and cutting is not easy. During a bulking
phase even casual bodybuilders are advised to eat 20 per cent more calories than usual. Some bodybuilders practise 'clean bulking', eating an
additional portion of lean protein; others favour 'dirty bulking', eating
large amounts of unhealthy food that create both muscle and fat, requiring a harsher cutting phase. Ryan Terry, a Mr. Olympia finalist,
recommends eating seven meals per day.[25] One doesn't always have the
appetite for that, so the Maximuscle website suggests supplements that
'can add calories to your diet without the need to force down a meal'.[26]
One serving of Maximuscle Progain Mass Builder contains 500 calories;
a single serving of Optimum Nutrition Serious Mass contains 1260!

The cutting phase requires creating a calorie deficit – using more
calories than you consume – while at the same time maintaining protein levels to nurture muscle, increasing fat levels to stave off hormonal
disruption, and setting carb levels 'as high as possible while still losing
fat', so that you can keep training.[27] It takes careful monitoring and a
lot of willpower.

You can make things easier by taking steroids.

Schwarzenegger himself is not puritanical about steroids. 'Too many magazines have been pretending the top bodybuilders don't use steroids,' he said in the late 1970s. 'Hell, they all do. And I realize it's stupid. Perhaps one of the best thing about my retirement from competition is that I don't have to take steroids as I used to.'[28]

Modern-day bodybuilders use vast amounts of steroids. A professional elite bodybuilder could easily take the same amount of synthetic testosterone in one month as an average man would produce in a lifetime.[29] And it's not only steroids: they also routinely use other performance-enhancing drugs, such as Human Growth Hormone (HGH) and insulin.

It's this cocktail of drugs, and particularly HGH, that is responsible for Roid Gut. HGH makes everything grow, not only muscles. So, when a bodybuilder takes HGH his internal organs and intestines grow along with his biceps. Combine HGH with insulin, used for its anabolic effects but bringing significant water retention, and you have the perfect recipe for a distended stomach.[30]

The cutting phase can also be drug-assisted. The aim of cutting is to lose the fat that was put on in the bulking phase without losing the muscle, to leave the muscles and veins clearly defined. Having a six-pack is far more a matter of having low body fat than it is about doing sit-ups. Elite bodybuilders, of course, need both.

Drugs that help with cutting are varieties of stimulants, such as clenbuterol (a bronchiodilator) or T3 (a hormone produced by the thyroid). These increase the body's metabolism, making the heart beat faster so that you lose fat even while at rest. Drug-assisted cutting can be just as dangerous as drug-assisted bulking: in both cases the body is forced to work well beyond its natural capacities. Cycling between steroids and stimulants is especially punishing. Elite bodybuilders maintain a gruelling drug regime that puts the body under constant stress.

All of which brings us back to our starting point: natural bodybuilding.

NATURAL BODYBUILDING

The concept of 'natural' bodybuilding emerged in the late 1970s and 1980s as a reaction to the drug-ridden state of the discipline. The first 'Natural Mr. America' contest was held in 1978, and the Natural Body Builders of America (NBBA) was formed in 1981. Natural bodybuilding has stayed popular as a contrast to drug-enhanced methods: the British Natural Bodybuilding Federation (BNBF), organizers of the Essex competition I attend, was founded in 2000.

Natural bodybuilding isn't natural like trees are natural. It's not about eating like a caveman or a yogic detoxer. It's not about developing a masculine physique as a side-effect of manual labour or weightlifting. Natural bodybuilding is most definitely a body modification practice: it's about going to great lengths to change your body to look a certain way. And it doesn't rule out the use of all sorts of artificial, processed substances. There's the fake tan, of course, but there's also a whole range of dietary supplements. The main sponsor of the BNBF competition is online retailer Viper Fitness, which sells a vast range of bodybuilding supplements and cautions on its website that its products must not be used by anyone under eighteen.

The website Evolution of Bodybuilding recommends that natural bodybuilders, or 'nattys', take a complex list of supplements.[31] First among them is Shred CBD, a 'cortisol killer'. 'If you don't know what cortisol is,' would-be nattys are told, 'then read up. Basically less cortisol = more testosterone and more muscle blah blah blah.' That 'blah blah blah' is a quote, not me editorializing. Bodybuilders are expected to become proficient in understanding the chemical underpinnings of muscle mass.

Next, the elixir of bodybuilding: protein shakes made from whey protein. These products, sold in powdered form, cost up to £50 per kilo on the high street. You mix them with water to make a shake with appetising flavours like Chocolate Brownie, Salted Caramel, or Strawberry Cheesecake. After whey protein, natural bodybuilders should look for BCAAs, or branched chain amino acids, 'generally the amino acids leucine, isoleucine and valine'. These are recommended for their contribution to protein production.

We're still not done. A natural bodybuilder should also get some 'Natural Test Booster' where 'Test' = testosterone. Evolution of Bodybuilding note that 'while a lot of the claims these companies make are pretty ridiculous (they won't have the same effects as steroids), you can still get some products that are packed with some decent vitamins and minerals to promote muscle growth.' Finally, a natty needs Creatine. This 'helps by increasing levels of phosphocreatine in your body. Which is used to create new ATP [adenosine triphosphate].'

It's all very high tech. It's very processed. And it's not obvious why this cocktail of supplements and shakes, pills and powdered protein, still counts as *natural*.

For a bodybuilder to count as natural, and to be eligible for natural competitions, he must not use very specific performance-enhancing drugs. In particular, he must not use steroids. The list of substances banned by the BNBF starts with anabolic steroids and testosterone: the key exclusions for any natural bodybuilder. Also banned are 'growth hormones, hormones and precursors, prescription diuretics, psychomotor stimulants, muscle implants of any kind, chemicals/drugs used to deceive or pass polygraph, clenbuterol and GHB', and anything illegal or banned by the US Food and Drug Administration or the International Olympic Committee.[32] The reference to the polygraph in the list of substances is because polygraphs, or lie-detector tests, are used to check that competitors really are natural. Their efficacy is controversial, but the urine tests also used generally cannot detect all banned substances, and they cannot detect whether banned substances have been used prior to the test date.

So why are these substances in particular the ones that are banned in natural bodybuilding? It's not because they are artificial: as we've seen, all sorts of artificial and processed supplements are allowed. It's not because they give an advantage: permitted substances also claim to do that. The best way of understanding it is that these are the substances that threaten the normative structure at the core of bodybuilding: masculinity.

NATURALNESS AS
AUTHENTIC MASCULINITY

Unlike the earliest competitions, no one today could simply turn up to a bodybuilding competition, show off their body and win. The modern bodybuilding physique, even the natural one, is created through conscious, concerted effort, focused on appearance rather than function. It requires an understanding of chemical and physiological processes and expert manipulation of both. But the built body can still be thought of as natural, according to the logic of natural bodybuilding, just so long as its modification has proceeded in a way that stays true to the ideal of masculinity. A masculine body, on this logic, is one that still makes its own testosterone. It is self-originating. It is independent. It is authentic.

Competitive bodybuilders have bulk. Natural bodybuilding implies that what they lack is authenticity. Proudly freakish, gloriously grotesque, bodybuilding on steroids is masculinity on – well, as the idiom goes, on steroids.

Unnaturally built bodies *mimic* masculinity, and they mimic with the aggressive excess of a caricature. 'The days when the Steve Reeves physique made a woman melt and a man burn with envy [are] gone,' said Jeff Everson, bodybuilder and owner of *Planet Muscle* magazine. 'Physiques now turned the stomach of the average woman and made most men snicker at the oddness of it all.'[33]

On this understanding, naturalness is compatible with a great deal of deliberate modification. The natural body as it is found in bodybuilding is *not* an unmodified body, literally speaking. It is natural not because it is unshaped, but because its shaping proceeds in accordance with its founding norms: masculinity and being the ideal man. A male bodybuilder identifies above all as masculine, as befits the sport's origins as the pursuit of ideal manhood. If he wants to be natural, he can do only whatever is compatible with that core, authentic masculinity. He must do nothing that suggests his masculinity is imported.

The socially constructed authenticity at the core of the natural bodybuilder stands in contrast to the unnatural bodybuilder's deception. The unnatural bodybuilder is cast as an illusion, a simulacrum of masculinity. 'Bodybuilding is a form of virtual reality that has degenerated into a cult,' writes John Fair, chronicler of the Mr. America contest.[34] He describes it as virtual reality because the strength the bodybuilder seems to have is illusory: by the day of a competition, an elite bodybuilder is so depleted from cutting and dehydrating that even standing is an effort. 'When we're up there (on the posing platform),' one competitor confessed, 'we're closer to death than we are to life.'[35]

The natural bodybuilder's body is heavily, effortfully modified, but it can be understood as natural because it epitomizes an image of authentic masculinity. Unlike the bodies of unnatural bodybuilders, its creation has not required importing testosterone, the paradigmatically masculine hormone. Unlike theirs, its creation has not produced feminization: breasts, a 'pregnant' belly, a small dick, shrunken balls.

NATURE AND NORMATIVITY: MASCULINITY AS POLITICS

To say that something is 'natural' is always to make a normative statement about that thing. Labelling something as natural usually indicates that there is something good about it, which is why we use phrases like 'natural remedies' and 'natural health' but not 'natural cancer' or 'natural illness'. The association between nature and goodness is not universal: sometimes 'natural' is understood as primitive, contrasted with concepts like 'modern'. But it is almost always bad to describe something as 'unnatural'.

Calling something 'natural' implies that it has ethical value along two dimensions: its origins and its durability. Something natural has supposedly emerged in some pure, authentic way: it is uncorrupted, non-artificial. Things that are natural may be in some sense the result of human labour, but they are the result of wholesome labour, not the product of meddling or corrupting interference. And something natural has a claim to durability: to continue existing in its natural state. Natural things may be fleeting, like blossom on an apple tree or the lifespan of a worker bee, but they recur: they are regular, returning with the seasons or the reproductive cycle. Things that are natural can be worked upon, affected, or defiled – their naturalness can be destroyed – but what it *is* for them to be natural, what is in their nature, endures.

This doesn't mean that assessments of naturalness, or the normative judgements that accompany them, always stand up to critical scrutiny. Allegations of naturalness have been particularly dangerous for women, who have found their unequal political status justified as natural in origin and thus both impossible and wrong to change. That's why feminists tend to be especially wary of claims about nature. Whenever something is labelled as natural we must always ask: what values are being invoked here? What political position is being protected and promoted?

The masculinity celebrated in modern-day bodybuilding is dominant. It is tough. The bodybuilder is no longer shaped and smoothed by wet hands running over the clay of his flesh, squeezing and sculpting a glorious, rippling figure. Now he is hacked by knives: he is 'cut', 'ripped', or 'shredded'. He is like a machine: he is 'yoked' or 'jacked'. He is pure flesh: he is a 'meathead' or 'beefcake'. He is, above all, big – but *dangerously* so: 'swole' or 'brutally huge'.[36]

He is *not* 'buff'. 'Girls use the term buff to describe their boyfriends,' says *Muscle & Strength*. 'If anyone describes you as buff, it most certainly means that you need to get your ass in gear. Time to start training hard and eating right.'[37] The bodybuilder is not here to attract women. He is here to be a man among men.

Steroids and other performance-enhancing drugs create the image of brutally huge masculinity that bodybuilding demands. But they do so by undermining norms of masculinity and femininity in a way that damages the core purpose of bodybuilding. Drugs undermine masculinity in part because they have 'feminizing' effects. With Roid Gut 'the gut hangs out like the abdomen of a pregnant woman', says bodybuilding expert Greg Zulak.[38] Taking steroids suppresses the body's own production of testosterone, leaving male users with breasts, shrunken testicles and erectile dysfunction.[39] The bodybuilder on steroids looks masculine, but his masculinity is inauthentic and corrupted. He is not self-made.

Natural bodybuilding seeks to restore authenticity. The concept of nature used in natural bodybuilding is best understood as being a claim about uncorrupted, self-made masculinity. Bodybuilding is natural, then, if it proceeds in a way that respects the core of the masculine ideal.

It's a separate question whether the masculine ideal is good or bad, and whether naturalness with respect to masculinity is to be sought or avoided. (Another separate question is whether we should be working to disrupt the gender binary entirely.) It's much better for your health to be a natural bodybuilder than to be either a steroid-using elite bodybuilder or an exercise-avoiding couch potato. But whether it's good or bad to be masculine depends a lot on the quality and characteristics of the prevailing masculine ideal. Masculinity, on its own, can be toxic or nourishing, aggressive or assertive, dominant or co-operative. It can be the Greek ideal of an all-round package of moral and physical virtue, or the limiting contemporary bodybuilding ideal of being nothing more than 'brutally huge'.[40]

Sociologist Scott Melzer argues that the ideal of masculinity in contemporary American culture emphasizes three areas in which men are expected to be dominant. We can think of them as the three Bs: breadwinning, body and bedroom. There are many esoteric practices of masculinity, such as barbecuing, DIY and mending cars, but failure in these minor ideals does not existentially threaten manhood. But breadwinning, body and bedroom are compulsory. As Melzer argues, 'physical, sexual, and economic competence and accomplishments are those to which men feel most accountable. Notably, a single perceived failure on these . . . is often enough to threaten one's manhood identity and status.'[41]

And yet failure is ever present. At its heart, the contemporary American masculinity ideal (one that also holds in many other countries) is about *control*: of oneself, one's environment, one's work, one's relationships. Men are expected to control themselves and their lives to an extent that is simply impossible, given socio-economic constraints and human limitations. As Melzer puts it, 'These body and breadwinner ideals are beyond even the reach of Tom Cruise and a 100-million-dollar budget. No man can possibly complete this mission.'[42]

When men fail at masculinity, as they inevitably must, Melzer finds that a common response is *internalization*. Rather than attribute their failure to live up to the requirements of masculinity to the impossibility of that ideal, or to uncontrollable socio-economic circumstances such as recession or austerity politics, men who internalize locate the source of failure within themselves. Internalization is a self-critical internal monologue suggesting to each individual man that he is to blame. It's his fault that he cannot find work, not the government's economic policy; he is to blame for his own physical inadequacy, rather than body ideals being unreasonable. Internalization accepts the authority of the masculinity script.

Internalization is the *feeling* of masculinity failure. Dealing with that feeling requires a strategy. Melzer identifies three: redefinition, repair and compensation.

Redefinition involves rejecting some aspects of masculinity, either by rejecting the idea that a man should be masculine, or by arguing that real men do things traditionally derided as feminine, such as looking after children, taking responsibility for housework, or treating women as equals. John Stoltenberg, feminist writer and activist, follows the redefinition strategies in his books *Refusing to be a Man* and *The End of Manhood*, the second of which ends with the radical claim that 'the beginning of selfhood means the end of men.'[43] Redefinition is a niche strategy, which is not to say that it is wrong. It is, though, highly demanding, and it places a great deal of strain on the individual. Redefinition is very difficult to do alone. Unsurprisingly, most men look elsewhere.

A second strategy for dealing with masculinity failure is *repair*. Repairing masculinity means making a deliberate attempt to rectify the perceived failure and meet the standard. In the documentary *Pumping Iron*, the bodybuilder Mike Katz, Mr. America 1969 and Mr. Universe 1972, describes how he was led into the sport after being bullied at school:

> I, I can remember, you know, back in my life, when, when, ah, I would be picked on quite often – I'm sure every kid's gone through it, but it just affected me more than I think it would affect other people. You know, 'hey four-eyes,' 'hey cross-eyes,' 'hey,' er, you know, 'you got rusty fenders on your bicycle,' you know, and 'your bike isn't as good as our bike,' and 'hey Jew-boy,' or, you know, 'hey, you're not, you know, Catholic, so you're no good.' I can remember times when kids would be going to dances, and, and I would leave a dance, you know, like eleven o'clock at night, I'd just leave a dance for no reason to say 'I'll show them,' you know, and, and go and run on a track, you know, for two or three hours, you know, and just go, or go home and lift weights.[44]

The taunts Katz reports go to the heart of the three pillars of masculinity ideal: the stigma of perceived bodily imperfections requiring him to wear spectacles, his relative lack of wealth as represented by his inferior bicycle, and the fact that he recounts being particularly compelled to exercise by the courtship ritual of the school dance. The anti-Semitic taunts remind us of the racist elements of the American masculinity ideal.

Katz's aim in pursing sports, culminating in bodybuilding, was to create a body so fearsome that he could never be picked on again:

> That was my biggest thing, you know, to go on a football field and be so feared. I wanted to be put in a cage, you know, and rolled out like a circus freak, you know: big bars, you know, and with chains and everything, and just hope like hell that everybody would just run off the field when they saw me coming.[45]

That this is an *image* of masculinity, an *act*, is revealed not only by the derogatory theatricality of Katz's description of himself as a 'circus freak' but also by his ultimate hope: that his masculine appearance is sufficient to scare away his opponents without actual engagement.

Repair means becoming a man, whatever the cost. But if repair is not possible, *compensation* may be the answer. If a man feels that he fails in one area of masculinity he may compensate by trying especially hard in another.[46] So a man who faces unemployment or career stagnation may turn his focus to working out at the gym; or a man who feels insecure in his sexual performance may prioritize status symbols and conspicuous consumption. This strategy features in the 1999 film *American Beauty* in which Lester Burnham, played by Kevin Spacey, deals with mid-life career failure by lifting weights in his garage in an attempt to seduce a much younger woman.

The heteronormativity of the masculinity ideal has a particular impact on gay men.[47] According to dominant homophobic narratives, gay men are not masculine, not real men. Some gay men reclaim the narrative of gay-as-effeminate by adopting a camp identity or performing drag. These practices and identities may be understood as redefinition of the masculinity ideal.[48] Other gay men reject the narrative of gay-as-effeminate by adopting a hyper-masculine identity and body. Their practices and identities affirm the masculinity ideal, prompting them to engage in repair and compensation to meet it.

As public health psychologist Perry Halkitis explains, the imperative to be seen as traditionally masculine, with big muscles and toned flesh, became particularly important for many gay men with the onset of the HIV epidemic. 'In the past two decades of AIDS,' he wrote in 2000, 'the desire to remain healthy and look healthy has worked in sync with attempts for men to construct a definition of gay masculinity.'[49] From the 1950s onwards, some gay men had affirmed their masculinity by adopting and eulogizing a muscular body aesthetic. But this 'subculture that so clearly associates masculinity with physicality, strength, virility, and sexual prowess' was accelerated by the AIDS crisis, 'driven and directed by a reaction to the seemingly endless sicknesses and deaths that devastated gay epicentres'.[50]

Many HIV-positive gay men engaged in bodybuilding practices of weightlifting and supplement use to counteract both the stereotypes and the physical effects of living with HIV. These compensatory and reparatory practices of body modification are understandable responses to a condition of unjust inequality, brought about by discrimination against gay men in society in general, and in the domain of medical research and treatment in particular. 'Perhaps, if we are able to eradicate the virus, then gay men can refocus their efforts in defining their masculine selves as individuals independent of their physical appearance,' Halkitis writes. 'Until then, the buff agenda provides a temporary patch for gay men who seek to maintain their health and be accepted by a society that views them as naturally weak, effeminate, sickly and deviant.'[51]

On Melzer's analysis, the three parts of the masculinity ideal (body, breadwinning, bedroom) vary in importance depending on the age and life-stage a man is at. For boys from puberty onwards the body ideal is the most important: being tough, being strong, looking older and bigger. As the boy grows into a teen and young man the bedroom ideal takes centre stage: to be a man now means to attract girls and women (according to heteronormative masculinity) and to satisfactorily *perform* sex (it's not so important, from the perspective of masculinity, to enjoy it). With the onset of adulthood, the breadwinning ideal takes centre stage: now, the most important thing for a man to do is to provide for his family and succeed in his career.

According to Melzer, boys who are not succeeding at sex and men who are not succeeding at breadwinning often try to compensate by emphasizing the physical aspects of masculinity: the ideal of the manly body. This is not to say that every man who pursues a manly body is compensating for masculinity failure; the body is an important site of masculinity in its own right, and men may focus on other aspects of the masculinity ideal to compensate for perceived body inadequacy. Focusing on the body as a compensation strategy may take relatively benign forms, such as natural bodybuilding or other sports, or it may take highly damaging forms, such as dangerous steroid use, domestic violence, or starting fights.

The body and bedroom parts of the masculine ideal intersect with the idea that a man should have a penis that is large – or at least not small – and that can perform sexually on demand and for an adequate length of time. Melzer describes an online community he dubs the Penis Health Club, in which members who are worried about their members interact and offer virtual support. This support comes in the form of a confusing combination: reassurance that size doesn't matter, alongside penis workout regimes that suggest it does. The workouts include manually stretching the penis and attaching weights to it. These regimes are time-consuming and demanding, sometimes so intense that they are 'on a par with those of bodybuilders'.[52]

The appeal of these penile workouts is not just the results that they may achieve. It is the simple idea that men can do something to change the culturally loaded body part, can change the physical flesh of the penis and the masculine identity it represents. 'Despair and resignation are replaced by hope and empowerment. A sense of control is restored and the work of restorative manhood therapy begins.'[53]

It's easier to achieve results with bodybuilding than with penile workouts. If you lift weights regularly, your muscles will grow. If you manage to stick to a restrictive diet, your body fat will reduce. And so the rewards of bodybuilding – the visible changes, the increased self-confidence, the respect of others – make it an appealing way to achieve masculinity ideals. At the elite level bodybuilding can be highly destructive, even dangerous. But at the amateur level, when it really is natural, bodybuilding can be good for both body and soul.

At the BNBF competition I am most surprised by the atmosphere. The event is all about judging and ranking bodies, and yet the environment does not feel at all body-shaming. I went to the competition expecting it to feel mildly threatening, to feel uneasy or ashamed of my own body, to feel guilty about participating in the objectification of the participants. But what strikes me most forcefully is how supportive the environment is.

The competition is divided into two sessions: the afternoon judging, and the 'evening performance' (actually running from 4 p.m. to 6 p.m. – a nice early night). The audience for the afternoon judging is sparse, and I can sit very close to the front next to the panel of judges. Proceedings are led by the head judge, the only woman among six men. The judges are current or former professional bodybuilders.

Competitors take the stage by class, and all in the class pose together. The first class is the men over fifty, followed by the men over sixty – two of whom, we are told, are actually over seventy! One of the over-seventies – by far the least muscular competitor of the day, his physique toned yet relatively slight – looks genuinely happy and carefree up on stage. Bodybuilding is clearly good for his spirit.

Other male competitors are divided by age and weight. There's a separate class for novices: bodybuilders who have never been placed first or second in any previous competition. Some of them have never competed before, we're told – they'll need extra cheering. It is the novice class whose entrants have physiques that most fit a conventional aesthetic: you could imagine them on the cover of *Men's Health* or in a Calvin Klein commercial. The novice category is also the male class with the most entrants. Bodybuilding is a popular sport with plenty of new recruits.

Once on stage, clad only in posing pouch and oil with fake tan for the white guys, the men are led by the head judge through the series of eight mandatory poses. First is *Front Double Biceps*: the classic strongman pose, with elbows bent and clenched fists held above the head. Next is *Front Lat Spread*: arms bent, fists on hips, chest broad. Then come two poses from the side (any side, competitor's choice): *Side Chest*, in which the shoulder is rolled back and the chest tensed to demonstrate its muscles, and *Side Triceps*, with the arm extended straight down and gripped at the wrist by the other arm, reaching round from behind the back.

Next come two rear-facing poses. *Rear Double Biceps Showing*

Hamstring & Calf is the classic strongman pose viewed from behind, accompanied with a slight lunge so that the muscles of the straight leg are emphasized. It's difficult to hold: wobbly, asymmetrical. *Rear Lat Spread* has hands on hips again: it makes the shoulders broad and shows a relatively smooth upper back.

Then the competitors turn to face the audience again for the final two poses. *Abs & Thighs* requires tensing the legs to show the leg and thigh muscles, while the arms are raised, hands behind the head, to reveal sucked-in abs and six-pack. This pose requires the vacuum that Schwarzenegger was talking about, lamenting its loss in elite competitions. It may be unachievable by those with Roid Gut but all the bodybuilders in the natural competition manage it fine. Some of them wiggle their hips, tilting from side to side to show the muscles on both sides of the torso.

Finally comes the *Most Muscular* pose, which looks the most aggressive. There are a few versions of this pose: to do one of them the bodybuilder clenches his fists in front of his body and leans forward towards the audience. The aim is to demonstrate sheer muscle mass along the shoulders, upper back, neck, arms and chest. This pose goes well with a fearsome facial expression: bared teeth, a grimace, or a roar. It's a stark contrast with the other poses, which are typically performed with cheerful, friendly facial expressions: broad smiles, twinkling eyes, maybe even a wink if the competitor is feeling confident.

The head judge leads the competitors through the poses, then rearranges them on stage and runs them through the poses several more times. She frequently exhorts the audience to cheer and clap for the bodybuilders. 'It's lonely up on stage,' she tells us all. 'Keep the noise levels up!' And the audience comply; most are there to support family, friends, or gym buddies. 'Go on, Dad!' someone shouts from the audience. It's a friendly, uplifting atmosphere.

The atmosphere ramps up a notch in the evening performance. In this part of the competition the lighting is more dramatic and dry ice makes an appearance: it's moody and theatrical. The auditorium, perhaps only a quarter filled for the afternoon judging, is now nearly full. There's a compère on stage, who takes up the task of keeping the audience participation going. 'The louder you are, the bigger these guys get!' We whoop enthusiastically.

The bodybuilders perform, one by one, to a 60-second piece of music of their choice. The music is eclectic: Michael Jackson, the *Back to the Future* soundtrack, some imposing classical, rap, trance, pop. Bodybuilders can perform in any way that they feel best complements their physique. Some of the competitors choose poses reminiscent of the Greek ideal. The over-seventy-year-old has mixed his own sound-track: it starts with music, to which he does some standard posing, and then cuts to some dialogue from the film *RoboCop*. He mouths along and pretends to be a cyborg. It's utterly delightful, and no one has to be reminded to cheer.

When the individual performances are complete all the members of the class take the stage. They repeat the poses they were judged on earlier for the benefit of audience members who are only here for the evening session. Then a piece of music is played and all the competitors take part in a Pose-Down, while the judges add up the scores. The judging is finished now, so the bodybuilders play to the crowd. They rush to the front of the stage and jostle for position, but it's all very good-natured. There's lots of smiling and joshing: some competitors co-ordinate their poses, others perform mock stand-offs.

When the Pose-Down is over there are lots of fist-bumps and hand-shakes. The competitors line up at the rear of the stage to hear the results. There's a feeling of camaraderie. All have performed success-fully. All have proved their masculinity.

UNNATURALNESS AS CORRUPTION

By the end of the twentieth century the Mr. America competition had all but fizzled out. Events held in the 2000s had dwindling audiences and little fanfare. The contest's downfall was, ultimately, its unnaturalness.

Throughout the 1990s bodybuilding was plagued by what Fair calls 'the steroid conundrum'.[54] On the one hand, the ubiquitous use of steroids was killing the sport. The bodies necessary to win in competition were unappealing to a mainstream audience: grotesque and freakish, not attractive and aspirational. The drugs being used had dangerous side-effects, as catalogued in articles with titles like 'Bodybuilders Who Passed Away Too Young',[55] 'Death By Muscle',[56] and 'Big Dead Bodybuilders'.[57] 'Try to find a dozen healthy IFBB [International Federation of Bodybuilding and Fitness] pros who successfully competed in the '90s,' Chris Colucci challenges readers of *TNation*. 'You won't have much luck.'[58] The winners of the first five Mr. America contests (1939–44) all lived to their late seventies or eighties; the average life expectancy of a Mr. America who won since the onset of the steroid era is fifty-three.[59]

On the other hand, efforts to clean up the professional sport with mandatory drug testing were largely unsuccessful. In practical terms, drug testing was too often ineffective. It was expensive and no one wanted to pay. It was virtually impossible for testing methods to keep up with the constant stream of new drugs being used. Competitions did not use the best testing protocols. And competitors found it fairly easy to avoid being tested or to cheat when they were. An IFBB bodybuilder, writing under the pseudonym Shadow Pro, reports:

> Here's the real story: Men and women can compete in a natural show and come up clean on drug tests just a few months after finishing a hard cycle. 'Natural' in this case simply means 'not currently on steroids and other drugs at this very moment . . . as least not the ones that can be detected by a lame drug test at a bodybuilding show.'
>
> Do you really think an athlete who was on drugs for years will lose all of his gains if he comes off steroids for a mere three or four months? Absolutely not! I sometimes look at these guys who claim to be natural and just laugh. They can't possibly think everyone around them is moronic enough to believe this, can they? . . .
>
> Sorry if I'm spoiling the fairytale you perhaps very much want to believe, but I'm here to speak the truth. Just so you won't think I'm a complete asshole, in the amateur level you might find some very good natural guys. But when it comes to the highest level in the world, meaning the pros and top level national competitors, you won't find anyone natural, even in the tested shows. That's the truth. If someone wants to prove me wrong, bring me a pro bodybuilder and I'll pay for their 'real' drug test.[60]

And, while no one other than a competitive bodybuilder wants to look like a competitive bodybuilder these days, it turned out that people didn't want to pay to look at less freakish competitors either. Audiences for professional bodybuilding shows *wanted* to see brutally ripped, violently shredded, grotesquely vascular guys. Men who didn't take steroids didn't live up to the ideal, and 'were stigmatised as losers'.[61] At the natural competition I attend the audience is almost all friends and family of the competitors. It's a great event for those in the sport, but natural competitions are not bringing in large outside audiences.

Steroid use in the women's sport undermines femininity, too, by creating a physique that looks more masculine. Bodybuilder Rachel McLish called for drug testing in her sport, saying, 'If steroid use isn't checked, people will keep asking "Is this a man or a woman?" Drug testing will legitimize our sport.'[62]

Top male bodybuilders are not real, authentic men, and top female bodybuilders don't look like women. This is a problem for the sport, which operates within dominant understandings of gender. The women's sport is at risk of requiring an unfeminine physique, one that is unappealing to both competitors and audiences.[63] One solution is categories for women bodybuilders that preserve their femininity.

The different classes in the male competition exist to make the competition fair. All of the men's classes are aiming at the same aesthetic ideal and are judged according to the same physical standards. In contrast, the women's classes are divided by aesthetic criteria. At the BNBF competition women compete in three different classes, defined not by age or weight but by aesthetic ideal. The classes are Bodybuilding/Physique, Athletic, and Figure.

The standard Bodybuilding or Physique class closely mirrors the men's competition. The same poses are used, and the women pose barefoot, with no jewellery permitted other than a wedding ring. The Athletic class also emphasizes muscularity but competitors 'should not be over muscular, heavily muscled athletes will be considered wrong for this class. The look should be athletic with long hard muscle rather than the bigger full muscle bellies of the Ms Physique.'[64]

The third category is Figure, which is closest to a glamour or beauty competition. Competitors in the Figure competition must pose in high heels and can wear jewellery. The criteria for this class emphasize femininity:

Competitors should show visible signs of strength training. Relative leanness means a competitor should show definition without striations[:] there should be a roundness to the muscle which accentuates the female form. There should be noticeable abdominal detail. There should be some visible lines in the quadriceps. Very hard condition and striated muscle will be considered wrong for the class. Posing form required is flexible ... [T]he athlete should display poses that accentuate their feminine shape and tone to their best advantage.[65]

These classifications and criteria demonstrate the tension between femininity and muscle. The more muscular the physique, the fewer feminine accessories are allowed (no shoes, no jewellery); the more feminine the accessories, the smaller the muscles must be. When they perform *Front Double Biceps* the women in the Physique category pose just like the men, with clenched fists, but the women in the Figure category pose with open hands and spread fingers. It's more a 'Ta-da!' than a 'GRRRR!'

These contradictions are explicitly acknowledged in Lianne McTavish's book *Feminist Figure Girl*, in which she details her personal journey into competitive bodybuilding. '[I]n my opinion while on stage I had never looked more conservatively lady like, displaying my

Bodybuilders in a range of categories posing at the BNBF

body for a panel of male judges while wearing a tiny bikini, delicate jewelry, heavy makeup, hair extensions, and high heels for the first time in my life,' she writes. 'Yet it seems that many outraged viewers had easily overlooked all of these gendered signifiers; these signs of femininity had in effect been overruled by my "manly" musculature, which sent mixed messages that were apparently disturbing.'[66]

As you'd expect, the most popular women's class in terms of number of entrants is the Figure class. These bodybuilders are the most conventionally attractive. But watching them makes me feel uncomfortable. For all the other classes, including the other women's classes, it's clear that we're watching athletes demonstrating their sport: it's no more sexual watching them in posing pouch and bikini than it is watching Olympic swimmers or runners in swimsuits and Lycra. The women in the Figure class are clearly accomplished athletes, too, but watching them pose feels closer to watching a beauty pageant. They feel more objectified, somehow, more sexualized. Perhaps it's only when a body is deliberately extreme that it feels OK to ogle it.

In patriarchal culture women are meant for display and objectified sexualization, so it follows – it's only natural – that the act of looking at women who most closely fit the prevailing norms of femininity feels objectifying. Constructing one's body can be empowering for a woman, but judging women's bodies on stage for their aesthetic appeal feels distinctly anti-feminist.

Bodybuilding is without doubt a body modification practice. It is absolutely a soldier in the war of *your body is never good enough*. But at least in bodybuilding the message and purpose are explicit. Everyone knows they are trying to shape their bodies in pursuit of an ideal; everyone knows they will be judged; everyone knows they can always be found wanting. Everyone knows this is not ordinary life.

Natural bodybuilding shows us that the concept of the natural body is not a straightforward proxy for the unmodified body. In natural bodybuilding 'naturalness' coexists with deliberate, effortful modification. What natural bodybuilding proves is that naturalness in relation to the human body always exists in reference to a norm – an ideal, an identity, a set of social standards.

Is it good to be natural? Is it better to have a natural body than an unnatural one? It all depends on the content and consequences of the regulating ideal.

In terms of physical health you could do a lot worse than being a natural bodybuilder. It's probably better to be a natural bodybuilder than to be someone who never exercises. You're certainly better off being a natural bodybuilder than an unnatural one.

In terms of mental health natural bodybuilding can be rewarding, supportive, communal, joyful and inspiring: a way of meeting masculinity ideals and boosting self-esteem. For some men, though, the standards set by natural bodybuilding are unattainable, and trying to meet them will only exacerbate anxiety and self-doubt.

Natural bodybuilding is a response to a masculinity ideal that is both immensely powerful and difficult to meet. Masculinity as an ideal cannot be assessed separately from assessing the system of gender as a whole. Masculinity can be toxic, but it need not be; and, certainly, *being a man* is compatible with both virtue and vice, both flourishing and suffering. As masculinity varies in both content and value, so too does the idea of naturalness that operates within it.

Natural bodybuilding is better than unnatural bodybuilding. But that does not mean that masculinity comes naturally. Building a natural body can be a valuable personal project, but it is also a deeply political practice.

2

Nature, Your Frenemy

Periods, Hair, Make-Up and Shametenance

A survey among students in Ethiopia showed that half of them have trouble concentrating during menstruation. Students in Sierra Leone have explained that they try not to answer questions in the classroom when they are menstruating – to avoid standing up. In a Kenyan study, a girl is quoted saying that during her period 'her whole mind will be centred there' and that she cannot feel free.

Anna Dahlqvist, *It's Only Blood* (2018)[1]

So much of what we are conditioned to believe is 'natural' is not. Certainly, it is not universal, nor 'just the way things are'. We have choices in what we collectively recognize as valuable. For me, great possibilities exist in my recognition that the society I live in was designed with my exclusion in mind. Never again will I mutilate any part of myself in an attempt to one day awkwardly almost-maybe fit in.

Emma Dabiri, *Don't Touch My Hair* (2019)[2]

While a natural look makes women feel better, 49 percent of survey respondents said aging has made it difficult to achieve.

Real Simple magazine (2017)[3]

Nature has been bad for women. It has given them the burdens and dangers of pregnancy and childbirth, a state that is responsible for the deaths of 830 women every day, 302,950 women per year.[4] It has given them the burdens of menstruation, something that causes monthly pain and psychological distress to the vast majority of women: studies find that up to 91 per cent of menstruating women experience period pain and approximately half suffer premenstrual syndrome (PMS).[5] It gives them the risks and consequences of unintended pregnancy, including taking prime responsibility for contraception and having to seek termination, adoption or take on the responsibilities of motherhood when pregnancy occurs. An article in *The Lancet* estimates that 44 per cent of pregnancies worldwide are unintended, making these burdens very significant indeed.[6]

With the hand that nature has dealt them, why would women want to preserve their natural bodies? Why wouldn't women want to modify their bodies as much as possible, if it could make their lives easier? Why give nature the time of day?

The real culprit, however, is not nature. It is *how society responds* to women's natural bodies. Maternal mortality is no more natural than mortality from any other cause, be it heart attack, cancer, malnutrition, or accident. These things really exist, and they're natural in the sense that they originate in our flesh and blood. But in every case, the issue that most affects mortality is how human societies are arranged: whether they're arranged in a way that encourages or prevents the emergence of life-threatening conditions, whether people live in conditions that hasten or slow the spread of disease, and whether the treatment of those conditions is prioritized in research, resources and medical settings. The World Health Organization says that most cases of maternal mortality are preventable; the problem is that societies don't prioritize their prevention. Whether a woman dies in childbirth depends not only on the country in which she gives birth but also on her class and race. In the UK and the USA, a Black woman is up to five times more likely to die in childbirth than a white woman.[7]

Menstruation, too, is a natural part of being female, but the way it affects a woman's life depends on social factors.[8] Right now, as you are reading this, 500 million women and girls are menstruating.[9] Perhaps you are one of them. But who else is? Look around the café, the library, the train; think back to the office, the shops, the school gates. Which of the people you encountered were bleeding? You almost certainly have no idea, and that fact probably strikes you as unremarkable. It would be much more remarkable if you *could* tell: if you saw blood-stained clothing, or a woman on her way to the bathroom with a tampon visible in her hand, or if a co-worker replied to your cheery 'How are you?' with 'Good, thanks – only moderate flow today, and the cramps have stopped!'

But have you ever acknowledged the enormous amount of *effort* that goes into keeping menstruation invisible?

Shame is built in from the start. Every girl learns, when she first gets her period, that she must keep it secret. Girls and women go to enormous efforts to hide their menstruation from others; collectively we keep it out of public life. We are complicit in practices that keep menstruation shameful for others, and we generally submit to personal feelings of shame or embarrassment.

We have little choice. Feminist philosopher Sandra Lee Bartky argues that shame is an emotion triggered not by one's actions but by one's status. 'Shame,' she writes, 'is the distressed apprehension of the self as inadequate or diminished.'[10] Feelings of shame are felt in relation to one's social status. 'What gets grasped in the having of such feelings is nothing less than women's subordinate status in a hierarchy of gender.'[11]

For shame to operate so effectively it has to be maintained. Systems of gender hierarchy are oppressively maintained in a vast variety of ways, including via legal structures, economic inequality, media portrayals and family life. Often women are explicitly shamed by others: for their inadequacies, for their failure to live up to required standards, *and* for their success at doing so. After all, if femininity is inferior, it is as much a diminishment to meet its demands as it is to fail them. Men and boys shame women and girls, whether on the playground, in the workplace, online, in government, or in the courts.

But for shame to persist it also has to be maintained by those who (are supposed to) feel it. Members of subordinated groups, including women and girls, effectively perform shame maintenance, or what I'll call *shametenance*. We engage in shametenance when we do things that maintain the social norm that something is shameful. We maintain shame by actively shaming others, or simply by keeping things private, silent, invisible, unsayable. And we engage in shametenance when we feel shame about ourselves, when we accept the idea that privacy is necessary or that silence is essential.

What is so notable about gendered shame is how readily it attaches to women's natural bodies. Gendered shame occurs in other contexts, too; Bartky's own example is the shame many of her female students express about their work, regardless of its actual quality. But the female body and its natural processes are a particularly rich source of shame.

Women perform shametenance about a great many things, including many aspects of female embodied experience: miscarriage, incontinence, stretch marks, menopause. All these experiences are incredibly common yet notably secret, as highlighted in the title of Nimko Ali's collection of women's stories *What We're Told Not to Talk About (But We're Going to Anyway)*.[12] Menstruation is perhaps the starkest example of shametenance. In all countries, menstruation is considered something to be kept private at all costs. This social shaming of menstruation affects all women, because it reflects and sustains their oppression.

Not everyone who menstruates identifies as a woman, because many trans men and non-binary people also menstruate. But I refer to 'women' and 'girls' because this discussion is about the specifically gendered nature of shametenance as it affects people who are socially identified as women and girls. Trans men and non-binary people may also feel they must conceal their menstruation, since menstruation is not generally thought compatible with those gender identities. For women and girls, though, menstruation must be kept secret even though – or precisely because – it is a fundamental aspect of womanhood.

Virtually everywhere it is imperative that women and girls conceal the fact they are menstruating. Most women and girls are filled with horror at the thought that others might be able to see their sanitary protection through their clothes, or in their hand; visible period blood on hands or clothes or furniture would be mortifying. When I was a civil servant a co-worker once asked me, in a whisper, whether I had a spare tampon. I did. She was horrified to find that I kept them in my desk drawer, not hidden in my handbag or briefcase. She returned the packet to me hidden inside a brown A4 envelope.

I bet most women have spent at least one day keeping their coat on or with a jumper tied around their waist to conceal a period stain. As a parent I spent a school sports day like that – *why* did I wear pale trousers?! A friend once told me that she had stood up at the end of a business meeting in someone else's workplace to see that her menstrual blood had leaked through her clothes and stained the fabric of the chair she'd been sitting on. 'What did you do?!' I asked, aghast. 'I pushed the chair under the table and left,' she replied.

I'd have done the same. But if I'd cut my hand in a meeting and blood had dripped on the chair I'd have asked for help, drawn attention to the stain, and apologized. It's only period blood that requires shametenance.

The need to conceal menstruation is clearly expressed in this clip from *The Archers*, the long-running BBC Radio 4 soap opera about life in a farming community in rural England. Mia has just started her first period. Mia's mother died suddenly of sepsis, and so her aunt Emma has come to visit with help and advice:

Mia: What's this?

Emma: Oh, now . . . I really wanted to find you one like I used to have, but then I saw this, with the sequins, and I thought 'Bingo!'

Mia: It's gorgeous!

Emma: So, you know when you're at school, and you've got your period? I remember I used to have this nightmare that someone would knock my bag over and all my sanitary stuff would fall out, and everyone would see.

Mia: I'm totally the same.

Emma: Exactly. Right? So. I bought a pouch, like this, just a simple zip-up, so it's nice and secure, and that's what I kept my stuff in. So if my bag ever did get knocked over, all anyone would see is this! And they'd think it was a purse, and move on.

Mia (emotionally): Emma, you're a lifesaver![13]

This depiction of shametenance is easily recognizable to anyone who has menstruated: we all have or had something to carry our tampons and towels in. I remember a bright yellow plastic box with a hinged lid that was perfectly sized to hold two Tampax tampons; the problem was that I, like every other girl in my class, had been given it when the Tampax Lady came to visit our school, and so we all knew precisely what the yellow boxes contained. Emma's sparkly sequined pouch is a much better idea.

Incidentally, you might think that the fact that this storyline featured on a programme as mainstream and Establishment as *The Archers* undermines the idea of shametenance. Doesn't it demonstrate that periods actually *can* be discussed openly; that it is only Mia's youth, inexperience and lack of a mother that makes them embarrassing for her? Well, no. Emma is presented as the 'lifesaver', the voice of frank, open advice and warm sisterly bonding. And yet the whole scene – which is played out, remember, on the radio, so there are no images to look at – takes place without ever once mentioning words like 'tampon', 'pad', or 'menstrual cup':

> **Emma:** Now, these are the possible choices of what to use.
> What you using at the minute?
> **Mia** (embarrassed): Errrmm . . . Er . . . These ones.
> **Emma:** They working out OK?
> **Mia:** Think so.
> **Emma:** Well, me and Mum bought you some different sizes and
> brands to try out.
> **Mia** (alarmed): Your mum knows?!
> **Emma:** It's OK, she helped me with mine. Now, we bought
> these, 'cause you might want something different when it's
> just started, or coming to an end – or, like on P.E. days, when
> you'll be running about and stuff, you might want these.
> They're cheaper, too. I swear, the price of ladies' things is
> such a rip-off![14]

Even in a dramatization designed to demonstrate the difficulties of discretion, we must make do with euphemism. 'Ladies' things' – a rip-off indeed.

Menstrual taboos exist around the world, dictating what menstruating women must not do: touch the Koran, receive the Eucharist, have sex, bathe, make mayonnaise.[15] In many places menstruation is considered so shameful that women and girls who are menstruating must seclude themselves during their periods, or ensure that the rags they use to catch their blood are washed and dried in a way that is not visible to anyone, even family members. The impact of this secrecy is significant: Anna Dahlqvist reports that the numbers of girls who do not attend school while they are menstruating, often for several days each month, varies 'from 20 per cent in studies from Ghana, Ethiopia, and Sierra Leone to roughly 30 per cent in Nepal, South Africa, and Afghanistan, 40 per cent in Senegal, and 50 per cent in Kenya. In parts of India, the number is as high as 70 per cent.'[16] Washing menstrual cloths quickly, for fear of being seen, and then drying them secretly in enclosed spaces rather than outside in the light and air means that they harbour bacteria that cause bacterial vaginosis or urinary tract infections, conditions that, if suffered repeatedly and left untreated, may cause the sort of fatal blood poisoning that killed Mia's mum.[17]

When a woman refuses to perform shametenance it makes the international news. In 2015 Kiran Gandhi ran the London Marathon

Kiran Gandhi, centre, after running the London Marathon

without using menstrual protection, to avoid the chafing and discomfort of tampons and pads. The image of her crossing the finish line with blood stains on her thighs was covered around the world.[18]

The rest of us are not so brave. Perhaps we feel we have more to lose; perhaps we have internalized shame more effectively. Some feminists have judged that it serves women better to downplay menstruation, to keep it invisible, since its existence can be used as a weapon against them. The writer Julian Barnes tells a story of this sort:

> Germaine Greer, when put up in debate against the sort of crusty old male who argues that women can't do really complicated and demanding jobs, like fly an aeroplane or run the country, because, well, er, you see, the fact of the matter is that ever so often, about once a month actually, they, how shall we put it, become a little unreliable – Ms Greer would on such occasions look the geezer magnificently in the eye and say, 'Am I menstruating now?'[19]

By naming it, Greer brought menstruation into view in that conversation, but her rhetorical question emphasizes secrecy. Greer's implication is that *of course one cannot tell* when a woman is menstruating. Greer's strategy may have been effective in the moments at which she reportedly deployed it, but the wider effects of a strategy of concealment are bad for women. As human-rights activist Archana Patkar puts it, 'By ignoring biology we are discriminating against half of the world's population. The silence is actually astonishing! . . . How are we supposed to access other rights if we ignore the daily and monthly needs of the human body?'[20]

But ignore them we do. 'In the UN's lowest standard for the treatment of inmates in prisons, the opportunity to manage facial hair is explicitly mentioned, but not menstrual management,' reports Dahlqvist.[21]

Valuing the unmodified body is about refusing to perform shame-tenance. It is about refusing to accept that our bodies are never quite good enough. It is about refusing to characterize our bodies in their natural state as gross or disgusting or dirty. In this endeavour, the concept of the natural body is our friend. It enables us to resist the oppressive social interpretations of our bodies and celebrate their simple, unarguable, naturalness. *IT IS NATURAL!* becomes a rallying cry, a poster slogan, an act of resistance.

Sometimes, though, the idea of nature is used to maintain hierarchy and to justify shame. A frenemy is someone who is friend and enemy together: at one moment boosting you up, at another holding you down. By the end of this chapter, we'll see why nature is a frenemy and how the idea of the natural body can be liberating *and* oppressive. We'll see the power of the idea of naturalness, and the various purposes to which that power can be put.

The idea of the natural body can be used to defend or to attack. It can be used to preserve, but it can also be used to destroy. When we describe something as natural we are wielding powerful rhetoric. We bring to bear ideas of purity, perfection and authenticity, ideas that can be used to reinforce structural oppression or to resist it.

NATURAL HAIR

Did bad mean Black? The endless scrubbing with lemon juice in the cracks and crevices of my ripening, darkening body. And oh, the sins of my dark elbows and knees, my gums and nipples, the folds of my neck and the cave of my armpits!
Audre Lorde, 'Eye to Eye' (1983)[22]

Natural/unnatural beauty continues to be the compelling binary.
Shirley Tate, 'Black beauty' (2007)[23]

Natural hair is an example of how the idea of naturalness can help secure justice. Natural hair fights on two fronts. First, it is a way for Black people, and especially Black women, to resist shametenance – to assert that *our bodies are good enough*. Secondly, it is a way to resist structural racism. The two are closely related.

'Natural hair' is the term used to describe Afro-textured hair that has not been straightened. Afro-textured hair is not just one thing: Black people have a variety of textures and curl patterns ranging from looser to tighter, rounder to kinkier. But it has long been the norm for Black people in Western contexts to straighten their hair, typically by using chemical relaxers but also with heated straighteners and styling products. It's a painstaking, arduous, expensive and even dangerous process, requiring frequent trips to the hair salon or at-home use of strong, burning chemicals.

The norm for straight hair is just one aspect of a racist aesthetic that associates beauty with whiteness, denigrating Black bodies and racialized features as non-beautiful, ugly, or deficient. As philosopher Paul C. Taylor puts it, 'the most prominent racialized ranking represents blackness as a condition to be despised.'[24] This racist aesthetic is one form of racism enacted on the body. Others included the pseudo-science of physiognomy, a doctrine based on the idea that physical features such as the proportions of the face or the length of the femur were indications of intellectual and moral qualities.[25] 'Thus it became part of the content of the standard thick, hierarchical racialism,' Taylor writes, 'that the physical ugliness of black people was a sign of a deeper ugliness and depravity.'[26]

The natural hair movement resists the imperative to straighten and encourages Black women and men to embrace their hair in its natural state. It allows Afro hair to retain its own texture. Natural hair is unmodified hair. It is hair that is allowed to be true to itself.

Sociologist Shirley Tate charts the development of 'black anti-racist aesthetics' particularly in the Caribbean, Britain and the United States. She describes how dominant white European standards of beauty impact upon Black people in those societies, so that Black women and men have tended to align beauty with straighter hair, paler skin and stereotypically white facial features. In the 1930s, the Jamaican Rastafarian movement developed an alternative aesthetic of resistance. That aesthetic emphasized the potential for resistance in valuing natural beauty. 'Wearing dreadlocks and praising dark skin and natural beauty was for Rastas a powerful symbol of freedom, defiance and being outside a white oriented aesthetics,' Tate explains.[27]

The Rasta understanding of the association between politics and beauty was not mainstream. But it returned to prominence with the anti-racist aesthetic developed in the Black Power movement of the 1960s and 1970s. According to that movement, 'Afro hairstyles ("the natural") became associated with political change and Black self love/ knowledge.'[28] The idea of naturalness, and natural hair in particular, thus became a form of resistance to colonial power, racism and white supremacy.

Natural hair, like natural bodybuilding, can take a lot of work. It is not natural in the sense of having been left alone. Natural hair usually has a great deal done to it: it may be braided, twisted, put in loc(k)s,[29] beaded, or coloured, and these processes take time, skill and effort. What natural hair scholar and advocate Emma Dabiri describes as the '"militant" Afro' of the 1970s, Afro-textured hair left unbraided, is a historical deviation from the more traditional African hairstyles practised for centuries and celebrated in the current natural hair movement. 'Within a traditional West African aesthetic, the idea of artifice was often highly valued, and we know that hair was rarely, if ever, left out in anything resembling a natural Afro,'[30] she writes.

> The natural hair movement that emerged [in the 1960s and 1970s] sought to avoid artificial manipulation of hair as a rejection of consumerism. Today's natural hair movement has been born out of a different cultural moment: a renewed confidence in our own worth driven in many ways by the revolution in social media.[31]

One influential source of information and advice on natural hair is the YouTube channel Green Beauty, run by Nikky Nwamokobia and watched by 267,000 subscribers. The channel showcases advice on how to style and care for natural hair. Every method involves regular sessions taking several hours. Microtwists are said to take three hours; in the comments viewers reckon that five to six hours is more realistic. Various cleansing methods are discussed, but viewers are told that long natural hair will take at least an hour to clean. Dabiri cautions us not to think of this as time lost or wasted – time spent styling hair can be a valuable source of bonding and sociability. But the point remains: natural hair is not hair left alone.

So, natural hair takes a lot of attention and skill: a lot of effort. But it does not involve a certain kind of effort. It does not involve shame-tenance. Natural hair is about refusing to be ashamed. It is about refusing the idea that Afro hair is bad hair. And it is about authenticity and the refusal of deception. Consider Dabiri again, describing her experiences as a Black Irish girl growing up in an overwhelmingly white community:

There is untold fun to be had experimenting with hair. But when I was in school it was emphatically not about fun. My actions were a bid for assimilation, by way of disguise. My efforts stemmed from a cardinal terror that people would catch sight of my real hair. From weaves, to extensions, Jheri curls, curly perms, straight perms and straighteners, my hair was hidden, misunderstood, damaged, broken and completely unloved. It is hardly surprising. I never saw anybody with hair like mine. Afro hair was – and in many places still is – stigmatized to the point of taboo.[32]

Natural hair is about letting the character of Afro hair shine through, working with the hair's texture and structure rather than against it. Twisting, braiding and locks may be involved, skilled processes that make the hair look a way that it wouldn't if left alone. But, crucially, these styles do *not* make Afro hair look like white people's hair.

In this sense it is unmodified. In this sense it is natural. The reason that straightening is different from other styling and treatment procedures has to do with racial and ethnic identity and the rejection of racism. Straightening directly targets Black identity. Afro hair that is straightened is hair that is being treated so as to fit in with a racist society, one that views white people's hair as the most beautiful or even the only acceptable form of hair. Natural hair involves painstaking care and highly skilled manipulation, but it is natural because it stays true to an image of Black/African identity that resists colonialism and white supremacy. These are identities that have been suppressed and denigrated by white people, designated inferior at the most micro and macro levels. Natural hair says NO.

In my discussion of natural bodybuilding I talked about *authentic* masculinity, a powerful and political idea. Natural bodybuilding involves excruciating effort and an array of products, but it is natural because it stays true to an image of authentic masculinity. The language of authenticity can be found in natural hair, too. As Tate explains, according to what she describes as a 'normalized racializing black beauty', 'the only authentic black hairstyles would be dreadlocks, afro, cane-row, and plaits. By extension, the only authentic blackness would be a dark-skinned one. These are the valorized signifiers of the ideal of "natural black beauty".'[33]

This language of authenticity is problematic when it implies that Black people who have different features or a different aesthetic are inauthentic or complicit. Natural hair is one way of resisting racist oppression, but it is not the only way. For some pioneering Black women, such as Madam C. J. Walker, an American entrepreneur who built a franchise business of hair salons and products for Afro hair at the turn of the twentieth century, straightened hair was a form of resistance since it offered African American women a way of being seen as respectable, and a route into the middle class.[34]

The association between naturalness and authenticity can also lead to the denigration of Black people whose natural hair is less curly, or whose skin is paler, than the standard of authenticity requires. There is a contradiction in an anti-racist aesthetic that frames the unmodified body as an act of resistance and yet, at the same time, excludes people with certain hair types or skin tone as 'not being really black'.[35] Tate describes how this phenomenon occurs when '"mixed race" straight hair is put outside of blackness', a process that involves shame-tenance. 'Having naturally straight hair which is therefore deemed to be unnatural,' she writes, 'means that you are subject to being checked by other black women, to being asked if your hair is real, to having it touched to see if it really is real.'[36] In this analysis, natural hair becomes associated with authenticity and realness. Hair that *looks* unnatural, because it is straighter than the viewer expects it to be, is denigrated as both unreal and inauthentic.

The challenge is to maintain an idea of natural hair as emancipatory and resistant that does not create new ways to denigrate particular Black bodies. Used with care, the concept of natural hair can be a friend rather than an enemy.

In 2019 New York City passed laws outlawing discrimination based on hairstyles. If you didn't think hairstyle discrimination was a thing, then you probably don't have Afro hair. Many employers and organizations have regulations that require certain hairstyles and forbid others, and the forbidden hairstyles are very often those that work on Afro hair. The New York legislation gave African Americans the legal right to wear their hair in styles such as Afros, cornrows, locks, twists, braids and Bantu knots, without suffering sanction from their employers or others.[37]

The 2016 video 'Locks in the Military (ARMY)', made by First Lt Whennah Andrews in partnership with Nikky Nwamokobia of the Green Beauty YouTube channel, is a lobbying film aimed at the US military. The video campaigned for the Army and Navy to join the other branches of the US military and allow service personnel to wear their hair in locks. The video succeeded: in 2017 the lock ban was lifted. At the time the video was made twists and braids were authorized, 'but locks are a no-no'. The video goes through the reasons given for the ban and shows that each one fails. For example:

> One of the concerns is about maintaining a neat and conservative appearance. According to the Army, 'neat' is defined as 'orderly and tidy in appearance' and 'conservative' is defined as 'conventional, traditional, and moderate in style and appearance; not extreme, not excessive, faddish, or intense'. And as you can see with these examples [photos of hairstyles appear on screen], micro-locks are very neat. Not only do they have meticulous, even parts, often referred to as a grid, if you take a closer look, the individual locks are very consistent, and altogether uniform. In fact, micro-locks make it a lot easier for naturally Afro-textured hair to be worn in conservative styles like buns and pony-tails.[38]

The video continues, moving through each of the hairstyle desiderata set out by the US Army and deftly showing how locks can meet them all. In particular, it shows how requiring Black servicewomen to wear their hair in styles better suited to non-Afro hair is burdensome, costly and stressful, since they must transport chemicals, products and styling tools as part of their kit and make time for straightening while stationed away from home.

I showed the video to my ten-year-old son. 'So basically it's racist,' he observed, meaning the ban. Correct. And sexist, too.

What the video shows is that the hairstyle standards weave racism and sexism in at the very start. The video demonstrates that Afro hair worn in locks can comply with Army standards, a crucial strategy for lifting the ban. But are those standards justified in the first place? Where do they come from? One Army requirement discussed in the video is that the hair should not stand out more than 2 inches from the scalp when it is styled. This requirement is clearly easier to meet for

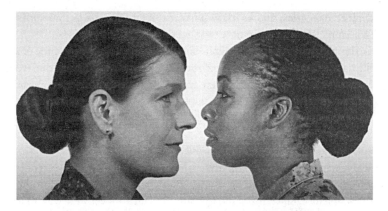

An image from 'Locks in the Military' showing that locks
can be worn in conservative hairstyles

people who have straight hair than it is for people with Afro-textured
hair. It would take effort for a person with straight hair *not* to comply:
they would have to dry their hair in a certain way and use firm-hold
styling products to maintain height. Someone with Afro hair, on the
other hand, has hair that naturally grows up and out rather than
down: to comply with the 2-inch height restriction they must either cut
their hair short or spend time making it lie flat.

Not only does the height requirement affect Black and white people
differently, the aesthetic it protects is inherently racist. Whether a style
that sticks out more than 2 inches from the head is considered conservative, or deliberately distinctive, or even rebellious, also depends on
whether the hair is straight or curly, and on the race of its wearer. A
white man wearing his hair more than 2 inches tall is likely styling it
in a way that aims to stand out, literally and figuratively – with spikes,
or a flamboyant quiff, or a Mohawk. A Black man with tall hair need
be doing no such thing.

More generally, the idea that hair should be 'conservative' is, as
Andrews notes, a value that invokes tradition and convention. Where
traditions are based on the assumption that only certain sorts of
people will be in the military, adopting a conservative attitude towards
them is to maintain those assumptions. In this case the paradigm soldier is both male and white. To be conservative, women must adopt

demure hairstyles, and Black women and men must adopt hairstyles that emulate those achievable with straight hair.

The intersection matters. White men are the default around whom the hairstyle rules are designed. Both Black men and white women are able to comply in ways that adhere to conservative gender norms: Black men by closely cutting their hair, white women by wearing their hair in styles like buns and pony-tails, styles that are recognized to be both feminine and respectable. Whether they should have to comply with these standards is another matter. There is ample scope for critiquing gendered appearance norms. But compliance is at least readily available for white people and Black men. Black women have no easy route to compliance, since the standards are difficult to meet in a way that reflects both femininity and Blackness, much less Black femininity.

At the end of the video Nwamokobia speaks to camera. 'American service members represent one of the most diverse countries in the world,' she says. 'We should be converging to a reality where a citizen can defend their country without having to sacrifice their personal ethnic identity.'

Nwamokobia's closing remark directly connects natural hair with *identity*. Nature, in this context, is all about being true to oneself, having an authentic identity. In the context of natural hair, the most salient identity is racial or ethnic. In another context, being natural might be about respecting a different sort of identity or source of value.

We've seen that the concept of nature and a natural body does a job. It invokes certain social and political identities, certain ethics, certain conceptions of value. This means that we cannot say clearly whether nature is good or bad, and whether having a 'natural body' is to be coveted and praised. It all depends on the view of nature being invoked, on the use to which that concept is being put, and the contrast it is being used to make.

In the natural hair movement, the concept of nature is, on balance, a friend. Other times, it's an enemy.

NATURAL MAKE-UP

When I was about twelve years old, a school friend said I had beautiful eyes.[39] 'You should outline them in black!' she said. Encouraged by the compliment, the next morning I attempted to follow her advice. I didn't own any black eyeliner, so I tried to create the recommended effect by layering blue and brown eyeliner on top of each other. On the school bus, my friend smiled and gave me the thumbs up. I had succeeded!

The pleasure was short-lived. Over the course of the day the liners separated and smudged, leaving me with multicoloured panda eyes. A boy with whom I was usually friendly passed me a note on which he'd written a humorous poem mocking my make-up skills. I was not a figure of beauty. I was a figure of fun.

Wearing make-up is risky, and putting it on is difficult. Nowadays help is at hand in the form of make-up tutorial videos. These have started appearing on my Facebook feed. I watch them, then more appear. It's a vicious circle.

There are two basic kinds. The first shows how to do the very heavy, artificial look that is currently fashionable. I recently watched one called 'This Fabulous Makeup Look' featuring C. C. Clarke.[40] It started with a woman who already had what looked like flawless make-up on – could that really have been her natural skin?! She then added a baffling, pass-the-parcel-worthy number of layers on top, until any semblance of nature was exterminated:

1. **Primer:** a transparent cream patted on with the fingers.
2. **Liquid Foundation:** skin-coloured cream (well, actually, not-quite-skin-coloured cream) applied with a brush.
3. **Contouring:** two different colours of concealer, one darker than the skin and one lighter. These are painted on in streaks and lines around the face.
4. **Blend:** the concealers are blended with a large brush. The aim is to make the face look a different shape (thinner cheeks, more prominent cheekbones, and so on). Some sort of powder is brushed on over the top.

5. **Powder foundation**: various different skin-coloured powders are applied here. Some are sponged on 'in the areas you need more coverage' – though it's hard to see how, since none of the actual skin is visible at this point. Others are brushed on to key areas.
6. **Blush**: again, several different pinkish colours are used for different parts of the face.
7. **Highlight**: back to the skin-coloured powders, applied with tiny brushes to the inner parts of the eyes, the tip of the nose. Didn't we already do this sort of thing when contouring?
8. **Brows**: first a brown pencil draws a line, then a black pen colours them in, then more pencil.
9. **Eyes**: eyeliner, mascara, false eyelashes, and a very dominant black cat-eye effect.
10. **Lips**: these are contoured, too, with different colours dabbed on in sections followed by lipstick over the top.
11. **Hair**: a wig, in this case. A 'style shortcut'. We need a shortcut, after all this.

There's nothing remotely natural about this look.

The second kind of make-up video showcases natural make-up. Natural make-up is make-up that is designed to look as though it is not there, or at least to contrast with heavy, obvious make-up. Someone wearing natural make-up hopes to appear beautiful, fresh, pretty and healthy rather than glamorous, overtly sexy, or dramatic. Natural make-up is make-up that does not advertise its presence.

You might think that natural make-up means no make-up, or at least minimal make-up, or surely quick-and-easy make-up. You'd be wrong. If you look at any beautician's guide to natural make-up one cliché is repeated over and over: natural make-up requires a lot of products and takes a lot of time. 'Barely-there, natural makeup is a look countless celebrities have been wearing in recent months,' *Glamour* magazine reports. 'But the au-natural, I'm-just-genetically-blessed, no makeup-makeup look takes more work than you think.' *Glamour*'s recommendations for achieving the natural look require a nine-step process and products costing between £200 and £300.[41]

Cosmopolitan concurs. 'In theory, natural makeup should be oh-so-easy – it's minimal, which means minimal effort, right? I wish . . .' Their recommended regime uses fifteen products and requires nine steps, many of which involve applying a product and then immediately removing most of it.[42] Make-up company Lancôme's 'nude makeup look', which they also describe as 'simple' and 'natural', involves fifteen steps and twenty products.[43]

The magazine ironically named *Real Simple* recommends a natural make-up routine using fourteen products. Eye pencil is indicated to be optional, and we're given permission to skip eyeshadow if we really must, but we're not allowed to miss mascara. 'Defined lashes are essential, even for a no-makeup look. "You can forfeit shadow and liner but never mascara,"' says their beautician.[44]

So natural make-up is not only compatible with artifice, it demands it. What makes it natural, then? In part it's that it *looks* natural: it looks as though it's not there. It *deceives*. Nature as deception – that's an odd conclusion. But of course you're not *really* supposed to look as though you've got no make-up on: you're meant to look turned out, put-together, professional. You've *made an effort*. But your effort fits within a certain aesthetic: one that prioritizes a fresh face, an image of health, the impression of effortlessness alongside the reassurance of effort. 'Today I'm going to share with you how to create a really youthful, wide-awake, and fresh look,' says make-up artist Katie of Beauty and the Boutique, 'but like you haven't tried too hard.'[45]

Philosopher Heather Widdows argues that beauty has become a moral duty: something that all women are expected to achieve. Girls used to be judged more on their character and virtues; now they are mostly judged, by others and by themselves, on their looks. Research consistently finds an epidemic of appearance-related anxiety. The Nuffield Council on Bioethics, an independent think tank and research organization, reports that

> a growing lack of confidence with respect to their appearance is hold-ing [girls] back from doing many things that they enjoy, such as wearing the clothes, they like, having their photograph taken, participating in sport or exercise, speaking up in class, using social media, socialising, or generally having fun with their friends.[46]

Appearance trumps everything else: 'a significant number of young people in their late teens report that they care more about their appearance than their physical health.'[47] And this imperative doesn't just affect girls: every woman, of every age, class and nationality, is expected to make herself beautiful.

Widdows demonstrates that this aspect of beauty renders us all vulnerable. If beauty were a demand of perfection, a standard to be achieved by the excellent, then it would be relatively easy to avoid simply by focusing on other goals. We might say that we choose to excel at work, or in caring for our children, or in sport, rather than in beauty, and so we have no need to pluck our eyebrows, wax our legs, enlarge our breasts, and refine our pores. Widdows shows that there may be some domains, such as academic philosophy, in which this sort of perspective is possible. But these are few and far between.

Beauty has become something that all women must achieve if they are to be good enough, where *good enough* should be understood as a moral requirement. And what is considered basic is increasing exponentially. As we've seen in the case of natural hair, beauty standards don't affect all people equally. The precise norms that apply vary. Make-up norms differ according to class and age, in particular. Those with bodies closer to dominant ideals need do less to be acceptable. But for most people, especially women, a quick wash and brush is no longer enough.

One of Widdows's key insights is this: when beauty is an ethical ideal, we are all vulnerable. Not one of us is good enough without work. No body can comply with beauty norms without considerable effort: make-up, diets, surgical and other procedures. So all of us are found wanting, are failing in some way, are letting ourselves go. This vulnerability is a serious public health issue on a global scale. And it's part of what makes the idea of valuing the unmodified body so appealing.

Most days I still don't wear make-up. Occasionally, though, I do apply it. Sometimes I regret it instantly: my skills aren't necessarily up to the job, and I end up wiping it all off. Other times, knowing my limitations and working within them, I achieve a passable effect. On those days, looking in the mirror immediately afterwards I experience a thrill akin to the school bus thumbs up. I've done it! I look great! I should wear make-up all the time!

But still the pleasure tends to be short-lived. Later in the day I catch sight of my reflection again. In the habit of touching my face freely, I have rubbed my eyes and smeared mascara underneath them. Not in the habit of reapplying, my lips are now devoid of lipstick except around the edges and in the creases. I look worse than if I had simply left my face bare as usual.

What these experiences bring home is the significance of *discipline* and *surveillance*, two key concepts in social theorist Michel Foucault's analysis of power. Sandra Lee Bartky's landmark article 'Foucault, femininity, and the modernization of patriarchal power' memorably applies Foucault's approach to the case of beauty practices. Bartky argues that the 'docile bodies' theorized by Foucault can be seen clearly in what she calls 'the forms of subjection that engender the feminine body', including make-up but also gendered rules of deportment, posture, body shape and dress.[48]

Discipline refers to the way that repeated, small practices coalesce into habitual norm-compliance. The fact of repetition creates actions that can be performed without conscious effort. Each individual practice on its own looks minor, but, together, they form a systematic and subconscious whole. Through discipline, Foucault argues, power is enacted on our bodies without requiring coercive enforcement. Conscious effort or coercive enforcement may be required for the process of discipline to begin; but once discipline takes hold it is self-perpetuating.

Since Bartky, feminists are used to thinking of the disciplinary aspect of beauty practices in terms of actions that must be performed: removing body hair, applying make-up, styling hair. Beauty is understood as practices, appliances and products to be mastered. But reflecting on my own use of make-up suggests that this is not the whole picture. Actions such as applying make-up, removing body hair and hairstyling are necessarily intentional: they are time-consuming, they require equipment that must be consciously purchased and maintained, and so even when they become routine, they lack the under-the-radar character of properly internalized discipline.

But beauty *does* require multiple unconscious disciplines. If you are going to wear make-up you need to look in the mirror repeatedly throughout the day, just to check things have not gone awry; you need to carry supplies with you to perform touch-ups; you need to become adept at speedy application. And significant beauty discipline is also required in all the things that must *not* be done. If you are wearing eye make-up you must not rub your eyes. If you are wearing freshly applied lipstick you must be careful when eating and drinking so as not to leave a print on a glass or a smear on a napkin. If you are wearing foundation you must not pull your top over your head without taking special care.

Using make-up frequently requires a great deal of skill, time and money, but it also requires many acts of *restraint*. To the seasoned make-up wearer these may become unnoticeable; to the occasional user they are unfamiliar and thus startling. Using make-up infrequently is hard work because the necessary acts of restraint have not been absorbed into the subconscious by the process of discipline. The occasional make-up wearer thus frequently fails and must confront her ineptitude.

The maintenance and restraint that make-up requires is also supposed to be invisible. Wearing make-up requires a lot of shametenance. Natural make-up doesn't create an overt aesthetic: it's not openly decorative. It's used because the face without it is not quite good enough. It's at least a little bit shameful. This may be why putting make-up on, or touching it up, is supposed to be done in private. In 2018 the BBC News website asked readers to write in with their tales of bad etiquette on public transport. Women putting on make-up featured highly, particularly for men:

> Michael, 59, said he was so offended by the sight he had moved carriages. 'I think once or twice I just stared at the person thinking that they would eventually notice and feel embarrassed. That never happened,' he said. 'It's something for someone's private space – their bedroom or bathroom. So to find myself sitting on a train and then suddenly inside someone's bathroom is very unwelcome.'
>
> For 60-year-old Gerard, a woman applying make-up in public is as bad-mannered as a man combing his hair in public. 'Why can they not get up 10 minutes earlier and do [their make-up] at home?' he asked. 'There seems to be something so totally "in your face" about females who insist on their dubious "rights" in this matter.'[49]

On one level, a woman who wants to wear make-up so much that she would rather apply it on the train than not wear it at all or spend the train journey reading could be interpreted as submitting to shametenance, because she is submitting to the idea that her bare face is shameful and must be concealed even if she lacks the time to apply it in private. But, on another interpretation, women doing their make-up on public transport are refusing to perform shametenance. They are refusing to accept the idea that it is shameful to wear make-up: that make-up must conceal its presence, must deceive the viewer, must pretend it is unnecessary.

Refusing to wear make-up at all is one sort of rebellion; wearing it proudly and applying it publicly is another. Wearing no make-up says 'my face is fine as it is'; wearing obvious make-up or applying it openly says 'it is fine for me to spend time on how I look'. Natural make-up applied in private says, 'my face is not fine how it is, and I don't want you to know what it takes to look like this.' This is shametenance.

The second key aspect of Foucault's account of power is surveillance. When I wear make-up I am reminded of this ever-present gaze of the other. Make-up takes my face out of easy existence and transforms it into an object of appraisal. Without make-up my face is just my face: it may look better or worse (than other faces, or than itself at different times) but its appearance is not likely to be embarrassing or humiliating. As long as it is clean, my face without make-up can go about its business untroubled. When it wears make-up, on the other hand, my face requires constant attention. It needs to be inspected in the mirror at regular intervals. It needs to be 'fixed'. It needs equipment. It draws attention to itself, not simply as part of a person but as a work of art, a product, as something adorned. A bare face says 'This is how I am'. A face with make-up says 'Don't I look good!' This feels like a lot of pressure.

Women who wear make-up every day often report that they feel unfinished without it. The use of the term 'my face' to describe make-up – as in 'I need to put my face on' – demonstrates this experience. For these women the thought of going out *without* make-up on may be shocking, humiliating, or unbearable. The condition of being made up feels normal, even natural; the condition of being bare-faced does not. It is reasonable to conclude that, for many women, the naked face feels like a face under surveillance: a face in which all the blemishes, dark circles and wrinkles are exposed for all to see.

The point here is that whether a person is aware of being under surveillance depends in large part on whether her face looks normal *to her*, which is related to (but distinct from) whether her face conforms to the social norms of her particular context. A full face of make-up is not normal for me. For this reason, I am much more comfortable wearing natural make-up than I am wearing overt make-up. Natural make-up is supposed to be invisible, and so I can apply it and be satisfied with the results. Shametenance works: my dark circles and red patches are covered up, and I look better. Heavier make-up, which I occasionally wear for a party or dinner, is clearly noticeable. If I've done a good job of application and maintenance, my made-up face looks better than normal; if not, it looks worse than normal. Either option makes me feel self-conscious and subject to surveillance. For other people, and other contexts, the opposite is true.

What this anecdote is meant to show is that significant aspects of beauty practices are *comfort* and *visibility*. Comfort relates to discipline: discipline makes some actions and inactions seem comfortable and others effortful. Visibility relates to surveillance: some beauty practices make us seem visible or hyper-visible, others make us feel invisible. Sometimes beauty practices aim at making the practitioner visible: she wants her appearance to be noticeable. But beauty practices can also aim at invisibility, at making a person blend in rather than stand out. Both the presence and absence of make-up can have this effect, depending on the person and context involved.

The era of social media, selfie culture and ever-more Orwellian technology is a context of ever-increasing surveillance. Our culture is a profoundly *visual* one. Everything we do has to be documented in images. What's the point of going to a restaurant if you don't Instagram the food? Why watch a firework display with your eyes alone if you can video it and watch it through your phone screen? Social media is making increasing use of video, with platforms like TikTok and Instagram encouraging us to submit ourselves for surveillance as we move and speak. The Covid-19 pandemic means more of our time is spent on videoconferencing platforms like Zoom and Teams, which confront us with our own image while we try to focus on others. These acts of self-display require even more work to perfect. Zoom provides various filters, including a pretty convincing virtual lipstick – although if you put your hand over your mouth there's a risk that

Zoom will draw lips on it. But if you want realistic eye make-up you'll need to do that yourself, perhaps following one of the online tutorials designed for videoconferencing. Either way, it is draining to cope with constantly seeing yourself on camera in meetings. As psychologist Jeremy Bailensen puts it, 'Zoom users are seeing reflections of themselves at a frequency and duration that hasn't been seen before in the history of media and likely the history of people.'[50]

In this context, it is hard to avoid feeling visible. It makes sense, then, that we might find solace in invisibility – however we manage to achieve it. Natural make-up presents itself as invisible, even while reminding us that we are constantly under surveillance.

Natural make-up is all about artifice. It is all about pretending that we really look this good, while at the same time locking us into shame-tenance. The idea of nature used here is an enemy. It doesn't help us resist the charge that *your body is never good enough*. It reinforces it.

NATURE AS FRENEMY

It's better to be a natural bodybuilder than an unnatural one, predominantly for health reasons. But a natural bodybuilder is not natural in many other ways of understanding that word. Is it better to wear natural make-up than unnatural make-up, or no make-up at all? Plausibly this is a matter of aesthetic preference and individual choice. But what about conforming to ideals of natural femininity, or following nature's guidance on sexual relations? It all depends on what you think they are. For nature does not reveal its instruction to us without first going through a hefty filter. We view nature only through human eyes.

The concept of nature is a frenemy. Nature can be a force for emancipation at one moment, a way of resisting repressive social meanings, but then constitute that repression in the next moment. This explains why being told 'it's only natural' can be either liberating or oppressive, inspiring or enraging. Imagine looking in the mirror and seeing more grey hairs than you thought you had. Imagine lamenting this fact to your best friend, who says, 'Don't worry! It's natural to have grey hair!' Do you feel better? Probably you do.

What about this scenario? You've just had a baby, and you're finding breastfeeding difficult and painful. The baby doesn't seem to want to latch, and when she does it brings a searing pain in your nipples. You're not sure if she is getting any food at all. You're not sure if you can cope. You express your fears to a midwife. 'Don't worry!' she says. 'It's natural to breastfeed!' Does that help? Or does it just make you feel more of a failure?

Both claims are true, in the sense that both are processes that have happened throughout human history and that female bodies are predisposed, in usual circumstances, to do. But they feel different. 'It's natural to have grey hair!' might be offered as a rebellion against compulsory concealment, a liberation from dyeing, and so it feels like a feminist thing to say. On the other hand, telling a struggling mother that 'it's natural to breastfeed' can make her feel helpless, desperate, or offended, because it can feel like blaming her for breastfeeding difficulties or for choosing formula-feeding.

The difference between the claims is not about whether breastfeeding or going grey *really* are natural. It's not that one of them was done by cavewomen and the other wasn't. (Presumably many more cavewomen breastfed than lived long enough to go grey.) The difference is all about context. In another context, the meaning changes. Imagine breastfeeding in public and feeling anxious about other people's reactions or disapproval. In that context, being told 'Don't worry! It's natural to breastfeed!' might be a great relief.

Consider another example of a naturalness claim: 'women are naturally weaker than men'. Is this a feminist claim? If it's used to justify excluding women from being firefighters, then no. If it's used to justify the existence of women's sport, then yes. Is it a true claim? It needs further specification. In every case? No. In most cases? Yes. Which matters? It depends.

Natural make-up looks like a good thing for women insofar as it allows them to appear as human beings, without excessive adornment, exaggerated features, or an explicitly decorated appearance. It suggests that just *being* is enough. But natural make-up is also bad for women, because just *being* is, of course, not enough. Natural make-up takes time, effort and money to apply, which is burdensome. But it also responds and contributes to the idea that the unmodified face is deficient and in need of rectification. More than that, natural make-up requires us to make it seem as though this were not the case. It requires us to perform shametenance.

It also asks us to participate in one or more lies. The first lie is that our faces really look like this. The second lie is that it doesn't matter how we look. The third is that we didn't have to do anything to look this way. The fourth thing that make-up shows – this one is actually true – is that we've made an effort. But natural make-up also implies a fifth claim of questionable veracity: that we're more liberated than our sisters whose make-up is more obvious.

Take another example: natural birth. This can be a liberatory rejection of a male-dominated, over-medicalized birth industry, or/and it can be another way for women to fail. Natural birth does not mean birth with no human intervention or action – after all, the mother is most definitely a human, and ideals of natural birth require her to do a great deal! Natural birth celebrates the mother's agency while also emphasizing the importance of support from midwives, doulas and loved ones. It also does not mean birth without medical assistance, a practice sometimes called 'free birth'. Instead, natural birth is vaginal birth that avoids unnecessary or superfluous medical intervention.

The ideal of natural birth is typically accompanied with a fear of what is called the 'cascade of interventions', a term used to describe the process whereby one medical intervention leads to another, then another, until the birth becomes completely medicalized. For example, one pregnancy website, tellingly called Mama Natural, advises against interventions by arguing, 'Induction increases likelihood of Pitocin; which increases likelihood of epidurals; which increases the risk of C-section (hence the cascade of interventions!).'[51]

This idea of natural birth has clear parallels with the ideal of natural bodybuilding. In both cases, some interventions are welcomed (creatine, whey powder, birth pools, hypnobirthing) while others are excluded (steroids, human growth hormone, epidurals, C-sections). In both cases the naturalness of the practices is related to strongly gendered ideals: masculinity for bodybuilding, femininity – and specifically mothering – for birth. And in both cases men and women can feel deep distress and even shame for failing to measure up to the relevant ideals, even when failure is outside their control.

When I was pregnant, I was very motivated to try to achieve a natural birth, but I did not succeed. My pregnancy was afflicted by placenta praevia, a condition that makes natural birth impossible. Even labour would likely have been fatal for first the baby and then me: the placenta would have ruptured, causing catastrophic haemorrhage. There was no sense in which I or anyone else was culpable for the situation, and there was no way of avoiding a C-section. And yet, despite knowing this rationally, I felt strongly as though I had failed to live up to the motherhood ideal. I even felt that there was a sense in which I was not a proper mother, a shame that lasted for years and could easily be triggered by hearing about a friend giving birth successfully.

The point of this story is emphatically *not* to endorse the idea that natural birth is morally superior to other births, or that women have a duty to attempt natural birth, or that a C-section should properly be thought of as a failure. I don't, and didn't, believe any of these things at the rational level. The point is rather to emphasize the power that normative ideals of naturalness have over us, and the ways in which they often relate to gender. Few of us can or want to reject gendered norms entirely: they are too deep, too hegemonic, and in many ways too appealing for that.

In all of the cases discussed so far, the claim that a body part or process is natural works in the context of a cultural imperative. Sometimes nature helps us to resist oppression, as with natural hair. Other times it reinforces oppressive norms, as with natural make-up. Nature sets itself apart from culture: something beyond cultural criticism, something to be respected, a trump card against oppression and constraint or, alternately, against licentiousness and indulgence. But nature *as concept* is, in fact, fully dependent on culture.

Nature is defined in opposition to culture. But what is true by definition is also false by definition. If nature is *necessarily* not-culture, then what nature is depends fundamentally on what culture is. And what culture is, of course, varies. In one sense, then, the natural body is permanent and unchangeable; in another sense, it is in constant flux.

What we've seen is that the concept of 'nature' and a natural body relies on a particular normative framework. We talk about something being natural when it stands in contrast with something we want to critique. We set up 'natural' bodies as being virtuous in contrast to something we oppose. What is natural for us in any given context depends on the parts of our identity that we are focusing on, the social and political structures that we are responding to.

Natural make-up is natural because it is designed to make women look as though they haven't worn it, while at the same time demonstrating that they've made an effort. It's natural because wearing make-up is an essential part of the norms of femininity in a sexist society. It's natural because women are supposed to look young, slim and flawless; because beauty is a requirement for all women. Natural hair, on the other hand, is natural because it represents rejecting racist appearance norms and embracing Black identity.

Nature, in other words, is inherently value-laden.

This is something that feminists have spotted. In the next chapter, we'll see how.

3

Killing the Enemy

The Feminist Case against Nature

> *Do you wish always to be well guided? Then always follow nature's indications. Everything that characterizes the fair sex ought to be respected as established by nature.*
>
> Jean-Jacques Rousseau, *Émile* (1762)[1]

> *There is no way to change the status of women in any society without dealing with basic metaphysical assumptions about the nature of women: what we are, what we want, what we have a right to, what our bodies are for, and especially to whom our bodies belong.*
>
> Andrea Dworkin, 'Feminism: An Agenda' (1983)[2]

Afghanistan is the worst country in the world to be a woman, according to women's rights experts.[3] The Taliban regime that ruled from 1996–2001 was notorious for its systematic subjugation of women, restricting every aspect of their lives and rendering them everywhere and always vulnerable to male domination. Intensely patriarchal practices persisted after the US-led invasion of Afghanistan in 2001 which toppled the Taliban.

Life expectancy for an Afghan woman is just forty-four.[4] The vast majority of Afghan women cannot read or write. Women and girls are still effectively confined to the home from puberty onwards, able to leave only with permission from their male relatives and, usually, with a male escort. Rape and domestic violence are rife. Marriages are forced. A bride is sold to her husband and his family, often while she is still a child, in order that she may bear him children and generally serve and obey him. He may have sex with her when he wishes and can be violent towards her with impunity.

An Afghan woman has a duty to provide her family with children. Or, to be precise, *sons*. Giving birth to a daughter – or, worse still, a succession of daughters – is a reason for mourning rather than celebration. Having only daughters brings a woman shame and even punishment. Many Afghan people believe that a woman can control the sex of her baby by will and prayer, and so a woman who gives birth to a daughter has simply not tried hard enough.[5]

In this intensely misogynist, stratified society there is a strong sense in which bodies are everything. Biology is destiny. Right from birth, whether you are a boy or a girl will determine how much you are fed or even whether you are fed at all. It will determine whether you are permitted to move freely and fully or whether you must constrain your body, restrict its functions, and conceal its form. Your nature will determine your whole life.

And yet. There is a way for an Afghan girl to escape the constraints of her body, just for a few years. She can become a *bacha posh*, a colloquial term in Dari meaning 'girl dressed as a boy'. A *bacha posh* (pronounced 'bat-cha posh') does not only dress as a boy; she operates in society exactly as boys do.

No one knows precisely how many *bacha posh* there are, because their existence is somewhat hidden. But journalist Jenny Nordberg, who chronicles their lives in her book *The Underground Girls of Kabul*, believes they are widespread. Their existence is an open secret. At one level, no one must know that a 'boy' is really a *bacha posh*, because a *bacha posh* undermines the strict system of sex-based hierarchy that Afghan society is built on. But often, others do know. They may have known the *bacha posh* as a girl: some children leave school as girls and return as boys. What is crucial for the system to work is that the pretence must be total.

Of course, it would be rational for an Afghan girl to want to be a *bacha posh*, because then she has access to the much greater freedoms given to boys. But it is not up to Afghan girls what happens to them. A girl can become a boy only if her parents decide to make her one. Nordberg identifies four reasons that families make one of their daughters into a *bacha posh*, and none of them have anything to do with the child's wishes or her sense of her own gender identity. First, families might make a girl into a *bacha posh* just so they can say that they have at least one son, something that is vitally important for the family's honour. Second, a son, even a little boy, can provide protection for the family as a whole and act as an escort for his mother and sisters when out of the house. Third, a boy can work in the family business or elsewhere for money, to support the family. A girl would never be allowed to fulfil this role, no matter how vital to the family's survival. Fourth, many Afghan people believe that a *bacha posh* can magically ensure that the next children to be born will be 'proper' boys. A *bacha posh* is better than nothing, but a *bacha posh* is always second best to a real boy.

So, parents of daughters will sometimes select one of them to grow up as a boy, at least until she reaches puberty. Her childhood will be shaped entirely by masculine norms and freedoms. She will wear trousers and have short hair.[6] She will play outside and be allowed to swing, jump and climb. She will fight and shout. She will sit in the front seat of the car, eat first at mealtimes, and boss her sisters about. If the magic works and a real son is born, he will take precedence over her, but she will continue to be more important than her sisters. She might even be given the job of protecting her little brother, who will take her place as the family's most important child.

All of this, the privilege and permission and priority, must be abandoned once her body starts to change. Once puberty begins, she must turn back into a girl and prepare to be married – which means, above all, she must become modest, shy and private, so that her virtue and thus her price is kept intact.

For many *bacha posh* this does not seem like a good prospect.

Usually, that doesn't matter.

Just occasionally a *bacha posh* is permitted by her parents to continue living as a boy and, ultimately, a man. This is a precarious and dangerous position for her to be in, as long as she is of child-bearing age, because it is much more difficult to maintain the total pretence that being a *bacha posh* requires when the boy she is supposed to be looks more and more like an adult woman.

Shukur is one *bacha posh* who continued her boyhood beyond

puberty. The risk of continuing as a *bacha posh* became very clear one day, as Nordberg describes:

> Shukur was seventeen on the day three mujahideen arrived at the door. Stricter dress codes for women had just been instituted in Kabul, with mandatory head coverings. The fighters had heard stories of a woman who dressed like a man and they had set out to correct the abomination. Shukur was at home in the Darulaman neighbourhood where she had grown up, in jeans, a slouchy shirt, and the Afro-like hairstyle she had cultivated. The fighters stood by the door and demanded to see the cross-dressing criminal they had been told lived at the house. At first, her father would not budge. But Shukur stepped forward and plainly said she was likely who they were looking for. The two men studied her and exchanged looks before one spoke up, in an authoritative tone: 'Okay. You look like a boy and you are completely like a boy. So we will call you a boy.'[7]

This event demonstrates the contradictions of Afghan systems of gender, and it also tells us something about systems of gender more broadly. The Afghan gender regime is highly restrictive and deterministic. It sets out rigid requirements for how women and men must act, allowing no room for self-expression or individual liberty. It is not sensitive to anything as esoteric as gender identity or as indulgent as diversity. And yet, confronted with someone they *knew* to be a girl dressed as a boy, the officials charged with enforcing the gender regime stopped short, swayed by the strong impression of masculinity that Shukur exuded. In the end, it was more important to them to maintain the strong boundary between the genders than it was to 'correctly' sort a person into one gender or another. Shukur performed masculinity so successfully that continuing to treat her as a man was the best way of maintaining the rigid gender binary.

Systems of gender in liberal democracies operate differently than they do in Afghanistan, but they operate nonetheless. And every system of gender has its own logic. It has gender practices that can be accommodated within its structures and those that cannot. It has rules for who counts as a girl and who counts as a boy: rules for whether the determining factor is genitals or clothing or behaviour or self-identification. Every human society has males and females, in the biological sense; every human society relies on sexual dimorphism to reproduce. But how that sexual dimorphism translates into a system of gender varies. The behaviours and sense of self that is expected of boys and girls depends on context, as does what is to be done with people who don't play by the rules.

Nordberg's account of the *bacha posh* is fascinating for many reasons – for what it tells us about Afghanistan, for its insight into the realities of living under extreme patriarchy, for its testament to girls' resilience and rebellion. But it also tells us something about the idea of nature, as it applies to our embodied existence. Afghanistan is a society in which women and men are expected to behave completely differently, right down to the level of the smallest mannerisms. Women must look down, must hunch over, must take small steps, must move in such a way that they won't trip even when wearing a face veil. After years of having these behaviours explicitly enforced, they become habitual: something that women can do without thinking.

Gendered behaviours become habitual for all of us, not only for Afghan women. Social theorist Michel Foucault described how social structures imprint themselves on our body. As I set out in the previous chapter, he argued that power operates through discipline: through the enforced repetition of bodily movements and deportment that eventually become subconscious.[8] Think of the way that schoolchildren are taught to sit up straight, to hold a pencil using a particular grip, to put up their hands before speaking. If you or your child has ever put up their hand before speaking at the family dinner table, you know how deeply discipline can embed itself. Foucault argued that this subconscious enactment of discipline is one way that power operates in modern societies. The child who automatically puts his hand up to speak, even at the family dinner table, is embodying the power structures that exist in school: the hierarchy between teachers and children, perhaps, but also the egalitarian requirement to allow speaking time to others, not to dominate the conversation, along with the requirement to do one's best – to pay attention, to have an answer.

Sociologist Pierre Bourdieu developed this idea into what he called the *habitus*: the way that our bodies take on a form that demonstrates their position in social hierarchies. One of his examples is the way that women's stride patterns differ from men's. Men tend to take long, free strides whereas women take shorter steps.[9] Bourdieu's analysis of the difference is that it stems in part from clothing norms: women sometimes wear restrictive skirts and high heels, clothes that require a restrained walking style, whereas men tend to wear trousers and shoes that allow open, expansive movements. Women's restrictive gait becomes a subconscious symbol of their inferior position.

Feminist theorist Iris Marion Young also developed this idea, prior to Bourdieu, in her landmark essay 'Throwing Like a Girl'. Young describes how girls are taught from childhood to use their bodies with restriction: to take up less space, to close their legs while sitting, always to limit their bodily functions. Men, on the other hand, can move freely, look directly, speak loudly. 'There is a specific positive style of feminine body comportment and movement, which is learned as the girl comes to understand she is a girl,' Young writes.

> The young girl acquires many subtle habits of feminine body comportment – walking like a girl, tilting her head like a girl, standing and sitting like a girl, gesturing like a girl, and so on. The girl learns to actively hamper her movements. She is told that she must be careful not to get hurt, not to get dirty, not to tear her clothes, that the things she desires to do are dangerous for her. Thus she develops a bodily timidity that increases with age.[10]

The term 'manspreading' was coined to describe the phenomenon whereby a man feels free to take up space: to s p r a w l. The Tumblr website Men Taking Up Too Much Space on Trains, sadly no longer online, showcased men sitting on public transport without a thought for their neighbours, basking in the unconscious glow of male privilege. They sit legs spread, arms outstretched, often while women next to them squash their bodies into the smallest possible space to avoid having to make thigh contact. As Young puts it, 'The woman lives her space as confined and closed around her, at least in part as projecting some small area in which she can exist as a free subject.'[11] Repeated experiences of unwanted attention and touching, often sexual, along with instruction from an early age, shape the way women and girls move and position their bodies.

These stark differences between the way men and women use their bodies – unconsciously, unthinkingly, in rest and in motion – exist even in liberal societies with formal equality between the sexes. In Afghanistan, where gender inequality is fundamental to the entire society, the way a boy lives in his body is just not comparable to the way a girl must live in hers. Girls have to learn their restricted embodiment over years before they can perform it to the required standard. It's hardly surprising that a *bacha posh* faces a huge challenge when she *suddenly* has to conform. After a childhood as a boy, the masculine way of being in a body seems like the *only* way of being in a body. It comes naturally. As Nordberg puts it:

> what is 'natural,' in the sense of presumably being innate, is not the same as what might *feel* natural. Acts or behavior can feel 'natural' to us after many years of performing them, because the brain has physically adjusted or developed in one particular direction. In other words: With time, nurture can *become* nature.[12]

Letting the body just be, letting it be good enough just as it is, is a luxury denied to most women. Our bodies, on this analysis, are never truly unmodified.

In a highly gendered context, women's and men's 'natural' way of being reflects the socialization they've been subjected to. And so one obvious feminist strategy is to work to destroy nature. At its simplest, this strategy means pointing out that what is often called 'nature' is not really natural at all. At its more complex, it means destroying the very idea of nature itself.

Within feminism the body is both basic and bothersome: to be transcended and respected, simultaneously. This is not easy.

Feminism grapples with two key claims. On the one hand, feminism rejects biological essentialism: the idea that biology is destiny, explaining our actions and determining our roles. There is no direct route from the uterus to the kitchen, from the vagina to prostitution, from XX chromosomes to XXX movies.

On the other hand, feminism insists on the political significance of embodied experience. Feminism rejects the philosophical dualism that separates mind from body and reifies mind, insisting instead that the physical reality of womanhood has implications for women's lives and status. The route from the body to social oppression is not direct, but it is well trodden nonetheless. Women are constituted and subjugated as a group because and by way of their sexed bodies. And women's experiences of bodily processes such as puberty, menstruation, abortion, pregnancy, childbirth, breastfeeding and menopause create a commonality and distinctiveness to womanhood. Not all women have all these embodied experiences. Some people who do have them don't identify as women. But everyone born female experiences some of them, or has to contend with their absence.

These two positions, the rejection of essentialism and the significance of embodiment, are both crucial to feminism. But they are in tension, as is demonstrated by current debates around trans identity and rights. Trans people want to be recognized by their gender identity rather than their birth sex, a desire that fits well with the feminist rejection of biological essentialism. But it is more problematic for feminism to accept the idea that there is *no* difference between being a trans woman or a trans man and being biologically female or male from birth, because embodiment matters. This tension between the rejection of essentialism and the significance of embodiment has posed problems for the development of feminist scholarship because both sides of a viciously toxic debate appeal to fundamental feminist principles.

And so feminists have a love–hate relationship with the concept of nature. At various historical moments they have found reason to reject or reclaim the concept, as the political significance of human nature, women's nature and the natural body ebbs and flows. Nature, and the idea of the natural body, has played a shifting role in the history of women's liberation. In this chapter I consider the feminist case *against* nature; in the next I reclaim nature for feminist purposes. We need both arguments to understand the value *and* the suspicion of the idea and reality of the unmodified body.

The concept of the natural body implies two rather contradictory things. On the one hand, saying that the body (or anything else) is natural suggests that it has a sort of perfection and deserves respect. If something is natural it seems to be in some sense *inevitable*: it was always going to be that way. It seems to some extent *immutable*: it cannot be otherwise, or at least not without effort. Something that is natural claims a certain *purity*: it is unadulterated, uncorrupted. All these ways of thinking about natural bodies suggest that we should value and protect them, supporting the intuitive value of the unmodified body.

On the other hand, the concept of *nature* is commonly contrasted with the concept of *culture*. The natural world is contrasted with the human, social world. On this understanding of nature, something that is natural is something that is yet to be developed, something that is yet to be civilized, something that is animal, that is base, that is unrefined. Only once culture gets involved will it be refined, developed, perfected. Natural things can even be deeply destructive, requiring human action to counteract them: vaccination against disease, engineering against natural disaster. On this understanding, valuing the unmodified body is a mere preference at best and a fetish at worst.

The contrast between nature and culture invites a choice: where is perfection really to be found?

Philosophers have argued on both sides. Sometimes the nature/culture distinction is used to critique nature and elevate culture, as when Thomas Hobbes famously described life in the state of nature as 'solitary, poore, nasty, brutish, and short'. Hobbes was certain we needed culture in order to tame nature.[13]

At other times the nature/culture distinction is used to elevate nature and de-emphasize culture. In particular, as we'll see in a moment, Enlightenment male philosophers used ideas of nature to justify sex inequality. Nature, on their account, not only divided men and women into two sexes, it also set out forms of behaviour appropriate for each group, and placed men in a position of natural superiority and dominance. The concept of nature at play in these accounts is one in which nature is to be respected, not corrupted.

As a result, feminists have often had to critique the concept of nature extremely forcefully. It has been a central task of feminism for much of its history to argue against the idea that women are natural subordinates. The main tool that feminists have used for this argument is the sex/gender distinction, which is a version of the nature/culture distinction. 'Sex' refers to the natural, biological differences between male and female; 'gender' refers to the cultural, normative differences between masculine and feminine. According to this distinction, women's inequality is a matter of culture, something that is determined by society not nature. Since inequality is a social phenomenon, it is open to social change. Feminism, then, provides both a normative critique of inequality and an activist programme for smashing it.

Feminists who use the sex/gender distinction in this way can be agnostic on the question of nature. They don't have to say what women are naturally like: they don't have to accept or deny that women are naturally weaker, more caring, whatever.

But, more recently, many feminists have argued that the sex/gender distinction relies too much on nature. Some feminists argue that the distinction should be abandoned in favour of the view that everything is, in some sense, culture. There is no natural body; there is no nature at all, except as viewed through the lens of human eyes, human societies and human norms. More radically still, the concept of the Anthropocene alerts us to the fact that humans are causally responsible for creating even the base conditions of the planet we live on: its climate, its ecosystem, its biodiversity or lack thereof.

In the last chapter I showed how the *idea* of nature is necessarily cultural. The question now is whether there is anything to nature *beneath* that idea. Can we get to a properly natural nature?

The feminist destruction of nature was necessary because, over centuries, a plethora of powerful men have insisted that male dominance is natural. We can find arguments for natural male dominance in a number of places. My aim here is not to present a full or complete history of the concept of nature (that would be impossible), but rather to provide a taster, an *amuse-bouche*, just enough to motivate the feminist critique. So let's start by going back 250 years to Western Europe. It's an era with many hierarchies to choose from: sex, class, race. Nature props up them all. If you're on the bottom, nature probably put you there and wants you to stay there. At least, that was the view of those on the top of the hierarchy: the rich white men.

THE LAWS OF NATURE

Enlightenment thinkers insisted on the significance of human reason, intellect and culture. Nature served as a contrast to culture. A state of nature, for these thinkers, was a mythical state without law or government. In one sense, the purpose of nature was to serve as a foundation from which humanity could develop and on which it could improve; but at the same time, nature served as something of a guide to morality and human behaviour.

John Locke's *The Second Treatise of Government*, published in 1689, used nature in this dual way. Locke understood the state of nature as a condition without human law and human enforcement – what he called a state of liberty. However, Locke insisted that the state of nature is *not* a state of licence in which anything goes, morally speaking. Even without human laws we are still subject to the law of nature. As Locke wrote, 'The State of Nature has a Law of Nature to govern it, which obliges every one: And Reason, which is that Law, teaches all Mankind, who will but consult it, that being all equal and independent, no one ought to harm another in his Life, Health, Liberty, or Possessions.'[14] Locke's interpretation of the law of nature would be influential in the drafting of the US Declaration of Independence a century later, which famously opens with an appeal to the 'Laws of Nature and of Nature's God', protecting men's 'unalienable Rights, that among these are Life, Liberty, and the Pursuit of Happiness'.[15]

Locke understood nature to be a blueprint for appropriate forms of family life and the relations between the sexes. He thought that human monogamy was justified by the reproductive and nurturing needs of the species, something that could be seen in contrast with other animals. The males of grass-eating animals, Locke opined, need stick around 'no longer than the very Act of Copulation'.[16] They were off the hook after that, Locke felt, simply because of their natural needs. Calves, lambs and foals can survive on their mothers' milk alone, and so there is nothing left for the father to do once he's impregnated his mate. But in humans the man cannot get away so lightly. According to Locke, 'the Father, who is bound to take care for those he hath begot, is under an Obligation to continue in the Conjugal Society with the same Woman longer than other Creatures.'[17] This obligation derived from nature: human babies remain dependent for a long time, during which their mothers may well become pregnant and vulnerable, and so fathers have an obligation to look after both mother and child.

Locke's conclusion that men have an obligation to contribute to the care of their children is laudable. But the thought that this conclusion can be derived merely from comparing the natural reproductive behaviours of different species is, well, odd. After all, even grass-eating animals need protection while young, and there is no reason why adult males could not contribute to that. At the same time, if adult male humans left women alone immediately after the 'Act of Copulation' there would be no danger of subsequent pregnancies interfering with the care of infants. Locke was committing a fallacy that would be repeated over and over again up to the present day: interpreting nature according to prevailing social norms.

Other Enlightenment philosophers understood nature differently, even as they stuck to the idea that nature was a guide to morality. Jean-Jacques Rousseau stated this point bluntly in 1762. 'Do you wish always to be well guided?' he asked. 'Then always follow nature's indications.'[18]

Nature's indications, of course, need interpretation. Predictably, the indications that Rousseau read from nature corresponded handily to many of the sexist morals of his time, including women's obligation to be sexually faithful. An unfaithful man, he wrote, 'is an unjust and barbarous man. But the unfaithful woman does more; she dissolves the family and breaks all the bonds of nature.'[19] Rousseau himself could hardly be described as a family man: he had five children with Thérèse Levasseur and abandoned all five of them to a Foundling Home, against her wishes.[20]

Rousseau thought that the lessons to be learned from nature included the appropriate treatment of the body. He did not think that nature required us to leave our bodies totally unmodified: he argued that the body had to be *cultivated* to develop the strength it needs to flourish. But Rousseau believed that the appropriate forms of physical development are naturally quite different for women and for men. 'Let us regulate [a woman's] views according to those of nature,' he wrote. 'Little girls love adornment almost from birth ... When the same motive is – very inappropriately – suggested to little boys, it by no means has a similar empire over them.'[21] And so, Rousseau concluded, men must focus on 'the development of strength', while women should focus on 'the development of attractiveness'.[22] Neither goal should be followed to the exclusion of the other: women need some degree of strength, men need some amount of attractiveness. But the focus for men and for women was, Rousseau thought, quite different and determined by nature.

Rousseau's nature-based views led him to some rather progressive conclusions. He regarded the overly restrictive clothing and lifestyles of the aristocratic women of his time as being a hindrance to nature, and thus to goodness, and harked back to the Greek ideal as bodybuilders would over 150 years later. 'It is known,' he wrote, 'that comfortable clothing which did not hinder the body contributed a great deal to leaving both sexes among the Greeks with those beautiful proportions seen in their statues.' Rousseau was scathing about the contemporary fashion for body modification using the 'gothic shackles' of whalebone corsets. 'I cannot believe that this abuse, pushed to an inconceivable extent in England, will not finally cause the species to degenerate, and I even maintain that the attraction that it offers is in bad taste. It is not attractive to see a woman cut in half like a wasp,' he proclaimed.[23]

Rousseau's diatribe against the corset invokes once again the connection between the idea of the unmodified body and *authenticity*. The corseted waist is a 'counterfeit' waist. It is not a true, authentic representation of the woman's real body. This idea of authenticity and its connection to nature is repeated when Rousseau invites the reader to consider what the corseted body looks like once adornment and concealment are removed. 'This defect would even be an assault on the eye when seen naked,' he writes. 'Why should it be a beautiful thing under clothing?'

Rousseau's critique of the corset is rather liberatory to women, viewed in isolation. But he continued to treat women as objects for male approbation and assessment. And, viewed in their entirety, Rousseau's dictates were hostile to women's equality, detailing as they did a myriad of ways in which women's natural place was different and inferior to that of men.

Reading Rousseau is troubling, because he combines a profoundly sexist understanding of women's nature and role with an instruction to value the unmodified body that resonates with the intuition that motivates my project here. Reading that intuition in Rousseau's words and within his normative context makes it seem less appealing, too moralizing, even dangerous. 'Everything which cramps and confines nature is in bad taste; this is as true of the adornments of the person as of the ornaments of the mind,' he instructs officiously.[24] But 'taste' has often been very bad for women; certainly feminists should not be afraid of being thought in breach of it.

EVERYTHING WHICH IS USUAL APPEARS NATURAL

Nature, or, to speak with strict propriety, God, has made all things right; but man has sought out many interventions to mar the work.

Mary Wollstonecraft,
A Vindication of the Rights of Woman (1792)[25]

So true it is that unnatural generally means only uncustomary, and that everything which is usual appears natural.
John Stuart Mill, *The Subjection of Women* (1869)[26]

Rousseau's views of women's nature did not convince everyone. Mary Wollstonecraft was particularly unimpressed with Rousseau's proclamations on the place of women. She vigorously defended women's equality in her landmark text *A Vindication of the Rights of Woman*, published in 1792. Wollstonecraft's strategy was not to deny the existence of natural differences between women and men, nor even to deny women's inferiority.[27] Her argument was that *natural* inequalities between men and women were not sufficient to justify *social* inequalities: an early version of the sex/gender distinction.

Wollstonecraft shared with Locke and Rousseau the idea that nature is prior to human action, and that it has its own ethical status. Our moral duties include allotting due respect to our natures. But we must avoid overreach. Wollstonecraft was particularly contemptuous of Rousseau's suggestion that women are naturally inclined to focus on their looks. His 'ridiculous stories, which tend to prove that girls are naturally attentive to their persons, without laying any stress on daily example, are below contempt,' she wrote:

I have, probably, had an opportunity of observing more girls in their infancy than J. J. Rousseau – I can recollect my own feelings, and I have looked steadily around me; yet, so far from coinciding with him in opinion respecting the first dawn of the female character, I will venture to affirm, that a girl, whose spirits have not been damped by inactivity, or innocence tainted by false shame, will always be a romp, and the doll will never excite attention unless confinement allows her no alternative.[28]

Wollstonecraft rejected Rousseau's version of nature, but in its place she put her own vision of what girls and women would always want. So still at stake is the question of what nature is and what it requires of us. Nonetheless, Wollstonecraft's analysis centred on issues of social inequality. She invited us to look critically upon our social arrangements, and not to be fooled into thinking that nature explains or excuses them. The feminist case against nature was under way.

Wollstonecraft's critical perspective on social norms was echoed by John Stuart Mill, writing nearly one hundred years later. In his book *On Liberty* Mill had attacked what he called the 'despotism of custom': the way that our freedom is limited by the concern to fit in with what others do and expect. *The Subjection of Women* focused that critique on women's inequality. Mill understood sex inequality as fundamentally a *social* system, and yet he argued that the system often used the concept of nature to try to excuse and explain itself.

Nature, Mill noted, is very often used in the service of discrimination. All forms of discrimination appear natural to those who perpetuate them (or perhaps they're just pretending; still, the result is the same). So it is unsurprising that men think that sex inequality is natural. Mill commented that slave owners from Aristotle in Ancient Greece to the plantation owners in the Deep South have often thought that their slaves were naturally inferior. We should be deeply suspicious of our views about naturalness: they are changeable throughout history, and they are generally employed in self-serving ways.

In general Mill argued that we use the word 'natural' where it would be more accurate to say 'customary': an analysis proven by the history of women's emancipation since Mill's time. Contemporary cultures still maintain many norms and inequalities of sex and gender, but liberal democratic societies don't any longer operate on the assumption that women are naturally unsuited to politics, or that nature prevents women having the vote, or a career, or an education. We tend to think things are natural if they fit with our own social practices.

Mill's own example of shifting ideas about women's nature was Queen Victoria, the British monarch when he was writing. 'Nothing so much astonishes the people of distant parts of the world, when they first learn anything about England, as to be told that it is under a queen: the thing seems to them so unnatural as to be almost incredible,' he wrote. 'To Englishmen this does not seem in the least degree unnatural, because they are used to it; but they do feel it unnatural that women should be soldiers or members of parliament.'[29] Mill alerts us to the political construction of 'nature': it is a concept that rests on our own experience and is deployed through our own norms.

Mill's most devastating argument against the use of nature to justify sex inequality is epistemological. *How do you know?* Mill argues that we simply have no way of knowing that the differences between women and men are natural, so we shouldn't claim that they are. We don't have examples of gender differences remaining constant throughout a variety of social arrangements, because every society we know of aggressively enforces them. To put it in contemporary terms: there is so much gender that we cannot isolate sex.

In a famous analogy, Mill compares women to trees that have been grown with one half in a greenhouse and the other half left outside.[30] Imagine the unfortunate inmate of this arboretum: half its branches carefully nurtured and luxuriously tended by the best botanists; the rest tortured by crazed plant sadists bearing ice, fire and secateur. No wonder, then, that the cosseted branches grow more readily than their mistreated counterparts. So why should we be surprised that women more easily develop those talents that society rewards compared with those it discourages, disdains, or disallows?

The tree is still a natural thing: it is still a tree, made of wood, bark, sap and leaf. It cannot transform itself into a tiger or a robot. But nature does not explain *everything* about its present form. As with trees, so too with women. That they are female and not male is not the result of society; but that women are *like this* and men are *like that* is society's doing.

Mill's philosophy was not without limitations. Perhaps the most glaring was that he only described *women* as subject to socialization. Men seem either to be untouched by society – the towering redwoods of a pristine Californian forest before the gold rush, perhaps – or else they are the all-powerful creators of it, the demonic gardeners with their crazed horticultural experiments. In reality, of course, men's position is no more natural than women's. Men also find some of their traits nurtured (dominating, deciding, drinking) while others are cut back (crying, caring, cleaning). In Mill's analysis, though, it is men who end up looking natural – ironically, since women are the ones who are usually allied with nature in the nature/culture distinction. But his insistence on the vagueness of nature was spot on. It was an insight developed to great effect by Simone de Beauvoir in the mid-twentieth century.

IN NATURE NOTHING IS EVER PERFECTLY CLEAR

All agree in recognizing the fact that females exist in the human species; today as always they make up about one half of humanity. And yet we are told that femininity is in danger; we are exhorted to be women, remain women, become women. It would appear, then, that every female human being is not necessarily a woman; to be so considered she must share in that mysterious and threatened reality known as femininity.

Simone de Beauvoir, *The Second Sex* (1949)[31]

The Second Sex is perhaps the most famous feminist exposition of the sex/gender distinction, though those are not terms used by its author, Simone de Beauvoir. She insisted, like Mill, that both the norms of gendered behaviour and the inequality between women and men are down to culture, not nature; going beyond his analysis, she argued that the very concept of womanhood itself is based on casting women as the Other. Woman is the *second* sex: the one that is defined fundamentally as not-man. Men are understood, in patriarchal societies, as the default humans. Men just are. In this sense, men are the ultimate unmodified bodies.

Womanhood, understood as a social identity, is not the result of nature. Hence Beauvoir's most famous line: 'One is not born, but rather becomes, a woman.' She continued: 'No biological, psychological, or economic fate determines the figure that the human female presents in society; it is civilization as a whole that produces this creature, intermediate between male and eunuch, which is described as feminine.'[32]

This is not to deny that nature exists. Our bodies have an awkward way of reminding us of their presence: needing things, wanting things, feeling things, doing things. We are all constrained and created, in part, by our biology. 'Woman, like man, *is* her body,'[33] Beauvoir pointed out. *Like man.* How refreshing it is to read an account that both recognizes and refuses women's othering.

But women's biology is, let's say, particularly insistent. Beauvoir was very aware of this. As a woman, how could she not be?

Beauvoir recognized that various biological processes and features – menstruation, conception, gestation, lactation – constructed the experience and reality of womanhood. Women's physicality differs from men's, and women's bodies provide particular challenges (and joys – it's important not to forget the joys). As Beauvoir put it, 'In the history of woman [bodies] play a part of the first rank and constitute an essential element in her situation.' The crucial point is that they don't explain everything. 'I deny that they establish for her a fixed and inevitable destiny. They are insufficient for setting up a hierarchy of the sexes; they fail to explain why woman is the Other; they do not condemn her to remain in this subordinate role for ever.'[34]

Crucially, Beauvoir rejected the idea that if something is natural then it can never change. She recognized the historical contingency of nature: of how we identify it and how we treat it. '[I]t might seem that a natural condition is beyond the possibility of change,' she wrote. 'In truth, however, the nature of things is not more immutably given, once for all, than is historical reality.'[35]

Like Mill, Beauvoir insisted that we cannot 'measure in the abstract the burden imposed on woman by her reproductive function'.[36] It is society, not nature, that urges women to have children, or prevents them from accessing contraception, or requires them to choose between motherhood and career. It is culture, not biology, that makes some practices taboo and others compulsory. Society's 'ways and customs cannot be deduced from biology,' Beauvoir argued. '[T]he individuals that compose the society are never abandoned to the dictates of their nature; they are subject rather to that second nature which is custom.'

The point is this: nature matters, sex matters, but neither nature nor sex adequately explain either the social situation and meaning of being a woman or the social dominance and default status of men. Sexist societies are rigid. But, as Beauvoir stated, 'In nature nothing is ever perfectly clear.'[37]

THE TERRAIN OF THE STRUGGLE

Women's biology is part of the terrain on which a struggle for dominance is acted out.

Catharine MacKinnon,
Toward a Feminist Theory of the State (1989)[38]

For radical feminist Catharine MacKinnon, Beauvoir did not go far enough in undermining the idea that women's inequality is natural. As we'll see in the next chapter, MacKinnon's account highlights the embodied nature of women's experience and subordination; here, we'll see how she furthered the feminist critique of nature.

Feminism centres women, but what is a woman?[39] Feminists have given various answers. At one extreme, there are feminist accounts in which womanhood is 'almost purely biological, in which women are defined by female biology'.[40] At the other, there is feminism that sees the category of women as 'almost purely social, in which women are defined by their social treatment'.[41] The case of the *bacha posh* illustrates the contrast: if womanhood is purely biological a *bacha posh* is a girl; if it's purely social, she's a boy, at least temporarily.

It's most common – most natural, perhaps – to think of 'woman' as a biological category: a woman is an adult human female, and a female is defined by physical features that biologists can explain and reliably identify. But what is the relationship between this biological category and gender inequality? MacKinnon identifies two possibilities. Female biology might be seen as the cause of women's subordination, or it might be seen as the subject matter of contestation, the thing we're fighting over.

MacKinnon strongly rejects the idea that biology is 'the source' of women's subordination. She attributes this idea to feminists such as Beauvoir and Susan Brownmiller, whose most famous work, *Against Our Will*, is an analysis of rape.[42] MacKinnon critiques Brownmiller's claim that the difference between male and female genitals is what makes rape possible. This claim relies on seeing the penis as in some sense necessarily active with the vagina passive; coitus is thus an act of penetration that can be performed aggressively. But MacKinnon notes that the mere fact of genital biology cannot explain rape, since it would be equally *biologically* possible for women to 'lurk in bushes and forcibly engulf men'.[43]

We might think that this image is somewhat over-optimistic about women's ability forcibly to procure an erection or proceed with coitus regardless, but MacKinnon's general point is correct: rape and sexual assault do not necessarily involve what Brownmiller calls the 'locking together' of penis and vagina, even when men attack women, and so the fact that women do not sexually assault men with anything like the frequency or ferocity that men attack women cannot be explained by their lacking a phallus. The existence of penises does not explain rape and sexual assault, and sexual assault does not require a penis.

In the social context of women's subordination, to be sexually attacked is to be attacked by or *as if by* a penis. The penis itself is not an aggressive organ. It becomes one only when accompanied with physical strength, brute force, intimidation, or humiliation. But any of these features could, in a different social context, accompany sexual assault by or as if by vagina. MacKinnon demonstrates this alternate social possibility with her use of the language of engulfment. It is society, not biology, that determines that we do not fear aggressive vaginal engulfment (or smothering, flattening, compressing, devouring, the tropes of the *vagina dentata* that have been used by women to assert power and discourage rape).[44] Rape is explained by doctrines of masculinity and male supremacy, not the existence of penises. These doctrines portray the penis as a powerful instrument of dominance, but they do not make it so. To paraphrase Andrea Dworkin, have you ever wondered why women do not frequently rape men? It's not because there's a shortage of dildos.[45]

Biology doesn't cause subordination, on this account. It's the other way round: biology subordinates only if it is socially interpreted as subordinating. As MacKinnon puts it, 'Social and political inequality begins indifferent to sameness and difference. Differences are inequality's post hoc excuse, its conclusory artefact, its outcome presented as its origin.'[46]

For MacKinnon, being a woman is not merely living in a female body, or merely being treated as a woman, or merely identifying as a woman. Instead – or perhaps additionally – MacKinnon argues that 'no woman escapes the meaning of being a woman within a social system that defines one according to gender.' Woman becomes a political category, and one with deep ontological significance: 'no woman is unaffected by whatever creates and destroys women as such.' A *bacha posh* fits this analysis: she may have a brief respite from particular norms of girlhood, but she has not escaped the social meaning of womanhood. As she ages, she will have to fit into that social meaning, and even as a *bacha posh* her experience is fully constrained by that meaning.

We can get a handle on this idea by considering the concept of biological essentialism. This concept has two main components. First, it invokes the idea that there is something about women's biology that *determines* their social position, in an inevitable way. MacKinnon strongly rejects this idea. But, secondly, biological essentialism invokes the idea of commonalities between women: that women exist 'as women', in the sense of having some experiences that transcend other significant differences such as race and class.

This idea of commonalities between women can be understood in different ways. One answer to the question of what women share 'as women' is that they share some biological feature. On this account, women share the experience of having female bodies, and female bodies have a variety of uniquely female experiences such as menstruation, gestation, childbirth and breastfeeding. Many feminists insist on the significance of these biological experiences both to individual women and to women as a group, and their work is vitally important. But though these experiences are shared by many women, they are not shared by *all* women. Some do not conceive, gestate, birth or breastfeed a child, and some do not menstruate.

The fact that some women do not share some or any of these experiences means that it is problematic to speak of them as phenomena that unite *all* women, but it does not mean that it is problematic to speak of them as phenomena that unite women. A significant part of the ordinary everyday life that feminist consciousness-raising uncovers as significant and as political concerns bodily experiences and the way they are socially treated – for example, the shame and secrecy associated with menstruation, together with the ways that it is used as a trope to undermine women as irrational or unreliable. The demonization of menstruation is an issue that affects *all* women by affecting their social and political status, regardless of whether they have ever menstruated or will do so in the future.

And the shame that is attached to female bodily functions also affects everyone born with a female body, including those who identify as trans or non-binary. For some, their trans identity is formed at least in part as a reaction against menstruation. 'I fell in love with the term "tomboy" the very first time it was ever used to describe me and I clung on to the label like a life preserver until I turned 14,' writes Cass Bliss, who now identifies as both trans and non-binary. 'It was getting my period that marked this transition the most directly for me. I saw my stained underwear like a bloodied flag of surrender I was forced to fly as I left behind the freedom of childhood androgyny.'[47]

When feminists, including MacKinnon, insist on the commonalities between women they predominantly mean that women share the experience of being socially constructed and situated as women. They share the fact that they are treated as inferior to men because they are women. This shared experience applies even if they are also treated as superior to some other women and men because of their position in another dimension of privilege, such as race and class. Fundamentally, though, this treatment is not caused by their nature.

NATURE IS NOT DISCOVERED NAKED

*Nature is constructed, constituted historically, not discovered
naked in a fossil bed or a tropical forest. Nature is contested,
and women have enthusiastically entered the fray.*

Donna Haraway, *Simians, Cyborgs, and Women* (1983)[48]

What does a monkey most want? What determines how monkeys live? For primatologists writing in the second half of the twentieth century the answer was *domination*. Primate lives were observed to be centred around alpha males, and the fight to become or remain the alpha male. In this story females and offspring are just along for the ride: they are prizes to be won, assets to be secured, followers to impress, genes to reproduce.

Primates have a special place in anthropology, the study of human nature. They have been used as the model of natural humanity. Primates have been studied as if they can show us what humans are naturally like: how they would be if society and culture didn't get in the way.

But this aim, the aim to find out about *human* nature, constrains and structures what is seen in animals. Feminist philosopher of science Donna Haraway described how different primatologists could see the primates they studied only through the lens of their own assumptions about human behaviour. Different studies of primate behaviour use, assume and reproduce different assumptions about 'nature'. Animal behaviours are observed, but which behaviours are deemed to be cause and which effect? Which observations are elevated to explanation? The answer inevitably relates to what are assumed to be facts about *human* behaviour.

In some cases, even observation cannot break through expectation. Haraway argued that the primatologists she studied had been unable to see the significance of mother–infant relationships in determining group structure because they had assumed, at a very fundamental level, that primate groups were determined by the alpha males. As Haraway puts it, writing about the primatologist Phyllis Jay, 'she literally, physically saw what almost could not figure in her major conclusions because another story ordered what counted as ultimate explanation.'[49] That other story was the imperative to understand what the primatologist understood to be the explanatory force behind *human* societies. 'All comparisons are not equal when the scientific goal is to know "man's" place in nature,' Haraway wrote.[50]

Haraway's radical critique suggests not only that we cannot use nature to tell us about society; it goes further, suggesting that nature cannot truly be seen at all. We can see things, of course, and some of those things occur in nature, or have natures, or could meaningfully be described as natural. But nature itself cannot be seen naked. It cannot be seen other than through our own, human, eyes.

This is not to say that nature doesn't exist. It just means that its existence must always be interpreted. Haraway didn't think that we should stop trying to see nature; she didn't advocate abandoning science. What science needs is self-awareness. We cannot 'pretend that science is either only discovery, which erects a fetish of objectivity, or only invention, which rests on crass idealism. We both learn about and create nature and ourselves.'[51]

One scientific discipline that attempts to uncover truths about the nature of humans and other animals is biology, a discipline that 'tells tales about origins, about genesis, and about nature'. But biology, even when it is pursued by women – even when it is pursued by feminists – is constrained by its origins in our own, unequal societies. As Haraway insists, 'modern feminists have inherited our story in a patriarchal voice. Biology is the science of life, conceived and authored by a word from the father. Feminists have inherited knowledge through the paternal line.'[52]

SEX PROVES TO HAVE BEEN GENDER FROM THE START

Sex itself is a gendered category ... As a result, gender is not to culture as sex is to nature; gender is also the discursive/cultural means by which 'sexed nature' or 'a natural sex' is produced.
Judith Butler, *Gender Trouble* (1990)[53]

One of the most important works in contemporary feminist and queer theory, Judith Butler's *Gender Trouble*, is the ultimate nature-killer. It has a good go at destroying the concept of 'woman', too – remarkable for a work of feminism. The central claim of the book is that the sex/gender distinction is untenable, because sex itself doesn't exist as a natural phenomenon.

Butler recognized, of course, that feminists would find her argument unsettling. 'Contemporary feminist debates over the meaning of gender lead time and again to a certain sense of trouble,' she wrote, 'as if the indeterminacy of gender might eventually culminate in the failure of feminism. Perhaps trouble need not carry such a negative valence.'[54]

For feminists, gender is indeterminate because it both exists and it doesn't. Feminism is about women: it's by them, and it's for them. And so feminism is grounded on the idea that there is such a thing as being a woman, most basically, and that there is such a thing as women's interests, even if those can be hard to define. At the same time, feminism's critical analysis of gender inequality is based on the rejection of the idea that women are naturally or essentially different from men. Women may do the vast majority of the unpaid domestic and caring work, but that's not because there's anything inherent to being female that makes women better at this work. A vagina isn't necessary for wiping bottoms; a penis shouldn't get in the way of the Hoover.

The sex/gender distinction allows feminists to say that natural sex differences do not explain or justify gender differences, because those are not natural. Butler certainly agreed that gender is not natural. But she argued that sex isn't, either. It's not just whether you're masculine or feminine that is down to culture rather than nature; it's whether you're a man or a woman; whether you're male or female.

How can this be? Butler observed that the sex/gender distinction has radical implications that are not always fully understood. The fundamental claim of the sex/gender distinction is that 'sex' and 'gender' are distinct. That's why gender cannot be fully explained by reference to sex. But if there's no necessary connection between sex and gender, it follows that there's no reason why the feminine gender should always accompany the female sex, or the masculine gender the male sex. Males can be feminine; females can be masculine. Moreover, if gender is not explained or caused by sex, there is no reason to think that there should be only two genders. If a female can be feminine or masculine, why could she not in principle be both, or neither?[55] The sex/gender distinction leads us, then, to the radical position that there can be more than two genders and that these genders do not need to map on to sex in any regulated way.

These ideas seem rather pedestrian now, when ideas like 'non-binary' and 'gender non-conforming' are becoming familiar. But in 1991 they were revolutionary.

Butler went further. Following MacKinnon, she argued that even the act of identifying people as female or male is inherently social. We choose which biological features count for making someone male or female: is it genitals, or chromosomes, or internal reproductive organs? And we choose to structure the world around sex categories, understood in a binary way. 'Because "sex" is a political and cultural interpretation of the body, there is no sex/gender distinction along conventional lines; gender is built into sex, and sex proves to have been gender from the start,'[56] she concluded.

Butler's aim was not simply to observe that there are non-natural, political elements to our practice of identifying sex and making it socially significant. Her aim was to critique that practice. Butler argued that the concept of nature is used in the service of what she calls 'the heterosexual matrix': a system of gender inequality built on compulsory heterosexuality. According to the heterosexual matrix, being lesbian or gay is marked deviant, a violation of some rule that is supposedly both biological and cultural. 'Paradoxically, homosexuality is almost always conceived within the homophobic signifying economy as both uncivilized and unnatural,' she wrote.[57]

The heterosexual matrix, the patriarchal gender binary that underpins gender inequality, rests on the idea that there are two distinct sexes that cause and explain two distinct genders. According to the logic of this oppressive system it is because a person is of the male sex that he will have the masculine gender, and one marker of maleness and masculinity is sexual attraction to persons of the female sex. In turn, persons of the female sex are (oppressively) understood as *therefore* having the feminine gender and *therefore* being sexually attracted to men. Sex, gender and desire become mutually supporting and causally linked under patriarchy. An essential part of Butler's critique is that the gender binary is both sexist and homophobic.

One puzzle for Butler's account is that it seems to posit an infinite regress. Which comes first, the idea of sex difference or the heterosexual imperative? If male and female come first then there is something prior, something primary, to biological sex difference, and that is precisely what Butler argues against. But how can heterosexuality even be defined, let alone enforced, without the recognition of male and female? Something must come first; there must be some pre-political difference that politics can get its teeth into. But Butler's central point is precisely that politics has teeth, and its bitemarks are everywhere.

REDUCING WOMEN
TO THEIR GENITALS

Where does this leave us? Contemporary feminism is in turmoil over three powerful questions:

1. Do women exist?
2. If so, who/what are they?

And, most profoundly of all:

3. Who is authorized to answer?

These questions, at least the first two, have been brewing in feminism for decades, centuries; what's remarkable at the present time is the orthodoxies that accompany them and the fear that surrounds them. People, especially women, are frightened to answer these questions, frightened to debate them, frightened of being ostracized and condemned for answering them wrongly. Needless to say, if there are women who are not authorized to give their views on what, who, or even *whether* women are, something has gone wrong.

The questions have been brought to the fore by the issue of trans identity, and particularly whether/how trans women are women. (There is much less debate about whether trans men are men.) That trans women *are* women is taken by many trans activists and supportive feminists, though not all, to be foundational, both premise and conclusion. The principle is intended to apply to anyone who identifies as a trans woman, regardless of their bodily characteristics or gendered appearance. For example, philosopher Talia Mae Bettcher argues that '"trans woman" applies *unproblematically* and *without qualification* to *all* self-identified trans women', and that 'being a trans woman is a sufficient condition for being a woman.'[58] In other words, self-identification governs both 'woman' and 'trans woman'.

On this view, having an unmodified body is cast as compatible with any gender identity, and also any legal and social sex status. This position both valorizes and downplays the unmodified body, both at once. It valorizes the unmodified body because it allows a trans person to assert their gender without undergoing any body modification. But it downgrades the unmodified body because it suggests that the natural body plays no role in generating a felt and socially recognized sex.

The supporting work for the principle *trans women are women* is found in the long tradition of feminist contestation of biological and natural explanations of women's position. The logical endpoint of that contestation is that biology plays *no role at all*. It describes neither women's role nor women themselves. Defining women in biological terms then becomes not only anachronistic but nonsensical; not only nonsensical but hateful; not only hateful but misogynistic; not only misogynistic but genocidal. Using biology as even part of a definition of woman becomes *reducing women to their genitals*; and that (no feminist would disagree) is *bad*.

If women aren't defined by their genitals, what are they defined by? Not their behaviours: to say that a woman is someone who acts like one would be to fly in the face of feminist critique of gender norms. And so various contemporary feminist philosophers have proposed alternative ways of understanding what 'woman' is.

For philosopher Sally Haslanger, it promotes social justice to define a woman as someone who is 'systematically subordinated along some dimension (economic, political, legal, social, etc.), and [who] is "marked" as a target for this treatment by observed or imagined bodily features presumed to be evidence of a female's biological role in reproduction'.[59] In other words, if people think you're female, and if they systematically subordinate you as a result, it doesn't matter what chromosomes you have or what your body looks like naked.

Haslanger's definition neatly captures the role of the body in defining women and setting them up for oppression while at the same time high-lighting the contingency of that connection. It has two rather radical (for the time, first published in 2000) implications: that someone who is biologically female but who is not systematically subordinated on that basis (so, a privileged woman who escapes sexism) is *not* a woman; and that someone who actually has male biology but who is widely presumed to have female biology, and is oppressed on that basis (so, some trans women) *is* a woman. It follows that womanhood can be hard to pin down, and it can be impermanent. A *bacha posh* really is first a girl, then a boy, and then a woman.

For Haslanger, the ultimate aim of feminism is the elimination of women. Her basic idea is that feminism is about ending the subordina-tion of women based on their bodies. This is the goal that has guided feminism for centuries. But describing this goal in terms of eliminating women rings alarm bells for many feminists. After all, it has been a central part of feminist struggle to make women visible. Women have very often been erased: from founding principles like 'All Men are Created Equal'; from basic rights like voting and owning property; from physical spaces like universities and golf clubs; from holding power as politicians and judges; and, as activist Caroline Criado Perez shows in her vital 2019 book *Invisible Women*, from the design and data collection of everything from town planning, car safety, personal protective equipment, mobile phones and public toilets.[60] Haslanger's aim to eliminate women *as a social category* is not as shocking as it first sounds – she's not trying to eliminate women as people or as sexed beings – but it's still a highly risky strategy. If a category is removed before the oppression that creates it, the oppression stays in place but the ability to describe it is lost.

However, Haslanger's account has fallen out of favour, not for weak-ening the category of women but for leaving too much of it intact. Philosopher Katharine Jenkins argues that Haslanger's account is transphobic. (More precisely, that it 'problematically marginalises trans women';[61] later, that 'failure to respect the gender identifications of trans people is a serious harm and is conceptually linked to forms of transphobic oppression and even violence'.[62])

Jenkins points out that Haslanger's analysis has the result that some trans women are not women. In particular, trans women who do not present as women (in other words, they make no attempt to comply with feminine appearance norms) are not women; trans women who are not accepted as women by others (they do not 'pass') are not women; and trans women who *are* accepted as women by others but who are *not* presumed to have female biology are not women. For Jenkins, this result is unacceptable because *all* trans women must be women as a matter of principle. It is also implicit in Jenkins's account that anyone who claims to be a trans woman is in fact a trans woman.

Jenkins thus advocates a definition of 'woman' that dispenses with bodies and biology entirely, depending on a combination of social position and subjective identity. In particular, Jenkins insists that the concept of 'woman' must include even someone for whom it is true to say not only that she does not have a female body (defined in terms of chromosomes and reproductive organs) but also that '*no one* around her is observing *or imagining* her to have a female gender identity'.[63]

In other words, it is crucial for Jenkins that any definition of 'woman' must include someone who 1) has a penis, testicles and XY chromosomes, 2) does not conform to feminine bodily appearance norms (for example, by having a beard), 3) does not conform to feminine beauty and clothing norms, 4) does not use a feminine name or pronouns, 5) is not even imagined by *anyone* else to have a 'female gender identity'.

It follows that the concept of 'woman' cannot be part of a political analysis of gender inequality, because we have no idea to whom it refers. The only way to find out who is a woman is by asking people, individually, and there is no way to test their claims or check for sincerity. Being a woman becomes purely a matter of self-reporting: not just pragmatically, as a way of getting round in-practice violations of privacy, but *in principle*. 'Woman' becomes a highly individualistic, even voluntaristic concept, not a concept that can be applied from outside as a part of a material analysis of either social structures or bodies. It is self-identification *all the way down*.

Self-identification is sufficient in some contexts, such as when setting the terms of a polite conversation. It's appropriate in that setting to defer to people's wishes. Gender self-identification takes on such importance because gender plays an extremely significant role in determining how other people relate to us. When we express or assert our gender, whether we are trans or not, we are in large part asking others to relate to us in a certain way. An assertion of gender becomes an ethical claim. It is a claim about an individual, about how they see themselves, and about how they would like to be treated. That claim is significant. Respecting it will often be an important part of respecting the person who makes it.

All of us make many different claims to be treated or related to in a certain way. We present different aspects of ourselves in different settings and ask that those be respected. Sometimes we wish to be treated as a professional, an expert, or a valued customer; other times we wish to be treated as a parent, child, or lover; other times as a patient or recipient of care. Sometimes our gender is of utmost importance in how we wish others to relate to us; other times, we feel insulted if our gender is highlighted. Many gender-non-conforming people report the immense difficulties they face in encountering people who do not know how to relate to them, gender-wise. 'Doing something as basic as going to the bathroom, anywhere that is public, is a nightmare,' writes philosopher Lori Watson, who is female, a woman, and not trans, but who is often wrongly taken to be a man.

> Few places have 'unisex' bathrooms. So here are my choices: go into the women's bathroom and face public shouting, alarm, ridicule, and confrontation. Or go into the men's bathroom, look down at the floor, walk quickly into a stall, and hope no one pays any attention to me but face the serious fear that they might.[64]

The need to support gender-non-conforming people, to afford them equal treatment and to treat them with respect, is what underpins a commitment to gender self-identification.

But in some contexts other considerations come into play. Self-identification can't be *sufficient* as an account of gender because it does not allow us to distinguish sincere from insincere claims, and it does not allow us to form policies that take adequate account of the many other aspects of sex and gender that have real political significance. Here's a real-life example. A student gym has hours when the gym is designated 'women only'. Some male students start to attend the gym during those times with the intention of making the women feel uncomfortable. The men are not trans; they are old-fashioned misogynists. In response to this problem, the women seek to strengthen and formalize the rule of women-only hours. In this context, self-identification would be totally inadequate. A rule restricting the gym to 'self-identified women' will be ineffective at keeping out the misogynist men, since they delight in attending during women-only hours, and since the new rule has no way of excluding them. If challenged, the men can simply claim that they identify as women. Their claim will be insincere, but the rule as it stands has no grounds for excluding them. In this context self-identification needs to be bolstered with objective criteria that can be used to exclude men.

This does not mean, to be clear, that the gym's rules must exclude trans people. Different rules will create different patterns of inclusion and exclusion. The students must choose whether their rules relating to women-only hours define 'women' as being legally female, or registered with the university as a woman, or usually living as a woman, or a variety of other possibilities. But whenever *any* sort of exclusion is warranted, self-identification is inadequate.

This result is totally generalizable and is not restricted to cases of sex- and gender-based exclusion. For example, if it were appropriate to exclude people from a job opportunity on the basis of a lack of qualifications, or from a school on the basis of age, that exclusion would not work if age or qualification status were *defined* via self-identification. The issue of how a category is defined is different from the issue of how it is usually identified. In practice, we often allow people to self-identify matters such as their gender, age, or qualifications: we don't typically have to show our birth certificates to access the gym, and I have never once been asked for my degree certificate. Self-identification can be used as a matter of trust and practicality. But that is not the same as saying that the characteristics in question cannot be defined, even in principle, by anything other than self-identification.

If gender were *only* a matter of self-identification, we would face two more general problems. First, feminist (and other) observers of gender would not be able to identify who the women are at the social level. A person's gender could be discovered only by asking them, and their answers might change. There would be no objective markers of gender, no reason why gender identity should be permanent, and no grounds for thinking that people were using the same criteria in identifying their own gender. So, it would be impossible to make political claims about the position of women (or indeed to make any general claims, be they sociological, economic, psychological, or statistical). How would we know if there were a gendered division of labour, or gendered patterns of violence, or a gender pay gap? Secondly, if women could be identified only by intrusive questioning and not mere observation, it seems unlikely that being a woman would be significant socially or politically. How could you discriminate against someone because of a characteristic you did not know they had? How could an unknown feature of someone explain their vulnerability to violence? If gender were a category that is neither socially ascribed nor socially identifiable, how could it be socially relevant?

The issue for this and other[65] avowedly subjective, voluntaristic accounts of what 'woman' is, is: what is the point of the concept 'woman'? What is it for? What does it help us understand? What does it do?

A concept's plausibility depends on its purpose. Before you can say whether you have defined something properly you have to be clear what you intend to use it for. Deployment is prior to definition.

The concept of 'woman' may need to be different depending on whether it is going to be used for the purposes of prescribing medical treatment, or recording crime, or allocating scholarships, or creating solidarity, or including, or excluding, or understanding, or overthrowing. A biological account of woman sometimes misses the mark, but other times it hits the X-ring. Sometimes what matters is a person's chromosomal biology or reproductive capacity. Sometimes what matters is a person's current anatomy. Sometimes what matters is their social identity – how they seem to others. Sometimes what matters is their self-identity. Elevating any one of these or other ways of thinking about sex/gender above the others in all contexts makes as little sense as eliminating any of them from view.

We mustn't give too much weight to the idea of the natural body, failing to see the social contingencies and political power that is overlaid on and beneath the skin. But we also need a full appreciation of the significance of unmodified embodiment, and the political role of socially and state-sanctioned body modification.

*

Azita was an educated daughter of educated, progressive parents. As an adult she was an MP in Afghanistan's parliament, under the rules for women's representation imposed by the American and European invaders following 9/11. As a child she had, for a time, been a *bacha posh*. Her father had wanted her to make something of herself; also, he needed a worker. Later, he would force her to marry her cousin, an illiterate farmer who already had a wife and who would subject her to violence throughout their marriage. But for a time, she enjoyed the privileges of masculinity.

What brought it to an end was her body, and its natural processes:

> Her stint on the other side came to an end when her father dismissed her early one afternoon when she was almost fourteen. Azita had begun to grow quickly; she was up two sizes in clothing in just a matter of months, and the day came when she complained of stomach pains. Too afraid to ask her mother, she learned the next day from a classmate what had happened. Neither of her parents said anything but it was apparent that they knew of the event that had turned her into a woman of childbearing age. Her father made it clear that she would no longer work at the store and that it was not a good idea for her to run around outside anymore, either.[66]

The start of Azita's periods was the end of her time as a *bacha posh*. More profoundly, it was the end of her freedom.

Here's something really important. All this problematization of the natural body does not mean that bodies don't exist, or that nature doesn't happen.

We can't deny the materiality of the body. Bodies do things, of their own accord, things which may liberate or constrain. Bodies age, they hunger, they put on weight, they fall ill, they die. Bodies menstruate, gestate, lactate, ejaculate, urinate, defecate. Bodies cry, sigh, sleep, lie awake and wonder why.

And bodies do these things whether we like it or not. We can stop them doing these things only sometimes, with effort, and often not at all.

Our bodies exist. They do things even without our culture's intervention.

But culture inexorably does intervene. It transforms our real, material bodies into subjects and objects, liberated and oppressed. It elevates some bodies and demeans others.

If men menstruated, feminists sometimes observe wryly, it would be a source of pride: a heavy flow a badge of honour, sanitary protection high-tech and ubiquitous, period pain over-researched and multiply treated.[67]

When menstruation is cast as shameful, requiring secrecy and silent suffering, insisting on its naturalness liberates. When menstruation is used to dismiss women as naturally unfit for public life, the opposite is true.

Either way, women bleed.

4

Weaving, Binding, Spinning

A Feminist Reclamation of Nature

> As 'essentialism' has become a brand, a stigma, a contagious
> disease that you have to avoid feminism to avoid catching, it
> has become one more way that the connections and coherence
> of the ways women are oppressed as members of the group
> 'women' can be covered up.
>
> Catharine MacKinnon,
> *Women's Lives, Men's Laws* (1997)[1]

> Biology will not simply go away, much as we might wish it to;
> it has to be theorized.
>
> Diana Fuss, *Essentially Speaking:*
> *Feminism, Nature and Difference* (1989)[2]

As I've mentioned before, the concept of nature is sometimes friend,
sometimes enemy. Feminist thought has identified nature's treachery,
enabling women to debunk, resist and overthrow naturalized accounts
of gender hierarchy. This work prevents the unmodified body from
being used to oppress and constrain.

But we are currently in danger of forgetting the ways that nature is
a friend. Nature reminds us that there is a material reality to our lives.
It encourages feminists to insist on the value and significance of
female-embodied experience in a world where male embodiment is
assumed as the default. And nature reminds everyone that women's
social subordination is not conjured out of thin air but is manufac-
tured from the systematic denigration of female bodies. A feminist

reclamation of nature can, then, be of great use to the project of *valuing* the unmodified body without fetishizing it.

Women's bodies are denigrated in so many ways that the process can become invisible. But think about three aspects of women's bodies that patriarchy targets: reproductive capacities, appearance, and sexuality. Each of these bodily aspects is weaponized against women. In every case, these features of women's bodies are at the same time elevated as the most important thing about them, used as an unattainable standard against which they will be found wanting, and derided as evidence of women's lack of seriousness, humanity, or equal status.

The basic mechanism is the same each time. First, elevate a woman's body or her bodily capacity to be the most important thing about her. A woman's main function is then to be a mother, or to be beautiful, or to be fucked.

Next, make the bodily standard unattainable. No mother is ever good enough, because mothers must be perfect. No woman ever looks good enough. And no woman is ever sufficiently sexually available and adventurous.[3]

Finally, weaponize the standard by punishing women for *meeting* it, as well as for failure. Are you a virtuous mother? Devoted, attentive, putting your children's needs before your own? Then you must be an inadequate worker: absent, distracted, uncommitted. Do you breastfeed your child? Then you are exhibiting yourself in public, making other people feel uncomfortable, putting on a disgusting display, or perhaps simply making other women feel bad.

Do you look good? Do you spend time, money and effort on your appearance? Then you are an airhead, a dumb blonde, someone obsessed with trivia. You take too long to get ready: men always have to wait for you. You're selling out feminism. Your clothing means you're asking for it.

Are you fuckable? Are you excellent at sex, with a voracious sexual appetite, someone who knows how to satisfy your partner and get satisfaction yourself? Then you are a whore, a slut, someone who cannot be raped, someone who needs to be raped.

Against all this, we must resist the patriarchal demand to denigrate and weaponize women's bodies. We must not allow them to be elevated so that they define everything about women. But nor must we allow them to be derided into insignificance. Our bodies are not everything, but they are *something*. We must assert the political principle of the unmodified body.

Women's value is not dependent on being mothers, or beautiful, or sexy, *but there is value in those things*. These bodily experiences, practices and goals are *significant* parts of women's lives. There is an embodied reality to being female, and there is a social reality to being a woman. These two don't always coincide. But, in a gendered society, the combination of female embodiment and social womanhood is significant, and it is precarious. The condition of being both sexed female and gendered woman has always been denigrated and always needs defending – which is not to deny the existence or the precariousness of other sex/gender combinations.

Not all women are mothers. It's not necessary to be a mother to have value. But motherhood is valuable. Without it, we cease to exist as a species. With it, we access joy and pain so exquisite that it is, for most mothers, utterly transformative. In it, we see aspects of human existence that disrupt some of the most fundamental and baseless assumptions of philosophy.[4] Women don't have to be mothers. But many women *are* mothers, and that is important. Moreover, everyone has a mother, even if not one who performed the act of mothering, and everyone is aware of the institution of motherhood. Those two facts act as the background for every woman's awareness of herself, and for everyone's expectations of women in general.

Beauty. Not all women are beautiful. Not all women should have to be beautiful. But all women are, in fact, expected to *try* to be beautiful.[5] And so we should not allow women's attempts to be beautiful to be mocked, used as an excuse to put them down. There is no reason to elevate men's visit to the pub and denigrate women's visit to the beauty salon – or, as the British government did in the Covid-19 pandemic, to allow pubs and men's barbers to come out of lockdown weeks before beauty therapists. Beauty practices can oppress, but they can also nourish. Heather Widdows points out that the beauty touch is one of the few sources of non-sexual caressing for many people, particularly elderly women.[6] Emma Dabiri describes the sociability and intimacy fostered by long hair-braiding sessions.[7]

And sex. Not all women have sex with men; not all women have sex at all. But many women do, and women's own experience of their sexuality must be taken seriously and respected. Women's physical and emotional responses have their own importance. Not all women like or want the same thing. But every woman likes or wants some things and dislikes others, *and that matters*. Every woman (and every man, actually) has the right to say no to sex, with anyone, at any time, and for any reason. And every woman has the right to ask for what she does want, and to have a sex life of her own devising: one based on her own fantasies, not someone else's.[8]

All of this implies the rejection of certain cultural ways of understanding our bodies – the rejection of cultural modification. It is a demand to be left alone, to be allowed to be who we really are, to be *unmodified*. Could it be understood as getting back to nature?

ESSENTIALISM AND INTERSECTIONALITY

In the last chapter we went on a whistle-stop tour through just some of the history of the uses and abuses of the concept of nature, and the ways that feminists have found it necessary to attack natural explanations. But have we moved too far away from the realities of our bodies? Do we need to reaffirm the significance of nature?

The natural body, it will turn out, is not the same thing as the unmodified body; but the idea of the natural body, and which bodies qualify as 'natural', gives us vital political insight. What is needed is a reclamation of nature; an account of the significance of biology that rescues it from essentialism.

Biological essentialism, when used in a pejorative sense, includes two ideas: determinism and universalism. As a whole, it is an idea firmly within the sex/gender binary. Biological determinism is the idea that biology explains behaviour. It is the view of women as naturally inferior that has existed for much of history, but it can also be found in some arguments for women's natural superiority. Biological determinism is a problem for everybody because it undermines the possibility of freedom and diversity; it's particularly a problem for women because they are standardly determined to be inferior.

Universalism, in this context, is the idea that all women are in some sense alike: that differences between women, though they exist, do not undermine the existence of women's shared experience. Universalism is related to biological determinism – if nature determines how women are, it stands to reason that they will all be the same – but the connection is not necessary, because women's common experience could be the result of their social status. Some degree of universalism is invaluable to feminism, but an uncritical or essentialist universalism is problematic because it seems to deny *intersectionality*. Intersectionality is a term that was coined by Kimberlé Crenshaw, originally to draw attention to the particular situation of Black women. Crenshaw pointed out a double bind faced by Black women: as *women* they all too often become invisible within anti-racism movements, and as *Black* they all too often become invisible within feminism. Black women thus suffer a double discrimination, and experience a form of oppression that is not reducible to either racism or sexism alone.[9]

In general, the concept of intersectionality emphasizes that women do not all stand in the same relation to power: other social locations, most obviously their race, class, nationality, sexuality, disability and gender identity, profoundly impact their experience, their needs and their political, economic and social status. At its worst, universalism can hide these differences and cast the experiences and needs of some women (typically, white middle-class women from the global North) as the experiences and needs of *all* women. This sort of universalism not only fails to attend to the needs of women cast as 'other', it also re-enacts the process of othering that caused much of their oppression in the first place.

What is needed is a balance between recognizing difference and commonality. As Audre Lorde puts it, 'Too often we pour energy needed for relating across difference in [to] pretending these differences are insurmountable barriers, or that these differences do not exist.'[10] As the opening quote from Catharine MacKinnon states, there is a danger in over-emphasizing the differences between women, and that danger is that commonalities are lost. 'Slowly I came to understand the paradox contained in "my" experience of motherhood,' wrote Adrienne Rich in 1976, 'that, although different from many other women's experiences it was not unique; and that only in shedding the illusion of my uniqueness could I hope, as a woman, to have any authentic life at all.'[11]

Women as people, and feminists as activists, experience (at least) three sorts of commonality. First, women are *treated* as a collectivity in patriarchal society, regardless of their individual uniqueness. Secondly, many women have shared experiences, whether by way of their embodiment, their social treatment, or their political situation. Identifying and articulating shared experiences is important not only to women's lives but also to feminism as a political movement, as the practice of consciousness-raising emphasizes. Thirdly, feminism is fundamentally a call to action, and this must be collective action to address a collective problem. The collective nature of feminism runs counter to the dominant capitalist ideology of the twenty-first century, which holds that the individual is unique, that choice is sovereign, and that an individual's particular situation of (dis)advantage is privatized. Feminism wants people to have choices – of course it does – but it recognizes that choices exist in a context, that choices serve conformity as often as they serve liberation, and that individuals' choices alone cannot overcome structural oppression.[12]

What I would like to do here is something rather unfashionable: explore the *value* of the concept of nature for feminism. If women's oppression is actually the result of culture, not nature, then nature can offer the prospect of liberation, of authenticity, even of sisterhood. It can offer a way of *living* in the body, while *leaving* it alone, while *loving* it. The concept of nature doesn't always have this progressive impact, as we've seen. But it can be put to good use; and right now, it must be.

WEAVING

It was a very gentle action. No one was waving or screaming or holding confrontational banners, it was just women using their bodies to block gates, which was highly symbolic.
                    Lynne Jones, Greenham peace protestor[13]

I remember the energy and desire and creativity and courage of women who were doing civil disobedience together; it was extraordinary. I was watching and photographing women who were laying bodies on the ground.

Paula Allen, Greenham peace protestor[14]

Feminist non-violence is active. Many women who came to Greenham had experienced male violence, so the passivity emphasised in traditional Gandhian non-violence was disempowering. Instead we developed creative ways to oppose nuclear weapons, which are the apex of patriarchal violence. For blockades we would dance or weave webs rather than just sitting down. If you were grabbed, you might sit or lie down, but others kept dancing.

Rebecca Johnson, Greenham peace protestor[15]

Greenham Common is a thousand acres of heathland just outside Newbury in the south of England. A walk through the common will take you among gorse, heather and bracken, past birch and alder woods, and through gravel beds laid down by the River Kennet millions of years ago. In the distance you may be able to see Watership Down, setting of the famously traumatic children's book in which a group of rabbits seek a safe home free from human cruelty and destruction.[16]

Greenham Common is notorious for the time when it was a military base – RAF Greenham Common – and, in particular, for the women's peace camps that grew up around it. These camps, interconnected but autonomous, existed throughout the Cold War period of the 1980s and the 1990s.

In 1980 the UK Defence Secretary Francis Pym announced that Greenham Common was to be the first UK site holding cruise missiles. NATO had agreed that a nuclear deterrent was necessary to counteract the threat posed by Soviet nuclear weapons, and Greenham had been chosen as the first location. Ninety-six American Tomahawk ground-launched cruise missiles would be housed at the base, missiles that would carry nuclear warheads and could fly for nearly three hours to detonate within Soviet territory.[17]

The base was converted into a maximum-security location. Arrangements were made to transport the missiles to the base by road, through the surrounding villages and country roads. Once at the base the missiles would be housed in massively reinforced structures, built to withstand conventional and nuclear attack. As the home of the West's nuclear deterrent, Greenham and the UK would themselves become targets.

In 1981, with Margaret Thatcher prime minister of the UK and Ronald Reagan the US president, a number of anti-war protesters went to the base to protest against the missiles. The number of protestors steadily grew, and many lived at Greenham in camps, engaging in what would be a mammoth and protracted act of civil disobedience as well as a powerful display of female solidarity and communal living. The protestors became known as 'peace women'.

The protestors' first prominent act was to chain themselves to the fence surrounding the base in 1981, an action undertaken by just thirty-six women. A year later, in 1982, 30,000 women joined hands around Greenham Common in the 'Embrace the Base' event.[18] One year after that, in 1983, 70,000 protestors formed a 14-mile human chain from the base to two other nuclear weapons' centres in the region.[19]

One photograph shows women taking part in Embrace the Base: many are dressed smartly, with dressy shawls and handbags among the woolly scarves and bobble hats.[20] Many women were inspired by the protestors and motivated to join the protest. 'People think everyone at Greenham Common was a hippy,' says Fran De'Ath, 'but many were ordinary women who did the cooking, and whose husbands played golf and didn't mind them coming because there were no men.'[21]

Some peace women would stay for over a decade. 'Katrina Howse, for example, first came to live at Yellow Gate in August 1982,' wrote Beth Junor in 1995. 'She made Yellow Gate her only home, and has remained working and living here permanently since: 9 of these 13 years in a tent.'[22] The camps were finally disbanded in 2000.

For the majority of their existence the peace camps were open to women only: men were not permitted. This contentious decision, made in 1982, garnered a great deal of press attention. 'The rationale was threefold,' reports Penelope Stokes, historian of the Common, 'first, that men were considered to have a tendency to take charge in mixed groups; second, that the group included teenage girls who might be at risk from male campers; and third, previous protest experience indicated that police reaction tended to be more violent against men.'[23]

Women at Greenham Common

Once established as women-only, the camps also became a hugely significant symbol of specifically female power and solidarity.

I was a young girl at the height of the Greenham Common protests, and was certainly aware of the camps. I remember my mother and her friends discussing them approvingly, even visiting for the day. The news reports of women linking hands around the perimeter of the base, scaling the fence, and blocking the entrance gates made a strong impression on me: women were powerful, they were brave, they were rebellious, they were resilient. Crucially, they *cared*. They wanted to protect the planet and the people on it.

Men made things dangerous. Women worked to make things safe.

This connection was explicit. 'Women could use their identity as carers and mothers to say, this is about the future safety of our children,' said a group of peace women in a 2017 interview. 'We weaponised traditional notions of femininity.'[24] Rebecca Johnson described another way the peace women used traditional women's roles. 'We taught ourselves to use authoritative "teacher" voices,' she describes. 'If women were being manhandled, we wouldn't shout but say, "Stop that now! You are not a violent man and you must not behave violently."'[25]

Ecofeminism is the view that there is a connection between the condition of women and the condition of the Earth. For ecofeminists, women's inequality is linked to environmental degradation, and, conversely, women's empowerment and feminist action is necessary for ecological rescue. Ecofeminism was at its strongest in the 1970s and 1980s, but it has gained new resonance in the current era of catastrophic climate change and resurgent climate activism.

Weaving is a metaphor used by ecofeminists, evoking women's creativity and the interdependence of life. Ecofeminists give nature a role in feminism in a very direct way, centring nature and weaving together the fate of the natural world with the condition of women. Weaving reminds us to value our unmodified bodies for their life-giving natural capacities, just as we value the natural earth.

Ecofeminists insist that feminists must work not to destroy the concept of nature, but rather to reaffirm its *value*. Nature is crucial to liberatory politics in general, on this analysis, but it's particularly important for women. Ecofeminists vary in their analysis of the connection between womanhood and nature. Some assert that women have a spiritual, elemental connection with the natural world, based fundamentally on the female body. Specifically female ways of having a body, particularly involving menstruation, pregnancy and breastfeeding, are understood as having a unique and powerful affinity with nature. This form of ecofeminism, associated with Earth mothers, Moon goddesses and crafts such as weaving, is often dismissed for being mystical at best, essentialist at worst: feeding into stereotypes of women's role that have served women badly for so long.

And yet ecofeminist activism based on spiritualism actually clashes with patriarchal understandings of femininity, because it involves women centring the planet and natural world, reuse and self-sufficiency, children's well-being, and bonds between women above men, consumerism, the house and the nuclear family. The peace camps at Greenham Common in many ways represent spiritual ecofeminism – which is not to say that the peace women all subscribed to that way of thinking – but the women in them were not praised by the male Establishment for conforming to their proper womanly roles. On the contrary. 'The peace women were seen as challenging traditional femininity by rejecting domesticity and leaving their children in the care of others,' notes Stokes.

'The prevalence of lesbianism in the camps was also a red flag, seen as a threat to the norms of family life.'[26]

Spiritual ecofeminism stipulates an essential nature for women, but it is not the nature that patriarchy assigns to them. A spiritual ecofeminist will not conform to Rousseau's vision of her nature as naturally inclined towards adornment, nor to the vision of woman as passive and apolitical. Spiritual ecofeminism urges us to respect the immense and unique power of the *female body*.

No feminist thinks all women are the same, nor wants them to be – but it can be difficult for spiritual ecofeminism to portray how differences between women coexist with claims about feminine and maternal nature. And so, this form of ecofeminism can seem dangerously or implausibly essentialist. As Mary Mellor puts it, 'This mixture of a near-essentialist conception of a woman-nature affinity and a non-gendered outcome is one of the most complex "weavings" of the ecofeminist web.'[27]

Adrienne Rich is one feminist who weaves this web most effectively. In her writings, particularly her 1976 book *Of Woman Born: Motherhood as Experience and Institution*, we find a deep appreciation of the significance and power of women's bodies – essentialist, if you like – together with a profoundly feminist vision for motherhood and womanhood that utterly escapes essentialism as a pejorative.

Rich urges us to respect and value maternity while at the same time arguing 'the institution of motherhood must be destroyed'.[28] She envisages a radically feminist world of egalitarian parenting: 'the assimilation of men in large numbers into a comprehensive system of child-care ... would be the most revolutionary priority that any male group could set itself.'[29] She is acutely aware of the differences in women's experience of motherhood, across boundaries of time, place, class and race. She is aware, too, of the different ways that women become mothers, that not every mother is a gestational mother, and that not every gestational mother remains a mother.

'What makes us mothers?' Rich asks, in a question that is posed to demonstrate the impossibility of answering it.

> The care of small children? The physical changes of pregnancy and birth? The years of nurture? What of the woman who, never having

been pregnant, begins lactating when she adopts an infant? What of the woman who stuffs her newborn into a bus-station locker and goes numbly back to her 'child-free' life? What of the woman who, as the eldest girl in a large family, has practically raised her younger sisters and brothers, and then has entered a convent? . . . Am I, whose children are grown-up, who comes and goes as I will, unchilded as compared to younger women still pushing prams, hurrying home to feedings, waking at night to a child's cry?[30]

So Rich in no way advocates an essentialist understanding of what makes a mother, or of who should nurture. She argues, also, that the institution of motherhood is profoundly significant for men as well as for women. But all women are profoundly affected by motherhood, in a way that marks them apart from men. 'The "unchilded" woman, if such a term makes any sense, is still affected by centuries-long attitudes – on the part of both women and men – towards the birthing, child-rearing function of women,' Rich insists. 'Any woman who believes that the institution of motherhood has nothing to do with *her* is closing her eyes to crucial aspects of her situation.'[31]

Rich expresses with great clarity the multiple connections between motherhood and patriarchy. As an institution, on her analysis, motherhood is an instrument of male dominance, wielded chiefly through multiple denials and suppressions of women's physical specificity. 'Patriarchal', she writes, 'means antimaternal.'[32] This is not to say that patriarchy is against women being mothers. On the contrary, motherhood is virtually compulsory in patriarchal societies. But patriarchy is anti-maternal because it stands fundamentally against recognizing the uniqueness and power of the female body, the only body capable of the awe-inspiring act of growing new life.

Hollie McNish's poem 'post partum' captures precisely how the body of the mother is valued only as a vessel or instrument. Once the baby is born the maternal body is cast aside. It becomes something to hide, to discipline, something to be pushed back into service and shape.

> they told me i was pregnant
> then told me i was glowing
> then told me i was blooming
> belly slowing growing life

> i gave birth to a baby
> i took the baby home
>
> they told me she was beautiful
> they told me, i agreed
> my body wrapped in silence now
> to lie and weep and bleed[33]

Rich fully recognizes, and endorses, the feminist critique of essentialist arguments that have reduced women to patriarchy's understanding of their nature. Motherhood 'has alienated women from our bodies by incarcerating us in them,' she writes. 'Women are controlled by lashing us to our bodies.'[34] But she is concerned that feminist critique has gone too far in its rejection of women's bodies. 'Patriarchal thought has limited female biology to its own narrow specifications. The feminist vision has recoiled from female biology for these reasons; it will, I believe, come to view our physicality as a resource, rather than a destiny.'[35]

That 'female biology' is something with immense power can be seen in the various attempts that all human societies have made to demonize or sanctify it, often both at once. At some times and places the female body, particularly the mother, has been venerated as the ultimate source of life, purity, fertility, a goddess; in other times and places she has been denigrated as dirty or devilish. Often these two configurations coexist, so that women can be sorted into Madonnas and whores, nuns and witches, wives and sluts.[36]

There are many examples of patriarchy's attempts to control the power of specifically female embodiment and thereby to suppress women's power. Taboos around menstruation are a pertinent example: making the menstruating woman into something dangerous, unclean, shameful, or embarrassing. Consider also limits on birth control and abortion, leading women to seek dangerous, mutilating, backstreet abortions or else to bear child after child beyond any ability to cope physically, emotionally, or financially. Women have suffered compulsory and alienated maternity: forced to breed for the slave trade, or the military, or family honour, or the church; forced to give their 'illegitimate' babies up for adoption, or their impoverished babies to the workhouse, or their female babies to be murdered, or their female children to the sex trade. Midwifery has been taken over by male physicians who have often lacked care and empathy for women and babies alike; male doctors introduced fatal germs, incapacitating procedures, painful positions and agonizing instruments to the birth process, with female experts demoted, banished, or burned as witches. Mothers have been expected to subordinate themselves to that role, with the house as the horizon, or else mothers have been expected to carry on labouring in the fields or the factories or the kitchens or the boardrooms directly after labouring to give birth, as though nothing had happened.

All these examples, and more, are detailed in Rich's work. Their sum total is this: 'Passive suffering has ... been seen as a universal, "natural," female destiny, carried into every sphere of our experience; and until we understand this fully, we will not have the self-knowledge to move from a centuries-old "endurance" of suffering to a new active being.'[37]

Crucially, we must distinguish between motherhood as an institution under patriarchy, and maternity or motherhood as embodied reality and experience. The institution of motherhood constrains, regulates and suppresses maternal power, making mothers into society's passive instruments rather than its ultimate source and motor force. On Rich's analysis, feminism requires both reclaiming the value of women's embodiment while rejecting entirely the institution of motherhood. Only then can women revel in their unique, natural relationship to maternity – a relationship that endures regardless of whether a woman herself becomes a mother – while rejecting both the patriarchal definition of motherhood and the reduction of women to their place in that institution.

As Rich puts it,

> The repossession by women of our bodies will bring far more essential change to human society than the seizing of the means of production by workers. The female body has been both territory and machine, virgin wilderness to be exploited and assembly-line turning out life. We need to imagine a world in which every woman is the presiding genius of her own body.[38]

Rich's reference to workers seizing the means of production brings to mind alternative versions of ecofeminism, which emphasize the socially constructed aspect of the connection between women and nature. Many ecofeminists take an anarchist, socialist, or Marxist approach, arguing that contemporary patriarchal Western capitalism constructs women and men differently with regards to systems of production and reproduction. For them, the capitalist political–economic order is run by men – men are and have been in almost all its positions of power since its inception – and it is run in ways that are detrimental to women and that fail to appreciate the realities of life as women know them. For social ecofeminists, women's affinity to nature is not inevitable or essential, but it is real and significant. The basic idea is that, while all humans are necessarily tied to nature, '(some) men have used their power to escape the consequences of their rootedness or embodiment'.[39]

Women remain close to the realities of embodiment because, in patriarchal societies, women are the ones charged with tending to everyone's bodily needs. Women create, grow, feed and nurture the bodies of others, using their own bodies. The fundamental embodiment of humanity is never more obvious than when one's own body is devoted to, devoured by, sometimes devastated by the creation and sustenance of life. But even aside from pregnancy, birth and breastfeeding, women are most often the ones charged with meeting others' bodily needs: providing sustaining, nutritious food and water, washing clothes, cleaning the home, tending to those who are ill or frail. In agricultural societies women also do a vast amount of nature-dependent work: tending the crops, tilling the soil, caring for animals.

Women's work thus makes women particularly attuned to the realities of embodiment, social ecofeminists argue. They are the first to notice when clean water and nourishing food are scarce, when illnesses are frequent or symptoms unusual. They are also the ones who suffer the most immediately from the destruction of the ecosystems in which they operate and on which they depend.

According to social ecofeminists, women's work under patriarchal capitalism means that women, and in particular poor women and women in the global South, are more likely to have an awareness of the significance of material reality and the constraints of embodiment than are rich people living in the global North, and men in general. It is not that women are more embodied than men, but that more of their time and attention is devoted to the realities of bodies.[40]

From this social ecofeminist perspective, a feminist rejection of the concept and significance of nature plays into the hands of patriarchal, colonial and elite rule. Denying nature enables political and economic structures that destroy the environmental goods that women rely on to keep themselves and their families alive. And denying nature also obscures this oppressive reality. As Mellor puts it,

> for women in other parts of the world and for poor women in western societies, embodiment is much more about obtaining basic sustenance and avoiding disease, disability through overwork and death. To discuss the woman-biology-nature debate within feminist thought is very much to embrace the concerns of relatively privileged western feminists with the danger of ignoring more fundamental problems which the majority of women face.[41]

In this context, thinking that feminism requires the destruction of the concept of nature is actually to deny intersectionality, because it is to imagine that the concerns of relatively privileged Western women are the same as, or more important than, the concerns of poor women the world over, and those in the global South more particularly. It is to ignore the ways that we all, ultimately, rely on the health and sustenance of our bodies.

The point is not simply that the feminist critique of nature distracts from other, more urgent matters; the point is that a wholesale rejection of the concept of nature renders those more urgent matters *indescribable, unanalysable*, and thus *unsolvable*. Rejecting the concept of nature and the realities of bodies makes us unable to theorize the way that those bodies operate in the world, the physical needs they have, and the way they are nurtured or harmed by the environment they live in and the politics that controls them.

Think of it another way. The dualism between nature and culture has traditionally been used as a tool of women's subordination, particularly in white European cultures. It has been used to identify women with nature and men with culture, and to justify women's social subordination. In this narrative, women are inferior to men because they are unable to access the various sophistications of culture: they are too irrational, too physical; they cannot think, because they bleed; they cannot produce, they merely reproduce. Moreover, describing these various imputed inferiorities as 'natural' is to suggest that they are inevitable and permanent.

If patriarchy says that nature is inferior to culture, and that women are nature and men are culture, feminists have two options. They can resist women's association with nature, or they can resist the idea that nature is inferior.

As we saw in the last chapter, feminists first sought to minimize the role of nature. They distinguished sex and gender, with sex representing nature and gender representing culture, and downplayed the role of sex. This method was strategically successful, but it came at a cost. Nothing was done to disrupt three patriarchal ideas: that nature as a concept is suspect in general, not just as deployed in any particular context; that women's nature, if it exists, must be inferior to men's; and, therefore, that any description of women's nature would be a justification of their subordination.

In other words, the strategy of distancing women from nature does nothing to undermine the patriarchal story in which nature is inferior to culture. Women thus remain at risk from being subordinated whenever nature resurfaces as part of womanhood. This feminist strategy requires the constant and complete annihilation of any hint of nature in women's experience – which explains why some contemporary feminists vehemently refuse to include biology or female embodiment as part of their understanding of womanhood or feminism. They are building on a feminist legacy that elevated women by denigrating nature. Recent feminist moves to destroy the concept of nature entirely, replacing everything with culture, thus retain the logic of natural female inferiority.

The alternative strategy is to reclaim nature. As ecofeminist Ynestra King puts it, women can 'recognize that although the nature/culture opposition is a product of culture we can, nonetheless *consciously choose* not to sever the woman nature connections by joining male culture'.[42] We could try to change male culture, by insisting that it includes us and everyone else and that it shifts from a logic of hierarchy to a logic of equality; or else we can insist that nature, including the specifically female and women-focused aspects of it, be respected.

Rather than expecting equality to be achieved only if women become like men, we could insist that equality become more woman-focused. We could insist that equality take account of the realities of bodies, rather than requiring their irrelevance. We could assert the political principle of the unmodified body.

One reason for pursuing an ecofeminist-inspired reclamation of nature is that the alternative – destroying nature in favour of culture – does nothing to destroy the hierarchical dualism between culture/gender/man and nature/sex/woman. Destroying the sex/gender distinction in favour of gender means that culture retains its role as something that transcends nature; and nature retains its role as something that limits, that constrains, that corrupts.

Women are in practice still allied with nature, both conceptually and practically. Women cannot escape their embodiment, their bodily needs, and their reliance on the natural world, and so feminists cannot destroy the concept of nature. Most likely, women will continue to be allied with nature, because that way men can remain allied with culture. Rather than brushing nature under the carpet as we go about our women's work, it is time we addressed its reality.

The strategy of *weaving* helps us to pull these threads together. It helps us reaffirm the value of our bodies just as we reaffirm the significance and value of the natural world. 'In arguing that we have by no means yet explored or understood our biological grounding, the miracle and paradox of the female body and its spiritual and political meanings,' Rich writes, 'I am really asking whether women cannot begin, at last, to *think through the body* ... There is for the first time today a possibility of converting our physicality into both knowledge and power.'[43]

BINDING

The bound foot existed for 1,000 years. In what terms, using what measure, could one calculate the enormity of the crime, the dimensions of the transgression, the amount of cruelty and pain inherent in that 1,000-year herstory? In what terms, using what vocabulary, could one penetrate to the meaning, to the reality, of that 1,000-year herstory? ...

> *But this thousand-year period is only the tip of an awesome,*
> *fearful iceberg: an extreme and visible expression of romantic*
> *attitudes, processes, and values organically rooted in all cul-*
> *tures, then and now. It demonstrates that man's love for*
> *woman, his sexual adoration of her, his human definition of*
> *her, his delight and pleasure in her, require her negation: phys-*
> *ical crippling and psychological lobotomy.*
>
> Andrea Dworkin, *Woman Hating* (1974)[44]

Andrea Dworkin was writing about foot binding, a horrific and excruciating mutilation of girls' feet that was practised in China from the tenth century until the twentieth. Foot binding typically started when a girl was between five and eight years old. The four smaller toes on each foot would be broken and forced underneath the sole; the toes and heel were then forced together, and the whole foot bound extremely tightly in cloth. The crushed feet were then forced into increasingly tiny shoes, and the little girl was forced to walk, despite the agony, to ensure that her toes were constantly forced as close as possible to her sole. Her feet would bleed, ooze pus, and smell horrific. Above all else, they would hurt. Usually, the person administering the torture was the little girl's own mother.

Some women with bound feet are still alive today, but the practice had ended by the time Dworkin was writing. Still, other binding practices exist. A woman who has given birth is supposed to devote her efforts to 'getting her body back' as soon as possible. The latest trend in post-partum penury is 'belly binding', whereby a woman who has just given birth wraps herself in an extremely tight band or corset to encourage her belly to shrink. The Belly Bandit is one brand: it uses a 'Power Compress Core™' and 'constant medical-grade pressure'[45] to help the woman 'struggling to regain her pre-baby body'.[46] Here's how it works:

> When you try on your Belly Wrap for the first time the ends should barely be touching. That's right if you can pull the Velcro closed it is too big! If the ends of the band are 1–2 inches shy of closing DO NOT EXCHANGE for a larger size. Simply lay down on a flat surface with the band beneath you and try closing it or get a little help from your

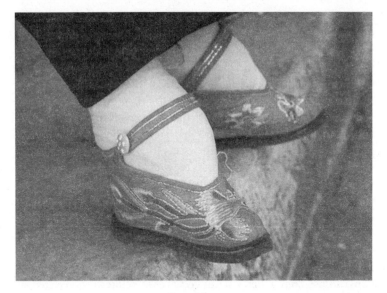

Bound feet

partner! If you find the band to be extremely tight you can wear it for a few hours each day until you begin to shrink into the size. You'll soon be wearing it around the clock!⁴⁷

The website describes the device as something to 'nurture the mother'.⁴⁸ Does this sound nurturing to you?

Of course, you don't have to have just given birth to bind your belly. There is a whole industry of 'shapewear' and 'tummy control'; you can find stomach-squeezing panels in swimsuits, underpants, tights, corsets, leggings. Anything that covers the belly can bind it at the same time. Underwear brand Triumph describes its Shape Collection, comprising 169 garments, as 'The sexy way to lose a few inches'.⁴⁹ Heist Studios promise 'HeroPanel technology that slims and shapes while keeping you comfortable'.⁵⁰ Marks and Spencer promise 'an extra dose of confidence when wearing your favourite outfits'.

The logic of the need to bind the female body is at its most complete in the contemporary practice of chest binding. Wrapping the breasts to conceal them is not new. 'In the early 1960s,' feminist psychologist Susie Orbach writes, 'the only way to feel acceptable was to be skinny and flat-chested with long straight hair. The first of these was achieved by near starvation, the second, by binding one's breasts with an ace bandage and the third, by ironing one's hair.'[51] Then, breast binding was a modification for the purpose of appearance; now, chest binding is a modification for the purpose of identity.

Chest binding is 'an integral part of the transitioning process for lots of trans men', according to *Pink News*.[52] Chest binding means strapping the breasts close to the body, to give the impression of a masculine, flat chest. According to the article, which is an encouraging 'how-to' guide for trans men, chest binding 'can be extremely uncomfortable and in some cases, very risky'. The guide reports that the dangers are especially high if binding is done with ordinary bandages or duct tape, because these practices risk 'forcing the weight of the breasts to break rib cages and, in some cases, puncture lungs'. People wishing to try chest binding are advised to buy a specially designed product and not to 'cut costs' – where the costs referred to are financial rather than physical.

Even an approved binder will hurt. 'Other health issues can include back pain, nerve damage, circulation issues and skin problems – for example, chafing, rashes, soreness and itching,' says *Pink News*. 'When you take your binder off, check your skin and make sure you're not bruised.' And remember, 'you should be able to take deep breaths when wearing one without difficulty. If you can't breathe, it doesn't fit.'

The first published medical research study of people who bind their chests (with various self-identified genders, but all born female) found that over 97 per cent of them experienced 'negative outcomes'.[53] Over half of people engaging in some form of chest binding experienced back pain and overheating; over 40 per cent suffered from chest pain, shortness of breath and itching. Around 40 per cent suffered postural problems – they were unable to stand naturally – and shoulder pain. Three-quarters of participants experienced pain and damage to their skin and soft tissue. Contrary to the *Pink News* advice, these problems were not lessened by using commercial binders rather than DIY methods.

Why, then, did the participants continue to bind? 'Although binding is associated with many negative physical health outcomes, it is also associated with significant improvements in mood and mental health,' the study reports.

> In response to open-ended questions about mental health effects and motivations for binding, participants consistently affirmed that the advantages of binding outweighed the negative physical effects. Many participants said that binding made them feel less anxious, reduced dysphoria-related depression and suicidality, improved overall emotional well-being, and enabled them to safely go out in public with confidence.

The researchers therefore advocate more research into how binding can be made safer.

Ultimately, chest binding may be the only way for a trans or non-binary person to feel psychological relief, short of mastectomy. That mental and physical pain characterizes both binding and being unbound is vividly captured in writer Maggie Nelson's description of her partner, Harry. 'Your inability to live in your skin was reaching its peak, your neck and back pulsing with pain all day, all night, from your torso (and hence, your lungs) having been constricted for almost thirty years,' she writes. 'You tried to stay wrapped even while sleeping, but by morning the floor was always littered with doctored sports bras, strips of dirty fabric – "smashers" you called them.'[54]

Chest binding has a different explicit aim from the 1960s beauty-motivated breast binding, but the way Orbach describes women's motivations then has striking resonance with the experiences of some trans and non-binary people now. Orbach writes that 'models of femininity are experienced by women as unreal, frightening, and unattainable',[55] meaning that women and girls sought ways of escaping prevailing standards of feminine beauty and sexuality. On her analysis, fat is a feminist issue because fat is one way for women to expand out of the bindings of femininity. Femininity, being a woman as prescribed by patriarchy, requires constriction; fat is an expansion of both body and possibility. 'For many women, compulsive eating and being fat have become one way to avoid being marketed or seen as the ideal woman,'[56] Orbach argues. Trans men and other people who bind their breasts are also seeking to reject the norms of feminine beauty, sexuality and identity: for them, binding offers a form of escape. 'I settled on the androgynous style that made me feel more like myself, and the binding that paradoxically left me able to breathe,' writes non-binary trans activist C. N. Lester, 'but still felt enormous pressure to present myself the way other people wanted me to be – to be found attractive.'[57]

In her professional experience as a psychologist working with compulsive eaters, Orbach had found that

> the most frequently stated advantage women saw in being fat had to do with sexual protection. It is almost as though through the protective aspects of the fat, women are saying they must deny their own sexuality in order to be seen as a person. *To explore their own sexuality means that others will deny them their personhood.*[58]

She describes how both compulsive eating and anorexia can develop in puberty, brought on by ambivalence about the girl's changing body and the social role it requires. For both anorexics and compulsive eaters, 'sensing something amiss at adolescence, they sought the answer in their individual biology. Their bodies were changing, becoming curvy and fuller, taking on the shape of a woman. They were changing in a way over which they had no control.'[59]

Puberty is an intensely difficult process, particularly for girls. Psychologist Karin Martin conducted a study into the experiences of puberty for boys and girls in the USA in the 1990s. Her striking finding is that it is *normal* for girls to emerge from puberty feeling bad about themselves and their bodies. Whereas boys tend to experience puberty as a good time in their lives, one that increases their agency, autonomy and self-esteem, for girls the opposite is true. 'In general,' Martin writes, 'puberty, for the girls in my sample, became associated with sexuality, and sexuality and the female sexed body became associated with dirtiness, shame, taboo, danger, and objectification. As girls internalized these meanings, they began to feel bad about their new bodies and themselves.'[60]

Martin attributes these outcomes for girls to the oppressive gendered norms that we attribute to female bodies and female sexuality. Developed breasts are associated with sexuality. Breasts bring unwanted attention from boys and men, the experience of objectification, and warnings from adults about the dangers of being sexually attractive. As comedian and fat activist Sofie Hagen puts it,

> Your teen years are full of warnings. All the monsters that you thought were under your bed when you were a child are suddenly real – and they are not under your bed where you can see and contain them. They are the reason you are asked never to leave your drink out of sight, the reason you don't walk home alone, and the reason you have to learn how to say no if there is something you don't want to do.[61]

Breasts are socially significant, to put it mildly, and so developing breasts is frequently a difficult process. Breasts are almost universally identified with shame. Martin found that pubescent girls virtually always felt ashamed of their developing bodies and wanted them to be different. This shame can't be avoided by having the perfect body, because the shame is caused by having *any* female body. 'With respect to breasts,' Martin writes, 'this usually means that flat chested girls want to have larger breasts and large chested girls want to have smaller breasts.'[62]

Periods are experienced as dirty, shameful and necessarily secret, and starting to menstruate is also associated with obligations to have sex and the dangers of unwanted pregnancy. Adult female sexuality in general feels to most adolescent girls like a dangerous, judgemental, pressured and objectifying space, and one they are pushed into not by choice but by their developing bodies. 'Girls come to associate sexuality with danger, shame, and dirt, and boys to associate it with masculinity and adulthood.'[63]

This needs emphasizing: the experience of danger, dissatisfaction and disconnect from their own bodies is *normal* for pubescent girls. The earlier they develop, the worse they fare.[64]

It is frightening to feel that you or your body are out of control. Ways of coping with this fear can include seeking methods of control, or adapting to powerlessness, or rejecting ideals of femininity, or rejecting womanhood as an identity. Both binding and (not) eating can be a way of gaining control and resisting a feminine sexual and social identity, with all the restriction and constraint that suggests.[65]

The answer is not to prevent chest binding, to force-feed anorexics, or starve over-eaters. These measures simply accentuate the idea that the failing is individual, reinforcing the cycle of shame. This isn't a problem that can be solved by individuals working on themselves, even with the help of psychologists (though such work may be a necessary coping strategy). It's a task for collective action, for feminist resistance. The answer is to demand political action to make living in a female body bearable. We have to target the cause of the problem: rampant male violence, sexual harassment, the objectification of female bodies, the denigration of motherhood, the industries that rely on us feeling bad about our bodies, the oppression of women in all its forms. We need to develop public policies that are effective in tackling body image and low self-esteem as public health issues.[66] We need to talk about the problem – between friends, in consciousness-raising groups, on social media and in public.[67] With this book I offer a framework for thinking about the unmodified body as a political concept, a way of illuminating the problem so that we can think about how to discuss and rectify it together.

A feminist reclamation of nature is, then, the insistence that the female body can be left unbound. This unbinding was, for Dworkin, a central part of feminism:

> A first step in the process of liberation (women from their oppression, men from the unfreedom of their fetishism) is the radical redefining of the relationship between women and their bodies. The body must be freed, quite literally: from paint and girdles and all varieties of crap. Women must stop mutilating their bodies and start living in them. Perhaps the notion of beauty which will then organically emerge will be truly democratic and demonstrate a respect for human life in its infinite, and most honourable, variety.[68]

Dworkin was most definitely not a biological essentialist. She rejected that charge in general throughout her writing and speeches, and specifically in several places, most notably in 'Biological Superiority: The World's Most Dangerous and Deadly Idea'.[69] In that work she rails against the claim, popular among some radical feminist separatists in the late 1970s, that women are biologically superior to men and so should rule over them, ultimately seeking to make men redundant via the development of new reproductive technologies. For Dworkin, ideas of biological superiority, even when they favour women, are deadly dangerous, as demonstrated in the ultimate doctrine of biological superiority applied by Adolf Hitler to justify the attempted extermination of the Jewish people.

So Dworkin had no time whatsoever for any feminism that postulates female biological superiority. She was also enormously sympathetic to trans people, writing that transsexuality (as it was then called) 'can be defined as one particular formation of our general multisexuality which is unable to achieve its natural development because of extremely adverse social conditions'.[70] These adverse conditions mean, for Dworkin, that 'every transsexual has the right to survive on his/her own terms', including with surgery where necessary.[71] Ultimately, though, Dworkin envisaged an androgenous utopia, in which the destruction of male supremacy and the enforced gender binary would mean 'the end of transsexuality as we know it', because trans people would no longer have to fit their gender and sexuality into constraining social norms.[72]

Dworkin would not endorse crude versions of spiritual ecofeminism, where women become the nature-given guardians of the earth. But she did make connections between women's condition under male dominance and the condition of the earth. 'Here we see the full equation: women = carnality = nature,' she wrote.

> The separation of man from nature, man placing himself over and above it, is directly responsible for the current ecological situation which may lead to the extinction of many forms of life, including human life. Man has treated nature much as he has treated women: with rape, plunder, violence ... In order to achieve proper balance in interhuman interaction, we must find ways to change ourselves from culturally defined agents into naturally defined beings.[73]

SPINNING

It's a question of strategy.

At a time of catastrophic climate change, is it wise to destroy nature?

At a time of continuing devastating violence against women and girls, is it wise to deny their distinct existence?

At a time of exponential growth in body modification procedures and an epidemic of appearance-related anxiety, is it wise to devalue the female body?

The reification of culture as nature served women badly, very badly indeed. But there is no evidence that the reification of nature as culture is serving them – serving us – any better. Instead, we need to spin nature. We need to take a political, pragmatic approach to the concept. We need to resist the reification of either side of the nature/culture dualism, without allowing either to become extinct.

In *Sex, Culture, and Justice*, published in 2008, I used the terms 'sex' and 'gender' interchangeably. I acknowledged the existence of bodily differences between women and men, female and male. But I noted, following MacKinnon, that the attention we give to those differences, the role they play in structures of domination, is entirely political.[74]

That framing seemed necessary at the time when sociobiological accounts of male dominance and female subordination were in the ascendant. Almost any aspect of gender inequality could, it seemed, be 'explained' by nature. A whole body of work by evolutionary psychologists had emerged, attempting to explain the existence of the corset with the claim that it created a waist-to-hip ratio that men were adapted to find attractive since it corresponded in some way to women's reproductive capacity.[75] Evolutionary psychologist Randy Thornhill and anthropologist Craig T. Palmer had argued that rape should be understood not as an exercise of power but, rather, as an evolutionary adaptation.[76] Clinical psychologist Simon Baron-Cohen had argued that sex differences in the brain meant that the male brain was 'programmed to synthesize and the female brain to empathize', a difference that he argued partially explained some forms of autism.[77] Kingsley Browne, 'American lawyer and evolutionary thinker',[78] had published a book arguing that 'much of the responsibility for differences in men's and women's earnings and status lies with evolved differences between the sexes'.[79] I sat in a seminar in which a fellow political theorist argued that evolutionary differences entirely explained pornography, including the fact that the women in it were 'low status'. It didn't seem to matter whether the author was a natural scientist or not: scientific explanations of gender inequality were percolating throughout the humanities and social sciences. In that context, the case had to be made most strongly that sex, biology and nature did *not* explain gender inequality.[80]

I believe the same things about sex and gender now as I did in 2008, when I wrote that the terms could be used interchangeably. But the political context has changed. At the time the significance of natural sex was so overrated that it was more provocative, more politically and pedagogically productive, to write as though sex were nothing at all. I could rely on my reader having a stable concept of natural sex differences, and the task was to disrupt that.

Now, most readers will of course retain a concept of natural differences. They will know that penises and vulvas exist, that sperm and egg are needed for reproduction, that male and female people can generally (not always) be identified as such by way of their visible bodily features, that some bodies can become pregnant while others cannot (and not just because of infertility). But the pressure is on to minimize the significance of these sex differences to the point of invisibility or, worse, to the point of making them disreputable. Now, the productive provocation is to reaffirm the reality and significance of the natural body, including within feminism.

I believe the same things now as I did then. I believe that bodies are real. They exist independently of our minds; they are the basic conditions of us having a mind. I believe that the human condition is one of embodiment: that we *are*, ultimately, our bodies. We cannot escape our bodily needs, we cannot experience the world other than through our bodies, our bodies are neither property nor a blank canvas but are intrinsically us. I believe that while we can suffer dysphoria, can deeply reject, regret, or disassociate ourselves from our bodies or body parts, we cannot literally be born in the wrong body, because there is no other body that 'we' could be born in. (If you had been born with a different body, 'you' would be someone else.) I believe that bodies create both commonalities and differences of experience: we can never truly know what it is like to exist in another person's body, either physically or mentally, but we can share our embodied experiences and find comfort and solidarity in similarity, as well as a greater awareness of social structures of power and freedom.

At the same time, I believe that culture is everywhere. We cannot access even our thoughts without cultural concepts, without language, without a socially mediated understanding of our own experience – or even what counts as an experience. Culture affects what we notice, what we do when we notice, whether we notice that we notice. Culture affects whether we find ourselves beautiful or ugly, whether we find ourselves to be natural or unnatural, whether we regard ourselves as normal or abnormal. Nature and culture coexist; nature and culture are interdependent; nature and culture rely on each other for contrast and distinctiveness even while they reveal that no sharp border can be drawn between them.

What does all this have to do with the concept and value of the unmodified body? The connection is this: valuing our bodies just as they are requires knowing what they are, what they do, and why that is valuable. Ultimately what we need is an egalitarian valuing of all bodies, whether male or female, and of any gender. Male bodies and masculine people are subject to cultural contestation and oppressive norms too, as we saw in the case of body building in Chapter 1. But since it is women's bodies that are most often devalued, it is women's bodies that need to be revalued, and that means engaging head-on with the idea of women's nature.

A feminist reclamation of nature is a reclamation of the value and specificity of female bodies. It is also an insistence that all bodies are primary rather than other: not all nature and no culture; not all culture and no nature; neither nature nor culture; both culture and nature.

PART TWO

Normal

At its core, the logic of the idea of naturalness is to resist culture: to be left unmodified. In this Part, I turn to the idea of normality, whose logic is very different. Normality is a concept that practically demands modification. Normality implies norms: rules about how we should be. Normality implies normalization: a process by which we are made normal.

And so, the idea of the normal body is a direct challenge to the political principle of the unmodified body. *Your body is good enough just as it is* – is that true only if your body is normal? Is there any reason to value an abnormal body, or to resist pressures to make it normal?

Three different values motivate body modification: identity, appearance, and health. A political perspective gives us the tools to criticize the idea that we should normalize our appearance or our identity. We can appeal to readily available arguments from feminism, queer theory, intersectionality and liberalism to show that we should be free to deviate from social norms – that freedom creates diversity and equality requires it. But these arguments seem much more problematic when we consider health. There doesn't seem to be anything valuable in refusing to change the body in ways that improve its function, cure it of disease, or keep it clean and maintained. These modification practices seem unproblematic; more than that, they seem virtuous. They seem like practices to be positively embraced and rigorously pursued.

It seems that we should want our bodies to be the best they can be – to improve their health and functioning as much as possible. There is a large literature on the ethics of enhancements: whether it is desirable, or even acceptable, to seek body modification that transcends both normal and natural and aims for perfection. I won't be going into that more speculative question, although later in the book I investigate the idea that we have a duty of self-care or self-improvement. Here I explore the far more moderate idea that it is good to be normal, and that modifications in the pursuit of normality are eminently desirable and ethically impeccable.

What we'll see is that the demand to be normal is rarely compatible with equality.

Our appearance-focused culture means that we make harsh judgements of 'abnormal' bodies. We judge people who look different or unusual – and we judge them in ways that go beyond the aesthetic. James Partridge, who suffered serious facial burns as a teenager, recalls the damning judgement he made of his own face when he saw it for the first time after his accident: 'Every fibre of my being told me *IT* was a thing I could never like or be proud of. Ever,' he writes. 'The "face values" that I had grown up with told me insistently and continually throughout that night that not only were my scars and distorted visage ugly and unappealing, but they also made me less of a human being, less worthy of being liked and respected.'[1] Partridge alerts us to the ways that the idea of the normal body actively hinders equality, by casting non-normal bodies and the people who have them as inferior. In Partridge's case, the need to be normal was a cause of suffering and shame.

Socially, we also judge bodies that are deemed to be abnormally unhealthy, particularly fat bodies.[2] As Sofie Hagen puts it,

> most people will have parents who tell them to 'never get fat', who will pinch their own stomach fat and say 'eww' and who will point at fat people in the shops and say words like 'lazy', 'stupid' or 'gross'. The negative attitude towards weight is so all-encompassing that the chances are that whoever you meet has been taught to hate fatness, long before they even had a chance to make up their own minds about what it is they like and don't like.[3]

Fatphobia is a socially accepted form of hatred in part because we attach blame to fat people, treating them as unethically unhealthy. This blame and derision are not compatible with treating people as having equal moral worth, and they rely on ignoring the political, cultural and economic structures that create both fatness and fatphobia.

At the same time, there is value in many of the things that the concept of normality tries to protect. Ideas of normality, including those relating to health and functioning, may be fundamentally social and open to question. But there is still a *reality* to a body's health and functioning. The body exists as a physical thing independently of its social place. Its constraints are our constraints; its possibilities are our possibilities. So, the idea that we should seek to achieve normality in terms of health and functioning can't be totally dismissed. The problem is that pressures to modify, including for health, often misfire. Constant pressures to modify our bodies have contributed to poor mental health: low body image, appearance anxiety, shame. Modifications aimed at health can be beneficial, but pressures to modify, even for health, may not be. And so, we need to find a path that recognizes the value of certain sorts of normality without trapping us in others. The political principle of the unmodified body is needed as a matter of equality, but also as a matter of public health.

At the start of the book, I described the pressure many women feel to 'get their body back' after pregnancy. The language of that phrase is so telling: it's not about anything as simple as losing weight or increasing fitness. When women try to 'get their body back' after pregnancy they are trying once again to feel and be normal, where normality is defined according to sexist standards. Getting your body back after pregnancy is about living up to standards of feminine attractiveness and youthfulness that society has set for women. It is about returning your body to its patriarchy-given place as sex object, decorative ornament and disciplined figure. It is about withdrawing your body from its subversively omnipotent role as creator of life, giver of sustenance, source of comfort.

But we can also reclaim the language of 'getting your body back' by understanding this imperative as a reclamation of the internal perspective. We can get our bodies back in the sense of allowing them, in their changed form and with their new experiences, to feel *like us*. Our post-pregnancy bodies may be stretched, cut, torn, sewn; but they are also mighty, life-giving, potent, nurturing. They are someone else's world, someone else's origin, our present, our reality. We can choose to accept them as they are, now. We can choose to recognize them as truly us.

We get our bodies back when we allow them to *feel* – and therefore to *be* – normal. But this is a project with certain political prerequisites.

5

The Normal Body

Is your body normal?

This might seem like an easy question to answer. You probably have a sense of whether your body is, roughly speaking, like other people's. Perhaps its size and shape seem to fit within normal parameters: you might know some people who are larger than you and some who are smaller, some who are paler and some who are darker, some who are prettier and some who are uglier. You're average? Then you're normal.

But perhaps you're not quite sure about every aspect of your body. How do your genitals compare to other people's? Are your labia longer or shorter than theirs? Is your penis larger or smaller? What do other women's faces look like without make-up? Do other women have to remove hair from there (upper lip, chin, nipples, arms)? Do most men your age have a six-pack? Are your stretch marks worse than other women's? Are you the only woman in her thirties whose hair is going grey? Is it normal for a man to start balding this young?

Beauty and appearance might seem fraught and subjective, not to mention strongly gendered, so perhaps you should look elsewhere for reassurance of your normality. You probably have a sense of whether your body is fully functioning and healthy, or whether you face physical impairments or disease. You might know, based on this understanding of what normal bodies can do, whether yours counts as one of them.

But even this idea of normality, one based on clinical assessment, is not simple. Even the concepts of disease and health are far more complex and subjective than they first appear. Before we think too much about it, most of us are probably what philosophers of medicine call naturalists: those who believe that there can be objective definitions of disease and health. If your body works, if it can do what most bodies can do, then it's healthy and it's normal.[1]

Against this naturalist view is the philosophical approach of normativism. Normativists argue that health and disease are essentially value-laden phenomena.[2] Saying that something is healthy or diseased, normal or abnormal, is not to state a fact so much as to make a *judgement*.

One way that normativists make their case is to point out that what counts as a disease changes over time. Some things previously labelled as diseases are now not, and such labelling has been discredited as invented or discriminatory. For example, the condition of hysteria is no longer recognized as a disease and is understood instead as an oppressive diagnosis, a sexist way to denigrate women's emotions and malaise.[3] Other things previously labelled as diseases now strike us as perfectly normal. For example, in countries such as Britain, the USA and Canada in the nineteenth and early twentieth centuries masturbation was considered by many doctors to be a disorder, one that could appropriately be treated by surgical intervention such as circumcision.[4] In those countries today masturbation is considered normal, and doctors who advocate circumcision tend to claim that it does not lessen sexual pleasure.

Changes in clinical responses to phenomena such as hysteria and masturbation demonstrate the culturally relative aspect of health and disease. Whether your body is considered normal, even in terms of health, depends on when and where you ask the question.

Value judgements are inherent in defining disease and abnormality, then. They also play a significant role in identifying bodies that are normal or better than normal. Whether the physical traits of your body count as beautiful also depends on when and where you are, and sometimes the norms change very fast. Buttock implants and labiaplasty are two popular cosmetic procedures that were unheard of relatively recently. Large buttocks and small labia are recent beauty trends whose popularity has developed alongside the surgical procedures that create them.

NORMALITY AS AVERAGE

What's the normal number of legs for a human? It's two, obviously. But the average (mean) number of legs for a human is fewer than two. Some people have only one leg, or no legs at all, and almost no one has three or more. So, if we calculate the average number of legs per person by adding up the total number of legs in the world and dividing it by the number of people, we'll end up with a number smaller than two, and the distinctly odd result that nearly everyone has more legs than average.

If we want to use averages to find the normal number of legs for a human, then, we need to use the mode: the most frequently recurring number. Then we'll get the correct answer of two. Most people have two legs, so having two legs is normal and having a different number of legs is not. In other cases, though, the mode gives the wrong answer. The average (mode) human has a penis, because there are slightly more males than females in the world (49.584 per cent of humans in 2019 were female, according to the World Bank[5]). If normality is determined by the average (mode), then it is normal for humans to have a penis and abnormal for humans to have a vagina. Again, that's the wrong answer. Having a vagina is perfectly normal.

If we want to use statistical averages to find out what's normal we need to know what sort of average to use in what context, and we need a reference class. We could use the mode to find out whether vaginas are normal for humans if we first restricted our investigation to the reference class of females. Then, we'd get the correct answer. And we could use the mean to find out the normal number of legs for a human if we started with the reference class of humans with a normal number of legs. But, of course, if we know what the normal number of legs is before we take the average, we don't need to use averages at all.

The naturalist philosopher of medicine understands clinical treatment as existing to create or restore a normal body, understood in statistical terms.[6] But even statistical definitions of 'normal' depend on a reference class. In other words, whether your body is normal depends on which other bodies you're comparing it to. It's not just legs that cause problems. What is statistically normal for men is different from what is statistically normal for women, including not only sexual and reproductive characteristics but also height, body composition in terms of fat and muscle, hair growth and loss, and susceptibility to disease. Physical conditions and susceptibility to some diseases vary by race and ethnicity, too. Whether a physical characteristic is regarded as a disability is open to contestation and change.

To see this, consider the ability to become pregnant and gestate a foetus. Almost all females of childbearing age have this ability. Some female people lack it, and we describe that lack as a medical condition, a detriment to health. If a post-pubescent, pre-menopausal female lacks the capacity to become pregnant and gestate a foetus we describe her condition as infertility, and we treat infertility as a disease and offer treatment.

However, we do not describe the inability to become pregnant and gestate a foetus as a disease or health condition when it comes to males. We consider this lack of functioning to be normal for them. Moreover, even though the ability to gestate a foetus is highly valuable to individuals and to society as a whole, we don't regard males as chronically disabled. Instead, we regard male people's inability to gestate to be normal – even though billions of people (females) do have that ability.

The obvious response to this point is to say that being unable to become pregnant and gestate a foetus is not a disability or health condition or abnormality *for males*, because this inability is normal *for them*. This is true, of course. But it is true of other conditions too, particularly those that are present from birth. Being unable to see is normal *for blind people*. Being unable to hear is normal *for deaf people*. Having difficulty understanding others' thoughts and emotions is normal *for autistic people*. And yet we often describe these things as disabilities, or health conditions, or examples of abnormality.

What this shows is that our conception of health, understood as normal functioning, depends on the reference class, and what we consider to be the correct reference class is often a normative decision. It is political, cultural and value based.

If we want to say that males are not disabled by their inability to conceive and gestate, we are relying on two claims. First, we are rely-ing on the claim that biological sex is a real or natural category that divides human beings into two classes with different standards of nor-mality. That claim seems obvious to many people but is deeply controversial to others – it is a claim with cultural specificity and pol-itical and ethical implications.

Secondly, our refusal to describe males as disabled by their male-ness rests on centuries of treating the male body as the normal body, the default body, from which any difference is seen as a deviation. If we considered females as the paradigm human, we might well describe males as disabled, since the ability they lack is so signifi-cant. But, since we treat maleness as both normal and normative, the functions that only females have are not seen as necessary parts of normal humanity.

In fact, as we've seen, it is female functioning that is cast as deviant or deficient. Pregnancy itself is often understood as being a type of disability – for example, it is treated as such in the USA, in lieu of statutory maternity leave. Disability theorist Jerome Bickenbach writes of pregnancy as one example of a 'health condition', which he defines as including 'states of the human body that characteristically create problems in functioning'.[7]

But, of course, pregnancy is much more aptly characterized as an extraordinary *ability*. Far from indicating a lack of functioning, preg-nancy is a unique and powerful function all of its own. It is the capacity to create, grow and sustain life; the ability to create other beings – the fundamental requirement for the existence of humanity. Despite its significance and wonder, however, the ability to become pregnant is also widely distributed among humans: about half of human beings will be able to become pregnant at some point in their lifetime. Why, then, do we not describe male people, who lack this vital and widespread human ability, as disabled or abnormal?

Ideas of normality rest on cultural assumptions. This cultural foun-dation means that conceptions of normality in health are often related to appearance and identity. Describing a body as normal or abnormal always implies a value judgement.

Value judgements are not always wrong, of course. Often, they are right. I aim not to reject all claims about normality but rather to uncover the hidden or not-so-hidden assumptions behind an attribution of normality. My claim is that body modifications are politically significant, and should be subjected to critical scrutiny, even when they aim to create or restore 'normal' health.

My claim is that the concept of the 'normal' body is never neutral.

> *For 2,400 years patients have believed that doctors were doing*
> *them good; for 2,300 years they were wrong.*
>
> David Wootton, *Bad Medicine* (2006)[8]

The most basic aim of medicine is to keep us alive. For most of human history it has not succeeded.

We are fortunate to live in an era in which medicine has become sufficiently successful at staving off death to turn its attention to the even more challenging task of making us healthy. Modern medicine is a practice of body modification – often very extreme modification, involving scalpels and stitches – but one that is directed towards normality, understood in a limited, health-bounded way.

Medicine modifies bodies according to conceptions of the normal or ideal body. Some bodies are acceptably within the limits of normal, but others fall outside those limits and require treatment. Examining medical practices can therefore show us what the concept of a normal body looks like when confined to the domain of health. Of course, what is considered properly within the purview of medicine is open to contestation and change. Does medicine include physiotherapy, acupuncture, yoga? Does it include paracetamol, vitamin supplements, a vegan diet? The barriers between medicine and lifestyle are fluid.

One practice that is paradigmatically medical is surgery, performed in clinical conditions by qualified surgeons. Surgery is a useful lens through which to view the medical conception of the 'normal' body because surgery is uncontroversially a medical procedure. So, an analysis of surgical modifications is one way to test the claim that there is something distinctive about health-based modification.

However, not all surgery is actually aimed at health, understood in a narrow sense. Legal practice, healthcare provision and philosophy often employ a distinction between types of surgery, and, in particular, between *cultural*, *cosmetic* and *clinical* procedures. Legally, states such as the UK prohibit female genital mutilation, designated as a procedure performed for *cultural* reasons, but permit or even provide labiaplasty, designated as *cosmetic*.[9] In terms of healthcare, both state and private providers tend to distinguish between *cosmetic* procedures, which are not usually covered, and *clinical* procedures, which are. In terms of philosophy, both sorts of distinction can be defended by reference to choice and necessity: *cosmetic* surgery is elective, chosen and unnecessary, and therefore permissible but not an entitlement; *clinical* surgery is non-elective, unchosen and necessary, and thus both permissible and an entitlement. The treatment of *cultural* surgery is often inconsistent and is affected by the culture from which it is drawn.

Some types of surgery are easy to classify as either clinical, cultural, or cosmetic. However, under scrutiny the clear distinction between these types of surgery blurs – and, with it, the idea of the 'normal' body as a neutral construction.

CULTURAL VS COSMETIC SURGERY

It is very tempting to distinguish between cultural and cosmetic surgery. On this distinction, *cultural surgery* is surgery that is performed to fit in with a cultural norm or practice. It is a modification motivated by *identity*. Paradigmatic examples of cultural surgery are female genital mutilation (FGM)[10] and religious male circumcision, both of which are performed in a variety of cultural and religious contexts.[11]

Cosmetic surgery, on the other hand, is surgery that is performed to make a body appear more beautiful, or to make a body appear less ugly. It is a modification motivated by *appearance*. Often, the cosmetic surgery project of making a body appear less ugly is framed as making it *more normal*. This effortless shift between beauty, ugliness and normality is very important, as we'll see. Paradigmatic examples of cosmetic surgery are breast implants, facelifts, rhinoplasty, liposuction and labiaplasty.

The distinction between cultural and cosmetic surgery is not merely conceptual. It also has implications for law and practice. For example, the UK Female Genital Mutilation Act 2003 states: 'It is a criminal offence to excise, infibulate or otherwise mutilate the whole or any part of a girl's labia majora, labia minora or clitoris. But no offence is committed by an approved person who performs a surgical operation on a girl which is necessary for her physical or mental health.' The guidance notes clarify: 'For the purpose of determining whether an operation is necessary for the mental health of a girl it is immaterial whether she or any other person believes that the operation is required as a matter of custom or ritual.'[12] So, the Act explicitly rules out *cultural* surgery on female genitals, whether those of children or adults (the Act refers to 'girls' but also applies to adult women).

However, the Female Genital Mutilation Act 2003 does *not* rule out *cosmetic* surgery on female genitals, including those of children. Some cosmetic genital surgery is performed on intersex girls and boys and recommended by doctors, even though intersex people who underwent such surgery as children often campaign against it.[13] One increasingly popular form of female genital cosmetic surgery is labiaplasty. To perform labiaplasty is precisely to 'excise . . . part of a girl's labia majora [or] labia minora'. Labiaplasty is thus explicitly covered by the definition of procedures that are presumptively illegal under the Female Genital Mutilation Act.[14] It follows that, in order for that presumptive illegality to be lifted, labiaplasty would have to be 'necessary' for the patient's mental health. So far, this necessity has not been tested in court, though legal firm Mills & Reeve describes the issue as a 'ticking time bomb'.[15] But the Act does stipulate that procedures that are necessary for mental health *can* include 'cosmetic surgery resulting from the distress caused by a perception of abnormality'.[16] Cultural surgery is explicitly forbidden; cosmetic surgery is explicitly permitted.

Since the Act requires only the *perception* of abnormality, not an actual abnormality or pathology, there is in practice no restriction on cosmetic surgery on the genitals. Labiaplasty is widely available and advertised, and this fact is recognized by government. The UK National Health Service's website aimed at patients, NHS Choices, states: 'Occasionally, a labiaplasty may be carried out on the NHS if the vaginal lips are obviously abnormal and causing the woman distress or harming her health. However, the NHS doesn't routinely provide this operation.'[17] NHS Choices does not advise that labiaplasty is illegal in other circumstances; instead, it advises women how to go about obtaining labiaplasty in the private sector. The UK government and law enforcement officials do not investigate cosmetic surgeons who provide the procedure, or prosecute those who provide it when it is not 'necessary' for the patient's mental health. In other words, while all forms of cultural FGM are explicitly illegal, all forms of cosmetic FGM are generally assumed to be permissible and treated as such.[18]

So, the distinction between cultural and cosmetic surgery is very important to the legal framework in the UK. However, the distinction is not sustainable. The basic philosophical reason is this: norms of beauty and appearance, including the closely related norms of *normality*, are fundamentally cultural. Cosmetic surgery is thus a form of cultural surgery. It is surgery performed to fit into the norms of a culture.

Cosmetic considerations are fundamentally cultural in two main ways. First, it is a matter of cultural difference what is considered beautiful. Globalization has made beauty standards increasingly homogeneous,[19] but, nonetheless, the content of beauty norms is cultural rather than natural or inevitable.[20] Beauty norms depend on culture for their existence, and their content may vary from culture to culture.

Secondly, it is culture that determines how important beauty is and whether beauty is considered more important than function. The relative weight given to beauty and function varies by context, body part and sex, although the significance given to beauty over function is usually higher for women's bodies. So it is culture that determines how significant beauty and appearance are in general, and which parts of the body are most susceptible for assessment cosmetically.

This fundamentally cultural aspect of beauty can be seen when comparing FGM with cosmetic procedures such as labiaplasty or breast implants. We can start by focusing on breast implants, since these are more common and less controversial than labiaplasty – at least in Western countries such as the UK and the USA.

There are, of course, many differences between FGM and breast implants. Most obviously, they affect different parts of the body. FGM is usually performed on girls who are too young to provide meaningful consent, and in any case their consent is often not sought at all, or it is far from fully informed since they may have no idea what is actually going to happen to them.[21] Breast implants, in

contrast, are usually performed on adult women, and those operations which are performed on children below the age of eighteen
are generally performed at the child's request.[22] FGM is usually
performed in non-clinical conditions, whereas breast implants are
medicalized procedures performed in hospitals and clinics. And
breast implants and FGM appear to track opposing norms, since
breast implants tend to be presented as a way of enhancing a
woman's sex life, whereas FGM is often justified as a means of preserving a woman's purity or chastity.

And yet many of the arguments in favour of an outright ban on
FGM also apply to some forms of cosmetic surgery, such as breast
implants.[23] The legal ban on FGM in the UK outlaws FGM even
when it is performed on consenting adult women in clinical conditions. But if FGM in that context is objectionable (and I agree that it
is), it is objectionable for reasons that apply to other cosmetic procedures such as breast implants and labiaplasty: it involves unnecessary,
risky surgery on women to make their bodies comply with a profoundly sexist set of norms about women's behaviour, sexuality and
value. If FGM should be illegal across the board, then so should types
or instances of cosmetic surgery that share those features.

Courtney Smith is a political scientist who conducted a series of
interviews with American and Senegalese women about breast
implants and FGM. She discussed each practice in the community
where it is rare: breast implantation in Senegal, and FGM (which she
calls female genital cutting, or FGC) in America. In each case Smith
started by describing the practice and answering questions about it,
and then asked her interviewees for their opinions. Smith's interviews
with American women about FGM were unsurprising: most were disturbed by what they felt was a barbaric practice that should be
stopped. What is perhaps more surprising from a Western perspective
is that many of the Senegalese interviewees had the same reaction
when learning about cosmetic breast implants. Smith writes:

> [W]hen I discussed breast implantation with Senegalese women, some
> of whom had experienced FGC, many of them reacted using the same
> rhetoric of barbarism that is traditionally used by some Americans
> (academics and non-academics alike) to describe FGC. Their words

challenged the notion that American women are simply freely choosing individuals with normal bodies, attempting to meet standards of beauty, while Senegalese women remain controlled, agency-less beings. For example, one Halpulaar woman commented upon breast implantation in this way: 'I have never heard of this practice and never in my life do I want to know about it. Women who do it aren't really women. It must be caused by a sickness.' ... Further, Senegalese respondents communicated disbelief—disbelief that people would travel across the globe to fight FGC in foreign lands, while the horrid, unnatural, and ungodly practice of breast implantation exists back home.[24]

For the Senegalese interviewees one of the most problematic aspects of breast implantation is that it is a potential impediment to breast-feeding. Several studies show that breast implants are associated with breastfeeding problems. Women with breast implants are much more likely to produce insufficient milk to feed their babies, and breast implants also have side-effects such as long-term pain and pressure that make breastfeeding significantly more difficult.[25] These problems with breastfeeding do not figure highly in Western discussions of breast implants, whether in the media or between women and their prospective surgeons.[26] But Smith reports that, for the Senegalese people she interviewed:

the central purpose of breasts is the nourishment of offspring; breast-feeding is part of being a woman and fulfilling the role of mother. For instance, one concrete symbol of the role of breast-feeding is the gesture of grabbing one's breast to signify the mother/child relationship. The fact that breast implantation often destroys the capacity to breast-feed is problematic and disturbs this established gender identity. Moreover, Senegalese interviewees were also disturbed that women would choose to destroy this important element of gender.[27]

What these interviews show is that the role that breasts play in signalling womanhood is deeply cultural. To generalize, in Senegal, breasts are fundamental to womanhood because of their function; in the USA, breasts are fundamental to womanhood because of their appearance. For American women who choose cosmetic breast implants, the appearance of their breasts is more important than their ability to lactate; for Senegalese women this judgement is a horrifying indication of warped cultural values. In American culture the function of the clitoris and vulva in providing sexual pleasure, and the need for uncompromised urination, menstruation, intercourse and childbirth, are paramount. Women who undergo cosmetic labiaplasty seek to preserve or enhance these aspects of their vulvas. FGM, which destroys or compromises many of these functions, is thus anathema from an American perspective.

All cosmetic surgery is also cultural surgery.

It does not follow that all cultural surgery is cosmetic. Surgery can be performed for cultural reasons that are not, or not primarily, cosmetic. For example, male circumcision in Judaism is traditionally performed not to produce a penis that is more attractive, but rather to indicate a religious covenant and community membership; in Islam, circumcision is seen as a natural practice required by God, and perhaps also a test of religious obedience.[28] It is therefore an example of cultural surgery but not cosmetic surgery. Similarly, many of the justifications offered for FGM in communities that practise it are not aesthetic but relate to other factors, such as a rite of passage, a protection of purity, or prevention of perceived dangers.[29]

However, notions of what is beautiful or aesthetically appealing are strongly connected to what is culturally normal. That is to say, features that are considered to be abnormal in any particular culture are often also considered to be ugly. Members of cultures which practise FGM may consider intact female genitalia ugly or disgusting.[30] Similarly, many people in the USA consider circumcised penises to be more attractive than uncircumcised ones.[31] In the UK, where circumcision is not routine, there is no generally accepted connection between circumcision and penile attractiveness. In Ancient Greece, the longer the foreskin, the better.[32] So there is a reinforcing feedback loop between bodies that are considered culturally normal or appropriate and those that are considered beautiful or non-ugly. Nonetheless, norms about appearance are only part of the full set of social norms that every culture maintains and operates within. Cosmetic surgery should be regarded as a subset of cultural surgery, not as a distinctive category.

Modifications aimed at appearance and modifications aimed at identity are closely connected. But is there a clear contrast between these forms of modification and those that are aimed at health?

CLINICAL SURGERY

It is commonplace to assume that there is a clear distinction between clinical surgery and both cosmetic and cultural surgery. For example, the NHS is in the business of providing clinical surgery, but it will not generally provide cultural or cosmetic surgery.

Clinical surgery can be defined as surgery that is performed to alleviate or prevent a medical problem or abnormality. NHS Choices states:

Cosmetic surgery is not routinely provided on the NHS.

Occasionally, it may be provided on the NHS for psychological or other health reasons. For example, the NHS might pay for:

- **breast implants** if a woman's breasts are severely underdeveloped or asymmetrical, and it's clear this is causing her significant psychological distress
- **nose reshaping** if the person has breathing problems
- **a tummy tuck** if the person has excess fat or skin after weight loss or pregnancy
- **a breast reduction operation** if the weight of a woman's breasts is causing her back problems

Generally, most people who wish to have cosmetic surgery will need to pay for this privately.

Reconstructive or plastic surgery can also be available on the NHS. This is different from cosmetic surgery; it's surgery to restore a person's normal appearance after illness, accident or a birth defect. It includes procedures such as rebuilding breasts after a mastectomy, or repairing a cleft lip.[33]

So, clinical surgery is performed by the NHS for 'psychological or other *health reasons*' (emphasis added), or to restore *normality* after an accident, illness, or a birth defect. This surgery is performed to alleviate, or possibly prevent, a medical problem.

But even the category of clinical or therapeutic surgery is not clearly defined. Take the case of male circumcision. The category of clinical surgery might seem clearly to include male circumcision in cases where the foreskin is causing medical problems. But this is not, in fact, straightforward. Phimosis is a condition where the foreskin cannot be retracted. Until recently, circumcision was a fairly common treatment for this condition.[34] But the NHS now informs patients that it is normal for a baby's foreskin not to retract for the first few years of life, and that most cases of phimosis will be resolved over time: 'It's rare for circumcision to be recommended for medical reasons in children. This is because other, less invasive and less risky treatments are usually available.'[35] Circumcision for phimosis is described as 'a treatment of last resort'. So, the NHS regards male circumcision as a necessary clinical surgery only in rare cases. It follows that, for the NHS, most male circumcisions are not properly regarded as clinical surgery.

As for routine male circumcision, NHS Choices mentions the existence of what it calls 'circumcision for cultural reasons' but does not discuss the procedure further; since it is not regarded as a clinical procedure the NHS neither provides nor recommends it. NHS Choices also does not consider whether healthy newborn baby boys should be routinely circumcised for health reasons. For the NHS, routine male circumcision is purely cultural and in no way clinical.

The American Academy of Pediatrics (AAP) gives a very different impression. In the USA, circumcision has become so thoroughly medicalized that, according to anthropologist Leonard Glick, even Jewish American parents will typically choose a hospital setting rather than a ritualized circumcision, and 'assume that the procedure is medically beneficial'.[36] The United States government and NGOs have also been at the forefront of a movement to export routine circumcision to other countries, particularly in eastern and southern Africa, establishing it as part of global health policy – a movement that critics describe as 'unethical human experimentation and Western neocolonialism'.[37]

The AAP's website entry on routine male circumcision states, prominently and emphatically: 'the health benefits of newborn male circumcision outweigh the risks.'[38] Here the AAP is not describing cases where there is a problem with the foreskin. It is referring to prophylactic removal of the foreskin in all healthy newborn boys. The AAP does not quite *recommend* universal infant circumcision, since, in their words, 'the benefits are not great enough' to do so. Instead, it concludes 'the final decision should still be left to parents to make in the context of their religious, ethical and cultural beliefs.' This is, on the face of it, a surprising position for a leading medical organization to take. The AAP does not say that parents should make this decision in the light of their assessment of the clinical evidence. Instead, the AAP – representative of the medical profession – recommends that parents make a decision about irreversible surgery on their babies based on culture, religion and ethics.

And the AAP very much assumes that circumcision is on the cards. Their parent-focused site HealthyChildren.org advises parents: 'If you have a boy, you'll need to decide whether to have him circumcised. Unless you are sure you're having a girl, it's a good idea to make a decision about circumcision ahead of time, so you don't have to struggle with it amid the fatigue and excitement following delivery.'[39] The remainder of the discussion on their page titled 'Should the baby be circumcised?' very much assumes circumcision will take place. Parents are told: 'In the United States, most boys are circumcised for religious or social reasons.'[40] A discussion of the medical risks and benefits then follows, but the risks are very much minimized: 'bleeding and swelling are rare', and '[a]lthough the evidence is also clear that infants experience pain, there are several safe and effective ways to reduce the pain.' The webpage does not mention the risks of anaesthesia, or provide the rate of complications and death. Perhaps most remarkably for a medical organization, it does not mention *at all* the function of the foreskin. That is to say, when discussing 'Should the baby be circumcised?', the AAP does not even mention the fact that circumcision has an inescapable negative cost: it entails the irreversible removal of healthy, functional, erogenous tissue.

The loss of the foreskin is mentioned on the AAP website for parents on a different page, titled 'Circumcision'. This page is notable because it considers the pros and cons of routine circumcision, unlike the page 'Should the baby be circumcised?', which does not. Yet even here the discussion is not even-handed and is skewed firmly in favour of circumcision. All the reasons given against routine circumcision by the AAP on this page are described as 'beliefs' or 'fears'. So it lists as the only 'Reasons Parents May Choose Not to Circumcise' the following: 'Fear of the risks', 'Belief that the foreskin is needed', 'Belief it can affect sex', 'Belief that proper hygiene can lower health risks'. On the other hand, the pros of circumcision are presented as facts rather than as beliefs or fears. So, for example, it lists 'A lower risk of getting cancer of the penis' rather than 'Fear of cancer of the penis' or 'Belief in a lower risk of cancer of the penis', and 'A slightly lower risk of urinary tract infections' rather than 'Fear of urinary tract infections' or 'Belief in a lower risk of urinary tract infections' or 'Fear of treating urinary tract infections through hygiene and antibiotics'.[41]

To sum up, although the AAP says 'the data are not sufficient to recommend routine neonatal circumcision of all boys', its advice in general does not mirror this evidence-based conclusion. Its discussion of the medical complications and issues is skewed strongly towards circumcision, in contravention of its own stated recommendation; and it actively recommends that parents make the choice based on cultural and religious reasons rather than medical ones, even though it is a medical organization, not a religious or cultural one.

So, is a parent who chooses non-religious routine circumcision for their baby boy after reading the AAP's materials choosing a cultural or a clinical surgery? Is the baby's body being modified for reasons of health, appearance, or identity? It may be hard to tell, even for the parent.

Regardless of whether a parent believes she is choosing for cultural or clinical reasons, or whether it is cultural or clinical reasons that loom largest in her mind, the fact that there is a choice at all, and the way that the reasons are presented to her and understood by her, is purely cultural. American parents are told by the American Academy of Pediatrics that they must make a decision about circumcision before the birth, even though the AAP also says that there is no clinical evidence-based reason to recommend routine circumcision. The same evidence is available to the NHS, and yet it does not even mention the possibility of clinically justified routine circumcision, let alone frame it as a surgery that parents should consider and decide about. This difference in framing both reflects and maintains the fact that 80 per cent of American boys and 6 per cent of British boys are circumcised.[42] In the USA, routine male circumcision is a culturally normal practice, whereas in the UK it is not, and that fact affects whether or not it is framed as clinical surgery.

But if it is culture that determines whether a surgical procedure is defined as clinical, then the distinction between clinical and cultural surgery is undermined. A modification that aims at health will also and already be a modification that reflects identity, in the sense that it will be a modification that *people like us* think of as beneficial to health.

This may sound like an incredible claim. Surely health is health, whoever and wherever you are? There may be differences in the practices that different cultures have invented or discovered to secure health, but isn't there some objective core? After all, the body lives, or it dies; it flourishes, or it falters; it works, or it cannot.

It is hard to deny that there is some objective core of health. A fully normativist position is implausible. I do not want to deny, at all, that there are real differences between living to old age versus dying young; living with daily pain versus suffering pain only occasionally; living as a neurotypical person versus dealing with problems of communication or concentration. My aim is to emphasize the significance of embodiment, not downplay it. Still, four considerations call into question the idea that health is objective.

First, there are often conflicts between different measures of health, and choices to be made about which to prioritize. Some treatments for chronic pain will also shorten life, and so a choice has to be made: is it better to live longer or to live with less pain? Different people may value these health-based considerations differently and opt for contrasting treatment protocols. Some of these differences will be down to individual preference, but some of them will be down to cultural questions, such as whether there is a prevailing (religious) belief in the afterlife, and whether suffering is regarded as noble or senseless.

Secondly, saying that a practice relies on culture, or that health is a value-judgement, does not mean that the practice or value are wrong. Some cultures prioritize longevity, others do not; from this difference it does not follow that either or both are misguided. Recognizing that our values are in some sense culturally dependent need not imply cultural relativism (the view that ethical judgements are true only in relation to particular cultures): we can see that we hold our values in some part because of who and where we are without thereby thinking that our values lack justification. It is simple fact that many of our most fundamentally held moral values were not shared by people in other times and places. Consider, for example, contemporary convictions about the wrongness of genocide, slavery, corporal punishment and women's subordination. That these values did not prevail in previous societies does nothing to undermine their status.

Thirdly, health problems can exist objectively in our bodies, but be caused by culture. Respiratory illness is a real health problem, but it is exacerbated by social phenomena: air pollution, cigarette smoke, asbestos. Anxiety actually exists, causing serious suffering for many, but the increase in clinical anxiety and depression is affected by societal structures such as overwork, job insecurity, the influence of the internet and the demands of social media.

Finally, even if there can be some objective measure of health, there are significant cultural elements to the practices used to secure health. For example, whether a practice is culturally normal affects whether the clinical reasons for or against it are even considered. In the UK the NHS does not consider whether there is an overall health benefit or health cost to prophylactic removal of the foreskin, because that is not a culturally normal practice. Similarly, in the USA the AAP does not consider on its website whether there are any health benefits to FGM with the aim of helping parents make a decision about it; on the contrary, the idea that we should consider or research any potential health benefits of FGM would strike most Westerners as horrific.[43] So too, prophylactic mastectomy or hysterectomy is not offered to women to reduce or eliminate the risk of breast or uterine cancer, unless they have a confirmed, serious and elevated risk for either disease. The search for clinical justifications for a practice varies according to whether that practice accords with a given culture.[44]

Routine male circumcision challenges the distinction between clinical and cultural surgery because male circumcision is regarded as clinical and cultural in some cultures, but as cultural and not clinical in others, meaning that an assessment of whether a surgery is clinical is already cultural. Other examples challenge the distinction between clinical and cosmetic surgery. One case is surgery to remove what is known as an 'apron' of abdominal fat and skin after significant weight loss. Where people have lost a large amount of weight they can be left with an overhanging fold of belly skin. This apron of skin can be unsightly, uncomfortable and cause problems of irritation and infection underneath. The NHS website, as quoted above, says that surgery to remove that skin 'might' be offered. But most NHS trusts will *not* offer abdominal surgery to alleviate such problems, since they categorize such surgery to be cosmetic rather than clinical.[45] So there is a distinction drawn between the 'cosmetic' tummy tuck, which the NHS will not usually provide, and the 'clinical' gastric bypass, which it will – even though both are required as the result of obesity, understood as a clinical condition.

In contrast, most NHS trusts *will* provide unlimited reconstructive breast surgery after a mastectomy. Reconstructive surgery is cast by the NHS as clinical rather than cosmetic, because the breast cancer diagnosis and mastectomy that precede it are clinical problems. But reconstructive surgery is not *clinically* required after a mastectomy. Viewed from a strictly clinical perspective, where the physical health of the patient is the only consideration, breast implants are actually contra-indicated, since they bring about the risks of surgery, complications and side-effects with no clinical benefit. Patients may *want* breast implants, and they may feel deeply distressed or dissatisfied with their appearance without them (breast implants may benefit mental health), but the same is true of patients seeking the removal of an abdominal apron after significant weight loss, or of many people seeking cosmetic surgery more generally. 'I lost a lot of weight a few years ago and have an abdominal apron,' says Owen.[46]

> There were multiple occasions where my body was seen by someone else and they responded with complete repulsion. When I go through metal detectors at airports, I am always pulled aside and patted down because scanners recognize excess skin as some foreign object. I could never comfortably go to the beach or the pool, as I feared that people would respond with repulsion to my body in the ways I had reason to believe they would. There was a sense in which I felt like less of a man because I was subjected to a gaze that men are typically not subjected to. It was markedly different from the gaze I was accustomed to as a fat man.

Why, then, does the NHS class reconstructive breast surgery as clinical but the removal of an abdominal apron as cosmetic? Cost is a factor, but why is the line drawn in that place? The answer is cultural.

The values or principles that underlie the distinction are unclear, and all are open to criticism. One possibility is that a distinction is made on the basis of presumed responsibility, with patients considered responsible for obesity and thus for having an abdominal apron, but not for having breast cancer and requiring a mastectomy. That distinction does not hold up to scrutiny: we know that obesity is significantly affected by social factors such as the price and availability of food of different types, industrial processing methods and ingredients, food marketing, whether town planning, work requirements and cost facilitate regular exercise, and so on.[47] But fat shaming is ubiquitous, and that cultural fact may explain the different treatment of reconstructive surgery and surgery to remove an abdominal apron.

Another possible factor is the cultural significance given to breasts as a marker of womanhood, where breasts are understood as visible adornments rather than functioning organs. The Senegalese women discussed earlier felt that breasts were essential to womanhood, but primarily as they relate to the ability to breastfeed. In the UK, as in many Western societies, women's breasts are seen as integral to their womanhood insofar as they are sexually attractive. In Western societies, to be a woman is to be sexually attractive, or at least sexually available, or at least open to judgement for being or not being sexually attractive and available. So reconstructive breast surgery after mastectomy becomes 'necessary' because a visible pair of attractive, matching breasts is culturally understood as essential to womanhood. It is less important, according to dominant social norms, whether those breasts are natural or the result of surgery; and, unlike in Senegal, it is practically irrelevant whether those breasts are functional and can lactate. This cannot be the whole picture – as Owen's story shows, an abdominal apron also affects gender identity. But the cultural significance of visible breasts surely plays a role.

A salient distinction in British medicine is that between cosmetic surgery and reconstructive or plastic surgery (both of which the NHS effectively categorizes as clinical surgery). NHS Choices defines reconstructive or plastic surgery as 'surgery to restore a person's normal appearance after illness, accident or a birth defect'. But here the category of 'normal' is deeply normative. If a person has a birth defect, then that 'defective' appearance is in fact that person's normal appearance. Normality is here related not to naturalness, but rather to commonness. And what counts as a common physical feature in any given culture depends on which physical features are left alone and which are surgically modified. So we have a vicious circle: if a bodily feature is viewed as abnormal by the medical profession and its surrounding culture, it will be surgically modified. If that bodily feature is routinely modified, unmodified bodies with that feature are abnormal. If bodies with that feature are abnormal, that justifies modifying them. This circle is another way in which culture determines whether an unusual feature counts as a birth 'defect', rather than just a difference.

Consider, for example, the condition of having an extra finger. The NHS Great Ormond Street Children's Hospital website states, 'Ulnar polydactyly or having an additional little finger on one or both hands is very common, especially in certain ethnic groups.' In many cases the extra finger is fully functioning and, even where it is not, '[t]he extra finger should not cause any problems.' However, the hospital reports that 'most parents ask for the extra finger to be removed, as it can lead to unwanted attention for their child as they grow older', and this operation is provided on the NHS.[48] Here again we see the blurring of the distinction between cosmetic and clinical surgery. An additional functioning finger can be an advantage, enabling greater skill at many activities, and may not even be obvious at first glance.[49] But neither this additional functionality, nor the fact that the condition is in fact common in certain groups, prevents the finger's removal from being provided on the NHS.

Similar considerations are also in play with the case of routine male circumcision in countries where it is practised. The AAP parent-focused webpage on male circumcision includes 'social reasons' among its reasons in favour of routine circumcision. It states, 'Many parents choose to have it done because "all the other men in the family" had it done or because they do not want their sons to feel "different."'[50] However, the AAP does not list any countervailing social considerations when considering reasons *against* circumcision. There is nothing along the lines of 'most boys worldwide are not circumcised', or 'many people find the natural penis beautiful', or 'there is no compelling reason for boys to have a penis resembling that of other men in the family', or 'having your son circumcised increases the social pressures on others to do the same'. Once again, the distinction between the clinical and the cosmetic is blurred, in this case by the fact that a medical association considers cosmetic and social reasons very partially.

SO, IS YOUR BODY NORMAL?

Disease often has a cultural element. Some phenomena that were once thought of as diseases or medical conditions are no longer identified that way, such as hysteria, masturbation and homosexuality. But some phenomena have only recently been recognized as diseases or medical conditions, or undergo shifting definitions. A key example is the diagnosis of conditions relating to gender identity, variously diagnosed at different times as transvestism, transsexualism, gender identity disorder, gender dysphoria, or gender incongruence.[51] Some of these terms are now considered to be offensive to trans people, with some arguing against any form of medicalization of trans identity.

Trans identity is not the only phenomenon whose status as a medical condition remains controversial. There is also deep disagreement as to whether deafness should be regarded as a disability or a cultural identity. From a naturalist perspective, deafness should be understood as a disability or impairment, a condition for which treatment should be provided. On this understanding, the right thing to do for a deaf child is to provide her with a cochlear implant, if doing so will help her to hear. But many people in the Deaf community campaign vigorously against the use of cochlear implants in children. For such campaigners, cochlear implants threaten deaf culture and language. Some even described the use of cochlear implants as an act of genocide.[52]

It is unsurprising that there are cultural differences and controversies surrounding the treatment of phenomena that are only controversially understood as diseases or abnormalities. But there are also cultural considerations in the clinical treatment of phenomena that are generally accepted to be diseases or abnormalities. This is because the concept of normality is itself inherently cultural, and because the treatments offered are cultural in nature. How unusual it is to have an extra finger depends on context, as does whether that condition is regarded as a disabling abnormality, or an advantage, or just within the range of normal. Doctors in the UK and the USA agree that UTIs, penile cancer and phimosis are clinical conditions, but they disagree about whether circumcision is an appropriate treatment for those conditions.

There can be various sorts of disagreement about treatment. Should we treat the person whose mental health is impacted by the physicality of their body with therapy, or by physically altering that body? Should the treatment be preventative or curative? Compare British and American approaches to circumcision, where the former favours leaving the foreskin intact unless absolutely necessary whereas the latter anticipates problems. How important is it to retain or enhance function? Compare cochlear implants, which are provided to enhance hearing, with the removal of extra fingers, which may reduce dexterity. How should we weigh competing functionings? Compare the ability to hear with the ability to use sign language as a first language.

Most profoundly, should treatment seek to change 'abnormal' individuals, or to change the social construction of abnormality?

If your body isn't normal, what should change? Your body, or the norm?

So far I've shown that there are many surgical practices, including mainstream ones, which cannot clearly be classified as only clinical and not at all cultural. If that's right, then we can't make a sharp distinction between modifications for health and modifications for appearance or identity. There's no reason to think that the political principle of the unmodified body must stop at the boundaries of health.

But maybe you're not quite convinced. That the boundaries are blurred does not mean that there aren't clear paradigm cases of health: clear cases where all cultures would regard a bodily condition as abnormal, modification practices that are clearly aimed only at securing health understood in the least controversial terms. In the next chapter I consider this challenge head-on.

6

Disability, Impairment, Identity

I found it impossible to say to others: Speak louder; shout! for I am deaf! Alas! how could I proclaim the deficiency of a sense which ought to have been more perfect with me than with other men, – a sense which I once possessed in the highest perfection, to an extent, indeed, that few of my profession ever enjoyed! Alas, I cannot do this!

Ludwig van Beethoven, letter to his brothers (1802)[1]

[T]o be physically disabled is not to have a defective body, but simply to have a minority body.

Elizabeth Barnes, *The Minority Body* (2016)[2]

The idea that the unmodified body has value seems to reach its limit when we consider disability. The concept of disability, after all, means some sort of hindrance or lack: the word is the negation of 'ability'. So it may seem odd to celebrate, or even be content with, a disabled body. Beethoven himself was profoundly affected by his deafness and tried to hide it for as long as he could. 'I beg of you to keep the matter of my deafness a profound secret to be confided to nobody, no matter whom,' he wrote to a friend. 'Oh how happy I would be if my hearing were completely restored!'[3]

Medical science is constantly developing new treatments for disabilities, aiming sometimes to eradicate them. Such treatments modify the disabled body. Surely, we might think, this is a good thing? Wouldn't it be perverse to think there is anything wrong with modifications that expand functions, remove restrictions, reduce suffering, enhance ability? Indeed, shouldn't we regard such treatments as entitlements, something that a just society has a duty to provide?

The political principle of the unmodified body is a resistance to pressures to modify and an insistence that *the unmodified body has value*. But that principle is challenged when the unmodified body is burdened by disability, ill health, or neglect. We raise money to support research into treatments to alleviate disability and provide modifying treatments through our health systems. We aim to treat or cure disease, letting nature take its course only when the prospect of health is gone. True, some religions forbid the use of specific medical treatments, such as the doctrinal prohibition against a Jehovah's Witness receiving a blood transfusion. And some people are sceptical about the safety or efficacy of even well-proven medicine, like vaccines. But there is no mainstream perspective from which *all* medical treatment should be refused, to leave the body utterly unmodified. And it may make little sense to speak of resisting pressures to modify when more effective modifications are urgently being sought.

In the last chapter I argued that even health has a cultural dimension. I showed that there are surgical, medical practices, such as male circumcision and cosmetic surgery on children, that blur the distinctions between health, identity and appearance. But I conceded that some aspects of health seem pretty objective. No one would deny that heart attacks, cancer and infectious disease are matters of health; no one would argue against trying to treat these conditions.

This is not to say that any treatment should be preferred, or that refusing treatment is never rational. Clinical treatment always brings risk, and the side-effects can be significant. Many people, reasonably and rationally, choose not to undergo treatments like chemotherapy, heart surgery, or resuscitation. Treatment is sensibly subject to cost–benefit analysis, and people reach varying conclusions about what's right for them. Still, there's no serious view that treating these diseases is wrong because it violates the value of the unmodified body; and there's no denying that treatment for these conditions is properly considered a matter of health.

So aren't these paradigm cases of modifications that are justified precisely because they are clearly health-based? If so, does that mean that the political principle of the unmodified body – the insistence that *your body is good enough just as it is* – doesn't apply to bodies burdened by ill-health or impairment?

My argument is not that modification is always wrong, or even that it is presumptively suspect. The unmodified body is neither a goal to be attained nor a purity to be preserved. I no more want to attach shame to a modified body than I want to defend its attachment to non-modification. In general, it seems better for a person to have more abilities rather than fewer, less suffering rather than more. Some bodies are easier to live with than others, and body modification may significantly enhance a person's quality of life. There's nothing inherently wrong about seeking such modifications.

At the same time, there is a long and continuing history of treating people with disabilities poorly, even as less than human. This ill-treatment includes religious accounts that viewed disability as punishment for sin, torturous mental asylums, abandonment to the street or imprisonment in the workhouse, neglect and isolation in residential homes, and the atrocities of eugenics. Even without such extreme injustice, disabled people's needs, status and contribution to society are rarely adequately acknowledged. The built environment is inhospitable to those with impaired mobility or vision, social communication is founded on the assumption of full hearing, employment is often denied to disabled people, the benefits system is inadequate.

Against this continuing context of discrimination, the political principle of the unmodified body states that there is value in the unmodified body, no matter what it looks like or what it can do, and that respecting this value is part of what it means to treat people equally. And the principle states that the current political situation is one in which pressures to modify have become overwhelming, in a way that threatens both public health and political equality. I do not argue that disabled bodies should never be modified. Instead, I argue that we must take collective action against the *pressures* to modify, and against a social and medical context that *assumes* that all disability is bad. In other words, the political principle of the unmodified body also applies to bodies that are affected by ill-health, impairment and disability.

DILEMMAS OF DEAFNESS

*I in no way see deafness as a disability, but rather as a way into
a very rich culture. Which is one of the reasons I was delighted
to learn when I gave birth that my baby was deaf.*
Sharron Ridgeway, herself deaf (2002)[4]

Sign language is not a simple word-for-word translation of spoken
language. 'What are you looking at?!' is a phrase used in British English to indicate anger at being stared at. It is a demand to be given the
respect of averted eyes. If you wanted to sign 'What are you looking
at?' in British Sign Language (BSL) you would *not* make a sign for
'what', another sign for 'are', a third for 'you', a fourth for 'looking',
and a final sign for 'at'. Instead, you would point at the person you
were signing at, wagging your pointing finger and ending with an
accusatory stabbing motion; you would then pivot your hand around,
point your first two fingers at your own eyes and draw them down

Interpreter for American Sign Language at the Independence Day
celebrations in Washington, D.C.

your body, ending at your feet. Throughout, you would add a facial expression to indicate indignation.[5] The result is a highly expressive dance; a use of the whole body that *enacts* rather than verbalizes the sentiment.

Sign languages have their own grammatical structure, too. 'ASL [American Sign Language] grammar is a locus of both precision and pride,' reports Andrew Solomon. 'The grammar is so conceptually different from oral grammar that it eludes even many people who study it closely. Fluent translators can find it difficult to rearrange ASL structures into English ones, and vice versa, and lose the patterns of meaning.'[6] Moreover, there is not one sign language but many, all with their own structure and vocabulary; even British and American Sign Language are so different that users cannot understand each other.

The profound differences between sign language and spoken language mean that it makes a great difference whether one grows up first with speech or first with Sign: whether one has a native tongue or a native hand. Languages can be learned at any age, but most of us will always be most proficient at a language we learned from infancy. 'Many linguists believe there is a "critical period" (lasting roughly from birth until puberty) during which a child can easily acquire any language that he or she is regularly exposed to,' says the Linguistic Society of America. 'Under this view, the structure of the brain changes at puberty, and after that it becomes harder to learn a new language.'[7]

With spoken vs sign language, the difference is even more stark. The two sorts of language are so different in their approaches that communication always feels easier in one rather than the other. Expressing yourself primarily through your hands and body, using gesture, expression and physical movement, is very different from expressing yourself primarily through your mouth and ears, using words, intonation and volume. It is of course possible for people to learn both spoken and sign language – many deaf and hearing people have some proficiency in both – but for most deaf people who learn it, Sign is a far easier form of communication than speech.

Unfortunately, deaf people are not always taught Sign; sometimes, they are even forbidden from using it in an attempt to ensure assimilation into mainstream hearing society.

'I couldn't learn to sign to save my goddamn life,' said Nancy, a hearing mother of a deaf child. 'But then we visited the public school oral programme, and we met kids who were not allowed to sign, and it was horrific. It was very clear to both of us that it was definitely child abuse to try to make a deaf kid oral.'[8]

Another family, hearing parents of two deaf children, followed an oral-only upbringing in the 1960s. Oral-only meant that Sign was forbidden. '"We would break Miriam's arms if she signed,"'[9] reported the father – metaphorically speaking, one hopes and presumes. His daughter Miriam became a competitive figure skater, which meant she had to perform to music she could not hear. When skating she needed some indication of the music's tempo, and she needed to know when to start skating, and so her parents permitted a very minor relaxation of the no-Sign rules. 'The coach was allowed to give her three signs: one to say when the music started; one at the halfway point to tell her to speed up or slow down; and one at the end to tell her the music was finished.'[10]

Miriam did eventually learn to sign in her late teens, when she started competing in sporting events for deaf athletes. Now that she was spending time around other deaf people her parents could no longer insulate her from Sign. Miriam found it humiliating and constraining to be the only deaf person in her circle who could not sign, giving her an overwhelming incentive to learn. Nevertheless, learning Sign was a struggle: she was already past the critical period for language acquisition, and her parents still disapproved. But it was worth it. To her parents' dismay Miriam ultimately chose to use Sign 80 per cent of the time, even though speech was her first language. '"But *all* my language would be better if I'd been allowed to sign as a child," she said.'[11]

It is easy to see the cruelty in these restrictions. If you are hearing, imagine how frustrating and soul-destroying it would be to be forbidden from speaking or communicating through sound, forced instead to communicate only through gesture. Such a restriction would seem cruel and nonsensical. It would also seem like an act of oppression: an act to suppress a form of cultural expression, or to destroy your identity as a hearing person. This is how the suppression of sign language feels to many deaf people. It's not only a limitation on their ability to communicate; it's an act of cultural aggression against Deaf people understood as a cultural and identity group.[12]

Deaf parents of deaf children are most likely to bring them up with Sign as their primary language, since Sign is most likely to be the language of a deaf household. In these cases, the communication needs of parents and children align. Hearing children of deaf parents generally become bilingual, learning Sign from their parents and oral language from their interactions outside the home: at school, with friends and wider family, and in the public sphere.[13] In this respect hearing children of deaf parents are much like conventionally bilingual children: both may speak a minority language with their parents at home but operate easily in the majority language elsewhere.

Hearing parents of deaf children face a more difficult choice. If they bring their children up primarily with spoken language those children may be able to operate in the mainstream hearing world. However, such children will likely find it more difficult to communicate with speech than they would with Sign. They will be constantly struggling to operate in a language that does not suit their bodies, and in a world that does not take them into account. Without Sign they will not be able to operate easily in Deaf contexts, as Miriam found, and even with excellent lip-reading skills they will be at a disadvantage compared to their hearing peers.

The effort of learning to decode and reproduce speech without being able to hear it is enormous: deaf children who are being educated orally generally fall well behind their hearing peers, because so much of their effort is spent on communication. 'It appears that it is extremely difficult to learn a spoken language like English to native proficiency through any other channel, except by simply hearing it,' report linguists Jenny Singleton and Matthew Tittle.[14] One hearing father describes how his deaf son, brought up with spoken language, was under-achieving at school. '"I didn't realise until later how much he was missing all the time," Bob said. "I knew how smart he was and he was not making it in algebra. I said, 'Let me sit in the class.' The teacher was writing formulas on the board and speaking with his back to the room."'[15]

So, bringing a deaf child up to use only or mainly oral language has serious disadvantages. But if a deaf child of hearing parents is brought up with Sign, the language that best suits her body and will best enable her to operate within the Deaf community, there may well come a time when communication between child and parents is limited, because her language ability will exceed theirs. 'While it may be difficult for deaf people to learn speech, it is also difficult for parents to learn Sign,' Solomon notes, 'not because they are lazy or smug, but because their own brains are organised around verbal expression, and by the time they are of parenting age, they have lost considerable neural plasticity.'[16]

The dilemma facing hearing parents of deaf children is how to educate their child. Should they choose Sign: a language that will make it easiest for the child to communicate, one that affirms their body, that nurtures their Deaf identity, and that gives them the best chance of a successful education, but that drastically restricts the size of their linguistic community? Or should they choose oral language: the language of the mainstream, in which the parents are the most proficient and that broadens their communicative circle, but that makes communication a constant effort for the child, that may hamper their educational development and separate them from their Deaf peers and culture?

The obvious answer may seem to be a drastic body modification.

Cochlear implants are devices permanently implanted in the skull, which translate sounds into electrical impulses that directly stimulate the auditory nerve without going through the inner ear. They are not a cure for deafness. 'The cochlear implant does not allow you to hear, but rather allows you to do something that resembles hearing,' explains Solomon. 'It gives you a process that is (sometimes) rich in information and (usually) devoid of music. Implanted early, it can provide a basis for the development of oral language. It makes the hearing world easier.'[17] Cochlear implants are life-changing, but they are not necessarily a straightforward improvement. They have risks and possible side-effects, including tinnitus, a damaged sense of taste and interference with balance.[18] They are highly visible, and mean living with a wire and microphone attached to your head. And the hearing that is achieved from them varies in its usefulness.

Cochlear implants can be very useful for people who face hearing loss at any age. If you have spent your life as a hearing person and

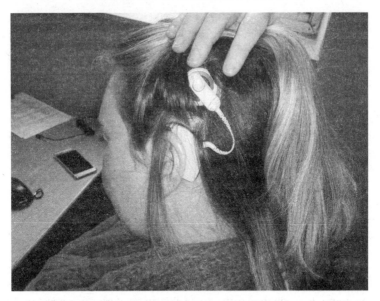

A cochlear implant

then suffer a degradation of hearing, you are used to operating through speech and sound and will probably welcome the restoration of that mode of communication. For people who are deaf from infancy, the considerations are different. Implants are then most successful when used on very young children, to take advantage of their neural plasticity and early language-learning ability. It is easier to interpret the sound given by a cochlear implant if it is the only sound you are used to, and it is easier to interpret sound at all if you have done so from infancy. 'People who have always been deaf and who receive the implants as adults often find them ineffective or just irritating,' reports Solomon, because 'a brain that has gone through development without sound is not organised to process it.'[19] Studies suggest that 50 per cent of deaf children who receive implants aged two will develop a spoken-language ability equivalent to hearing children, whereas if the implant is delayed until age four, only 16 per cent of children reach equivalent proficiency.[20]

Moreover, children who have cochlear implants cannot rely on oral communication. Implants do not provide the same quality and nuance of sound as hearing ears do, 'and therefore children with the implant receive fewer fine distinctions of spoken language than their hearing peers. This means that some implanted children, not exposed to Sign because they are expected to develop speech, may fall into that frightening category of the needlessly impaired who have meagre primary language.'[21] Best practice is for children with implants to be brought up with both spoken language and Sign, until it becomes clear which language is easiest for the child. But it is hard to bring up a child bilingually, especially when one of the languages is not your own, and so hearing parents often rely on the implant and don't use Sign.

Cochlear implants are a decision that parents must make for their children. And they are not a body modification that merely improves health or functioning. They do not make a deaf person into a hearing person, because they do not create full hearing. But they also do not leave the deaf person intact, just adding an extra ability, because they destroy all residual hearing. Many deaf people make considerable use of their residual hearing for communication or sound-detection: how useful that residual hearing will turn out to be cannot be determined in infancy.[22]

If a child receives a cochlear implant, then she will probably be educated with spoken language rather than Sign, and to choose a language for a child is to make a decision about her communicative peers, her lifelong culture and her identity. The language we learn shapes us as people: it shapes our concepts, our communication, our sense of self. And since language is a cultural mechanism, something that operates between people in a linguistic community, the languages we use determine to a great extent our cultural identity.[23] It follows that the language we teach our children, whether it be English, Spanish, Mandarin, Urdu, ASL, or BSL, will strongly shape their identity. This is the case for any child and any language: a child brought up to speak English will have a different communicative community and culture than a child brought up with French or Russian or Danish; but usually the choice of language is simple, because the language of the parents is also the language of the wider community, or else community immersion will teach the mainstream language. With spoken language for hearing children there are no special considerations about the child's individual communicative abilities and how they relate to her peers.

Different considerations apply for deaf children in a world where deaf people are in a minority, spread across linguistic communities. As Singleton and Tittle put it, 'ASL functions as the primary language for many Deaf adults in America today, serving as the symbol of identity for membership in the Deaf culture and the store of cultural knowledge (values, customs, and information).'[24] And so modifying children's bodies by giving them a cochlear implant, something that affects which language they can and will use, is to a significant extent an act of body modification for the sake of identity. It is not a simple health measure, or a mere extension of functioning.

The complex issues at stake are illustrated in the story of Ethan, a deaf child of hearing parents. 'We were accepted on to the implant programme when Ethan was about six months old, and magnetic resonance imaging showed thin auditory nerves,' Ethan's mother recounts.[25] 'Two radiologists recommended that we didn't proceed, but our wonderful consultant sought a third opinion, and, aged 15 months, Ethan had a unilateral implant.' The fact that they sought a third opinion, rather than taking the advice of the first two specialists, suggests that Ethan's parents were strongly motivated to pursue the implant route, and that this motivation was primarily cultural and identity-based rather than medical. 'We were firmly of the mind that he would be living in a hearing world and Ethan should be given any available opportunity to access sound,' his mother explains.

Although Ethan was originally brought up with sign language, once he received the implant his parents and doctors expected him to assimilate into the hearing world. It was not entirely successful. 'We were encouraged to stop signing and we attended Auditory Verbal Therapy sessions,' his mother remembers. Ethan initially attended a school that took an oral approach:

> He had a wonderful year there, the school worked hard with him and were very knowledgeable. In a very thorough annual review, along with the school we decided Ethan would be better off with sign support. We moved him to the 'half-way house' school and began BSL

classes and signing at home again. However, although they professed to use both BSL and English in every class, it was . . . overall not a high level of sign. We also found that Ethan was not pushed, and very little was expected of him. His education eventually stalled and his behaviour deteriorated. We removed him, having to home-school him briefly, and then enrolled him at the final school with strong BSL. It was life-changing. His academics and language improved dramatically and he responded really well to a very structured approach with high expectations.[26]

Ethan's mother says that she remains happy with the decision to give Ethan a cochlear implant. But it is clear that supporting Ethan's Deaf identity, and protecting his ability to use Sign, was essential to his flourishing.

There are two conclusions to draw from these stories. The first is that modifying a deaf person's body so that he can hear changes his identity. Giving a child a cochlear implant and educating him orally, as opposed to leaving his body unmodified and educating him in Sign, affects who he will grow up to be, because it affects everything that shapes his identity: his language, his peers, his culture, the way he reflects on the world and on himself. This is not to say that cochlear implants are bad, or that there is anything disreputable in parents making choices that affect their children's identities. All parents make such choices, by choosing or imparting their values, their habits, their religion, their hobbies, their emotions. But modifying a body to improve its functioning is often – very often, in the case of static impairment – to modify it for its identity as well.

The second conclusion to be drawn from the case of cochlear implants is that there is no simple answer to the question of whether a modification is valuable. It is not easy to tell whether a body with a cochlear implant is more beneficial, even to the person themselves, than the unmodified body it replaced. Treatment is not always improvement.

MODELS OF DISABILITY

The aim of research should not be to make the legless normal,
whatever that might mean, but to create a social environment
where to be legless is irrelevant.

Michael Oliver, 'Medicine and Disability' (1978)[27]

There are two dominant models of disability: the medical model and the social model. The medical model is the mainstream understanding of disability by people who are not themselves disabled. It understands disability as a feature of bodies. What it is to be disabled, on this account, is to have a certain kind of body – more pejoratively, to have something wrong with your body.

The medical model makes a commitment to the unmodified body look like a fetish. It encourages us to see our bodies as limitations, with modification the liberation. It suggests that the most effective way of helping disabled people is to search for a cure – a search that helps them by eliminating them physically and socially.

But from the perspective of disability theory and activism, the search for a cure is problematic. At a practical level, a focus on cure can distract attention and resources away from those who are living with impairments that cannot currently be cured. It probably does disabled people more good if that money is spent on helping them to live with their impairments, particularly if the search for a cure is unlikely to be successful any time soon.

Objections to the medical model go beyond the practical. Many disability rights advocates argue that a focus on cure, on modifying the disabled body, is incompatible with granting disabled people the respect and dignity they are owed. That is to say, they endorse the founding value of this book, that *the unmodified body has value just as it is,* and critique the search for a cure as incompatible with that value.

The medical model has been rejected by disabled people and disability rights advocates for the past half century for its demeaning and impoverished understanding of disability. 'A cure may exist now or in the future for some disabilities, and may be important in the lives of some disabled people,' writes disability activist Eli Clare. 'But by and large we are not waiting to be cured. To frame disability in terms of a cure is to accept the medical model of disability, to think of disabled people as sick, diseased, ill people.'[28]

Instead, in its place is put the social model, first developed by Michael Oliver in the 1970s. The heart of the social model is the claim that disability is the result of social structures, not bodies. To quote Clare again, 'The disability rights movement, like other social change movements, names systems of oppression as the problem, not individual bodies. In short it is ableism that needs the cure, not our bodies.'[29]

The social model distinguishes between impairment, which is about what bodies can do, and disability, which is about what society does. The inability to hear is an impairment, but the disadvantages and barriers of deafness are a disability. Disability becomes the product of society because our societies – the built environment, social norms, infrastructure, methods of communication – are centred around the bodies of the majority. The concept of the majority here indicates both numerical and structural dominance. Because the majority can hear, communication is focused on sound, whether spoken language, automated announcements, or warning sirens. Those who cannot hear are therefore disabled. If communication were always visible as well as audible, deafness would not be disabling. Because the majority can walk unaided it is common for buildings, streets and public transport to have multiple steps. Those who cannot easily navigate steps are thereby rendered disabled. If steps were replaced by ramps or elevators fewer people would experience disability.

Moreover, the social model points out that this socially created disability is not even dependent on impairment. Some people who can't navigate steps are hindered by an impairment (something that would be understood as a disability on the medical model). But there are many people who find steps difficult even though they are not impaired. Babies cannot navigate steps, which means that steps also become difficult for anyone who is pushing a baby in a stroller or pram, but this disability does not mean that babies or their carers are impaired. Their disability is caused by society, not their bodies. Most people pushing babies are women who, as a subordinated group, are less influential in architecture, town planning and transport engineering.[30] Steps can also become difficult for people who are pregnant, or elderly and infirm – again, groups dominated by women. Steps suit some people and not others, and their existence causes some people to experience disability regardless of impairment.

The same can be said of many other impairments. If everyone were blind then being blind would not be a disability, because society would not be structured around the assumption of sight. Braille would be the only written language, voice recognition software would be faultless, cities and transportation would be designed in ways that could be safely negotiated without sight. Similar stories can be told about neurological or educational impairments and differences: if these were more common (not a numerical minority) or more accepted (not a dominated minority) then our social norms, educational institutions and workplaces would be vastly more hospitable to behaviour that is currently coded as challenging, anti-social, or defective. It's not that these physiological conditions would not exist – they would, of course. But they would not be represented as disabilities.

A humorous illustration of the social definition of disability is found in *The Carnivorous Carnival*, a children's book in Lemony Snicket's A Series of Unfortunate Events. The carnival has an old-fashioned freak show, which includes Hugo the hunchback, Colette the contortionist and Kevin the ambidextrous person. The story demonstrates the social contingency of who is labelled a 'freak' with Kevin's absurd lamentations: '"You're whispering about me, aren't you?" Kevin called out from the other end of the caravan. "I bet you're saying, 'What a freak Kevin is. Sometimes he shaves with his left hand, and sometimes he shaves with his right hand, but it doesn't matter because they're *exactly the same!*' "'[31]

Disability theorist Tom Shakespeare points out that there is an analogy between the impairment/disability distinction and the sex/culture distinction. Both separate a social identity into its constituent parts, one physical and one cultural, and emphasize the significance of the cultural part. In his words, 'sex corresponds to impairment, and gender corresponds to disability. The disability movement was following a well-established path of de-naturalising forms of social oppression, demonstrating that what was thought to be natural was actually a product of specific social relations and ways of thinking.'[32]

Disability and gender intersect with each other, too. Models of masculinity and femininity are premised on bodies that are not disabled. As Clare writes:

> The mannerisms that help define gender – the ways in which people walk, swing their hips, gesture with their hands, move their mouths and eyes as they talk, take up space with their bodies – are all based upon how non-disabled people move. A woman who walks with crutches does not walk like a 'woman'; a man who uses a wheelchair and a ventilator does not move like a 'man'. The construction of gender depends not only upon the male body and female body, but also upon the nondisabled body.[33]

Thus gender and disability work together and against each other. Each sort people into social categories that purport to be a simple reflection of the body. But the reflection is distorted: each is refracted through the other, and the final image is heavily filtered.[34]

The social model encourages us to see disability as a feature of societies, not of bodies; it therefore reveals that liberation and equality require changes to society rather than to bodies. This is a good result for disabled people, identifying a strategy for liberation that is not dependent on clinical science. It's also symbolically empowering.[35] Just as women are empowered by the realization that their gendered oppression is not straightforwardly caused by their embodied sex but is the result of that sex's mediation through gender, so disabled people are empowered by the realization that their physical capacities are not the cause of their social incapacitation.

Shame works on disabled people just as it works on women and girls. The bodies of disabled people are heaped in shame by mainstream society, whether through the institutions of the freak show, the asylum and the nursing home, the slurs, jokes and insults, the objectification of medicine, or through their exclusion from education, employment and wealth. The antidote to shame is pride, and the principle of the unmodified body is a generalized form of the movement for disability pride. 'Pride works in direct opposition to internalized oppression,' Clare writes in his book, which is called *Exile and Pride*.

> To transform self-hatred into pride is a fundamental act of resistance . . .
> I need to stare down the self who wants to be 'normal', the kid who

thought she could and should pass as nondisabled, the crip still embarrassed by the way her body moves. I can feel slivers of shame, silence,
and isolation still embedded deep in my body.[36]

The point is not that individuals must overcome their personal
shame by taking on a private attitude of pride. That strategy is too
individualized, too removed from the realities of structural oppression. The point is the recognition that shame is socially created. It is
the result of being consistently situated as an unequal. And so pride as
an act of resistance can be attempted at the individual level, but it
must be accompanied with social change. These two movements, the
personal and the political, enable each other in a conscious movement
of resistance.

BUT WHAT ABOUT THE BODY?

The social model of disability has vital lessons for the principle of the
unmodified body. At the same time, it risks going too far. The body –
every body – is a social phenomenon, but it is not only social. It is also
a material reality, its own constraint, a sensory, fleshy, feeling physicality. Throughout this book, I urge the reclamation of the body from
both pressures to modify and attempts to deny its significance. The
social model of disability succeeds admirably at resisting pressures to
modify. It is a vital tool for understanding and countering disabled
people's oppression. However, it struggles to capture the significance
of the body and, with it, the full range of disabled experience.

The social model imagines a world in which impairment does not
cause disability. But such a world may be hopelessly utopian, because
some impairments would be disabling in any realistically possible
world. Certain kinds of mental and physical impairments are so significant that anyone who lives with them is severely limited in their
ability to work or live independently: large areas of human functioning and flourishing are simply closed to them.[37]

Clare captures both the utility and the limitations of the social
model reflecting on his own life with cerebral palsy (CP). 'To neatly
divide disability from impairment doesn't feel right,' he writes. 'My

experience of living with CP has been so shaped by ableism – or to use Oliver's language, my experience of impairment has been so shaped by disability – that I have trouble separating the two ... Both center on my body.'[38] Clare describes how both social constraints and bodily limitations create physical experiences that in turn provoke emotions such as frustration, embarrassment and anger.

> On good days, I can separate the anger I turn inward at my body from the anger that needs to be turned outward, directed at the daily ableist shit, but there is nothing simple or neat about kindling the latter while transforming the former. I decided that Oliver's model of disability makes theoretical and political sense but misses important emotional realities.[39]

Shakespeare, who shares Clare's concerns, proposes what he calls a critical realist model as a solution. This model recognizes that both bodies and societies contribute to disability. In order to count as disabled you must have an impairment *and* you must suffer social constraints as the result of that impairment. Both are necessary. The critical realist model allows us to distinguish disability from other kinds of social oppression that reference bodies, like gender and race. In a sexist society a woman suffers social constraints because of her embodiment, but that does not mean that being a woman is a disability, because femaleness is not an impairment. And the critical realist model allows us to distinguish disability from other kinds of bodily limitations that don't give rise to social constraints. No human beings are able to fly – in that sense we are all impaired – but the inability to fly is not a disability because it prompts no socially imposed constraints.

The fact that disability is a matter of both physical and social constraints means that there are two ways of potentially enhancing a disabled person's life: changing society or changing their body. The social model of disability places the emphasis solely on changes to society. It demands that social structures, norms and the built environment change, allowing *disabled people* to become *people with impairments*. Impairment then becomes just the human condition. We all have limitations to our physical capabilities. Impairment is normal. What isn't normal, or what shouldn't be accepted as normality, is that impairment creates disability.

But this optimistic view of the potential of social change to eliminate disability simply cannot work for all impairments. As Shakespeare puts it, 'the social model works from the perspective of someone with a stable physical impairment', but it is less apt for 'people with mental health issues, people with learning difficulties, or even people whose physical impairments involved more intrinsic suffering'.[40] There are some bodies, some ways of existing in the world, that can hardly fail to impose serious limitations on how one can live.

In part the significance of the body is a matter of the form and degree of impairment, in part it is a matter of how the impairment comes about. As we saw in the case of deafness, cochlear implants are more clearly beneficial for people who lose their hearing later in life, because they are already neurologically and psychologically accustomed to navigating the world by sound. For them, the preferred solution to their acquired disability will often be a change to their bodies. In contrast, people who are born deaf start out with a different relationship to the hearing world, meaning that for them social measures such as the easy use of Sign may be more effective.

Different forms of impairment suggest different strategies for improving the lives of disabled people.[41] Static conditions of impairment present from birth, such as deafness, blindness, or restricted growth, are often inherited, creating kinship and community networks of people with the same impairment. Some static conditions of impairment cause suffering or pain, experiences which everyone wants to avoid. But for people with static impairment, Shakespeare writes, 'impairment becomes a part of personal identity, to the point that the person cannot conceive of themselves without their impairment.'[42] To treat such conditions medically is to try to create a state of bodily functioning that the person has never previously had: one that is normal in social terms but abnormal for them. The principle of the unmodified body is a highly apt principle of resistance for people in this category.

Other people suffer a deterioration in their usual state of health, or acquire a new impairment as the result of disease or injury. Medical treatment in these cases aims to restore their previous state of health: to return them to their normal. People's attitudes to such impairment vary, in part according to whether they interpret the impairment as a natural part of ageing, for which a cure is unlikely, or as a shocking disruption of normal life. Both groups have previously experienced their bodies as normal and been socially read as having normal bodies before the onset of impairment. According to Shakespeare, people who acquire age-related impairments such as arthritis, rheumatism and Parkinsonism 'are less likely to identify as disabled or as part of the disability community, retaining their lifelong sense of themselves as normal'. People who acquire a static impairment such as a spinal cord injury vary in their identity. Some of them come to identify with their new embodied state, while others continue to find it 'unfamiliar and devastating',[43] and desperately search for a cure. For people in this group, body modification in the form of medical treatment, plastic surgery and rehabilitation may be an absolute necessity. However, at some point the quest to return to a previous normality must give way to acceptance of a new normal, and at that point the principle of the unmodified body again comes to the fore.

Finally, some people have acute degenerative conditions: conditions that predictably worsen over a lifetime, such as multiple sclerosis and muscular dystrophy. People with these conditions are aware of what they are losing: they are aware of an ongoing deterioration in their health and functioning. For them, Shakespeare notes, 'Impairment may not be seen as part of personal identity: it may be seen as an external threat or as an illness for which cure is hoped for.'[44] That the body is in constant flux is very obvious to people in this category, and its changes may be particularly distressing. The principle of the unmodified body seems less apt for this group: what they want is not necessarily an acceptance of their deteriorating bodies but, rather, resistance to that decline, by whatever means. Social measures play their role – an essential role – but ultimately it is the body that betrays.

And so there is no simple answer about the value or status of the unmodified body and its relationship to normality. Whether a body is normal depends on whether the comparison is to other bodies or to one's own experience. Normality is not just a matter of what a body can do now but also about what it has ever been able to do. Similarly, modifying a body to remove impairment may be a matter of restoring normality or a matter of creating a new normal – a state that feels profoundly abnormal from within.

DISABILITY AS NEUTRAL

We've seen how the search for a cure can be harmful to disabled people, whether by diverting resources into medical research and away from helping them now, or by portraying disabled people as pitiable, failing, expendable. But we've also seen how some disabled people long for a cure. And so we might ask: if a cure were discovered from nowhere, without its creation having had negative effects, wouldn't that be wondrous? Is the principle of the unmodified body anything more than a consolation prize?

It's common, at least for people who aren't disabled, to assume that a modification that removes or lessens an impairment is a straight-forward improvement: an increase in welfare or flourishing, an enhancement of ability. But this isn't always true. 'The non-disabled appear to be bad at predicting the impact of disability on the disabled, and tend to systematically overestimate the bad effects of disability on perceived well-being and happiness,' writes philosopher Elizabeth Barnes.[45] On her view, disability (and also impairment: she does not distinguish the two) is 'neutral with respect to well-being'.[46] For some people, being disabled makes their lives go worse; for others, it makes their lives go better; for many, disability makes life better in some respects and worse in others.

To make the case for the neutrality of disability, Barnes draws an analogy between disability and sex. Being female may make your life go worse in various significant ways: it makes you vastly more suscep-tible to domestic and sexual violence, puts you at the disadvantaged end of the gender pay gap, and brings physical risks and burdens asso-ciated with menstruation, childbirth and menopause. But femaleness also brings with it special abilities, unique experiences and opportun-ities for flourishing: pregnancy, childbirth and breastfeeding can be profoundly joyful; femininity or womanhood can be a source of soli-darity, creativity and identity. For some women the burdens of being female will far outweigh the benefits: whether because of preference, social context, abuse, or misfortune they would have been better off if they had been male. For other women, the reverse is true. For most women, it is incredibly difficult to tell, because womanhood is not an attribute they can imagine themselves with or without; it is part and parcel of what it means for them to exist at all.

The same is true, Barnes argues, of disability. Disability should never be thought of as a simple lack, because the experience of disability opens one up to experiences that are not available to people without that disability. This point is easy to see in the case of deafness. Deafness is not merely the inability to hear; it is also the ability to communicate through body rather than sound, membership in a rich cultural community, an experience of the world that is profoundly unavailable to someone who has hearing. But the same is true, according to Barnes and other disability pride activists, of other disabilities. She argues:

> Disability can make it harder to feel certain kinds of self-consciousness or engage in certain types of prejudice, disability can offer a sense of liberation from cultural norms about how your body should look or behave, disability can help you develop an appreciation for a different pace of life or give you a new or different aesthetic appreciation for the varieties of human body.

Disability can be, Barnes continues, 'an "epistemic resource" and a "narrative resource": it can expand the scope of what we can know and what we can experience, in ways that disabled people often find very valuable.'[47]

What Barnes wants to show is that there is no necessary or universal answer to the question of whether disability makes one better or worse off, and thus no universal or easy answer to the question of whether it is a benefit or a burden to modify a disabled body. The principle of the unmodified body, we might say, can be first prize in its own right.

Barnes's argument is important, but does it prove too much? After all, we might object, any adversity can reveal reserves of human adaptation and resourcefulness. That people can find the good in adversity does not mean that it was not adversity in the first place, nor does it mean that we shouldn't try to prevent or alleviate it. To argue by analogy: conceivably Nelson Mandela would not have become the first democratically elected president of South Africa had he not endured decades of political imprisonment for campaigning against apartheid, and, conceivably, the achievement of becoming president added greatly to his life and well-being. But that does not make his imprisonment any less unjust, and it does not mean that it would have been bad to release him earlier.

Or perhaps Barnes's argument proves too little. Her argument is that disability can be in some ways good and in some ways bad, for some people good and for some bad, in ways that depend on myriad factors including social context, the particular embodied experience of each person, and an individual's goals and preferences. It is much worse to be Beethoven, musician and composer, going deaf in a world that is inhospitable to deafness, than it is to be a Deaf child of Deaf parents in a flourishing community of Deaf people within an accepting wider community. In other words, much of the badness of disability may be the result not of the disability itself, but rather of the way that disabled people are treated socially; and in any case people differ in what is important to them.

But then, of course, anything can be sometimes good or sometimes bad depending on a multitude of factors. Being very wealthy is good if one is able to use that wealth for great personal advancement, but bad if it plunges one into depression or drug addiction, or makes one the victim of kidnapping or gold-digging romantic partners; and it may be indifferent if one decides to give all the money away and live a frugal life. If disability is a neutral feature, because what it adds to a life cannot be determined in advance or for everyone, then almost everything will be neutral in a similar way. So it seems that Barnes's argument removes our ability to say anything meaningful about which features make lives go better or worse, and that removes our ability to create societies, practices and procedures that support flourishing rather than suffering.

Barnes offers two counter-arguments to these objections. The first is that there is a difference between an experience of adversity *causing* something good and in itself *being* something good. Mandela's imprisonment may have caused something good – becoming president – but it was not in itself something good. But for some disabled people, Barnes argues, 'Their experiences of having disabled bodies, rather than simply, say, life lessons about perseverance or courage or what have you, are of value to them.'[48] One example she gives is Dostoevsky, who felt extreme euphoria from his epileptic seizures. 'All of you healthy people don't even suspect what happiness is, that happiness that we epileptics experience for a second before an attack,' Barnes reports him as saying.[49]

But for other disabled people, such as Beethoven, their experience of their disabled bodies causes great distress. In Beethoven's case, Barnes argues that

> it wasn't that deafness *by itself* caused such a severe reduction in well-being. It was deafness combined with a career as a composer and a conductor, a love of the auditory experience of music above almost anything else, and an intense creative drive to compose music that was devastating. Deafness by itself doesn't entail a reduction in well-being.[50]

Let's grant that Barnes's claim is true. Even so, the same could be said of almost anything. It wasn't Dostoevsky's seizures *by themselves* that caused him such joy; it was his seizures combined with his openness to experiencing sudden and uncontrollable emotions, the fact that he did not live in a social context that demonized or incarcerated epileptics, the fact that he did not long for a job that was incompatible with epilepsy (being an anachronistic fighter pilot, perhaps).

So there are problems with Barnes's general claim. Nonetheless, she is surely right to say that disability is not always bad for a person. And this means that modification of disabled bodies to make them less disabled is not always good either. Even where modification is largely focused on functioning it cannot help but impact a person's identity, and even where modification improves some kinds of functioning it involves different sorts of loss. And social pressures for disabled people to modify their bodies, along with the assumption that modification is always the answer, undermine their equal status.

The principle of the unmodified body recognizes the material significance of the body, and this means recognizing the reality of bodily impairment as something that can cause suffering and constraint. But the principle also insists that *your body is good enough just as it is*; that equality requires resistance to the idea that bodies are defective or that modification is necessary. These two parts of the principle are in delicate opposition, and achieving them both is something of a philosophical and political balancing act.

The search for a cure illustrates the problem. If disability and impairment were only about bodily function, then cures would be straightforwardly good. But since impairment and disability also invoke identity the position is far less clear. Curing an impairment is to disrupt or even destroy the identity that forms around it. And, since most disabling impairments cannot in practice be cured, a public, vocal search for a cure is at the same time a denigration of the value of the disabled body. Why cure something if it is not defective? And how can a disabled body be both defective and equally valuable?

At the same time, many people do in fact want their impairments to be cured. People whose impairments cause pain and suffering might long for relief. People suffering from degenerative conditions and people whose impairment was acquired later in life may see the search for a cure not as a destruction of their identity or a denigration of their value, but as a longed-for modification that might restore normality. If we distinguish between the *body*, or a particular physical *condition*, and the value of the *person*, surely we can say that a desire to change the body is compatible with valuing the person?

It's true that wanting to alleviate suffering, cure impairment, or enhance an ability does not mean that the person has no value as they are. Sometimes people are treated unequally by being *denied* healthcare or pain relief, as when women are expected to undergo invasive procedures or childbirth without adequate analgesia, or when people of colour are denied proper treatment as the result of systemic racism, or when doctors fail to acknowledge that weight loss is not the solution to every health condition faced by a fat person.[51] But it is important to acknowledge too the damage done by presenting modification as the only proper response to difference; damage which affects bodies, minds and social standing. We must recognize the multiple ways in which people with impairments have been treated as inferior and, in this context, the principle of the unmodified body is an assertion of equal status.

So far I've focused on people whose disability is stable and permanent, part of what is normal for that person. But for many people disability is the disruption. Impairment is the modification, and not a welcome one. For people in this position, the unmodified body is the body they had *before* the onset or worsening of impairment. Medical treatment, although a modification, is then actually in the service of the unmodified body, because it is a restoration of normality understood subjectively. In the next chapter, I investigate modification as restoration.

Disability is not just about the body. And it's not just about impairment. Disability is also significantly about identity. It intertwines with other identities, including those with a bodily element. It mediates and is mediated by identities of sex/gender, sexuality, class, race and age. Neither the concept nor the experience of disability can be understood by looking at the body alone.

At the same time, the fact of bodily impairment remains fundamentally significant. Being impaired affects many people's lives profoundly. The aim of this chapter is not to prescribe a particular approach to disability and injury, still less to advocate for any particular treatment protocol. My aim, instead, is to show how the motivating claim of *Intact* – the principle that the unmodified body has value, that the body you have, right now, whatever it is, can be *good enough* – can and should also apply to the disabled body. There is no equality unless the political principle of the unmodified body applies to disabled people, too.

7

Choosing to be Normal

*Reconstruction, Objectification
and the Internal Perspective*

*I had a labiaplasty in my late teens because I thought my
longer left labia was unsightly and it was painful in tight jeans.
I hadn't enough life experience to realise it was completely
normal. I think drawings in biology textbooks and porn were
the only times I had seen labia and mine did not look like the
ones shown. [Now] I feel robbed of a part of me. If a sexual
partner comments positively on my genitals I feel odd about it
because it's not really how I look.*

Survey respondent, Nuffield Council on Bioethics (2017)[1]

*I'm being offered many ways to keep looking normal and avoid
offending the eye of the average man in the street, but zero ways
to just be myself: a woman, like thousands of women in the UK,
with one breast.*

Diana Harrison, post-mastectomy (2018)[2]

When Hannah was pregnant she requested a C-section.[3] She did not
have a specific medical condition requiring a surgical birth, but she
felt it was the right choice for her. Hannah had researched the risks
and benefits of various birthing methods. 'An uncomplicated home
birth seems like the best possible outcome,' she tells me, over lunch in
a busy restaurant.

But of course not everyone who wants that sort of birth can have it. I
looked into the risks of complications: what happens in the worst-case

scenario, when a birth goes wrong. The risks of a complicated vaginal birth seemed worse than the risks of a complicated C-section. I cared more about the prospect of being incontinent than the prospect of losing my womb, for example. So I chose the C-section.

Hannah researched the pros and cons of different ways of giving birth, and she also researched NHS protocols. 'I did my homework,' she remembers. 'I went on the NHS website and found all the phrases about patient choice, and all the reasons that entitle a patient to a planned C-section. So when I went to see the midwife I was ready.'

By that point in Hannah's pregnancy she was suffering from Symphysis Pubis Dysfunction (SPD). It's a relatively common complication of pregnancy that can cause severe pelvic pain and temporary disability; it usually resolves after giving birth. 'My SPD was really bad at that point, and so I was actually on crutches when I went to see the midwife,' Hannah recalls. 'I think it helped. The midwife took one look at me on crutches and said "OK" to the C-section.' Hannah had a successful Caesarean birth and is pleased with her decision.

Hannah's story may strike you as remarkable, even extreme. Many pregnant women research childbirth options, but it's less common for a woman to make such a pessimistic and precise assessment of the risks and choose on the basis of worst-case scenarios. And while some women are wary of the medical profession, as Hannah was when she prepared her case before consulting the midwife, they're more likely to take that scepticism as a sign that they should choose minimal medical intervention, not elective surgery.

Hannah's choices seem less surprising, though, once you know the story we've met to discuss. A few years before becoming pregnant, aged twenty-seven, Hannah had a double mastectomy.

A family history of breast cancer and genetic testing showed that Hannah was almost certain to develop aggressive breast cancer in her lifetime. Her mother had developed the disease aged just thirty. Doctors advised Hannah that the only real option was to have a precautionary double mastectomy as soon as possible and hope that cancerous cells had not yet developed. This treatment protocol was made famous when Angelina Jolie followed it in 2013 and went public about her experience.[4] Hannah agreed to the surgery. She is still in no doubt that she made the right decision.

What she is less pleased with, though, is what happened next. 'My surgery was not an emergency: I didn't yet have breast cancer,' she explains.

> So once the decision was made I was put on the waiting list for a mastectomy. I was referred to a surgeon, and I looked up his credentials. He was extremely qualified: very senior in his field, with publications and a lot of experience. I was very happy to be referred to him. My genetic profile was so serious that it really mattered how good the mastectomy was. I really wanted to make sure that as much as possible of the potentially cancerous tissue was removed. So I wanted a surgeon who would do as good a job as possible on the mastectomy itself.

By the time her first appointment with the breast surgeon came around, Hannah had thought a lot about the procedure. 'My first instinct was that I wanted to be flat-chested after the mastectomy,' she says. 'I had quite small breasts anyway, so I felt that being flat-chested would be most similar to my natural appearance. I tend to wear quite androgenous clothes. I didn't really want additional reconstructive surgery, and I didn't like the idea of implants.'

I ask Hannah if she had researched her rights, and the various forms of reconstruction available, before she visited the surgeon. 'Not at that point, no,' she says. 'I didn't anticipate a fight. I thought the surgeon would be on board with doing a mastectomy without reconstruction – after all, it would be saving the NHS money.'

But Hannah was wrong about the surgeon's support. He talked about various different options for reconstruction: whether to have reconstruction using artificial breast implants or using fat from elsewhere on her body, and whether to have reconstruction at the same time as the mastectomy or in a subsequent operation. But he did not mention the option that most appealed to Hannah: being flat-chested. 'I was shown a binder full of photos of women who had had different forms of reconstruction,' she remembers. 'It showed the different shapes and sizes of implants, and the different places where scars might be. But I was not shown a single picture of a woman who had opted for no reconstruction at all.'

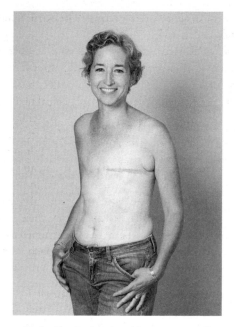

Gemma Cockrell, who has faced breast cancer three times

Hannah's surgeon also didn't tell her about the different options for wound closure. A mastectomy wound can be closed in a way that leaves it smooth and taut, or it can be closed in way that leaves a section of loose skin and fat. If you ultimately want to be flat-chested, as Hannah did, it is better to have a smooth wound closure. If you are planning subsequent reconstruction then having loose skin is best, as it leaves space for an implant.

'Reconstruction was presented to me in a completely normalizing way,' Hannah recalls. 'It was implied that everyone has reconstruction, so the only question is what sort of reconstruction you want.'

This way of proceeding doesn't only fail to cater to those women who already know they want to be flat-chested. It means that many of them won't ever choose not to have reconstruction, because they won't consider it as an option. As Hannah puts it, with great insight, 'Presenting the options frames the choice.' If you're told that your options are reconstruction now or later, reconstruction this way or that, that's likely what you'll choose.

Hannah *had* considered an alternative. She went to the surgeon already feeling that she wanted to remain flat-chested. So perhaps the surgeon's way of framing the options didn't affect her?

On the contrary. Hannah's surgeon and medical team very strongly pushed for reconstruction. 'They assumed I'd be willing to take on a large amount of risk to have a reconstruction,' she tells me. 'They saw the value of a good aesthetic result as very high. I didn't. It was more important to me to have a full range of movement, and to be free from pain. They never asked me about what mattered to me.' Hannah felt that her medical team had strong preconceptions about what women wanted. They didn't feel the need to check that their preconceptions applied to Hannah, specifically, because they assumed that all women were the same. As Hannah puts it, 'Their approach didn't seem very patient-relative.' She continues:

> I get the feeling that things might have been different if I'd presented as an athlete. Perhaps then they'd have believed that I truly did value a full range of movement over aesthetics. I am quite outdoorsy – I even turned up to one appointment with a backpack, because I was going camping afterwards. But no one ever asked me what my values were, or believed me when I tried to tell them. I tried to say why I was making the choices I made, why I weighed these outcomes as I did, but they didn't seem to believe me. I was actually told I was being irrational.

In the end, Hannah's surgeon gave her an ultimatum. 'He said he would not do the mastectomy unless I consented to reconstruction at the same time,' she tells me. 'I needed the mastectomy, and I believed he was the best surgeon, and I didn't want to go back on the waiting list. So in the end I gave in.'

When I first heard Hannah's story I was profoundly shocked. Why on earth would an NHS surgeon – one bound by the ethics of patient-centred care and evidence-based medicine – want to push a clinically unnecessary surgery? I have heard many accounts of malpractice in the *commercial* cosmetic-surgery sector, of clinics offering multibuy offers on a range of cosmetic procedures, of misleading and unethical advertising, of sales staff masquerading as clinicians.

Where surgeons stand to profit financially from performing a procedure it is easy to see why they might promote it, and then push it to patients. But this surgeon stood to make no personal profit from Hannah having reconstruction. Why would he issue such a cruel and unethical ultimatum?

Of course, neither Hannah nor I know why the surgeon acted as he did. Hannah doesn't tell me the surgeon's name and I deliberately do not ask; this is not an exercise in holding an individual to account. I want to hear about breast reconstruction from a patient's perspective, and I want to consider the general principles to be learned.

How does Hannah interpret the surgeon's actions? Does she feel the surgeon was acting in good faith, trying to promote what he thought were her best interests? 'Yes, I do think he was,' she says, fairly confidently. 'I think he was trying to help me. But he was very paternalistic. He kept repeating that I was an excellent candidate for a very successful implant. And there was also a lot of ego there. He also kept saying that he was sure he could do a very good job.'

It was clear to Hannah the surgeon trusted his own aesthetic judgement very deeply, and that he felt his judgement was more important than her own. 'It was all about his ability to create a good aesthetic outcome,' she says. 'I heard a few times that perhaps some *elderly* women might choose not to have reconstruction, but that a young woman like me should certainly have the procedure. He didn't seem to care or accept that I might value other things more than aesthetics.'

In the end, the surgeon's faith in his own aesthetic judgement above Hannah's own won out – not once, but twice. First, she had breast implants despite wanting to be flat-chested. And then, she ended up with breasts that her surgeon chose for her.

'In the end, I consented to reconstruction,' Hannah says, ruefully.

> It seemed the only way of getting the mastectomy without having to go back on the waiting list and being transferred to a less experienced surgeon. So I told him that I would have reconstruction, but that I wanted the implants to leave me with breasts that were the same size or smaller than my natural breasts.

The surgeon did not follow her wishes.

'When I woke up from surgery, I thought that my breasts looked massive,' Hannah recalls.

> I told the surgeon, 'my breasts look bigger'. He said it was just the swelling. But by the time the swelling had gone down they still looked bigger. I asked the surgeon about it. He told me that he had tried various implants on me and had chosen the larger ones. He said, 'These looked good on your frame.' He had made this decision against my explicitly stated wishes, while I was unconscious on the operating table.

Hannah pauses.

> Breast implants don't come in cup sizes, so I asked him how the weight of the implants compared with the weight of breast tissue that had been removed. They know, because they weigh both during the operation. He admitted that the implants he'd chosen were twice as heavy as the breast tissue that had been removed.

When Hannah heard this she was furious. The surgeon had gone against her explicitly stated wishes to be the same size or smaller than her natural breasts. But even having to admit that he had not done as she asked, and even seeing Hannah's reaction to his revelation, did not make the surgeon realize that he had overstepped the mark. 'He was baffled,' Hannah says. 'He could not understand why I was so cross that he'd made them so big.'

SURGEONS' STORIES

Every cosmetic surgeon has a story about the patient they refused to operate on. I've spoken to quite a few surgeons about the ethics of their profession, and they liked to tell me these stories. I'll tell you some, too. They fall into three categories.

1. Unwilling children

These are my favourite 'I wouldn't do it' cosmetic-surgery stories. In them the surgeon refuses to perform cosmetic surgery on a child, even though the parents want them to.

You might be astonished to think that cosmetic surgery is performed on children. But in fact, it's quite common. Some cosmetic procedures performed on children are completely routine and normalized.

Cosmetic orthodontics is an example. It's not normally surgical, but wearing braces is a long-term, inconvenient, expensive and often painful project. It requires visits to the orthodontist every six to eight weeks for about two years.[5] Adult patient Michael Thomsen describes having to focus elsewhere as 'the brackets were applied and the first uncomfortable sensation of tightening pressure began to radiate through my skull' – a sensation he had to become accustomed to over the three years that he wore braces. Removing the braces, finally, 'felt like a 10-pound weight had been removed from the front of my face'.[6]

Cosmetic orthodontics are normally performed on children. According to the NHS, 'The ideal age to have braces is usually around 12 or 13, while a child's mouth and jaws are still growing.'[7] Orthodontic treatment for under-eighteens is available free on the NHS for those who need it – which, according to the NHS, is one-third of all children.

Even surgical cosmetic procedures are routinely performed on children. Otoplasty or pinnaplasty, surgeries that pin back protruding ears, are also offered by the NHS and 'usually done on children or young teenagers'.[8] In the USA the Mayo Clinic reports that this surgery can be performed on children as young as three and that splinting can be performed 'immediately after birth'.[9] Other cosmetic procedures routinely performed on children include removing extra fingers and toes,[10] removing webbing between fingers and toes,[11] laser treatment for port wine birthmarks,[12] routine male circumcision,[13] and cosmetic surgery on the genitals of intersex children.[14]

Cosmetic surgeries on children are instigated and consented to by parents, with or without the child's input depending on age. Clearly babies cannot consent at all. Older children may be capable of expressing an opinion but not giving full autonomous consent. The point at which a child is considered to be capable of giving autonomous consent to medical treatment is known as 'Gillick competence' in the bioethical literature, after the UK House of Lords court case *Gillick v. West Norfolk and Wisbech AHA* set out principles by which children under the age of sixteen could be given contraception without their parents' consent.[15] Gillick competence is a relative, context-dependent state, taking into account the child's maturity and intelligence and the urgency and seriousness of the procedure.[16] When children are not yet Gillick competent, parents are considered legally able to consent on their behalf.

But some cosmetic surgeons refuse to operate on children, even very young children below the age of Gillick competence, if the child does not want the procedure. Mark Henley is a senior consultant plastic surgeon who treats a lot of babies and children with cleft lip and palate. He also does commercial cosmetic surgery, and was president of the British Association of Plastic, Reconstructive and Aesthetic Surgeons (BAPRAS) 2019–20. Henley was a colleague of mine on the Nuffield Council on Bioethics Working Party on Cosmetic Procedures, and over the years he's shared many stories of his profession. Henley is one of the good guys of cosmetic surgery.

Henley tells me that he refuses to operate on unwilling children. One of his stories goes like this. A very young child, four or five years old, was booked in to have his ears pinned back. He'd had several preliminary consultations in which the child had been willing to have the operation. On the day of the surgery, the child was brought in by his parents – but he'd changed his mind. 'I don't want it done!' he said. And so Henley refused to do the procedure. The parents were livid.

Another surgeon tells me a similar story.[17] Parents brought in a three-year-old boy and asked for cosmetic surgery to remove the boy's moles. The surgeon didn't think it was necessary. 'Let the boy come back when *he's* got a problem,' the surgeon said. 'When he's got psychological problems and worries about his appearance. I'll do the operation when *he* wants it.'

The tricky thing, of course, is how to make sure the parents don't give the child those problems and worries. It's likely that parents who think that a child's appearance is a problem will make the child feel the same way. Still, in the meantime, a surgeon can refuse to operate. And refuse they should: bodily integrity dictates that cosmetic surgery should not be performed until the child is old enough to consent, which may mean not until the child becomes an adult.

Or even later. One junior plastic surgeon, who specializes in treating burns and facial scarring, tells me he hates purely cosmetic surgery and won't do it. 'I helped my consultant do a private breast augmentation once,' he says.

> I never met the patient – my boss did all the consultations – so I didn't see her until she was all covered up by drapes in the operating theatre. We did the implants, then removed the drapes. I saw her face for the first time. She was only eighteen. I was disgusted and vowed then that I'd never do a private cosmetic procedure again.

2. Don't get sued by a SIMON

Cosmetic surgeons don't want to be sued. (Does anyone?) They also want to avoid complaints, and they want to avoid unsatisfied customers. Complaints are bad for business, and job satisfaction, and surgeons' consciences.

Complaints and litigation can happen because of botched procedures, but they can also happen when the operation has gone well. 'Lots of surgeons ask me "Why are patients still dissatisfied after surgery, even when the outcome is excellent?"' says Nichola Rumsey, Professor Emerita of Appearance Research.

> The answer is that psychology plays a huge role in the process. Most patients have cosmetic surgery for psychological reasons – to make themselves feel better about their appearance, or because they think evaluations of them by others will be more favourable. Cosmetic surgery can improve a patient's satisfaction with a specific body part, but there's no evidence that it has a sustained impact on patients' overall body image or mental health. There is a considerable body of evidence linking body image dissatisfaction with psychological distress. And people don't graduate from low body confidence.[18]

In other words, psychological distress is what makes you unhappy with your appearance, not the other way around. If you're dissatisfied with your appearance, then, more often than not, changing how you look doesn't make you feel better long term. Cosmetic surgery treats the symptom, not the cause. Body image dissatisfaction is not, ultimately, caused by how you look.

Surgeons see this effect in their practices: patients who are dissatisfied no matter how good the aesthetic outcome from a clinical point of view. And so, many surgeons try not to operate on people who seem likely to be dissatisfied and liable to complain even after successful surgery.

Surgeons will standardly try to identify patients with Body Dysmorphic Disorder (BDD), a psychiatric condition defined in the *Diagnostic and Statistical Manual of Mental Disorders* (DSM-V) that leads patients to feel sustained and deep dissatisfaction with their bodies. The UK's National Institute of Health and Care Excellence (NICE), the government body that provides care and treatment guidelines for the NHS, recommends that cosmetic surgeons screen for BDD and offer psychological rather than surgical treatment.[19] BDD is regarded as a contra-indication for cosmetic surgery in many countries, including the USA.[20] But it's not only BDD sufferers whom surgeons regard as mentally unstable and better avoided.

The question is, how do you tell? 'You can smell it,' says one surgeon, 'from the way they say "hello", the way they shake your hand.' Another describes how she and a colleague act as each other's second opinion, someone to whom they can refer patients they are uneasy about. Patients who've already had a number of procedures with surgeons they don't want to go back to are a particular red flag.

Henley tells me that he never does cosmetic surgery on patients who have just divorced or been bereaved without first referring them to a psychologist. These major life events leave people unsteady, disoriented and looking for a change that will solve everything. Sometimes, a change of appearance seems like the answer. How they look becomes a proxy for their emotional distress. But it is, ultimately, only a proxy, and so surgery fixes the symptom but not the cause.

It's understandable for people in emotional turmoil to seek a change, but it's dangerous when that remedy is cosmetic surgery. A post-divorce haircut can always be grown out, but cosmetic surgery can't be undone when the grief has worn off.

I always feel self-conscious when talking to cosmetic surgeons, wondering whether they are expertly scanning my features for aesthetic imperfections. I meet another experienced senior surgeon at a major plastic and cosmetic surgery conference, where I've been invited to talk to the practitioners about problems with the idea of the normal body. This surgeon is taller than me, and he wears spectacles on the end of his nose: sometimes he scrutinizes me through the lenses, at other times he peers over them. Is his gaze flitting between my facial flaws?

The surgeon thanks me for my lecture, and tells me his 'I wouldn't do it!' stories. He tells me that he uses what he calls the 'SIMON principle' to identify patients in the 'might sue' category. The SIMON principle is well known among surgeons. It stands for: Single, Immature, Male, Obsessive and Narcissistic – and they're trouble. Often, they come in for a rhinoplasty (nose job), and rhinoplasties are already some of the riskiest procedures on a cosmetic surgeon's menu. The risk is not so much to the patient's health but to his or her peace of mind – and with it, the surgeon's post-surgery complaints list.

Rhinoplasties are technically very difficult to do, and it can be difficult to control the result very precisely. Moreover, the nose is such a central part of the face that reshaping it has a profound effect on how a person looks. This means that a surgeon can perform a rhinoplasty which in his (or her – though over 75 per cent of plastic surgery consultants are male[21]) estimation has an excellent result – clinically perfect, aesthetically as intended – and yet the patient can still be deeply unhappy since the face they see gazing back at them in the mirror does not feel comfortably theirs.

So, surgeons try not to operate on people they think might cause them trouble afterwards. One technique for getting out of doing the operation is for the surgeon to say that he or she is not skilled enough to get the results the patient wants. But this consideration is a delicate balance, because of course commercial considerations push in the opposite direction.

British cosmetic surgeons fall into two categories: those who operate wholly in the commercial sector, where profit is paramount, and those who perform plastic and reconstructive surgery on the NHS and then perform private cosmetic surgery on the side. The latter category, the NHS plastic surgeons, think of themselves as fundamentally more *ethical* than their purely commercial colleagues. In fact, it's common for NHS plastic surgeons to describe commercial cosmetic surgery as a cowboy industry, full of malpractice, unethical selling and shoddy work. Many surgeons strongly support tighter regulation of the commercial side of their industry. For example, in 2012 several members of the British Association of Aesthetic and Plastic Surgeons (BAAPS), including the president, signed a letter calling on government to outlaw advertising for cosmetic surgery.[22]

The UK government is reluctant to regulate, however. A series of independent inquiries and reports into scandals has given them ample opportunity, but government has chosen to pass. So the cosmetic-surgery industry remains astonishingly underregulated. The NHS does not train specialist cosmetic surgeons (as opposed to plastic and reconstructive surgeons), since it does not offer cosmetic surgery, and so there's a saying in the industry that 'the first facelift you do is your first commercial one': commercial practitioners must learn on their paying clients. Unscrupulous business practices abound – financial incentives such as o per cent finance, two-for-one offers and 'refer a friend' schemes;[23] freelance surgeons who rent operating space in clinics with prestigious Harley Street addresses and then cannot be found when problems arise; poor record-keeping and treatments that are not evidence-based.

One mechanism Henley advocates, in the absence of government regulation, is regulation via insurance. All cosmetic surgeons need indemnity insurance so they can compensate patients if things go wrong (perhaps when a SIMON slips through the net). The Plastic, Reconstructive and Aesthetic Surgeons Indemnity Scheme (PRASIS) is a specialist insurance scheme that gives surgeons lower premiums if they adhere to a Code of Practice.[24] The idea is that surgeons who follow the Code have a lower complaint risk, and thus can pay a lower premium. The Code of Practice covers all aspects of cosmetic practice. It includes the requirement that surgeons 'Not offer financial or other incentives – including the return of consultation fees – to patients to commit to treatments', the recommendation of a four-week cooling-off period, and it reminds surgeons that 'you are under no obligation to undertake surgery or treatments, that you believe will be against a patient's best interests.' This nifty solution restores the connection between profit and ethics. Ethical practice means a lower risk of being sued, which means a lower insurance premium and a healthier balance sheet.

One of the reasons that surgeons who focus on NHS work but practise commercially on the side generally think of themselves as more ethical than their purely commercial colleagues is because the bulk of their work is not cosmetic: it's reconstructive or plastic surgery, providing help for those disfigured by illness, injury, or disability. But it's also because their NHS work brings with it a non-commercial framework for surgical practice: a framework centred on patients, not profit. The wholly commercial surgeons don't have regular interaction with the ethical framework that shapes NHS practice, focused on patient-centred care and evidence-based medicine, and so they are perhaps less used to thinking outside commercial logics. At least, that's how the NHS surgeons see it.

One issue of contention between the commercial and the NHS surgeons is this: what do you do if a cosmetic-surgery patient changes her (or his – although over 90 per cent of cosmetic-surgery patients are women[25]) mind on the day of the surgery? Of course, you don't operate without her consent; but does she get her money back?

For large commercial providers, the answer is often no.[26] Operating theatres have been booked, doctors and nurses have been paid, and so the patient must bear some of the cost. For Henley, the answer is yes, the patient must get her money back. After all, he points out, cosmetic surgery is clinically unnecessary, irreversible and risky. There's no way it should go ahead unless the patient is fully on board, and a patient who goes under the knife so as not to lose a deposit is not. For Henley, giving patients who change their mind their money back is good ethics *and* good business. On his assessment, patients who are not totally happy about going ahead are patients who are likely to cause surgeons problems later. It makes sense to avoid them.

A surgeon's approach to potentially troublesome patients affects his or her 'conversion rate': how many initial consultations with prospective patients are converted into actual procedures. For commercial-only practitioners the goal is to increase the conversion rate as much as possible. 'Have you ever heard American surgeons boasting about how high their conversion rates are?' one British surgeon asks another over conference canapés. 'Terrible!' Another surgeon tells me how appalled he was to hear a surgeon brag about his 95 per cent conversion rate. 'There's no way 95 per cent of the people going to see him really want cosmetic surgery,' he says. 'My conversion rate is around 40 per cent, and that's good.'

It's significant that the SIMON principle highlights *men* as potentially unstable candidates for cosmetic surgery. The implication is that it is not quite right – not normal? – for a man to be concerned about his appearance. Men are traditionally supposed to be concerned with what they *do* rather than how they *look*: what they earn, what they lift, who they screw. A man who wants cosmetic surgery seems automatically suspect. SIMONs aren't anxious, or cowed, or embarrassed, or ashamed. They're Single – why can't they find a partner? They're Immature – why haven't they graduated to manlier worries? They're Obsessive – women may worry about their appearance thirty-six times a day,[27] but why haven't SIMONs got more important things to worry about? They're Narcissistic – why do they direct the male gaze inward, rather than outward where it belongs? And they're Male, which is what makes all this a problem.

3. I'd say 'Fantastic!'

The third type of patient that surgeons are proud of not operating on are the ones who, in the surgeon's judgement, don't need surgery.

A cosmetic surgeon probably has a strong aesthetic. Hannah's surgeon had a very strong sense of how her breasts should look, insisting on reconstruction and performing an illicit augmentation. And remember Dr Romo, the surgeon who upsold fourteen-year-old Nadia from having her ears pinned back to having her ears pinned back, her nose straightened and her chin made less pointy? Dr Romo didn't like pointy chins. Hannah's surgeon didn't like flat chests or small breasts.

Most surgeons know what they like. And patients tend to listen. Sociologist Debra Gimlin points out that differences of class and social status tend to work in surgeons' favour. The cosmetic surgeon 'occupies a higher social status (associated with gender, occupation, and professional position) than do most patients' and this, coupled with the power the surgeon has to deny treatment, means that 'the cosmetic surgeon wields far greater influence over his clientele' than do other professionals such as beauticians and hairdressers.[28]

Surgeons' aesthetic sense is most often used in recommending procedures, but it is also sometimes used in refusing to perform them. One surgeon describes how she responded to a man who wanted surgery to remove the stretch marks he was left with after losing a lot of weight. 'There was nothing more he could do with exercise; by now it was just down to the knife,' she tells me.

> I told him I could remove the stretch marks, but he would be left with a scar from hip to hip. He said that didn't matter, because a scar could be removed with Photoshop. I didn't think that was right. Photoshop would be a temporary solution to a permanent problem. I persuaded him to have a different operation that would leave a smaller scar that could be hidden by his boxers. The final result was extremely good, if I say so myself.

Another surgeon, this one retired, regales me with his 'I wouldn't do it!' story. It's about breast augmentation. As he tells the story his eyes keep flitting to my own breasts. It's very disconcerting.

'I was in consultation and an eighteen-year-old girl came in with her mother, wanting breast implants,' he tells me. 'And I wouldn't do it! She was perfect! She had an amazing figure! OK, her breasts weren't particularly big – but they weren't too small either! I mean, I'd have done it if she was really flat-chested, or really horrible-looking, or something' – at this point he wrinkles his nose and turns away from my own breasts, for which I am thankful – 'but she wasn't! If she was my daughter ... well ... I'd have said "Fantastic!"' His eyes sparkle.

'So, I wouldn't do it. I said, "I won't operate on you, you're perfect just as you are." She stormed out. And her mother flung her arms around me and said, "Thank you doctor."'

Fin.

Actually, not quite *fin*. These stories always come with a postscript.

'Of course, someone else would have done it,' he says, ruefully.

The postscript is necessary because that's what demonstrates the narrator's ethical virtue. (Sometimes they're used the other way: 'Better that I do it and do a good job – otherwise she'll just go off to some cowboy who would take her money no questions asked!') If every surgeon would refuse to operate then the storyteller loses their bragging rights. To work, the 'I wouldn't do it!' story has to be a tale of selfless sacrifice: of refusing to take the money in pursuit of a greater ideal. The problem is, the ideal isn't the patient's. It's the surgeon's own.

OBJECTIFICATION

We tend to think of objectification as something that others do to us. Objectification is a critical term describing the process whereby someone treats our body as a mere object: for their pleasure, their perusal, their use. A paradigmatic example of objectification is street harassment, where a man loudly comments on the appearance or facial expression of a passing woman. The man treats the woman he shouts at as an object for his own enjoyment or amusement. Models are objectified, too: they are valued simply for their appearance, in or out of clothes. And prostituted women are objectified, since they are treated by johns as *things*, things to be used sexually, rather than as autonomous people with their own sexual desires and boundaries.

Feminists have used the concept of objectification to protest against these sexist and misogynist ways of using women, of treating them as things rather than as full human beings with equal status. Used in this way the concept of objectification is something one person does to another person, from outside.

This way of thinking about objectification is important and does useful analytical work. But we can also think of objectification as something we do to ourselves. Objectification is perhaps at its most complete when we think of our *own* bodies as mere objects. We objectify our own bodies when we value them for what they *look like* from the outside: how they look to others, or in a photo, or in the mirror. We objectify our bodies when we value them for what they can be *used for*, understood in an instrumental way.

We avoid objectification when we treat our own bodies not as *things* but as *us*. We reject objectification when we reject the idea that our bodies are not, could never be, good enough just as they are. We refuse objectification when we refuse the idea that our bodies need to change to fit a social standard. This is not an easy thing to do for most people, and it becomes ever harder the more a person's body deviates from those social standards. Sometimes the only liveable solution, from an individual point of view, is to do whatever is necessary to fit in. But from a collective, political perspective, we must work to make it easier to refuse objectification, whether by working together to change social standards, or by engaging in collective deliberation and consciousness-raising about the pressures to modify and their significance. One example of collective action is the body neutrality movement, which advocates acceptance of the body you happen to have.[29]

Objectification takes an external perspective: it views the body *from the outside*. The opposite of objectification is taking an internal perspective: considering the body, its feelings, experiences and needs, *from the inside*.

Consider make-up. Wearing make-up is very strange, when you think about it. It's one of the very few forms of optional bodily adornment that is only seen by others. Some sorts of bodily adornment cannot easily be avoided. Hair has to be cleaned and styled in *some* fashion, whether that style is a short haircut, or longer hair styled or tied off the face, just so that you can see, move and eat easily. Being presentable and professional requires additional effort. Clothes have to be worn to keep warm and maintain decency. But it's perfectly possible never to wear make-up. Most men never wear it, and many women get by without.

Once you've put your make-up on and left the mirror it becomes purely for others to see and experience. You see your clothes and shoes on your own body throughout the day; you feel their texture and warmth. Jewellery and nail varnish flash in and out of your vision as you move. Hair falls into your eyes, or doesn't; it brushes your neck or lets in a breeze.

Make-up does none of these things. It sits on your face entirely out of view – until you accidentally smear it on your hands or catch a glimpse of it in the mirror (or, since the pandemic, go into a Zoom meeting). Wearing make-up is a nuisance and the aesthetic effects are solely directed at others. There is nothing else like this, nothing that demands such constant attention from the wearer but yet is almost entirely for others' eyes. Even a back tattoo, something that only others can see unless its wearer contorts in front of a mirror, demands minimal attention or maintenance from its wearer after the initial application.

Wearing make-up is a way of objectifying ourselves. When we apply make-up, we see ourselves as others see us, and we treat their perspective as the one that counts.

THE INTERNAL PERSPECTIVE

The idea of normality is very much an objectifying idea. 'Normal' takes our bodies and then compares them to others. It takes an externalizing perspective. Not being normal comes to mean *not being like others*.

But most of the time our own bodies are completely normal *to us*, once we take an internal perspective. Once we refuse the external, objectifying point of view, anything our body is usually like is normal, because it is normal *to us*. It doesn't much matter, from a purely internal perspective, whether our bodies are like other people's. From the inside, our own body is the only one we know. Its sensations are our sensations. Its way of moving is our way of moving. When our body is cold, we are cold. Its surface and shape – how it looks – is its normality.

From an internal perspective, how our bodies are *to us*, our bodies might stop being normal in two ways. First, our bodies become abnormal to us if they go through sudden or drastic change. Suffering illness or injury, having successful treatment for a chronic condition, going through a major bodily change like puberty, pregnancy, or menopause – these things change the ways our bodies feel and make them abnormal to us, at least for a time.

This internal abnormality is not the same thing as external, objectifying abnormality, because a new sense of internal abnormality does not mean that our bodies have become unlike others. Going through puberty is entirely normal from an external perspective: everyone who lives long enough does it. From the internal perspective, though, puberty is not normal, because the body no longer feels the way it did before. Now it has hair in unfamiliar places, it has pains, it bleeds regularly, it ejaculates often, perhaps even its voice can no longer be relied upon.

One cross-cultural study of girls' experience of their first periods found that most of them experienced only negative emotions about that event, including feeling 'embarrassed, ashamed, scared, awful, shocked, confused, terrible, miserable, frightened, depressed, and freaked out'.[30] This finding is echoed in other studies. Psychologist

Karin Martin finds that negativity characterizes girls' experience of puberty in general. Puberty, Martin argues, is a time when girls become aware of their own objectification. This objectification is chiefly associated with breast development and weight. When girls start to grow breasts, they are subjected to sexual comments from boys and men, and their parents and other adults are likely to see them as potential targets of sexual attention – something that can feel dangerous or scary.[31]

For girls, puberty heralds a *reduction* in their freedom. Boys are generally given more freedom, in line with their developing maturity, but for girls this maturity is associated not with greater responsibility but with greater risk. Although they are developing emotionally and intellectually just as boys are, becoming increasingly capable of making rational decisions, looking after themselves and taking responsibility for their actions, girls tend to be treated as though this intellectual maturity is irrelevant. What matters, pubescent girls learn, is how their bodies look to others and the treatment they'll receive as a result.

The social reaction to their developing breasts also caused the girls in Martin's study to feel shame. This shame was applied generally to their bodies, regardless of what they looked like. Girls with small breasts felt they should be larger, and vice versa: 'girls often want their breasts to be *different*.'[32] This dislike of their bodies was also especially evident in adolescent girls' attitudes to their weight, another bodily characteristic on which they took an external perspective. Girls were displeased by what they perceived as their overweight bodies, and then disgusted with themselves when their attempts to lose weight failed. After puberty, Martin writes, 'girls, in general, do not like their bodies at all.'[33]

What is so disheartening in Martin's findings is the fact that this overwhelming dislike and even disgust with their own bodies is *normal* for adolescent girls. In other words, the feeling of bodily failure is the usual response to puberty, for girls. Boys can also find puberty difficult, and developing masculinity presents its own challenges. But the boys Martin studied did not generally experience the same damage to self-esteem and sense of personal agency as the girls: they experienced puberty as an enhancement of freedom, a welcome path to the privileges of masculinity. The reason for the gendered difference, according to Martin, is partly the physiological differences between male and female puberty, but it is much more significantly the cultural norms that surround those differences. Women's bodies are objectified far more than men's, their experience of sexuality is far less free and autonomous, and they are expected to perform shametenance about their experiences: keeping quiet about menstruation, not engaging in or discussing masturbation, not even becoming familiar with their own genitals.[34]

So, girls going through puberty face a social context that is virtually guaranteed to push them to take an external perspective on themselves and their bodies: to view themselves as others see them, to judge themselves harshly, to keep quiet about their experiences. The external perspective becomes normal for girls. One might even say it is normal for girls to feel abnormal. Certainly, it is normal for girls to feel *wrong*.

Conversely, a person with a congenital difference or impairment may have a body that is abnormal from an external perspective, because it is unlike most other bodies; but from an internal perspective that body is absolutely normal, because it has always been that way. Consider the following passage by Tom Shakespeare, an academic and broadcaster who has achondroplasia, a condition that affects bone growth:

> I feel me. I really do. I don't feel Other. I believe without thinking that I am just like everyone else. Like all of you. I may look out through these distinctive green eyes, but I think with this normal brain. I speak, the same. Hear, the same. Feel, the same.
>
> How wrong I am! I don't look the same. I have always been obviously different. From infancy, I grew up, or didn't grow up, like this. So shortness of stature, this restriction of growth, this, say it, *dwarfism*, has always been my ordinary. I can't help it, I can't escape it. This is who I am. It's all I've ever known. I always forget the most unusual thing about me. It's certainly the first thing you're aware of. But I'm often as surprised as you.[35]

External abnormality and internal abnormality are not at all the same. Whether you feel normal, in the internal sense, has very little to do with whether you are normal, in the external sense. Looking different does not mean you feel different, and it does not mean you will necessarily feel bad about how you look. Looking the same does not mean you feel normal, and it is certainly no guarantee that you will feel OK about yourself. This is a vitally important fact.

Because the second way our bodies can become abnormal to us is when we take an external, objectifying perspective. We look in the mirror, inspect our features, and think 'Do I look right?' We look down at our genitals, unsure how they compare to others, and worry 'Am I normal?' Often this objectifying perspective is forced on us by others. Nadia became worried about her ears only when another child commented on them. Your vulva becomes abnormal when labia in porn don't look like yours. Anxiety sets in when a sexual partner expresses surprise about the appearance of your genitals: the presence or absence of pubic hair, the presence or absence of a foreskin, the length of penis or labia. Shakespeare again:

> Whoever they are, however kind, however thoughtful, I always want to say to people: Get up! Please! Don't squat or crouch or kneel. It looks painful, you wobble, we two make a fine sight. Don't make a fuss. If it's hard for you to crane your neck downwards, we could sit together on chairs, so we are at the same height. Don't draw attention to my difference, please.[36]

A normal body from the objectifying point of view is 'one like others'. A normal body from the internal point of view, from the perspective of lived experience, is 'one like mine'. So, too, shifting from the objectifying perspective to the internal perspective changes the meaning of abnormality: from 'not like them' to 'not like me'.

The question then becomes: what is truly, genuinely, really *me*? Where is my authentic self located?

Answering this question can also be done in an external, objectifying way or in an internal, non-objectifying way. The woman who undergoes a mastectomy undergoes a drastic and sudden change in her bodily appearance and experience. Her chest looks different, and it feels different. Things it may have been able to do before – feel nipple sensation, breastfeed – it can no longer do. Things that endangered it before – tumours, cancer – are removed. The post-mastectomy chest is not normal in either the objectifying or the non-objectifying sense. It is not like most other women's chests, and it does not feel like this specific woman's own chest.

Rectifying this abnormality can be done in different ways. From an external perspective, reconstructive surgery restores normality. It makes the chest look like other women's chests, at least when clothed. If the reconstructed breasts closely resemble the woman's natural breasts, then reconstruction makes her look more like her, too; but this may not be the case, as happened with Hannah. Surgeons and patients who use reconstruction as an opportunity for enhancement are pursuing normality from the external, objectifying perspective but not from the internal point of view.

From an internal perspective, the reconstructed breast may do little to restore normality, because reconstructed breasts may not *feel like me* from the woman's perspective. They will not have the sensations of natural breasts, and they may have new sensations not previously felt: pain, hardness, pertness. This is not to say that reconstruction is bad – certainly not morally speaking, but also not from the internal point of view of normality. Because the post-mastectomy chest most probably does not feel normal to the woman herself either way: with or without reconstruction. Mastectomy is a drastic change. And so, if this analysis is correct, the post-mastectomy woman is in a position of existential abnormality.

A similar phenomenon confronts those who experience facial disfigurement as the result of injury or illness. As you may recall, James Partridge suffered serious facial burns in a car accident at the age of eighteen. He writes about the experience of first looking in the mirror after being facially injured:

> Steel yourself, then do it. Have one quick look. Take the mirror away. Then look again but don't stare at yourself. Get a general impression. Then put the mirror away.
>
> 'Is that really me,' shouts your inner voice. Your face's symmetry is grossly distorted. The colour of the skin, the swelling, perhaps the missing parts, the scars and unhealed wounds, the surgical metalwork, the stitches – there is so much that is wrong. And yet it is still you. You know you are intact behind this mask.[37]

And, in his recent book *Face It*, Partridge describes the profound disruption of identity caused by his burned face, something he referred to initially as '*IT*'. 'What I had thought of my self-image was now

IT, not Me,' he writes. '*IT* could not possibly be me . . . The old 'Me' had gone. But *IT* wasn't Me. I had no identity.'[38]

Partridge's account details the process of dealing with facial disfigurement: a process that involves both others and self. Coming to terms with facial disfigurement partly requires external treatment: plastic surgery, rehabilitation, perhaps camouflaging make-up in the early stages. Partly it is dependent on the reactions of others. But in large part it is about one's own attitude to oneself. 'Successfully changing faces,' Partridge writes, 'amounts to completely facing up to your new face and wearing it in public with pride and confidence, and effectively persuading all those whom you meet that behind your mask is a perfectly normal person with normal human emotions and mental abilities.'[39]

It is very uncomfortable to be, and feel, abnormal. Most of us want to be normal: it is within the logic of normality that it is a condition to be aimed at and achieved. Queer theory situates the problem of abnormality with the concept of normality, rather than within the abnormal person. When abnormality is understood in the external, objectifying sense that is the right way to proceed. We should refuse

James Partridge

categories of normality that compare and contrast, requiring homogeneity and punishing diversity. But from the internal perspective the aim of feeling normal, of feeling *like me*, is one that we can scarcely abandon. We all want to feel at home in our own skin.

So how does someone who suddenly does not feel normal, such as a post-mastectomy woman, feel normal again? If we take an external, objectifying perspective we make her feel normal by making her look normal. We perform reconstruction, or we give her a prosthesis. But if we take an internal, non-objectifying perspective we help her to *feel* normal, properly like herself. What she needs will differ from woman to woman, but likely includes emotional support, professional therapy, role models, other visibly or openly post-mastectomy women, support groups, and time.[40]

These are important strategies that an individual can use. But individual actions are not enough. Since normality is a socially constructed concept, our best individual efforts to feel normal are likely to fail if they are not supported by a social context that allows us to *be* normal, however we compare to others.[41]

This is where the political principle of the unmodified body comes in. The unmodified body is precisely about asserting the value of the body just as it is. It is about taking an internal perspective on one's body, allowing its familiarity to be a virtue, and allowing its changes to be acceptable.

At the same time, the unmodified body is meant as a call to collective action, a principle to guide policy. I'm not a psychologist and *Intact* is not meant as a self-help book: I don't presume to diagnose or treat anyone's personal struggles with body image. What I'm trying to do is convince you that a problem exists, and offer a way of thinking about it.

The principle of the unmodified body can be brought in at many levels and through many practices: yoga, mindfulness, gratitude, body positivity and neutrality, consciousness-raising, activism, policy. It is a response to a social and political context, and it's that context that needs the biggest change. It is not easy to change a social context, and some well-meaning attempts fail. For example, psychologist Amy Slater was an advocate of using labels on advertising and marketing images to show when they'd been photoshopped – until research showed that to be an ineffective strategy. If advertisers continue to use models who look 'perfect' according to a narrow, unattainable standard, then labels don't do anything to disrupt that ideal or the power it holds over us.[42] But it is important to keep trying, and to support research into effective policy interventions and cultural changes.[43]

For some of us, feeling normal comes easily, whether as the result of how we are treated socially or how we feel internally. The two are connected. If we have a majority body, one that looks like most others, and one that is socially coded as normal by virtue of its sex, race, lack of impairment or disfigurement, gender conformity and so on, it is easier to feel normal. 'There are unquestionably minimum social standards of facial acceptability to which it is important the disfigured conform,' Partridge writes,

> but you may find it difficult to decide what they are. A few years after my accident, still looking very badly disfigured, I travelled to India. There, and in Iran and Afghanistan, my face was rarely given the slightest attention. Heavily scarred faces are regular sights, as disfiguring diseases and accidents are commonplace, while plastic surgery is not widely available in those countries [Partridge is talking about the 1970s and 1980s]. I could quite easily have lived and worked there with no further surgery. But on my return, a trip on the London Underground was enough to convince me that I needed more reconstruction to live and work in Britain.[44]

There's no objective truth about what is needed to be treated as normal, from an external perspective. And whether we feel normal is not a simple matter of willpower. How others treat us is crucial. But the connection between being treated as normal and feeling normal is not rigid, because our own individual psychology plays a role too. Feeling normal is much harder for people with gender dysphoria or other forms of body dysphoria. Feeling normal after injury or illness may be harder for people who are shy or introverted.[45] We must not dismiss the effort, the struggle, the burden of choosing to feel normal just as we are. Sometimes, conforming to an external standard of normality is easier to deal with, a better course of action – even if that means undergoing body modification.

*

We left Hannah's story just after her operation, when her surgeon gave her larger implants than she had consented to, already under duress. But worse was still to come.

Complications can occur with any operation; one study found that 13.8 per cent of implants used in reconstruction have to be removed within the first eight years.[46] That's what happened to Hannah. One of her breast implants became infected soon after the operation and had to be removed.

Hannah lived for a full year with one implanted breast, the other side flat. During that time Hannah did a lot of research into her options: whether it was possible to have the remaining implant removed to give her the flat chest she had wanted, or whether she would be better off having the failed implant replaced.

'The problem is,' she explains to me,

> that once you've had a reconstruction it's then very difficult to achieve a flat effect. The implant stretches the skin, so that you're left with rippling and unevenness. It would have been straightforward to give me a flat chest immediately after the mastectomy, because my natural breasts were small. But now my skin has been stretched around an implant – and one that was bigger than my previous breasts – the outcome would have been much less successful.

Up to this point Hannah's treatment had been on the NHS. She paid privately for a second opinion, still hoping to find a surgeon who could provide her with the flat chest she had always preferred. 'The second surgeon was no better,' she remembers. 'He confirmed that the first surgeon had done an excellent aesthetic job with the remaining implant. Again, it was all about the look, and it was all about what the surgeons could create rather than what I wanted. The original surgeon was very proud of his first breast and wanted to match it.'

It's only afterwards, when typing up the notes of the interview, that I notice that Hannah calls her successful implant 'his' breast. It is his, not hers: both the surgeon and, ultimately, Hannah herself take the objectifying perspective on her chest.

Hannah lived with one breast for a year before returning to the original surgeon to have a second implant. I ask her how that year was for her. 'It was surprisingly fine,' she says. 'It was actually much easier than I thought it would be.' A charity sent Hannah a knitted prosthesis, which she wore once or twice; otherwise, she was visibly one-breasted.[47] 'I actually felt more comfortable, during that year, with my flat side,' Hannah recalls. It was her flat side that felt more like her, more normal.

When the year was up Hannah returned to her surgeon. I'm curious how that went. 'He was so confident that you had to have reconstruction,' I say, 'that he must have thought that living with only one breast for a year would have been terrible for you. Did he ask how that had been?'

'Not at all,' says Hannah. The medical team had given her a silicone prosthesis, and so Hannah thinks they must have assumed that she had been wearing it. She hadn't, not only because she didn't feel the need from an aesthetic point of view, but also because it was uncomfortable. The knitted prosthesis that Hannah found herself felt much nicer. That would have been useful information for the medical team to know: knitted prostheses instead of plastic ones might be a way for the NHS to improve patient experience. They might even save money. But no one did ask Hannah about it. No one wanted to know what her experience of living with one breast had been like. 'In fact none of the medical team showed any interest in my experience,' she says.

The second implant was successful, from an aesthetic point of view. But it left Hannah with a chronic pain condition from the repeated surgery. Hannah's implant had been placed under her chest wall muscles, not on top of them. Sub-muscular implants like Hannah's tend to look better, and they have a lower risk of capsular contracture. Capsular contracture is a condition that affects many breast implants – some studies say all of them – at some point; it's when scar tissue contracts and stiffens around the implant, making the breast uncomfortably cold and hard. But sub-muscular implants have the disadvantage of causing greater pain, and they are more likely to restrict the full range of arm movement.

'This was a reconstruction decision that they presented to me as not really a choice at all, because it was obvious to them what was best,' Hannah explains. She repeats the thought that only looking more athletic would have enabled her to achieve a different outcome, because only then might the surgical team have seriously contemplated the idea that she might genuinely prioritize function over form. 'I get the feeling that if I had presented more as an athlete, they might have made a different recommendation. They never asked me what sorts of activities I did, or might want to do after the surgery.'

Because Hannah's implant was sub-muscular, and because the surgery had to be repeated, her chest wall was cut and re-cut several times. It's taken extensive physiotherapy and regular yoga to restore movement, and she still has to deal with pain.

Hearing Hannah's story fills me with such a range of emotions. Shock, first, and then anger, and a great sadness in thinking about what she has had to go through and how she has suffered. Hannah tells her story with great courage and equanimity: she frequently talks about what she should have done. 'If I'd known it was going to be so hard, I'd have gone to the surgeon prepared,' she says. 'I'd have had a list of statistics and risks, ready to argue my case. I would have known the relevant bits of NHS policy so that I could assert my own choice.'

Hannah could have done all this, of course, but *she should not have had to.*

Is it any wonder that this is precisely what she did later, when requesting a C-section?

Hannah can think of various things that she could have done differently. But she can also think of lots of things that the surgeon and nurses should have done. 'They should give patients the facts about the number of women who choose to have no reconstruction at all,' she says.

> They should present no reconstruction as an option. The binder of photos should include post-mastectomy women with flat chests. They should talk about the different options for wound closure. They should be careful to perform the mastectomy in a way that makes it possible to have a flat chest afterwards, not just in a way that is prepared for an implant.

Surgeons should also realize that not everyone has the same lifestyle or values; not everyone will make the same choices about how to balance appearance and function. 'They should check what sorts of activities you do now, and what sorts of activities you might want to do,' Hannah argues. 'Do you lift weights, do you want to wear a bikini or go topless? They should run through the possible effects of the various options. They assumed that women would be willing to bear a high level of risk to get a good aesthetic. I wasn't. I am much more concerned about pain and function.'

Another of Hannah's recommendations is one that is repeated by a number of experts and studies. Surgeons should follow up their patients and find out if they're happy with the outcomes, not just immediately after the surgery but a year later, or longer. 'It really puzzles me,' she says. 'Why don't they want to know? They didn't have the evidence base to answer my questions about after-effects. They didn't know how many patients were left with pain, or how many were happy with their surgery. They assumed women were happy if they didn't come back to complain.'

But why would a woman go back to complain? What would be the point? Hannah repeatedly asserted her wishes, repeatedly asked not to have an implant, expressed her anger that the surgeon had increased her breast size without her consent. It made no difference then. What difference would it make a year later? She has not been back to complain. But nor is she happy with her treatment. Her body does not feel like her own.

An external perspective on normality invites the abnormal person to change so that they become normal. An internal perspective on normality invites the abnormal person to seek support and time to allow themselves to feel normal again. Alternatively, it invites *norm critique*. It invites us to reject the idea that we must fit a standard, a template, for our bodies. It encourages us to reject alienation from our embodied selves.

The principle of the unmodified body is the assertion that *your body is good enough, just as it is*. The concept of normality is, in many ways, anathema to the unmodified body. Normality means normalization, and normalization means modification. And so, normality is a concept to be viewed with suspicion when it is deployed from an external, objectifying perspective – including when we adopt that perspective towards ourselves. But normality becomes a concept to be embraced, even actively pursued, when viewed from an internal perspective. Viewed from an internal perspective, being normal is about allowing one's own internal normal experience to take the role of just *being* normal. It is to allow normality to be a subjective feeling, not an objective standard. It is *choosing to be normal*, just as you are. Which, of course, raises the question: how? Or, more aptly: under what social conditions is this possible?

PART THREE

Whole

Throughout this book I've defended the political principle of the unmodified body: a principle that urges conscious resistance to the dominant refrain that *your body is never good enough*. This principle is necessary to counteract the pressures, practices and psychological problems that plague our health; and it's necessary to defend equality for all of us. The unmodified body is not a perfectionist ideal: it's not a goal to be strived for or a standard to be measured against. It's a base to fall back on, a foundation to rely on, a territory to be inhabited and defended where necessary. It is a political premise.

So, the political principle of the unmodified body doesn't rule out modification. It invites us to reflect on the reasons for modification, and to ask ourselves whether they are justified. Questioning the reasons to modify our bodies takes on a different force depending on whether we are applying it to ourselves or to others. If we are considering modifying our own bodies, we are not concerned about permissibility. Assuming we are adults of sound mind and with full information (not easy to achieve), we should be at liberty to modify our bodies as we see fit. Part of our basic freedom and status as moral equals is the right to be free from coercion when acting in matters that primarily concern only ourselves.[1]

We should be free to modify – or, more accurately, seek to modify – our own bodies.[2] But we can still engage in critical analysis of our decisions and practices. The questions to ask yourself if you're considering modifying your own body are: to what extent are your actions shaped by or reacting to dominant social norms? How are you acting autonomously and how are you pushed towards this modification? Is this modification necessary for you to gain social status or acceptance? Are you pursuing this modification as the result of socially induced shame? Do the social pressures that you're reacting to fit within a structure of norms and institutions that undermine your equality? Does the modification that feels necessary to you harm or enhance your health? Will being modified make you feel better? What is the evidence for that? The aim of these questions is not to find definitive answers but to engage in a process of reflection.

In the following pages I discuss this question of choosing to modify oneself. I don't attempt to consider all motivations for self-modification, and certainly I don't claim to speak the truth for all people or for any specific person. Instead, I consider three logics of self-modification that I haven't yet fully addressed: the idea that self-modification is a virtue, a laudable way of making an effort; the idea that self-modification can be a necessary act of self-care, one that nurtures the soul or affirms one's identity; and the idea that modification can be an act of creativity. These logics can be found in many modification practices, including those already discussed, but I focus on modifications for gender identity.

There's an important difference between an individual's freedom to modify her own body, and the rights or duties that other people have to help or modify it for her. There are many practices which are wrong to perform on another person, and this wrong does not always disappear if the practice is asked for. And so, in the last chapter I discuss the conditions under which intervention in others' bodies is and isn't permissible. In that context, the principle of *bodily integrity* applies.

Modifications to other people's bodies are justified only if they don't violate their bodily integrity. For adults, bodily integrity is usually secured by deferring to choice, although this approach has problems. For children and severely cognitively disabled people, the concept of bodily integrity takes on a special importance because they are not (yet) capable of giving or withholding autonomous consent.

Bodily integrity has the distinct advantage of being a widely accepted principle, one often deployed in discussions about bodily interventions. But philosophy deplores a clique. From the outcasts' corner we'll see that the content of this principle is too often vague and its prescriptions contradictory. The principle of bodily integrity, properly defined, should offer guidance on controversial cases. It should tell parents, guardians and doctors what to do when there is disagreement about what is in the best interests of a child, or when there is uncertainty about what the child will want when she or he is an adult, or when there is no way of knowing what a cognitively disabled person would want.

My argument suggests, of course, that controversial cases should be decided in favour of the unmodified body. Integrity as a concept is close to wholeness, remaining intact. And so in the final chapter I set out an idea of bodily integrity that captures the value of the unmodified body. True to philosophical form, along the way I will point out problems for my position, reasons to be cautious about the view I am also urging you to accept. More precisely, these will be reasons to recognize that any defence of the unmodified body is necessarily nuanced, never straightforward, inescapably subtle.

8

Deciding to Modify

Self-care, Dysphoria and Creativity

Over himself, over his own body and mind, the individual is sovereign.

John Stuart Mill, *On Liberty* (1859)[1]

> *Don't hide yourself in regret*
> *Just love yourself and you're set*
> *I'm on the right track, baby,*
> *I was born this way!*
>
> Lady Gaga, 'Born This Way' (2010)[2]

If you've visited a Disney theme park or resort, you'll have noticed the attention to detail. Every aspect of the Disney experience is carefully managed, themed, 'imagineered'. This micromanagement is part of the success of the parks. Once inside, the rest of the world disappears.

How people look is an important part of the fantasy. Most Disney staff wear costumes, whether to operate the rides, serve food, or sweep up litter. They are allowed to wear some jewellery with their costumes, such as wedding rings or earrings. But Disney instruct staff that 'Cause bracelets, which remind our Guests of the realities of the outside world, are not permitted.'[3]

Disney has always imposed strict appearance rules for its employees, or 'Cast Members'. Fingernails must extend no more than a quarter of an inch past the fingertip. Sunglasses must not have opaque or mirrored lenses, and should be removed during any 'extended interaction' with customers. Facial hair, forbidden for many years, is now allowed but must be 'neatly groomed and well maintained'.[4]

In 2021 Disney announced a major overhaul of its appearance policies. *Disney Look*, the employees' rulebook, was revised to allow greater flexibility, particularly around gender expression. One significant change was that visible tattoos became permitted.[5]

Disney was following shifts in public opinion and behaviour in the USA. According to a 2019 IPSOS poll, 30 per cent of Americans had at least one tattoo, with the average tattooed person having four.[6] Tattoos were most common in those aged under thirty-four, and more popular among people with college degrees than those without. Most tattooed people do not regret their body art, but there are various websites and TV programmes dedicated to tattooing disasters, such as *Bad Ink*, *Tattoo Fixers* and *Bodyshockers*, which keep tattoos firmly in the mainstream.[7]

One emerging trend is the post-mastectomy tattoo. Women who have had mastectomies may choose to cover their breasts, chests and scars with ornate tattoos, often depicting flowers and plants, wildlife, or even bras.[8] Many women report that these tattoos are emotionally healing. 'Tattooing enabled me to put my own stamp on my scar,' said Diane, who chose an abstract design.[9] Others choose highly personal imagery. 'In honour of my paternal grandmother, Iris, who survived breast cancer in the 1950s, I had a beautiful flow of irises as my design,' said Kerry. 'Instead of a scar slashed across my chest, I had a beautiful, personal piece of art; I couldn't be happier with it.'[10]

Interviews with women who have chosen post-mastectomy tattoos reveal recurring themes of control, agency, femininity and self-esteem. Many women describe the process as a way of reclaiming their bodies from both the cancer and the ensuing treatment. They are a way of taking back control. 'I love my tattoo. I adore it,' said Elaine, whose tattoo shows flowers and birds in bright, beautiful colours. 'It's me claiming me back from cancer. Not the consultant's way, not the plastic surgeon's way. My way.'[11]

Other women relate the sense of control to a reclaimed femininity. 'I thought I was comfortable with my body post-mastectomy, but having the tattoo has transformed me,' Sarah G. described.

As I started to recover, I thought about how I didn't have a nipple there now, and it felt as if my femininity had been stripped away . . . I'm more body-confident now than I have ever been. I feel as if I've taken control not only of my body, but of myself as a woman. I've taken a life-changing and potentially detrimental experience, and turned it into a real positive.[12]

Juanita, whose post-mastectomy tattoo is an enormous pair of feathered wings covering her entire chest, gives a powerful message of unity.

My angel wings are a symbol of solidarity with my sisters around the world who have had breast cancer. There is beauty after breast cancer; it's a painful journey, and in some ways beauty hurts. But I feel happy and sexy when I look in the mirror now. I feel proud to be a woman – like I have been reborn.[13]

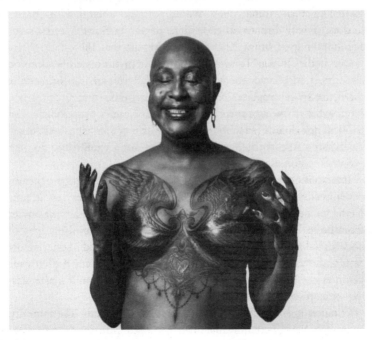

Juanita with her post-mastectomy tattoo

Modifying the body isn't all bad. We cannot live without ever modifying our bodies, and there's no reason why we should. At the most fundamental level, our bodies are ours and we may use and change them as we see fit.

As a political principle, the claim of the unmodified body is meant to be asserted as a defence. It defends each of us from the cultural pressures to feel bad about our bodies and therefore ourselves. It defends us from the social pressures to make changes to our bodies. It asserts our political equality. It is a demand to be accepted just as we are.

But is asserting the principle of the unmodified body too risky? One fear is that the principle of the unmodified body might be taken too far; used against someone who genuinely wants or needs modification. Not all desires for body modification are driven by social pressure alone. Some desires to modify seem to emanate from the body itself. 'Our bodies are not merely blank slates upon which the powers-that-be write their lessons,' writes Eli Clare, a writer, speaker and activist on disability and trans issues. 'We cannot ignore the body itself: the sensory, mostly non-verbal experience of our hearts and lungs, muscles and tendons, telling us and the world who we are.'[14]

Our bodies lead us to seek treatment for disease, modification for discomfort, surgery for enhancement. People's lives are transformed for the better by hip replacements, organ transplants, cancer treatments, tooth extractions, laser eye surgeries, hysterectomies, vasectomies. The political principle of the unmodified body neither condemns such treatments nor advocates withholding them. No one is expected to become a martyr to non-modification.

The political principle of the unmodified body asserts a premise, not a goal. The unmodified body is not a state of purity to be preserved, or a state of perfection to be attained. It's a foundational claim of value, a baseline to be protected. We can and should grant the unmodified body the status it deserves without suggesting that modification is never justified. We grant the unmodified body the status it deserves not by preventing or refusing all modification, but by resisting *social pressures to modify*.

Pressures to modify can be physical, mental, or social. The three are connected. Mental suffering and physical suffering are closely connected, and both can be caused by social pressure. Sometimes, the best way of alleviating suffering, distress, or simple dissatisfaction is by modifying the body. Body modification can be an effective coping strategy. But it's important to know whether the modification really is proven to relieve suffering, whether it's an evidence-based treatment. And it's important to ensure, at a political and social level, that we are not creating and recreating a society that causes suffering and then pushes modification as the only solution.

Often, the social pressures to modify are intense. When people are under strong social pressure to modify their bodies we should not condemn them for choosing to do so. Very often, submitting to a social norm is the most rational response to it. We don't necessarily do a person any favours if we deny her the means to fit in, to become socially acceptable, to feel comfortably invisible.

So the principle of the unmodified body must not be used by political or medical institutions to deny evidence-based procedures to people who genuinely need and want them.[15] It is a political principle of resistance that can be used by individuals to resist procedures that are not evidence-based, or that they don't really want. It urges restraint when acting on others, pressuring or persuading them that really their bodies ought to be different, to look better or to fit in with the group. And it demands collective forms of resistance against a culture of bodily inadequacy.

It's not always easy to tell the difference between interventions that really will help people live easier, healthier, more flourishing lives, and those that simply heap on anxiety and increase feelings of inadequacy. Sometimes, our best intentions backfire. This is particularly a problem for public health campaigns. Well-meaning attempts to improve public health sometimes make things worse. For example, attempts to reduce obesity by labelling foods with their calorie content can cause an increase in eating disorders, which are in themselves disastrous for both physical and mental health. Public health campaigns that aim to reduce obesity levels seldom succeed even on their own terms.[16] So, we must tread carefully when urging body modification on others, even where we think that modification would be health- and welfare-enhancing.

But what if the pressure to modify comes from within? What if our bodies simply don't feel normal to us, even if they are just like everyone else's? What if we feel that the body we are born with does not reflect who we truly are? What if we have the profound feeling that we were born in the wrong body, such that any authentic expression of identity, perhaps even any bearable existence, requires extensive surgical modification? This idea is perhaps the deepest challenge to the principle of the unmodified body.

Alternatively, what if we simply have the desire to change our bodies? What if we view our bodies as blank canvases, opportunities for creativity and self-expression? People with this perspective need not think that their bodies are wrong in any deep sense, need not view their bodies as somehow mistaken or inauthentic. They may simply see the body as one of the many ways in which they can express themselves; just as we choose our clothes and hairstyle, shape ourselves around our hobbies and allegiances, so too we may work on the body as one way of creating and communicating who we are. On this perspective, modification is a choice and should be respected as such. What then is the status and value of the unmodified body?

These ideas, the idea of being born in the wrong body and the idea of the body as the canvas for self-expression, are in tension: one portrays body modification as a free choice, the other portrays it as a necessity. And yet they are often found together, for example in transgender experience and theory. I'll investigate the political conditions that make both discourses possible, and the political implications of adopting each.

First, though, I'll consider a different logic of body modification: the idea that it is virtuous to make an effort, and that this virtuous effort applies to our bodies just as much, if not more, as to our minds.

SELF-CARE AS DUTY AND VIRTUE

I respect the time I spend each day treating my body, and I consider it part of my political work. It is possible to have some conscious input into our physical processes – not expecting the impossible, but allowing for the unexpected – a kind of training in self-love and physical resistance.

Audre Lorde, 'A Burst of Light' (1986)[17]

*The new emphasis on self-care represents a long-overdue rec-
ognition that a person's health and well-being is crucial.
Healing from traumatic life experiences, eating properly, keeping fit, making time for personal grooming – none of these are
extravagant or unreasonable aspirations.*

Emma Dabiri, *Don't Touch My Hair* (2019)[18]

Make it burn!

Jane Fonda, *Workout* (1982)[19]

It's good to make an effort. In life generally we praise effort and condemn laziness. We celebrate ambition and lament inertia. It's virtuous
to make the best of ourselves, to try to make ourselves the best we
can be.

That it is considered virtuous to make an effort to improve ourselves can be seen in all sorts of domains: in education, where we are
expected to work hard to improve our knowledge and qualifications;
in the disciplinary environments of school, family and prison, where
we are expected to conform or improve our behaviour and teach
others to do the same; in therapy and self-help, where we are expected
to introspect and question ourselves so that we can improve our mental health and emotional resilience; in our careers, where we are
expected to strive to improve our skills, status and salary in a steady
upwards trajectory; in our hobbies, where we are expected to improve
our accomplishments and smash our personal bests.

These generalized forms of virtuous effort are also found specifically in the bodily domain. We readily apply the ideas of virtue and
vice to the project of changing our bodies. It is considered morally
good to try to improve our health and hygiene, and morally bad to
refuse to do so. We praise each other for exercising and offer prizes
for physical fitness. We feel justified in judging someone who doesn't
bother to wash themselves, or wear clean clothes, or combat body
odour. We feel entitled to criticize people who smoke, eat unhealthily,
or do no exercise: some even advocate limiting access to healthcare
for people with bad habits.

We also readily apply a moralizing attitude to changes to the body
that aim at changing its appearance or identity. Norms of appearance

vary by class and context. It seems perfectly justifiable to criticize someone who makes no attempt to look smart and presentable in a work environment, despite having the means and know-how to do so. We expect people to dress appropriately for the occasion, which means different clothes for work, weekends and weddings. We often expect people to wear uniforms, to put forward an impression of identity, belonging, branding, or smartness. Someone who deliberately flouts a dress code, turning up to a traditional formal wedding in jeans and T-shirt, is doing something wrong. Conforming to norms like these can be a way of showing care and respect for others, showing solidarity by participating in a communal social event.

Of course, ideas of virtue and appearance can easily become oppressive and normalizing. Norms maintain their dominance when doing nothing to comply with them is interpreted negatively – as a sign of laziness, giving up, letting oneself go. Requiring everyone to fit a certain aesthetic has its limits: most of the time we should be free to make these choices for ourselves. As we've seen, appearance norms are very often deployed in the service of sexism, racism, classism: conformity to ideals that do not stand up to scrutiny.

But isn't it *good to make an effort*, whatever your aesthetic? If it's virtuous to strive at things like learning a language, practising a musical instrument, beating a personal best running time, or gaining a promotion, why isn't it similarly valuable to strive to improve your appearance? It's typical for the intellectual or academic to praise effort in matters of the mind but sneer at effort in matters of the body. But is that attitude really anything other than snobbishness, anything other than prejudice against those with different priorities?

Philosopher Heather Widdows argues that a significant part of the appeal of the beauty ideal is that it offers the chance of self-improvement, because the self, according to the beauty ideal, is 'always in progress'. The act of posting selfies on social media, which requires preparatory beauty work before the photo and then digital modification afterwards, demonstrates how beauty can give a sense of goal-directed achievement. 'The status of such images is illuminating; they stand between the actual self and the imagined self, steps upon the way,' she writes. 'Such images, like the engagement in beauty practices, can serve to prove that the self is improving and that we are doing what we should.'[20]

That virtue is generally assigned to effort in the domain of appearance is clear when we notice that we apply a different moral assessment to body modifications that have been worked for and those that haven't. If someone has put effort and hard work into body modification, we think of them as deserving the results. If their body hasn't required effort of the right sort – if it's the result of genetic good luck or some sort of cheating – then our moral assessment is harsher. On this logic, a dieter deserves more praise than someone who is naturally slim, or someone who has lost fat through liposuction, because the dieter has made more effort. The natural bodybuilder is more virtuous than the steroid user because the former has had to create his body with hard work, whereas the steroid user has taken the easy option – not in terms of health and side-effects, but in terms of time in the gym. 'People always ask me, when they saw me in the gym in the *Pumping Iron* days, they say "Why is it that you are working out so hard? Five hours a day, six hours a day, and you always have a smile on your face?"' says Arnold Schwarzenegger, in a video described on YouTube as 'the speech that broke the internet'.

> I said, 'Because for me, I am shooting for a goal! In front of me is the Mr. Universe title. So every rep that I do gets me closer to accomplishing that goal: to make this goal, this vision, turn into reality. Every single set that I do, every repetition, every weight that I lift will get me a step closer to turn this goal into reality.' So I couldn't wait to do another 500-pound squat! I couldn't wait to do another 500-pound bench press! I couldn't wait to do another 2000 reps of sit ups![21]

So, does the idea of body modification as virtuous effort, enjoyable goal-directed action, undermine the political principle of the unmodified body? On one level, not at all. The principle of the unmodified body says nothing about the virtue or otherwise of engaging in acts of modification. It does not assert that modification is bad or that the unmodified body is superior. Its focus is less on the process of modification than on the motivation and context for that modification. Its target is what happens, politically speaking, when modification becomes the standard response to social pressure, and when modification is motivated by the need to change in order to be treated as something approximating an equal. None of this need say anything against engaging in body modification as an act of self-improvement motivated by pleasure in doing your best.

On another level, though, it is very hard to disentangle social pressures to modify from personal motivation, because the two so often work in tandem. Take dieting. A recent survey by Girlguiding UK found that half of girls aged eleven to twenty-one had been on a diet, and 40 per cent of girls aged between seven and ten felt they should lose weight.[22] This feeling is not confined to young girls: one UK poll found that the average person tries 126 fad diets in their lifetime.[23] According to the *Washington Post* 45 million Americans go on a diet every year.[24] Some of them probably do need to lose weight for health reasons – 70 per cent of adults in the US are overweight or obese[25] – and some of them will probably feel better if they do so. After all, what you eat really does affect your health and your well-being: whether you feel sluggish or energized, whether clothes fit or chafe, whether exercise is invigorating or hellish, whether your immune system is robust or struggling. It would be odd to imply that dieting is always bad, or that people who are trying to lose weight are just deluded victims of social pressure.

But it is also true that diets simply don't work. In fact, nearly 95 per cent of diets fail.[26] Of course, you can lose weight by following a diet, and almost any diet will work in the short term. But diets are not generally something that people can follow for long periods. Sooner or later eating patterns return to normal and the weight returns. To embark on a process of dieting is almost inevitably to embark on a process of anxiety and guilt. It is to succumb to precisely the pressures that the principle of the unmodified body seeks to counteract. And it is to succumb to a cycle that is entirely counterproductive. Poor body image and shame about your body are more likely to lead you to engage in harmful behaviours: you're more likely to eat unhealthily, smoke, take illegal drugs and get inadequate exercise if you feel bad about your body.[27] Long-term food restriction can leave you feeling hungry all the time, and plays havoc with metabolism and menstruation. Some leading fitness YouTubers like Stephanie Buttermore have advocated going 'all in', eating without restriction as a method of resetting appetite. It's important for our health to respect and take care of our bodies, not punish them with cycles of dieting and feelings of shame.[28]

The idea that it is an act of self-improvement to work on our bodies all too easily morphs into the idea that a sub-optimal body is evidence of personal failure and inadequate effort. As Widdows notes, selfie culture rests on the idea that we can measure progress in our self-improvement quest by monitoring our appearance and inviting others to rank it. This practice, of submitting images of oneself for surveillance and ranking, spans many body-modification practices, including dieting and weight loss, fitness and bodybuilding, hair and make-up, and gender transformation.

The discussion board at bodybuilding.com includes a popular forum, 'Post Your Pictures and Introduce Yourself', where new members are encouraged to post their photos and receive advice on how they should start or change their bodybuilding routines. The threads are full of photos of men in their underwear, posting with questions like 'Is my overall physique alright in terms of bodybuilding?' and 'Critique my physique what do I need to work on?'[29] 'Legs', says the first response. 'Chest and arms if going for aesthetics', says the second. 'Arms' says the third. The fourth reply is more reassuring, but he's not so kind to himself.

> Hey man! First of all, great stuff, man! You are right where I want to be. We even have the same arch on the back is that Normal? Since you already have the legs part covered, I don't think anything else needs work. You look perfect, brother! Keep it up! How long have you been working out?[30]

Body modification itself can be felt and experienced as an act of self-care. Having a haircut, manicure, or tattoo; going to the gym, a yoga class, or for a run; spending time on make-up or shaving – all these can be forms of nurture. They can be a way of giving our bodies, and thus ourselves, due attention. Spending time on our bodies is spending time on ourselves. I once took a yoga class with a teacher whose captivating words during the final guided relaxation were 'No one needs anything from you . . . No one wants anything from you.'

It's in this spirit that Emma Dabiri takes the phrase 'Reclaiming My

Time', used iconically by US Representative Maxine Moore Waters in response to the evasive answers given by President Trump's Treasury Secretary, and re-applies it to the theft of black people's time more generally. 'These three simple words,' Dabiri writes, 'were a subversion. They represented the reversal of the weight of generations of accumulated violence, of centuries of free black labour that still remain unpaid.'[31] This theft of time can be measured in large and small ways, but Dabiri uses the idea in part to push back against the perception, particularly popular among white people, that styling and caring for natural Afro hair takes too long. 'On a practical and basic level,' she insists, 'reclaiming my time is rejecting a lifestyle that prevents us from doing our damn hair.'[32]

Why is it that self-care so often focuses on changing the body, particularly for women? Masculine modification discourses are more usually framed around goals and results: achievement rather than self-nurture. It would be all too easy to see only the pernicious aspects of the idea that body modification is self-care for women. Because a woman's body is never good enough, any investment in changing that body can be soothing. It is a reassurance that something is being done, an alleviation of guilt, a feeling of virtue that is in itself a relief. Because the appearance and attractiveness of a woman's body is the most important thing about her, synonymous with her very identity and worth, time spent on the body truly is time spent on the self. To buff the thighs is to buff the ego.

But there are also positive aspects to the common alliance between body modification and self-care. The principle of the unmodified body is about rejecting the idea that the appearance of the body is the most important thing about it – rejecting the idea that who we are is how we look – but at the same time, it asserts the connection between our bodies and our selves. The sorts of body modification that are routinely undertaken as part of self-care don't only make our bodies look good; many of them make it feel good, too.

Beauty procedures like haircuts, manicures, pedicures and facials can be enjoyable from a sensuous perspective. Often these procedures are not entirely pleasurable – exfoliation and cuticle work can be uncomfortable, sitting under heat lamps or foil at the hairdresser's can be tedious – but they include a good amount of what Widdows calls the 'beauty touch'. 'The importance of touch for human beings is hard to overestimate,' she writes. 'In a world where touch is often [only] sexual, or between parent and child, the beauty touch is a permitted and acceptable form of touch, and one where prolonged adult-to-adult touch is allowed.'[33] Touch is nurturing, and beauty practices are one way, perhaps the only way, for women to experience nurturing touch uncomplicated by sexual obligation.

There's also an embodied reality to the pleasure of other forms of body modification and body work, including the form most socially acceptable for men. Fitness and weight training bring not only the social and identity rewards of conformity to masculine norms. They also bring a significant physical and mental boost. There is ample evidence of the impact of physical exercise on mood.[34] In fact, exercise is one of the best evidence-based treatments for low mood and depression.

You don't have to be depressed to get joy from exercise. One of the most memorable scenes in the bodybuilding film *Pumping Iron* is Schwarzenegger's gleeful description of the thrill of the pump:

> The greatest feeling you can get in the gym, or the most satisfying feeling you can get in the gym, is the pump. Let's say you train your biceps. Blood is rushing into your muscles and that's what we call 'the pump'. Your muscles get a really tight feeling like your skin is going to explode any minute: you know, it's really tight, it's like somebody blowing air into your muscle, it just blows up, and it feels different, it feels fantastic. It's as satisfying to me as coming is, you know, as having sex with a woman and coming! So can you believe how much I am in heaven? I am like, uh, getting the feeling of coming in the gym, the feeling of coming at home, the feeling of coming backstage when I pump up, when I pose out in front of 5,000 people, I get the same feeling, so I'm coming day and night! I mean that's terrific, right?[35]

Choosing to modify our bodies can have many benefits. It can be a virtuous act, one that shows respect for others or a way of making an effort to improve. It can be an act of self-care, reclaiming time and attention for oneself and feeling good in the process. I don't want to dismiss any of these ways of choosing to modify your body. But I have tried to show how norms can be oppressive, how effort can become punishment, how pleasure can be elusive if the body is never allowed to be good enough just as it is.

But what if the body simply *isn't* good enough as it is?

BORN IN THE WRONG BODY

I was born with the wrong body, being feminine by gender but male by sex, and I could achieve completeness only when the one was adjusted to the other.

Jan Morris, *Conundrum* (1974)[36]

I didn't make changes to my sexed body so as to conform to gendered ideas of what my body should look like. I did it so that I could finally be complete in myself, and free from the shock of being divided in presence that had plagued me since I entered puberty.

C. N. Lester, *Trans Like Me* (2017)[37]

The idea that a trans person is someone who is born in the wrong body is a familiar trope of early trans writing and theory, and one that is still used today. It can be traced back to the late nineteenth century, when Havelock Ellis popularized the concept of 'inverts' to describe people who rejected heterosexual sex and/or gender norms. 'Many women in the 1920s did effectively change sex inasmuch as they passed as men, took wives as men, and lived lives as men,' writes gender scholar Jack Halberstam (writing as Judith).[38] Whether today's greater tolerance and technology would lead such women to identify as lesbian or as trans is difficult to tell; most likely, experiences would vary.

Humanities professor Bernice Hausman analyses several autobiographies by celebrity trans pioneers. Most described themselves as 'transsexuals', meaning a person who has had, intends, or desires to have surgical modification (usually breast implants or mastectomy, and genital surgery). Hausman shows how many of those trans pioneers deployed versions of the *born in the wrong body* narrative. One clear statement of the principle is found in Jan Morris's autobiography, just quoted. Another example is Nancy Hunt, who in her autobiography *Mirror Image* declares:

> Women do differ from men, quite apart from anatomy. And I always sensed which one I was – again, quite apart from anatomy. I was not a man. I was a woman. And if my anatomy did not confirm this classification, then in the final event it was going to be easier to change my anatomy than to change myself.[39]

Historian Joanne Meyerowitz finds similar accounts in her studies of trans people in the 1950s and 1960s. She describes how, in the very early years of what was then known as sex change or sex reassignment surgery (SRS), 'hundreds of people wrote to, telephoned, and visited doctors to inquire about sex change surgery'.[40] They were motivated by a strong feeling that the bodies they had were wrong. Their ultimate desire was not to change that feeling by coming to a place where they felt better about the bodies they had, but rather to change their bodies. Crucially, this strong desire for body modification was not experienced by these early seekers of surgery as merely a desire for cosmetic change. Instead, it was closely allied with a very deep sense of *identity*. As Meyerowitz argues, 'many transsexuals simply rejected the notion that the bodies they were born with represented their true or permanent sex. For many, the truth of sex lay in the sense of self, not in the visible body.'[41]

Born in the wrong body discourses include accounts of dysphoria that are not put in those precise terms, and so I will sometimes refer to them as dysphoria discourses. Trans writer C. N. Lester sought surgery as part of their identity as genderqueer. Through surgery, Lester writes, 'I learnt what it was to feel comfortable in my own skin. That basic and extraordinary freedom – of finally feeling at peace in my own body.'[42] Lester describes dysphoria as a 'savage pain' that, for some people, only surgery can salve.[43] 'For me,' Lester writes, 'it becomes an issue of personal alignment, of revealing the body already felt to be there.'[44]

Similarly, trans woman Michelle O'Brien writes:

> Every morning, when I wake up, I swallow a single pill of Proscar, a five milligram dosage of Finasteride. Every two weeks I give myself an intramuscular injection of one ml of Delestrogen, a synthetic hormone.

I do these things because I like what they do to my body. I take these drugs because my body, for as long as I can remember, never fit quite right. And I believe that these drugs will help me find myself, be myself and live as myself.

Eventually, I developed a story about my gender to talk about this bad fitting, this mismatch between what I felt and what people saw. This story helped me to understand that I wanted to use these drugs, that I wanted to grow breasts and experience their other effects. It's a story I've encountered elsewhere, that other people I've met also tell about themselves. A story about being trans.[45]

As Humanities scholar Jay Prosser puts it, 'My contention is that transsexuals continue to deploy the image of wrong embodiment because being trapped in the wrong body is simply what transsexuality feels like.'[46]

Born in the wrong body/dysphoria discourses share three features: the experience of dissonance between body and mind, locating the problem in the body not the mind, and concluding that body modification is the solution.

First, there is the experience of dissonance between body and mind. The bodies that these trans people had did not feel right to them: did not feel authentic, did not feel comfortable, did not feel truly theirs. This experience is verifiable only by taking an internal perspective. It is something that must be experienced for oneself. 'Those looking to know how it feels, to have a chance at life in a congruent body, free of dysphoria?' writes Lester. 'Just listen to trans people and what we know of our own lives.'[47]

Second, *born in the wrong body*/dysphoria discourses include the claim that the cause of the distress is the body rather than the mind; or, to put it another way, that the true, authentic self is the one found in the mind. If there's a mismatch between the body and the mind it could in principle be either the mind or the body that's wrong. Sometimes, we locate the fault squarely in the mind. The layperson's understanding of anorexia is that is a form of deep distress caused by a mismatch between body and mind: put crudely, an anorexic wants to be much thinner than she is. In this sense the anorexic is like the person with gender dysphoria. But the usual response to the anorexic is to say that it is her mind that is at fault, because her body is plenty thin enough already. So, treatment for anorexics acknowledges their distress as real, but locates the problem in the mind. The goal of treatment is that the mind should change to accept the body. According to *born in the wrong body*/dysphoria discourse, the opposite is true for trans people: the mind is authentic, and the body is wrong. 'Coming into myself after physical transition was the most extraordinary sensation,' writes Lester. 'It was like waking up well after interminable illness.'[48]

Third, *born in the wrong body*/dysphoria discourse concludes that the correct treatment is body modification. This is a distinct claim from the previous one – that the source of the problem is the body rather than the mind – because one possible response to the first two features (dissonance between mind and body, locating the problem in the body) would be a determination to make the best of a bad situation. In other words, one could in principle believe sincerely that one's body was not a correct fit for one's identity, that one's body was flawed or did not adequately represent one's authentic self, but nevertheless recognize that changing one's body was difficult or undesirable and that work on the mind was the best solution. Changing the body could, in principle, be rejected as too risky, too painful, too costly, or unlikely to succeed.

Many burns victims experience strong dissonance between body and mind and locate the problem in the body, especially those who suffer facial burns. The suddenly damaged face no longer represents the authentic identity of the person inside. Recall that James Partridge felt so alienated from his burned face that he called it *IT*. Such burns victims will undergo many rounds of plastic surgery to repair their injuries, but, despite all this, they have to accept that their faces are never again going to match their previous incarnation or their sense of self, and so they will need to learn mental strategies for coping with and, ultimately, embracing their bodies. Partridge argues that work on their own mental and social attitudes is the only solution for burns victims' dysphoria.

In contrast, *born in the wrong body*/dysphoria discourse concludes not only that the body is the true source of distress, but also that the best form of treatment is body modification. As Meyerowitz puts it, 'most [transsexuals] had what they described as deeply rooted, long-standing, and irrepressible yearnings, and they wanted medical treatment, sometimes with an urgency that bordered on obsession.'[49] For Prosser, 'what makes the transsexual able and willing to submit to the knife – the splitting, cutting, removal, and reshaping of organs, tissues, and skin that another might conceive as mutilation – is the desire to get the body back to what it should have been.'[50]

Jake Edwards, who identifies as non-binary, rejects the phrase *born in the wrong body* but describes their experience using the three features I've identified as part of dysphoria discourse. 'Personally, I absolutely do not think my body is wrong; I don't feel that there was a mistake when I was born, and I don't think I needed to "fix" myself,' Edwards writes.

> As someone who has taken hormones and had surgery, I view those things as ... how can I put it? ... kind of personal upgrades to who I was supposed to be, if that makes sense? Not that they'd be right for other people. Sure, I may have seen those upgrades as essential, but my body wasn't wrong without them. Surgery was essential for me to live my happiest and most fulfilling life, because I could look at myself in the mirror and see something that reflected the inside.[51]

Edwards's account is from the blog of Mermaids, a charity and campaigning organization that exists to support and affirm gender-diverse children and their families. Mermaids describes a shift in its own practices regarding the use of *born in the wrong body* discourse. In September 2020 Mermaids announced that it would no longer use the phrase. 'We recently posted that "no child is born in the wrong body", which is our broad position as a charity,' the organization's blog says. 'Why? Because we believe that transgender people shouldn't be expected or encouraged to reject their entire amazing, intelligent, beautiful, creative bodies, simply because of gender incongruity. Still, we also know some people – including some of our amazing patrons – do use that phrase to express who they are.'[52]

As Mermaids notes, some trans people do still find the phrase apposite, and many trans people who dislike the phrase still describe an experience of gender dysphoria that uses the same logic. For example, the Mermaids blog entry includes a personal account from celebrity trans activist Munroe Bergdorf:

> Model, campaigner and Mermaids patron, Munroe Bergdorf used to say she was born in the wrong body but then decided it wasn't right for her: 'I've come to understand why the phrase "born in the wrong body" is unhelpful to me. I know why I used to use it; because other people struggled to understand, but looking back I know it did me harm. Saying you have the wrong body feels like a kind of self-abuse, and it's not the same as saying "I need to adjust my body to be my true self". That's a different thing.'[53]

Bergdorf's account is puzzling because she describes *born in the wrong body* terminology as 'self-abuse' yet thinks of body modification as necessary to adjust the body to her 'true self'. But if her unmodified body was not her true self, how could describing it as wrong be an act of *self*-abuse? Similarly, Edwards states that their unmodified body was not wrong, and yet describes body modification as 'essential'.

The puzzle is partially explained when we realize that *born in the wrong body* discourse is particularly associated with the medicalization of trans identity, and the diagnostic criteria used to gate-keep access to medical treatment, especially genital surgery. Many trans theorists argue that *born in the wrong body* discourse is learned by trans people and repeated as a necessary fiction to access surgery.[54] Trans people describe how treatment protocols restricted access to hormones, and especially surgery, to people with a clinical diagnosis of dysphoria – and the conditions for obtaining such a diagnosis have traditionally been oppressive and reductive. In particular, trans activists strongly criticize medical and legal protocols that require trans people to 'live as' their preferred gender for prolonged periods of time before accessing surgery. These protocols are intended to ensure that trans people are serious about transition, that they will not regret irreversible surgery, and to prepare them for living in their preferred gender. Critics argue that these requirements force trans people to adapt gender stereotypes of clothing and deportment rather than live in an authentic way, and that they put trans people at risk of harm since they require them to present themselves as a member of their preferred gender before they have undergone the physical transitions necessary to do so without being challenged or threatened. So *born in the wrong body* talk becomes associated with an unwelcome medicalization and pathologization of trans lives.

The medicalization of trans identity can be oppressive and insulting, but it can also be useful from a trans rights perspective to retain a sense that gender identity is a medical issue. If hormones and surgery are nothing more than a preference or an enhancement there's no reason to consider them anything more than a luxury; if dysphoria is a medical condition, they become an entitlement. Medical gatekeeping is the price that must be paid for receiving hormones and surgery as a medical treatment, paid for by health insurance or socialized medicine.

Moreover, *born in the wrong body* discourse, complete with its medicalizing and pathologizing overtones, seems necessary if one is to justify medicating trans children with puberty blockers and, ultimately, cross-sex hormones, a treatment protocol that Mermaids defends. *Born in the wrong body* discourse implies that there is an objective, clinical truth to gender identity; that some people are clinically transgender, in a way that can be diagnosed even in childhood; and that the appropriate treatment for gender dysphoria is not psychological (changing feelings) but physiological (changing bodies). Since this is Mermaids' view, its recent use of *born in the wrong body* discourse is unsurprising.

Adopting this perspective implies accepting that trans identity is a clinical or psychological condition, justifying gate-keeping and diagnosis by physicians. Clinical diagnosis and prescription are necessary to allocate treatments fairly in the context of scarce resources for healthcare, and to ensure that treatments are only provided when there are sufficient clinical indications for them, to avoid harm to people who are wrongly diagnosed by themselves or others. These practices are appropriate, just as they are with all other clinical conditions and treatments, if modification for gender identity is understood as a treatment for dysphoria. On that understanding modification treatments such as surgery and hormones should never be given to anyone, adult or child, just on their say-so. Doctors retain their traditional role as experts whose job it is to diagnose and prescribe treatment. The diagnostic criteria, and the prerequisites for transition, may need to change in accordance with improved scientific, sociological and ethical evidence. But clinical oversight is a necessary implication of *born in the wrong body*/dysphoria discourse.

What are the political conditions that make *born in the wrong body* discourse possible? The feeling of distress with one's own body is in no way unique to trans people, although it is typically much more intense for them. It is the generalized condition of modern society. It is a position particularly sold to and adopted by women and girls, as I've shown throughout. Girls who go through female puberty *normally* (in the sense of typically) emerge feeling profoundly wrong in their new bodies. Of course, most girls don't ultimately seek body modification to distance themselves from womanhood. But the number of people born female who identify as trans or non-binary has soared: in the UK, official figures showed that the number of born females receiving gender treatment rose 'more than 4,000% in less than a decade'.[55] And body modification for gender identity does not just affect trans people. Virtually all girls and women engage in multiple modifications, both surgical and non-surgical, to *conform* to gender roles. Becoming a woman, in the gendered sense, is not easy for anyone.

Body image anxiety and modification for gender is also experienced by many men and boys. 'Shame and masculinity have a reciprocal relationship,' writes David Adjmi in a piece describing his attempts to conform to masculine gender norms through bodybuilding. 'Men are shamed into hating anything feminine in themselves and the world, and if they dare to question that hatred, they are forced to relive the shame.' For Adjmi, this shame accompanies body modification rather than being alleviated by it. 'The more I tried to perfect my body at the gym, the more wrapped up I got in all this shame.'[56]

As we've seen, there are countless ways that we are taught that our bodies are wrong, countless bodily standards that we are compelled to meet, countless connections drawn and barriers erected between looking one way and being another. To be a man you must be masculine, to be masculine you must be strong, to be strong you must be muscly. To be a woman you must be feminine, to be feminine you must be beautiful, to be beautiful you must be thin. If you're thin you're not manly;

if you're fat you're not feminine. There is always something else we could and should change: more or less hair, muscle, or make-up; darker or lighter skin, a taller or shorter body, larger or smaller breasts, thicker or leaner biceps, fatter or thinner buttocks, more or fewer piercings, presence or absence of a foreskin, looser or tighter vagina, larger penis or no penis, breast enlargements or chest binding, packing or tucking, facial hair or electrolysis ...

There is no end to body dissatisfaction, and no end to the ways in which we can be improved. In this context, trans people's experience of dysphoria should not be considered as evidence of pathology but as evidence of humanity. That some feel it more than others, that for some the feeling is fleeting while for others it is all-consuming, is evidence of our individuality. It is evidence of the host of ways in which we all have different psychological, social and material resources to deal with cultural imperatives. It is also evidence of the constraints we live under. As pioneering trans theorist Sandy Stone writes, 'Under the binary phallocentric founding myth by which Western bodies and subjects are authorized, only one body per gendered subject is "right". All other bodies are wrong.'[57]

So, the first premise of *born in the wrong body*/dysphoria discourse, that the body is wrong, is part of the general social landscape. And the same is true of the second and third premises: that the authentic self is the one found in the mind rather than the body; and that the proper solution is to change the body. Feminist philosopher Cressida Heyes argues that these, too, are reflective of the modern condition more generally, part of the social norm of *care of the self*.

This norm has a rather contradictory character. On the one hand, the idea behind *care of the self* is that we must each discover and create our unique, authentic inner selves. This authenticity and uniqueness mean that our created and curated self should be different from anyone else's. On the other hand, since we must all engage in the project of *care of the self*, self-realization itself becomes a normalizing goal. All of us must do the same thing. There's a tension, in other words, between the goals of conformity and the goals of uniqueness: to fit in, we must be different; to be different, we must act like everyone else.

The dominant norm of *care of the self*, as Heyes understands it, relies on the premise that we all do in fact *have* an authentic inner self.

According to the norm, this inner self is something that is inherent within us: an essential part of who we really are. It's not open to us to create any sort of self we wish: we must become our real, true selves. 'You do you!' as the saying goes. At the same time our true, authentic self is not something that announces its presence without help. Our inner self may be hidden, even from ourselves; certainly, it is not always obvious to others. And so we must *work*: first to identify our inner selves – the work of self-knowledge – and then to reveal that self to others.

Heyes points out how the contemporary norm of *care of the self* requires that the visible, external self – the body – is brought in line with our discovered inner identity. Body modification becomes an individualized project that everyone must participate in. In other words, the current social norm in Western societies synthesizes several apparently conflicting values: authenticity; an inner essence, nature, or core; transformation; individuality; and conformity. Everyone is expected to transform or modify themselves, especially their bodies, in order to reveal their own inner essence, their authentic selfhood. Our chosen methods differ. Some use dieting, others bodybuilding; some use cosmetic surgery, others clothes and make-up; some conform to their sex/gender role, others seek to leave it behind. But we are all engaged in the same, socially mandated project: constructing authenticity, conforming to uniqueness.

We're left with two conflicting ideas:

1. Your real self is to be found within, possibly deep within, and will require work to be revealed. This work may need to be psychological, physical, or both. You will need to work on yourself to find yourself, and then you'll need to work on your body to make it fit the self you have discovered. *This is the logic of the modified body.*

2. Your real self is whoever you actually are, right now, including what your body is like. You do not need to do any work to be truly you. You are already you, and you always will be. *This is the logic of the unmodified body.*

These ideas conflict, but each is hard to let go of entirely. The reassurance offered by the principle of the unmodified body is up against the transformative potential of the ideal of *care of the self*.

Kate Bornstein perfectly illustrates the dilemma. Bornstein's account of her own trans identity centres the experience of wrongness. 'I've no idea what "a woman" feels like,' she writes. 'I never did feel like a girl or a woman; rather, it was my unshakeable conviction that I was not a boy or a man. It was the absence of feeling, rather than its presence, that convinced me to change my gender.'[58] So, for Bornstein, being trans meant rejecting the gender into which she was originally placed, which in her case meant being classified as a boy/man as the result of being born with a male-sexed body. Bornstein reveals that her own identity as a woman was based on antipathy not (just) towards masculine roles but towards her own male body parts, in particular her penis. 'I never hated my penis,' she writes.

> I hated that it made me a man – in my own eyes, and in the eyes of others. For my comfort, I needed a vagina – I was convinced that the only way I could live out what I thought to be my true gender was to have genital surgery to construct a vagina from my penis. Fortunately, I don't regret having done this.[59]

In this respect, Bornstein employs the logic of the modified body.

But at the same time, Bornstein endorses the principle of the unmodified body. She recognizes that sex/biological gender *is in fact* used as a highly salient cue for gender as a whole, but she argues that it *should not be*. This is unsurprising: rejecting the connection between biological sex and experienced gender is essential to trans identity and theory. After all, if one's biological sex did in fact determine one's gender, than being trans would be either impossible or pathological. Since being trans is certainly possible, and since trans people, theory and activism strongly reject the idea that trans is pathology, the connection between biology and gender must be forcefully denied. 'Belief in biological gender is in fact a belief in the supremacy of the body in the determination of identity,'[60] Bornstein writes. She is clear that this belief is not one she shares. 'In the mid-80s, when I first got involved with women's politics, and gay and lesbian politics, I saw these buttons that read "KEEP YOUR LAWS OFF MY BODY!" or "BIOLOGY IS NOT DESTINY!" I thought they were particularly relevant to my situation as a transsexual.'[61]

Bornstein does not fully explain how these two parts of her account are compatible. But her analysis is essentially political. She ultimately makes a feminist argument for the end of gender as a political system, something she sees as being oppressive to everyone, trans or not. At the same time, she recognizes that the gender system is pervasive and powerful: virtually everyone has to participate in it so as to survive physically and emotionally. So, one might reject a system in political terms, while feeling compelled to submit to it in personal terms.

In the face of the onslaught of a gender system that requires us to fit our identities, personalities, preferences and power to match our sexed bodies, we can either submit or we can resist. Submission to gender norms may be possible within our unmodified sexed bodies, or it may be possible for us, personally, only by modifying our sexed bodies. There should be no shame in modification. Very often, finding a way to conform to norms as dominant and consequential as gender norms is the only realistic option. But the possibility of resistance should always be upheld.

For some people, body modification *is* their form of resistance.

CREATIVITY AND
THE BODY AS BLANK CANVAS

Carnal art is self-portraiture in the classical sense, but realised through the possibility of technology ... Carnal art transforms the body into language.
ORLAN, 'Manifesto of Carnal Art' (1989)[62]

ORLAN is a performance artist famous for undergoing repeated plastic surgeries to transform her face and body. ORLAN constructs these surgeries so that they are works of art in the process, not just in the product: the procedures are filmed, she remains conscious throughout, she lies on the operating table wearing clothes designed by fashion designers. ORLAN had nine different cosmetic surgeries between 1990 and 1995, some of them aiming to recreate facial features found in classical art, others more bizarre. Her most notorious surgery gave her implants in her forehead like little horns.

ORLAN understands her work as both a practice and a critique of body modification: it is, as her manifesto states, interested in 'the spectacle and discourse of the modified body'. She identifies as a feminist artist, and describes her work in the following terms, as related by journalist Stuart Jeffries:

> Was she trying make herself more beautiful? 'No, my goal was to be different, strong; to sculpt my own body to reinvent the self. It's all about being different and creating a clash with society because of that. I tried to use surgery not to better myself or become a younger version of myself, but to work on the concept of image and surgery the other way around. I was the first artist to do it,' she says, proudly.[63]

Body modification can also be valued as creativity or self-realization: the body is a blank canvas, a project to be worked on, a way of coming into being as piece of art or self-made identity. The idea that the body is a blank canvas for self-expression can be seen most clearly in modification practices that literally inscribe themselves on the body: paradigmatically tattooing and piercing. These practices cast body modification not as normalizing, but as autonomous, individualized, free. Counter-cultural modifications seek to set the subject apart from others, or perhaps to situate her within a sub-culture understood as importantly distinct from the homogeneous mainstream.

According to this logic, a creative modification will be one that is self-directed, unique, one that contributes to diversity, perhaps one that is explicitly rebellious, one that is driven by pleasure or else aimed at a *telos*, a purposeful goal. An uncreative modification is one that is normalizing, that aims at conformity, one that is insufficiently motivated and not thought-through, or driven by self-loathing or fear of being different.

Some people who pursue body modification as creativity describe the process as changing the self. One striking case is Sylvain Helaine, a man who has tattoos covering every part of his body. Even the whites of his eyes have been surgically dyed black. Helaine's body is about as modified as it is possible to be. In an interview with CNN, he described his tattooing journey as beginning when he had an 'existential crisis', meaning a crisis about his own sense of self and existence.[64]

Creativity is also available in the everyday, routine forms of modification such as hairstyling and make-up – at least insofar as the make-up is decidedly non-natural. Both hair and make-up offer low-risk ways of experimenting with your appearance: they allow the creative use of colour and form, integrate brushwork, artistry and maths.[65] The creativity and empowerment involved in hairstyling and make-up can be illusory but it can be genuine too, sometimes both at once. I have a lipstick with the shade name 'SUCCESSFUL': when I wear it, I mock its pretension at precisely the same moment I allow it to give me a boost.

Body modification for gender identity can be understood as creative, too. Some trans people and theorists reject *born in the wrong body* discourse not just because it has been used as a way of gate-keeping treatment or pathologizing trans people, but because they see it as distorting trans experience and denying trans people agency over their bodies. According to this view, body modification for gender identity can be an end in itself, not merely a clinically prescribed treatment for a psychological disorder. Treatments such as puberty blockers, cross-sex hormones and surgery are, on this account, legitimate choices for anyone to make for whatever reason they see fit. And so, hormones and surgery for gender identity should generally be available on demand. Many people with this perspective explicitly compare body modifications for gender with cosmetic surgery. For example, trans activist and academic lawyer Dean Spade notes that critics of transgender body modifications 'fail to include in their analysis the fact that people (trans-sexuals and non-transsexuals) change their gender presentation to conform to norms with other technologies as well, including clothing, makeup, cosmetic surgery not labelled SRS, training in gender-specific manners, body-building, dieting, and countless other practices'.[66]

One striking example of conceptualizing the body as a blank canvas, the raw material from which to craft a persona, is found in queer theorist Jack Halberstam's account of undergoing 'top surgery' or a double mastectomy, a procedure Halberstam chose as part of his gender identity. Halberstam describes a conversation with his mastectomy surgeon, Dr Li:

> Doctor Li was calm and reassuring. 'Why did you become a plastic surgeon?' I asked him moments before going under. 'I always wanted to become an architect,' he answered. 'And plastic surgery allows me to build structures out of flesh.'

Some people might have found this response odd, but Doctor Li's answer thrilled me. It only raised my confidence in his abilities and in his understanding of me, and my body. Together we were building something in flesh, changing the architecture of my body forever. The procedure was not about building maleness into my body; it was about editing some part of the femaleness that currently defined me. I did not think I would awake as a new self, only that some of my bodily contours would shift in ways that gave me a different bodily abode.[67]

This metaphor is not body-as-canvas but body-as-building: a structure that can – should? – be architecturally designed, a home made out of flesh and blood. There's a clear distinction between Halberstam's account and *born in the wrong body* discourse, because Halberstam does not expect surgery to create a new self, nor does he use the language of a true self. Instead, he is excited by the thought of having a 'different bodily abode'.

Thinking of modification for gender as a form of creative expression invites the analogy between gender-affirming surgery and cosmetic surgery; and, of course, both are performed by cosmetic surgeons. Hugh McLean is a Canadian cosmetic surgeon well-known for his surgeries on trans people. His website's home page features a glittering green banner advertising 'current promotions' – something that professional cosmetic-surgery associations in the UK regard as unethical. His description of what he calls 'FTM top surgery', meaning double mastectomies on people born female in response to their masculine gender identity, smuggles in a sentence about side-effects in the midst of a heady set of promises. It's a sort of 'Where's Wally?' of informed consent. See if you can spot it:

FTM Top Surgery is designed to remove breast tissue and create a flatter, masculine appearing chest. There are 2 most common surgical techniques that can be used to achieve this: a 'double incision' and 'keyhole or peri-areolar'. Regardless of which technique is used, the aim is the same: to help your body conform to your self-image. No procedure is able to assure that sensation is retained and the main difference in the procedures is the amount of scarring. People who have top surgery often say that they are finally able to get on with their lives, that they now appear the way they should, and that they are more confident in their role in life.[68]

Although he mentions the specific needs of trans and non-binary clients, and although his website strongly suggests that the procedure will alleviate gender dysphoria, it is clear that McLean sees top surgery as just another form of cosmetic surgery. 'For us,' the website says, 'the diagnosis is made by the patient, not the doctor, in the same way that a patient seeking breast enlargement is the one who diagnoses her own breasts as too small.'[69]

The idea that modification for gender should be a matter of choice, just like other cosmetic surgery, is found in the writings of many trans theorists and activists. For Halberstam,

> to the extent that trans* bodies are subject to psychiatric scrutiny for the choices people may make about body modification, it should only be for the same reasons that other non/trans bodies fall into at-risk categories. That is, while currently non/transgender men and women do not have to undergo psychiatric evaluation before having any kind of cosmetic surgery, so transgender men and women should be able to elect body modifications without psychiatric evaluation unless they too exhibit unstable behaviors.[70]

If body modification for gender identity should be considered a free choice akin to cosmetic surgery, then trans people should be considered *consumers* of hormones and surgery, with their preferences the only prescription needed. That view may be appealing from a trans rights perspective, since it casts trans people as autonomous choosers rather than disordered victims. However, the free choice view has a disadvantage from a trans rights perspective: if modification for gender is comparable to cosmetic surgery, then surgery and hormones become a discretionary lifestyle choice. The implication then is that they should be funded by individuals, rather than by state health services or insurance companies.

The free choice perspective also suggests that the category of 'trans children' is suspect, because being trans is no longer a clinical condition that can be objectively diagnosed. If modifications for gender are just expressions of creativity and autonomous choice, the implication is that gender non-conforming children should not undergo them, since they are not yet of an age when they can give autonomous consent to such drastic and irreversible changes. Just as children are not appropriate candidates for tattoos or facelifts, so they should not be appropriate candidates for puberty blockers, cross-sex hormones, or surgery understood merely as a creative expression of gender identity.[71]

The analogy Halberstam draws between surgery for gender identity and cosmetic surgery may be apt for many trans people, though not all; it is ill-suited to trans children and may not be adequate for trans people suffering from dysphoria or body anxiety, either. But even where the analogy holds, it need not imply unfettered access. An alternative implication of the analogy is that everyone, trans or not, should have to undergo psychiatric assessment before undergoing cosmetic surgery. Indeed, that's a treatment protocol that is recommended by many experts in cosmetic surgery, including some surgeons themselves.

In the end, the use of gender modification surgery as an act of creativity and self-expression must be up to (adult) individuals to decide for themselves. What must be recognized, though, is that trans people who use surgery in this way are just as subject to the demands and constraints of gender norms and the pressure to modify as everyone else. That observation creates a political imperative to reduce the pressures for trans people to modify their bodies, simply as part of the *general* imperative to reduce all pressures to modify.

Patrick Califia, a feminist theorist whose book *Sex Changes* was first written when Califia identified as a butch lesbian and then reissued when he identified as a trans man, neatly sums up the dilemma:

> In the end, I decided that I could not separate my personal ambivalence about being female from the misogyny and homophobia of the surrounding culture. I could not tell if I wanted to have a cock because I wanted to be a man, or because I had been told all my life that any real sex had to involve a penis and a vagina. Did I hate my tits because I was transsexual, or did I hate them because I was sick to death of being leered at, grabbed, and ridiculed? I went around and around with this question for months, and could not come to any honest answer.[72]

All of us, when contemplating modifying our bodies for any reason, might well be similarly perplexed. Are we modifying because we really want to, or because social conditions make life intolerable for bodies like ours?

At the individual level, we can do our best to introspect. At the clinical level, doctors must ensure they practise evidence-based medicine and do their best to offer only those treatments that have been shown to be beneficial for patients with the relevant set of symptoms and characteristics – a requirement that applies to both cosmetic surgery and treatment for dysphoria. But, most crucially, at the social level, we must work together to reject the idea that body modification is necessary to fit in: to disrupt discourses of bodily inadequacy and assert the political principle of the unmodified body. Only then, once all these measures are in place, can we be sure that choices to modify really do serve the bodies they change.

9
Bodily Integrity, Intervention and Resistance

Consider the following children and their loving parents. They are all based on real cases.

Ashley is an American girl. She has static encephalopathy, meaning that she is severely cognitively and physically disabled. She is unable to move, to hold up her head, to turn over in bed, or do anything necessary to care for herself. She is also profoundly limited intellectually: she cannot talk or communicate beyond making facial expressions and expressing distress or pleasure non-verbally. When she is six years old her parents authorize a range of surgeries and interventions designed to keep her permanently the size and shape of a child, so that she can continue to be lifted and carried by her parents and so that she will not go through puberty and become a sexually mature adult. These include the removal of her breast buds (early mastectomy), hysterectomy rendering her infertile, and growth-limiting hormones. Ashley will never be able to express her views about her treatment.[1]

Charlie is an American baby boy. When he is three months old his paediatrician tells Charlie's parents that he is developing a flat spot on his head as the result of lying on his back. The doctor recommends that Charlie wear a helmet for twenty-three hours a day to correct it, a treatment that should take place before the age of six months. The helmet will be tight-fitting to restrict the growth of Charlie's skull everywhere except in the area of the flat spot. Charlie's parents take the doctor's advice and use the helmet, although they find it distressing.[2]

CX is a British boy who suffers from lymphatic cancer. At the age of fourteen he becomes gravely ill and in need of chemotherapy if he is to survive, which will in turn require a series of blood transfusions.

He and his mother, both of whom are Jehovah's Witnesses, withhold consent on religious grounds: they believe that having a blood transfusion is against God's will. The NHS Trust responsible for treating CX take the case to court. The judge rules that CX should have the treatment, saying 'the anger and upset he may well feel' will be 'eclipsed by the ultimate benefits of the proposed potentially lifesaving treatment'.[3]

Eilish and *Katie* are Irish conjoined twins, joined from the shoulders down. Each is born with her own head, neck, heart and lungs, but their lower gastrointestinal tract and reproductive system are shared. They could live permanently conjoined, but when they are three years old their parents decide to have them surgically separated. The surgery would leave each girl with one leg, half a uterus, half a vagina, and half a vulva. One girl would keep the bladder and urethra, the other would get the anus and rectum; both would always need to wear colostomy bags. The twins are hospitalized for months before the surgery, undergoing invasive and painful procedures to prepare their bodies for their separation. The operation takes place when the twins are three years and seven months old. Four weeks later Katie dies of heart failure, brought on by the surgery. Eilish survives. At the age of six she is fitted with an artificial leg, which she names *Katie*. At the age of twelve Eilish does not want to speak to a newspaper reporter about the separation, but her mother does. 'We think in years to come that Eilish will appreciate the decision we made,' she says.[4]

Ethan is a British boy. He is born deaf; both his parents are hearing. At the age of six months old two doctors examine Ethan's auditory nerve and recommend that he does not receive a cochlear implant. His parents are unhappy with this recommendation and seek a third opinion: this doctor recommends an implant, which Ethan receives aged fifteen months. Initial attempts to shift Ethan from Sign to oral language are unsatisfactory and Ethan's education and behaviour deteriorate; he flourishes when he attends a primary school that focuses on Sign. Later, he attends an oral secondary school and does well there. His mother says, 'We have always been happy with our decision for Ethan to have an implant . . . Our ethos has always been to give him the opportunities and see what happens.'[5]

Luna is a seven-year-old American child whose gender is disputed.

Luna is biologically male and so Luna's father identifies Luna as a boy, but Luna displays persistent preferences for feminine-coded clothing and toys and so Luna's mother identifies Luna as a girl. Luna's mother says she is following the advice of doctors: Luna was diagnosed with gender dysphoria aged five and doctors have reported that Luna consistently identifies as a girl. Luna's father says that Luna is happy identifying as a boy with him, and cites evidence that most children identified as trans grow out of it and identify as their birth sex after puberty. Luna's parents, who are separated, disagree about how Luna should be identified at school, about what pronouns should be used to refer to Luna, and how Luna should dress. In time they will disagree about whether Luna should take puberty blockers, which have been suggested for Luna from nine years old.[6]

Priscilla is a Latinx baby girl. In her culture, girls usually have their ears pierced. Her parents research the best age for piercing children's ears and decide to pierce Priscilla's when she is two months old. They reason that babies of that age are unable to pull their ears to alleviate the pain, unlike older babies aged five or six months, and that they will not cry in fear when they are about to be pierced, unlike older children aged four or five years. As an adult Priscilla is happy with her pierced ears.[7]

Rosie is an American intersex girl. She has two XX chromosomes but she has genitalia that are atypical for girls. When Rosie is born the doctors strongly recommend that she undergo surgery as soon as possible, ideally at six months old, to reduce the size of her clitoris and create a vaginal canal; their rationale is that it would be better for Rosie to look 'normal'. Rosie's parents decline the surgery. They say that if she expresses a desire for surgery on her genitals when she's older they will first arrange consultations with a therapist, an intersex person who has had surgery, and an intersex person who hasn't had surgery, to help her make a fully informed choice.[8]

Tom is a British boy. Most boys in Britain are not circumcised unless they are Jewish or Muslim; Tom's family identify as neither. Still, his parents decide to have him circumcised, believing it to be more hygienic; also, his father is circumcised. The circumcision is successful with no complications. However, as an adult Tom is deeply psychologically affected by his circumcision and regards it as a violation. He devotes significant time, resources and effort to coping with the physical and emotional impact of his circumcision.[9]

What should parents be allowed to do to their children?

How can we explain the legal permissibility of circumcision and the removal of children's extra fingers, but the illegality of child tattoos? Is cosmetic surgery on children any different from parental choice in early education and upbringing? If parents can meticulously shape their child's fundamental, profound beliefs about existence and the afterlife in accordance with their preferred religious ideal, and if they can surgically shape their child's features to make them more 'normal', why can't they surgically shape their child's features to more perfectly match their personal ideal of beauty? If parents' wishes about bodily interventions or medical treatment of their children can be overridden in cases where treatment (or non-treatment) is in the child's best interests, why are parents allowed to do many other things to their children that aren't in their best interests, like feed them unhealthy food, let them lead inactive lifestyles, or teach them falsehoods?

In this chapter I consider how the principle of the unmodified body can be used to formulate policy on intervention in others' bodies. As with earlier parts of the book, I proceed via a proxy concept that is more familiar than the deliberately novel idea of the unmodified body. This time the proxy concept is *bodily integrity*.

Bodily integrity is a concept that is used in philosophical and legal analysis of bodily interventions, paradigmatically (but not only) medical interventions. It is particularly important in cases where an intervention hasn't been consented to, perhaps because the patient is unconscious and in urgent need of medical attention, or because the patient is incapable of giving autonomous consent due to youth or cognitive impairment. At its heart is the idea that there is something sacrosanct about the body: some special status that should not be violated.

The concept of bodily integrity is used in a great deal of philosophical, political and legal discourse. But despite its familiarity there's significant debate about its meaning and what it implies for cases like those at the start of the chapter. For some philosophers, bodily integrity is best understood as a principle that protects current or future autonomy; for others, it's about acting in someone's best interests or doing what they would have wanted. These considerations are important parts of the ethical picture. But they leave many of the hard cases unresolved. So in the first part of this chapter, I'll set out an account of what bodily integrity *is*.

Once we know what bodily integrity is, we need to know what it *does*. How important is the principle, especially when compared to other values such as public health or religious community? I won't answer that question in full here, but I'll discuss it in the second part of the chapter. Ultimately, the principle of bodily integrity should act as a *defence* against wrongful bodily intervention. That's the purpose of the principle. It exists to draw a protective circle around the body, to act as a boundary that cannot be crossed. Where there's a pull in favour of some unconsented-to bodily intervention, the principle of bodily integrity should push back. It should offer resistance. Any intervention into someone else's body needs a very clear justification; if there's significant doubt, intervention shouldn't occur. In this way bodily integrity acts like the principle of the unmodified body: not as a conclusion, as a barrier to all modification, but as a morally weighty default position. When it comes to others' bodies it's better to err with too little intervention than too much.

AUTONOMY

There is an important but often fine line between surgery and assault. That line is marked, at least in the case of patients competent to make decisions for themselves, by informed and voluntary consent.

David Benatar, 'The Ethics of
Contested Surgeries' (2006)[10]

When it comes to adults, the ideas of autonomy and of bodily integrity seem to do much the same thing. If something violates my bodily integrity it will also violate my autonomy; conversely, if I consent to a bodily intervention then standard theories of freedom say that it will, for that very reason, violate neither my bodily integrity nor my autonomy.[11]

But this doesn't mean that bodily integrity is just the same thing as autonomy. Many people don't or can't have bodily autonomy, but they're still entitled to bodily integrity because they still need its defensive powers.

Some people who need the defensive powers of the principle of bodily integrity lack the mental capacity for autonomous action. Children are not autonomous. Babies are clearly not competent to decide even the most basic things for themselves, meaning that parents must take charge of every single decision about babies' bodies. As babies grow into children, they gradually become capable of taking on greater control, but their decisions are not always wise or in their best interests, meaning that parents must be in charge of their children's lives and their bodies for many years. So children do not – cannot – have bodily *autonomy*. But we should still respect children's bodily *integrity*. We need to be able to say that there are things that parents and doctors cannot do to children's bodies. We need to be able to defend children's rights not to be subjected to a range of physical interventions, even if their parents want them.

Sometimes, children ask for interventions and parents and doctors need to decide how to respond. A child may ask for a cosmetic procedure, such as ear piercing, Botox, or cosmetic surgery, to deal with social pressure or bullying, or to achieve a certain aesthetic. She may ask for contraception, or abortion, or medical treatment relating to gender identity. Depending on the age of the child, her reasons for wanting treatment and the nature of the procedure in question, sometimes it will be appropriate for doctors and parents to refuse on the grounds of bodily integrity.[12] Children may not be best placed to assess their own needs as they develop and shift over time, or to predict or prioritize their long-term interests.

We need to be able to defend children's bodily integrity as a principle that protects them from certain forms of medical treatment, cosmetic intervention, religious ritual, physical punishment, or physical neglect. So, we must concede that children do not have autonomy, including many forms of bodily autonomy. But we must not concede their bodily integrity. The two concepts are distinct.

Children are not the only people who lack bodily autonomy but should still have bodily integrity. Severely cognitively impaired people may lack autonomy entirely, if they are unable to make decisions or control the course of their lives in any meaningful sense. They too need the defensive powers of bodily integrity, to protect them from wrongful intervention.

Other people need the protective principle of bodily integrity not because they are incapable of acting autonomously but because they have no choice but to submit to physical intervention. Most of us will need physical care at some point in our adult lives, and we may be dependent on physical interventions that we cannot fully consent to. We may be critically ill in hospital or after an accident, requiring life-saving treatment that we temporarily lack capacity to give permission for. We may suffer from age-related decline of our mental capacities, such as dementia, meaning that we must be forced to submit to physical procedures, such as help with basic hygiene and toileting, that we vehemently resist. We may suffer from physical illness or disability that gives us no choice other than to submit to ingress into our bodily sphere that we would much rather repel; in other words, we may have no reasonable choice but to comply with intimate care and clinical procedures, such that we give our consent but lack full autonomy.

'I have to attach a lot of things to my penis,' says an anonymous disabled contributor to Laura Dodsworth's collection of men talking about their penises. 'Since I was a child I've had something attached to my penis most of the time. I have visible scarring down the side of my penis from one of the continence devices I had as a child. Also, because of medical tests, I am exposed a lot. My penis is public property.'[13] This man had no choice but to undergo interventions on his penis – he could not exercise autonomy over it – and so he was in great need of the protection of the principle of bodily integrity to mark out the ethical interventions from the unethical ones.

For all these people, which is to say virtually all of us at some point or other, the capacity to autonomously direct the course of their lives, including what happens to their bodies, is restricted. But this should not mean that they are not granted bodily integrity. They still need protection against illegitimate bodily interventions and procedures. They still need respect for the wholeness of their bodies and their bodily boundaries. They still need the defensive force of bodily integrity.

Ambulance crews and hospital staff may legitimately administer many physical procedures to an unconscious and clinically unstable patient, including serious procedures such as surgery, intubation, or CPR. But they cannot legitimately perform extra procedures that are not urgent and necessary, no matter how well-intentioned. You would have no legitimate complaint if you woke up in hospital after a near-fatal car accident to find that doctors had performed life-saving surgery on you without your consent; but you *would* have a legitimate complaint if you found that they had also performed a vasectomy, or a circumcision, or even removed your verruca.

Similarly, a person with severe cognitive and physical impairment, someone who lacks capacity to grant consent to anything that happens to her, must necessarily submit to a variety of intrusive bodily procedures. But her rights are still violated by physical or sexual abuse, even if she is not aware of what she has endured, or even that it was abusive.[14]

So, bodily integrity is not the same thing as bodily autonomy. Nonetheless, the value of autonomy does need to be taken into account. Controlling our lives matters. Doing things for ourselves matters. Having options left open matters.

THE RIGHT TO AN OPEN FUTURE

The mature adult that the child will become has a right to self-determination, and ... that right is violated in advance if certain crucial and irrevocable decisions determining the course of his life are made by anyone else before he has the capacity of self-determination himself.

Joel Feinberg, 'The Child's
Right to an Open Future' (1980)[15]

Parents must necessarily make a huge number of decisions for their children, while knowing that they will likely mature into adults who value autonomy highly. One way of dealing with this fact is to think in terms of what philosopher Joel Feinberg describes as 'the child's right to an open future'.

Some rights apply only to people with certain capacities, such as the capacity for autonomous thought and action. These rights include the right to vote, the right to consent to sex, and the right to make everyday decisions. These are rights that children will have only when they grow up. Feinberg argues that parents, and other adults, hold those rights *in trust*. Adults must keep those rights safe for the children in their care, by preserving the conditions that keep them intact until they can be claimed by their rightful owners.

The right to an open future captures the idea that we should leave as many choices as possible *open*, for the child herself to make when she's old enough. Parents and others will have to make many choices for her along the way – that's unavoidable. Sometimes it's clear that an intervention is in a child's best interests. But we should make choices that don't foreclose options unnecessarily; and where we can delay a choice and save it for her, or make a choice that will *expand* her options, we should. For example, parents may force a child to attend school (and governments may legislate to require children to be educated) as part of what is necessary to secure the child's right to an open future: to ensure that when she reaches adulthood, she has the personal skills and available options so that she can exercise autonomy.

Education and upbringing have been the areas where most of the philosophy of a child's right to an open future have been done. Philosopher Claudia Mills makes one important objection to the principle of the open future in that context, which is that there can be disagreement about what counts as an option, or a valuable option, or a good range of options.[16] It's generally agreed that it's more valuable to have a smaller number of meaningfully different options than it is to have a large number of very similar options. For example, it's better to have three options than 20,000 options if the first choice is between going to see a football match at Wembley, a Shakespeare play at the Globe, or Dolly Parton at Glastonbury, and the second is any seat you like to watch Jordan Peterson at the O2 Arena. It also matters whether the options are valuable: a choice between worthless options is worse than having only one valuable one. Given that parents have to make choices whatever they do, how should they navigate these issues? Would it better promote the child's right to an open future to bring her up firmly within one religion but with a wide range of musical and cultural opportunities, or with no religion but a firm emphasis on sport over art? Is the choice between ten different musical instruments more or less open than the choice between one religion and atheism? Dilemmas such as these complicate the idea of maximizing a child's future options.

But the right to an open future can also be applied very usefully to the body.[17] Here, the options are more clear-cut because the unmodified body presents itself as a default. It's easier to see what happens to the body if we do not intervene in it, and it is much easier, and more ethical, to parent in a way that intervenes minimally on children's bodies than it is to parent in a way that intervenes minimally on their mental, social and educational development. Some important decisions about children's bodies can't wait, such as the treatment of childhood conditions like asthma or eczema that worsen or cause suffering if left untreated. But in many cases children will be capable of making decisions when they're older; and they'll have an opinion about the decisions made on their behalf when they were younger. And so decisions about a child's body that can reasonably be delayed, should be; and any decision that can't be delayed should be made in a way that maximizes the options that are left open for her (or is very clearly in her best interests – more on that later).

Most cosmetic interventions can safely be delayed until the child is old enough to choose or reject them for herself. Piercings, tattoos, breast implants, nose jobs – procedures like this can be done at any age, and so the right to an open future tells us that parents should not choose them for their children. The reason that parents shouldn't choose these procedures for their children isn't that there's something wrong with them. There's no need to show that having pierced ears or tattoos or breast implants is bad. It's simply that decisions of this sort should be made by the person whose body it is.

I'm not going to attempt to answer the question of at what age a person becomes competent to choose body modification for herself. There's a large literature, philosophical and legal, on the question of children's autonomy, and delving too far into it would be a distraction.[18] One influential approach is the previously mentioned legal concept known as Gillick competence, which states that children can reach competence to make autonomous choices at different stages, depending on both their own intellectual and emotional maturity and also on the significance and risk of the choice involved. Plausibly, a child can make an autonomous and informed choice about whether to have her ears pierced at an earlier age than she can decide about more major procedures like breast implants or tattoos. The central point is that, in all cases, the choice should be *hers*.

Of course, some interventions are clinically urgent: without them, the child will die or suffer serious loss of health or functioning. Thinking in terms of the child's right to an open future helps us to see why these interventions are permissible: they're necessary to keep the child's future options open. A life-saving heart transplant on a baby preserves her right to an open future. Without the surgery, her future is closed.

Thinking of bodily integrity in terms of the right to an open future also helps us to understand why parents may legitimately authorize some clinically unnecessary interventions on their children but not others. Consider the contrasting cases of routine vaccinations and routine circumcision. David and Michael Benatar argue that parents may legitimately authorize clinically unnecessary circumcision on their children – a position I disagree with – because they can also legitimately authorize vaccinations – a position I endorse. In their view, you can't have one without the other. A child can't give autonomous consent for a vaccination and so, they argue, if parents are entitled to vaccinate their children it must be because they have the right to act in what they perceive to be their child's best interests. And if parents may make that judgement in the case of vaccination, the Benatars argue, parents may make it in the case of circumcision and most other procedures. According to the Benatars, the limits of parental authority are reached only with interventions that are 'unequivocally harmful to their children', not merely those about which there may be disagreement.[19]

But once we think about bodily integrity in terms of the child's right to an open future, the equivalence between circumcision and vaccination disappears. Vaccination protects the child's right to an open future by maximizing the chance that he will survive to adulthood, and it does so without closing any of his options (other than the ability to be infected with a deadly disease, which is not an option that any reasonable person values). In contrast, even on the most favourable reading of the benefits of circumcision, circumcision secures no health benefits that can't be obtained in other, non-invasive ways (such as condom use or antibiotics) or by the boy choosing circumcision for himself when he is old enough.

So not circumcising keeps the most options open: it allows a boy and the man he becomes to enjoy the benefits of an intact foreskin, and it also allows him to access the benefits of circumcision. Fundamentally, it gives him the irreplaceable benefit of being able to make a *choice* about his own body for himself.[20]

Men have a wide range of feelings about being circumcised. Many accept it without much thought. Some are positively happy with the choice their parents made for them. Others are dismayed or traumatized. For example, in Dodsworth's book *Manhood: The Bare Reality*, one circumcised man comments: 'I really, really like that I am circumcised. I don't like the look of foreskins . . . I understand that foreskins are a pleasure zone, but they just look odd to me.'[21] But another says: 'I've got all sorts of issues about my genitalia! . . . Being circumcised and having one fewer testicle than most men I feel slightly . . . what's the word . . . mutilated. I'm not all that I came into the world with. Hacked at.'[22]

Many men express some ambivalence:

I've struggled to come to terms with my body . . . I was circumcised and most other boys weren't. I don't have a problem being circumcised. I am Muslim, and circumcision was the practice of the Prophet, so I think it is a requirement to be circumcised. I don't know any Muslim men who aren't.[23]

I am Jewish and circumcised. I didn't really think about it until I had my son, and thought, 'Oh well, he needs to be circumcised,' just as a part of being a boy. But the mohel, that's the rabbi who does the circumcision, didn't want to do it because his mother's not Jewish and therefore the boy is not Jewish. He refused to do it. So I thought, 'Oh, OK, well maybe that's not a bad thing.' I didn't really have a choice when I was circumcised and maybe I would like to have had. He can choose to have it done if he wants, but I don't think he will. I'm OK with being circumcised. My parents did it automatically as part of their culture.[24]

It's impossible to say whether most men feel happy or unhappy with their circumcision, not least because there are complex emotional and psychological factors that affect a person's attitude to their own body. It is psychologically safer to adopt a position of acceptance.[25] But this diversity of experience, the unknowability of how a bodily intervention will be experienced by the person whose body it is, is not a signal that it doesn't matter whether the intervention is performed or not. It's a signal that we should leave the decision to the person whose body it is, because we lack a sure enough conviction that any decision we make will be the right one for them.

The right to an open future can answer many of the cases set out at the start of the chapter. Priscilla was happy with her ear piercing; Tom was deeply unhappy with his circumcision. But this difference doesn't mean that the ear piercing was justified and the circumcision not: their reactions couldn't have been known in advance, and others feel differently. In both cases, their right to an open future would have been better secured if their parents had not modified their bodies, leaving the decision to them when they were older.

Similarly, the cases of Eilish and Katie, the conjoined twins, and Rosie, the intersex girl, look clear from the perspective of the right to an open future. Since it would have been possible for Eilish and Katie both to survive while conjoined,[26] it was wrong to separate them. That decision should have been left for them to make when they were old enough. (Most likely they would then have chosen to remain conjoined, as we'll see.) Rosie's parents make the right call, from the perspective of the right to an open future. They left Rosie's genitals as they were, something for her to make a choice about as she matures.

The right to an open future also suggests that it was right for the court to overrule CX's wish and force him to have a life-saving blood transfusion, at least insofar as it was right to consider him too young to make his own autonomous choice. Having the transfusion best protected his right to an open future and his right to make his own decision later. Cases like CX's become more difficult the closer children come to autonomous adulthood. But the general principle that courts may overrule parents' refusal to authorize life-saving treatment on their child for religious reasons falls well within the scope of the right to an open future.

However, not all the cases are clearly decided by the right to an open future. Ashley, the girl with static encephalopathy, will never be able to make decisions about her life. Her parents don't hold her rights in trust for her to take over when she's old enough; they will *always* have to choose for her. So, the right to an open future doesn't seem to apply.

The right to an open future is more applicable in the cases of Ethan and Luna, because both can be expected to grow into autonomous adults. But it doesn't clearly decide either case. Will Ethan's future choices be widened by having a cochlear implant in infancy and integrating him in hearing society, or by retaining his residual hearing and supporting his Deaf identity? Will Luna's future autonomy be better supported by going through male puberty, keeping Luna's fertility intact and possibly prompting Luna to identify as a boy, or will Luna be more autonomous if Luna does not go through male puberty and undergoes hormonal and surgical treatments to create a more feminine body? I suspect each of us has an intuition, probably a very strong intuition, about the best course of action in each case. But our intuitions won't all be the same. Both cases are deeply controversial, and so we need further guidance on how to resolve them.

REVERSIBILITY

Respecting the unmodified body as part of the right to an open future has close connections with the idea of *reversibility*. Reversibility is one way of measuring the significance of a bodily intervention. Many of our intuitions about bodily interventions are explained by that concept. Reversibility explains why tattoos are treated differently from haircuts. If an intervention is reversible, we're likely to be more relaxed about it.

Reversibility is an important point when considering any bodily intervention. It plays a role in our understanding of what it is to respect or violate bodily integrity. A reversible modification will generally be more in keeping with the child's right to an open future than an irreversible one. But it doesn't tell the whole story, for three reasons.

First, reversibility doesn't seem to give the right answer in many cases: there are both ethical irreversible interventions and unethical temporary ones. Vaccinating a child against deadly diseases like polio, diphtheria and pertussis (whooping cough) is irreversible. Once vaccinated, a child can't subsequently be made vulnerable to the disease once again. (Some vaccines may lose their potency, but you can't deliberately become un-vaccinated.) But the irreversibility of vaccines doesn't mean that it's unethical to vaccinate infants. In the case of vaccinations, the benefits to individual and public health are so overwhelming, and the risks and side-effects so minimal, that it is a justifiable practice. Cost–benefit analysis doesn't settle all cases, as we'll soon see, but it is enough to justify an overwhelmingly beneficial intervention or to rule out a disproportionately costly one. The same is true of other life-saving medical treatment such as blood transfusions, the removal of an infected appendix, or the removal of cancerous tissue. The irreversibility of these interventions is actually an advantage. It's much better if the diseases can't return.

There are also plenty of examples of reversible bodily interventions that are unethical. In one sense nothing is reversible, in that we can't turn the clock back and prevent an act from ever having happened. But there are many bodily interventions that leave no lasting mark on the body. Bruises, cuts and broken bones heal. Sexual activity need leave no permanent physical injury. Weight can be gained or lost. But it is still a serious violation of bodily integrity to beat or stab someone, to sexually assault or rape them, to starve them or to force-feed them – even if their bodies recover.

Second, parents are permitted to do many irreversible things to their children, meaning that it is difficult to specify what is different about bodily irreversibility. Parents determine what language their children speak, whether their children have the chance to become virtuosic in activities like piano playing or ballet dancing, and whether they grow up with or without religion. Parents make choices for their children that can have a profound impact on the entire course of their lives, such as how to educate them, which tastes, preferences and hobbies are introduced and nurtured, and whether to make them into child actors or pop stars, possibly making them rich and famous in a way that will shape their lives for ever. Reversibility can't explain why some parental actions are legitimate and others are not.

Third, both intervention and non-intervention can be irreversible, meaning that questions of reversibility don't always resolve controversial cases. Vaccination is irreversible, but so is death or impairment from a preventable disease. Separating conjoined twins is irreversible, but so is the death of a twin whose organs cannot sustain both her and her sister. Many interventions are *irreversible either way*.

Some interventions can be safely delayed until the child is adult, old enough to make the choice for him- or herself, without any deterioration in the benefits of the intervention. The presumed health benefits of circumcision, such as treatment of phimosis (tight foreskin) or minimizing the risk of some sexually transmitted diseases, can be accessed at whatever age the operation is performed. There's no need to circumcise all boys just in case, particularly since the relevant diseases are unlikely to affect children.

But some interventions only work if they're performed on children or babies. Charlie's baby helmet therapy only works if used before brain growth is complete in toddlerhood, so it's not a procedure we can get his consent for. And there's significant disagreement about baby helmet therapy. It's another example of a procedure on which the British NHS and the American Academy of Pediatrics (AAP) give very different advice, with the AAP endorsing it and the NHS being considerably more sceptical.[27]

One disagreement is about whether the helmets work. A recent study by researchers in the Netherlands suggests they don't: it found that there were no significant differences in the outcomes achieved by babies who did or did not undergo helmet therapy.[28] If helmet therapy isn't an evidence-based treatment, if it doesn't achieve what it claims, then it shouldn't be used at all. But what if it does work? What if it does, as the AAP claims, achieve significant improvement of a flat spot? Is it a violation of the baby's bodily integrity, or a justifiable treatment?

Reversibility won't give us the answer. If the treatment works, as the AAP claims, then the treatment is irreversible – you can't recreate a flat spot in adulthood once the skull is hardened. But then, the effect of no treatment is irreversible, too. One mother, Deana Morton, describes how the irreversibility of no treatment led her to consent to helmet therapy for her baby boy, against her strong instincts:

> At our three-month appointment, the doctor began discussing helmet therapy—called cranial orthosis—with us. Our son had a cranial deformity. I was shocked—truly in disbelief—because all I could see was a beautiful baby who was perfect in every way.
>
> Our paediatrician's son wore a helmet as a baby, so she didn't sugar-coat the process. 'It's going to be tough,' she said. 'But your son might thank you for his round head later in life.'
>
> Except I was opposed to putting a helmet on my son and immediately said no to the idea. It seemed unnecessary and cruel—we would be confining our child's head, and it looked uncomfortable.
>
> I sat awake that night with thoughts of the helmet swimming through my head. Would my son feel insecure about the flat spot when he was older? Was the flat spot my fault? Why can't my son talk so he could let me know what he prefers? Helmet or no helmet?
>
> I decided to go through with helmet therapy because I feared my son would hold the flat spot against me when he was older.[29]

Morton's account of helmet therapy is distressing. She describes how her baby 'began to whimper' and was 'fussy' when the helmet was fitted; how it took only a week until 'he began to have abrasions on parts of his head where the helmet rubbed against the skin'; how the helmet therapy worsened her own post-partum depression, frequently causing her to have emotional breakdowns in public and with her therapist; and how it was a source of conflict with her partner. Part of her trauma came from the agony of decision-making: was the helmet the right thing to do, or not? Did wearing a helmet violate her baby's bodily integrity? Would leaving his flat spot untreated and permanent do the same? The principle of reversibility can give no answer to these fraught questions.

Reversibility gives no clear guidance in other controversial cases too. It doesn't help with the case of Ethan. Cochlear implants, as we saw in Chapter 6, work best if they are implanted in children aged just two. Having a cochlear implant is irreversible, but so is not having one. Parents must choose between giving a young child a cochlear implant and irreversibly destroying his residual hearing, or not giving him one and irreversibly removing the opportunity for developing high levels of oral language capability. The concept of reversibility gives no guidance on which to choose.

Reversibility is also indecisive in the case of Luna. A trans person will have a better chance of physically inhabiting their preferred gender, and will need less surgery to do so, if they are treated in childhood with puberty blockers to prevent them developing the sexually mature physical features of their birth sex. Puberty blockers only work if they're given before children complete puberty, at an age when children are unlikely to be capable of fully appreciating the ramifications of treatment,[30] and when children's durable gender identity is not yet fully clear to themselves or others. If puberty blockers are delayed until the child can give autonomous consent, it will be too late for them to work. Puberty itself, and many of the physical changes that occur then, is irreversible.

But the drugs themselves cause irreversible changes. The NHS recently revised its public guidance on puberty blockers, noting that little is known about their long-term physical and psychological side-effects. What is known is that a high percentage of children who receive puberty blockers go on to receive cross-sex hormones from the age of sixteen – almost 100 per cent, according to some studies.[31] And cross-sex hormones cause irreversible changes such as breast development, deepening of the voice, and infertility.[32]

Many studies find that the process of puberty itself tends to consolidate gender identity, meaning that a child is less likely to identify as trans or wish to transition if she or he has gone through unmedicated puberty.[33] If that's true, then how should we state things? Should we say that puberty blockers make people trans, or that puberty makes people cis? Either way, something irreversible happens. We need a way of deciding between irreversible treatment and irreversible non-treatment. The principle of reversibility doesn't help on its own.

If someone reaches adulthood wishing they had a more rounded head, or wishing that they were hearing rather than deaf, or wanting to be read by others as a woman rather than a man, they are likely to wish that their parents had made the decision to authorize bodily intervention on them as a child. But the opposite holds too. A gender non-conforming girl may grow up to be a woman who doesn't identify as trans, in which case she may deeply regret hormonal or surgical intervention received as a child that has left her irreversibly infertile, without breasts, or with facial hair.[34] A deaf person may come to identify more fully with Deaf culture than with hearing culture, regretting the loss of residual hearing caused by her cochlear implant. And an older child or adult may learn of procedures performed on him as a baby, such as the use of helmet therapy or a circumcision, and wish that his body had been left alone.

When considering a bodily intervention on a child, then, parents and doctors are making difficult choices. They are trying to weigh up the competing costs and benefits of action and inaction. They are considering whether delay is possible, or whether some intervention is truly urgent. And they are trying to make a best guess about what the child's preferences are likely to be for the long term – something which they are quite likely to be wrong about, particularly in cases where they don't themselves have the same physical condition as the child. Whichever way they choose, parents have to confront the irreversibility of their choices. Irreversibility cannot solve these dilemmas of bodily intervention.

However, the concept of reversibility does have ethical significance. Sometimes the balance of reversibility between action and inaction is not equal. In those cases, the principle of bodily integrity suggests we should prefer the course of action that is more reversible. In the case of circumcision, for example, the principle of reversibility tells us to prioritize non-circumcision, because most of the benefits of circumcision can be achieved by delaying the practice until it can be chosen. Non-circumcision is reversible, but circumcision is not.[35]

Some of the circumcised men in Dodsworth's book mention how much more difficult it is to choose the procedure as an adult than to undergo it non-consensually as a baby. Adult circumcision, they say, would be 'too painful and traumatising';[36] it was 'difficult' to shift from having a foreskin to not having one;[37] being circumcised as a baby means 'it's not something I think about';[38] if a boy is given a choice 'I don't think he will'.[39] Do these considerations show that it is better to circumcise a boy when he is an infant, so that he will be spared the burdens of a later circumcision?

No. For one thing, the fact that most adult men don't choose circumcision for themselves shows precisely that they value their fore-skin, or the simple fact of being intact, more than any benefits that being circumcised might bring; and if that's true for a man when he's an adult, why wouldn't it also be true for him while he's still a baby?

But, an objector might say, what if a man develops a medical con-dition for which circumcision is the best treatment? Wouldn't it then have been better for him if he'd already undergone the procedure when he was too young to remember it, too young to notice the loss? Well yes, perhaps, in the sense that he wouldn't have to undergo the procedure now. But the same could be said of any medically necessary bodily intervention. If you have to have a testicle or a breast removed because of cancer, for example, it might be easier to cope if you'd always lived without it. But that's no reason to prophylactically remove everyone's breast tissue or testicles in infancy just in case they need a mastectomy or orchidectomy later on.

Even if it is easier to deal with the loss of something you've never had than something you've always had, it's a different thing entirely to come to terms with the fact that a part of your body has been removed with-out your consent. A man who's been circumcised doesn't just have to come to terms with not having a foreskin. He has to come to terms with the fact that an adult restrained him and cut off part of his penis when he was a baby, and that his parents not only allowed this but actively sought it out. 'I used to do stand-up and I'd say that when your first memory is of a bearded man coming to your cock with a knife you tend to be a bit neurotic for the rest of your life,' says one man.[40] Another comedian, Tom Rosenthal, includes in his routine 'Manhood' a photo-graph of the invoice his parents received for his circumcision, something he finds deeply poignant. It is this lack of control and invasive interfer-ence with their bodies that leads some men to describe their infant circumcision as an act of abuse and to suffer lifelong emotional trauma.

And so keeping the whole body intact allows more time: for more truths to be known, for the important context to be found, for diver-sity and life experience, for the person to be sure of their identity and values, and for the person whose body it is to take ownership of the whole process.

BEST INTERESTS

The right to an open future helps solve the dilemmas of intervention in some cases. It tells us what to do in cases where an intervention can be delayed until the person whose body it is can decide for herself. But it doesn't help in cases where treatment is urgent; it doesn't help in cases which are irreversible either way; and it doesn't help in cases where the person whose body it is won't ever become autonomous, because they have a severe cognitive impairment that's unlikely to improve.[41]

One plausible candidate for dealing with these cases is the idea of *best interests*. Philosopher Joseph Mazor takes the view that bodily integrity justifies intervention that's in someone's best interests.[42]

On Mazor's view, a life-saving heart transplant performed on a child would *not* count as an infringement of bodily integrity, even though it's a serious, unconsented-to encroachment, because it's clearly in the child's best interests. Life-saving surgery can be justified without using the idea of best interests: usually the right to an open future will be enough. But the best-interests conception does look useful for cases where there is no likelihood of a person becoming autonomous. For example, consideration of best interests shows why it's justifiable to provide pain relief for someone at the end of life who can't consent, and why it's justifiable to intervene with toileting and hygiene assistance for people with dementia. These interventions can't be justified by appealing to an open future, but it's clear that they're in the recipients' best interests. In these easy cases it seems right to say that the principle of bodily integrity should not rule out intervention.

Mazor points out that there are two ways of justifying interventions like these. One way is to say that these interventions are violations of bodily integrity, because they are non-consensual, but they are justified all things considered. Another way, which Mazor prefers, is to say that an intervention that's justified all things considered is therefore *not* a violation of bodily integrity. But that's a mistake. Politically speaking, Mazor's approach has the effect of legitimizing more bodily interventions. It weakens the defence against body modification, and capitulates to the social context of increased pressures to modify.

For that reason it's better to say that an intervention can still be a violation of bodily integrity even if it is, to the best of our understanding, justified. This way of thinking about unconsented-to bodily interventions alerts us to the *contingent* nature of their permissibility. It reminds us that intervening in someone's body without their consent is a kind of violation, and so it's justified only if there is strong evidence that it's in the person's interests – and that evidence must be robust, up-to-date and subject to revision.

Moreover, the concept of bodily integrity needs to do more than give us the right result in easy cases. It needs to help with controversial, difficult cases. If it's to do that effectively it needs to offer guidance based on reasoning that is less controversial than the raw case itself. But often the best-interests approach relies on reasoning that's just as controversial as the cases it needs to solve, meaning that it simply shifts the dilemma to a different stage of the argument.

The case that Mazor uses to illustrate the best-interests approach to bodily integrity is infant male circumcision. As we've seen, there's considerable controversy about the advisability and permissibility of this practice. For infant male circumcision to be permissible on the best-interests approach to bodily integrity, it must be in boys' best interests. But it's difficult to know what that would mean. In the case of circumcision we might say that a boy's relevant interests include health and the avoidance of disease, which includes both his own health and also the health of any future sexual partners he may have; his own sexual functioning and satisfaction, including sensitivity to touch and stimulation, ability to orgasm, erectile function and ability to engage in the sexual practices he desires; his feeling of being socially accepted, which may include being recognized and welcomed into a religious community, or feeling his body to be acceptable or attractive; relationship success, including being considered attractive to partners; and good mental health, including self-esteem, body acceptance and being content with his parents' decision to circumcise him or not.

What we can see straightaway is that the determination of what counts as being in someone's interests is itself not a question of science or medicine, but rather a question of value: it is a matter of ethics and politics. And the best-interests account of bodily integrity risks simply reflecting the social pressures to modify. It will be in someone's interests to have a body modification if they live in a social context that requires that modification. If a modification is necessary to meet a standard of social acceptability, then the modification will likely be in the person's best interests, since being socially acceptable is very important for well-being. This means that a best-interests standard of bodily integrity won't do the job required of the principle of the unmodified body. It won't provide the philosophical resources to resist political pressures to modify.

There are many ways that social norms affect what's in someone's best interests. A broadly liberal, sex-positive perspective tells us that it is in a person's interests to experience sexual satisfaction and the ability to participate in desired sexual practices; but in a different time and place we would take a different view. Two hundred years ago in the USA circumcision was routinely performed precisely in order to *reduce* sexual desire, as a means of preventing 'disorders' like masturbation and erotic dreams.[43]

The effects of a given intervention depend to a significant extent on the cultural context within which the person will live. In other words, whether an intervention produces an outcome depends not only on the intervention itself, but also on how society works, and in which social groups a person operates. For example, whether circumcision is necessary for a boy to be accepted as a member of his community depends on which community that is (Jewish, Muslim, or neither); whether circumcision is considered an enhancement to his sexual attractiveness (circumcision is regarded as enhancing penile attractiveness in the USA but not in Europe); whether he develops sexual preferences and behaviours that are helped or hindered by having a foreskin (will he seek to delay or hasten his orgasms, will he wish to engage in direct stimulation of the foreskin or in practices like docking?).

Circumcision is just one example of a body modification that can be in someone's interests if and because it's socially required. James Partridge, who suffered serious facial burns as a teenager and who spent decades campaigning for 'face equality', argues that people with facial disfigurement suffer from 'faceism', a discriminatory attitude against those whose faces are deemed imperfect.[44] According to Partridge, faceism consists of three social stigmas. First, there's the stigma that people with facial disfigurement are 'sad and second-rate', meaning that they won't have happy and productive lives. Second, there's the stigma that facial disfigurement reveals moral deficiency, as in the repeated fictional representations of villains as being scarred or disabled. Facial deformities, scars and burns are legion among the villains in Bond films, superhero films, Star Wars films, fantasy films like *The Lord of the Rings*, animated films like *The Lion King*, and, of course, horror films. Third, people with facial disfigurement are subject to the 'Why don't you fix it?' stigma: the idea that they both could and should undergo (more) surgery to make their face 'normal', implying that their continuing disfigurement is in some sense their fault.[45]

These stigmas are widely believed among the general population and can also be shared by people with facial disfigurement. But the stigmas are untrue. People with facial disfigurement can have exceedingly happy and productive lives, as the many case studies in Partridge's book show. Having a facial disfigurement has no bearing whatever on your moral character. And, while plastic and cosmetic surgery can do incredible things, it has its limits – as do the people who undergo repeated rounds of it. So, the three stigmas are false, but most people believe them.

When combined with the three stigmas the best-interests conception of bodily integrity would conclude that it is not in someone's interests to have their facial disfigurement left alone, and that it is no violation of bodily integrity to subject children with facial differences to repeated cosmetic surgical procedures. And that is, indeed, what happens: parents and doctors tend to opt for surgical 'correction' of facial differences over and above what is necessary for good functioning.

Partridge argues strongly against faceism, calling for concerted social change, legislation and individual action to combat the stigma and discrimination faced by people with facial disfigurement. His charity Changing Faces campaigns to raise the visibility and acceptance of people with a wide variety of facial conditions. Partridge himself calls for a future of face equality, one in which 'We would all thrive unfettered by messages that we don't look good enough. People would be judged on their personality, talents and qualities and would be met by others with open minds and arms and with civilized twenty-first-century face values.'[46] In other words, Partridge wants a world in which a perfect face is not a necessary part of one's best interests.

And yet, despite his compelling insistence that societies must change to destroy the three stigmas of faceism, Partridge also recognizes that people with facial disfigurement must do some work on themselves. A great deal of his work has been developing an education and support programme that helps people with facial disfigurement develop the social and communication skills they need to overcome the reactions of those they encounter. As he puts it, 'to create the best prospect of positive interactions as a person with a disfigurement, you need to be willing to take the initiative in most social encounters, especially first time meetings of any sort.'[47] People with disfigurement 'have to get used to being inspected and you have to get used to being stared at, because it is essential that people become accustomed to your new face'.[48] And 'as a disfigured person, your problem is how you can calm the anxiety of the people you meet without making them feel even more awkward.'[49]

The strongest message Partridge emphasizes is that a person with facial disfigurement must come to terms with their face and act in a way that means that others will too. Still, he recognizes that bodily intervention may sometimes be necessary to gaining acceptance. 'Changing faces is not something you will go through in isolation from the rest of humanity,' he writes.

> Facial disfigurement is, above all, a social handicap, and your course of surgery to try to diminish it must at least partially respect the wishes of the wider society in which you will circulate. This may suggest that you have to fulfil certain minimum social standards when deciding on how much plastic surgery to receive – and these are not easily discovered.[50]

Part of this process, Partridge argues, may involve surgical changes or camouflage make-up.

Ultimately, the social conditions must change to accept people with all sorts of faces, but in the meantime, the onus is on individuals who suffer from the status quo to change. 'It's unfair to have to do all this, but necessary,' Partridge writes. 'Until the campaign for face equality is successful, it will be an effort.'[51]

What's in someone's best interests is not a fixed, scientific fact. It's a contingent, shifting goal, one that depends on how we structure our societies, on the options and norms we create, on the values we endorse,

BODILY INTEGRITY, INTERVENTION AND RESISTANCE

and on how we weigh competing considerations. A person with facial disfigurement suffers in a faceist society. We might improve their life by changing either their face, or our faceism. A best-interests account can't distinguish these two strategies: which is better depends only on the costs and benefits involved. It may be easier, all things considered, for an individual to conceal, camouflage, or surgically alter their face than it is to effect thoroughgoing social-norm change. But placing the burden on the individual is hardly fair.

The principle of the unmodified body tells us that social-norm change is better than surgery, ethically speaking, even if it is more difficult. Bodily integrity must be able to follow suit. If bodily integrity is to be a distinct ethical principle, one that is really about the *body*, not just a restatement of utilitarian cost–benefit analysis, it must be a principle that prioritizes keeping the body intact wherever possible. Best interests are important, but they are not the same thing as bodily integrity.

There's no fixed, objective answer to what a person's interests are, or how to weigh up conflicts of interest. There's also no fixed, objective answer to what the outcomes of intervention and non-intervention will be, since much depends on the social reception of a person with a given body, and the resources that are available to them.

Still more difficult is how to determine which balance of outcomes counts as being in a person's *best* interests. What if a given intervention, such as circumcision, works to reduce disease but also decreases sexual satisfaction? Does that intervention then count as being in the person's best interests? Answers to questions like this depend on how one weighs each value, and this judgement will vary from person to person. For some people a large increase in health or the avoidance of disease is needed to justify even a minor decrease of sexual satisfaction; others reasonably make a different trade-off. We cannot straightforwardly say whether an intervention is in someone's best interests without knowing how they themselves weigh up competing values.

The best-interests approach to bodily integrity looks for an evidence base and defers to scientific process. This is an admirable way of proceeding, and evidence-based medicine should be regarded as a minimum standard for interventions. But the reasons behind the evidence, the outcomes that are obtained, are not pure science. They depend on the social context and social facts, on normative judgement and values, and on what sort of evidence is even looked for.

So, the best-interests account of bodily integrity is either indeterminate, or else simply reflects dominant social norms. In the case of infant male circumcision, it might simply reflect the social status of the practice and conclude that being circumcised is in a boy's best interests if he lives in a circumcision-practising community. Alternatively, if the best-interests account of bodily integrity is to be used as an objective standard, one that can counteract social norms, it won't be conclusive. Disagreement about whether circumcision is in the boy's best interests is *precisely* the question that makes the practice controversial in the first place. And the problem isn't that we lack sufficient evidence about the costs and benefits of circumcision, or that we haven't run enough opinion polls that tell us whether most men value their foreskin or value their circumcision. The problem is that there is no one balance of reasons that should dominate; no one decision that is right for everybody. Whether the costs of circumcision are worth the benefits, and indeed what counts as a cost and what counts as a benefit, is something on which reasonable people disagree.[52]

A principle of bodily integrity should remind us that decisions about other people's bodies should be taken only when absolutely necessary. Wherever possible, the decision should be left to them – which, in the case of circumcision, means delaying the procedure until the boy is old enough to decide for himself whether it is in his best interests (which may not be until he becomes adult). This is the principle of the unmodified body.

HYPOTHETICAL CONSENT

Philosopher Brian Earp argues that bodily interventions in cases where people are unable to consent because they are children or incapacitated in some way should be dealt with using a notion of hypothetical consent. What *would* they consent to, if they could? Earp acknowledges that it is very difficult to know what someone would consent to in many cases, and that we can often be wrong. That's why, he argues, it's better to err on the side of caution and wait until a person can choose for themself if at all possible. Earp is a powerful voice against routine infant circumcision, a topic on which he's one of the leading bioethical experts, for precisely this reason.

Nevertheless, Earp argues that there are some 'easy' cases in which nearly everyone says they would consent to an intervention. In his account, it's acceptable to perform an unconsented-to bodily intervention on someone (in his terms, an *infringement* of bodily integrity will not be a *violation* of bodily integrity) if that intervention 'is almost universally regarded as something that promotes well-being'.[53] This standard seems to give the right answer in cases like emergency life-saving surgery. But it won't work for difficult, controversial cases – and those are the cases we need help with. In controversial cases there's no accepted answer about what someone would want, and it's not always possible to wait until adulthood (as in the case of cochlear implants).

Moreover, there are some cases where almost everyone agrees about what they say they would want in a certain situation but this universal intuition is out of kilter with the views of the minority who actually *are* in that situation. A striking example is the separation of conjoined twins. Conjoined twins don't have conjoined parents.[54] And people who aren't conjoined assume that being conjoined must be a terrible state, with separation far preferable and certainly in the children's interests. But this assumption is highly suspect.

Some separation surgeries, known as 'sacrifice surgeries', necessarily kill one twin to save the other, and so certainly aren't in the sacrificed child's interests. Other surgeries proceed with the aim of saving both children but do in fact result in the death of one twin. Clearly separation is not in the best interests of twins who die as a result.

What of cases where both twins survive? Conjoined twins who have been separated are usually left with serious impairments, often in worse health and with reduced functioning compared to their conjoined state, since separation almost inevitably leaves each twin without a fully functioning set of organs and limbs. So, life after separation is often a life of increased and significant disability, which must be taken into account.

It's a moot question whether it's better to be conjoined or separated and disabled. Parents and doctors often assume that separation is preferable at almost any cost. But this assumption is not warranted.

Conjoined twins who are left intact can live flourishing, independent lives together. Conjoined twins always have each other, and this togetherness can be a source of great emotional and physical support. And, if left to make the decision for themselves, conjoined twins almost never choose to be separated.[55] According to historian, journalist and activist Alice Dreger, 'conjoined twins often explicitly say they do not ever want to be separated, since this would result in a profound change of identity or the death of a twin's "other half".'[56] This desire to remain together, Dreger reports, is 'practically universal'.[57]

So, parents and doctors, and the rest of us who are not conjoined, may feel that it is obviously in conjoined twins' best interests to be separated if possible, but that judgement is likely to be based on our own prejudice and perspective, not on any genuine understanding of what it is like to be a conjoined twin. Still less do we understand what it is like to be a conjoined twin who has been separated. And our judgement is not a judgement shared by conjoined twins themselves. Hypothetical-consent accounts are problematic because it doesn't just matter *how many* people think an intervention is justified. It also matters *how much they know* about what it is like to live with, and without, the intervention.

Most of us don't know how conjoined people feel about their anatomy, because we aren't conjoined and we haven't researched people who are. Disability is much more common, but non-disabled people make false assumptions about what disabled people experience and want all the time. Philosopher Eva Feder Kittay shows that the best-interests account is particularly limited in the case of disabled children, and that the difficulties increase the greater the disability. The problem, Kittay argues, is that 'the new parent, if not herself disabled or already the parent of a disabled child, is likely to bring her own ableist biases to the situation.'[58] As we saw in Chapter 6, people who are not disabled are systematically bad at assessing the quality of life of people who are, tending to assume that being disabled is significantly worse than it really is for people who actually experience it. So, parents without disabilities are biased towards intervention for their disabled children. Parents tend to assume that intervention is in a disabled child's interests, when it may not be.

Parents are supported in this assumption by doctors, whose focus is always on what they can do to modify or 'improve' bodies. Doctors' instinct is to offer treatment and to medicalize conditions, rather than to counsel acceptance and inactivity. As Kittay puts it, 'the physician is professionally liable to see disability as a medical condition only.' She suggests that no decision about the treatment of a disabled child should proceed without 'information from those better situated to provide a perspective from a life lived with disability'.[59]

These misunderstandings could perhaps be rectified with humility and careful listening. But some things are simply unknowable. We just don't know what a severely cognitively impaired person desires, feels, or wants. We don't know this about any individual, and we can't know this about such people as a group. Possibly they have very diverse perspectives, as is the case with people's views about circumcision. Possibly they have very consistent preferences that diverge from the assumptions of people without impairment, as is the case with conjoined twins. Often, we don't even know how much a severely cognitively impaired person feels or thinks at all.

As Kittay emphasizes, discussing the case of Ashley described at the start of this chapter:

> What we know of are the capabilities that allow the brain to direct the rest of the body in certain ways. We do not yet know enough about what is actually going on in the (bodily) brain and the subjective world of people with severe cognitive disabilities. As Ashley will have hormones produced by intact ovaries, she may well experience the sensations of bodily maturation. What will it mean to her not to have breasts? Do we know? What will it mean to her to be a woman? Do we know? How will she experience bodily growth? Can we say? No, no, and no. It is the misleading image of a fertile, full-grown woman with the mind of a baby that makes us think we know something about which we, at the current time, have not a clue.[60]

The hypothetical consent approach to the principle of bodily integrity is appealing, but it ultimately will not do. It suffers from the fundamental problem that there is just as much uncertainty about what someone would consent to as there is about what is in someone's best interests. And a best guess on either matter risks simply reflecting the dominant social pressures to modify, pressures that a principle of bodily integrity ought to offer a defence against.

So far, we're left without clear guidance on the cases of Ethan, Luna and Ashley. In all three it's not possible to defer to future bodily autonomy, either because the person in question is likely never to become autonomous, like Ashley, or because decisions have to be made before they do, like Luna and Ethan. In Luna and Ethan's cases, it's deeply controversial whether intervention or non-intervention will best preserve their right to an open future. And it's not possible to defer to best interests, because the controversy about the proposed intervention is also a controversy over whether that intervention is in their best interests.

In these sorts of dilemmas, the considerations discussed so far are inconclusive between modification and non-modification. My claim is this: in hard cases such as these, bodily integrity means ruling in favour of non-modification. To respect bodily integrity as an ethical principle is to respect the value of the body understood as whole, complete, or intact: to leave others' bodies alone in cases where there is significant doubt as to whether intervention is justified.

To put it another way, the principle of bodily integrity says that you should *not* intervene in someone else's body without their consent unless 1), the evidence that the intervention is in their best interests is beyond reasonable doubt, or 2), there is clear and convincing evidence that intervention best secures that person's right to an open future. A higher standard of evidence is needed to justify intervention based on best interests because we are more likely to make mistakes about what is in someone's best interests than we are to make a mistake about whether an intervention opens or closes options, increasing or decreasing the choices left for them to make in the future. Interventions that are reversible are more likely to pass this test than are interventions that are irreversible, but reversibility is not itself part of the definition of bodily integrity. If there is doubt about whether a proposed intervention meets this standard, then the principle of bodily integrity rules against it.

Now we have an account of what bodily integrity is. How important is it?

Bodily integrity is not the only ethical value. Other values may conflict with it. For example, the value of the common good means that public health considerations may sometimes have to be set against, or even override, bodily integrity. It may be justifiable or even ethically required to administer vaccines to children that benefit the wider population more than children themselves.[61] To take another example, I've argued that bodily integrity rules against routine circumcision; but that argument has to be set against other values like religious tradition and non-discrimination.[62] Cases like these will need careful discussion and argument and can't be resolved here. There will be many occasions where bodily integrity has to be balanced against other, competing values, and sometimes those other values will win. However, the principle of bodily integrity is ethically very significant. In the final part of the chapter, I'll offer three reasons for thinking that bodily integrity should be given serious weight.

RESISTANCE

The principle of the unmodified body is a political principle of resistance. My claim is not that the unmodified body should be regarded as sacrosanct. I don't claim that parents can never legitimately authorize bodily interventions on their children, nor that doctors can never rightly suggest or perform such interventions. Instead, I claim that the intact body should be treated as a morally privileged baseline,[63] given a weighty moral status that can be overridden only in very clear cases. If there is any serious doubt as to whether some bodily intervention should be performed, it should not be. The whole body should be treated as the default that it is.

The principle of the unmodified body should be adopted as a political act of resistance against the overwhelming pressures to modify. These pressures to modify undermine our health, because they create an epidemic of appearance-related anxiety and related mental health problems, and because they encourage us to undertake modifications that can be physically harmful. And the pressures to modify undermine our equality, because they are applied to us unequally, in ways that entrench existing inequalities, and because appearance norms are often discriminatory in content (sexist, racist, ageist, ableist).

In a similar vein, the principle of bodily integrity operates as a way of resisting pressures to modify. In some of the hard cases of intervention in children the pressures to modify are the same as those I discuss in the book as a whole. The idea that Luna and Rosie should be modified comes from dominant norms of gendered bodies. Trans theorist Sandy Stone describes 'the binary phallocentric founding myth by which Western bodies and subjects are authorized,' according to which 'only one body per gendered subject is "right". All other bodies are wrong.'[64] Rosie's body is wrong, on that myth, because it doesn't have the genitals that accord with its chromosomal sex; Luna's is wrong, on that myth, because its maleness doesn't accord with the dominant gendering of Luna's behaviours and preferences. Resistance to the myth enables us to leave Rosie's and Luna's bodies alone, without making assumptions or impositions about their future gender presentation and identity. It tells us that, regardless of their gender, their bodies are 'right' just as they are.

The idea that Ethan should have a cochlear implant, or that Katie and Eilish should be separated, rests on the assumption that impaired, disabled and visibly different bodies are inferior; that it is objectively better to be even partially-hearing rather than deaf, better to be separated even if severely impaired rather than conjoined. Resisting those assumptions means remaining fully open to the idea that modification may not be justified. This is not to assert that it is certainly or always unjustified. For some people, cochlear implants may clearly secure their right to an open future because of their physiology or because of the lack of support for Sign and Deaf culture in their community. Or, the technology of cochlear implants may improve such that it becomes much clearer that they best serve the right to an open future. I'm not arguing that treatments like cochlear implants are never justified. But when we're considering cases that *aren't* clear, bodily integrity properly rules in favour of non-modification. In all cases, the principle of the unmodified body urges us to support all children in feeling positive and confident about their bodies: that their bodies are good enough just as they are.

INTRINSIC VALUE AND EQUALITY

But why should we say that all bodies are good enough just as they are? What if some bodies aren't good enough? The principle of the unmodified body tells us that we do something *wrong* if we deride others' bodies. The best way of understanding what is wrong with criticizing the intact body is by recognizing its interconnectedness with respecting others' basic moral equality and value.

The body is not a mere tool, or object. It is inextricably bound up with our own experience and identity. Your body doesn't just belong to you; it *is* you. I don't mean this to be a metaphysical claim about the nature of personal identity, although of course we experience the world only through our bodies. On the ordinary, day-to-day level we associate our bodies very deeply with our selves, and understand our bodies either as simply being our selves, or as being something that ought to reflect our selves, even if they need work to do that properly. We understand criticism of our bodies to be criticism of our selves, and we imagine our changed bodies to be reflective of our changed selves. We experience and express our identity through our bodies. Pressures to modify our bodies are also ways of undermining our selves, of undermining our basic moral worth and sense of equality.

Another way of seeing this point is through the literature on the experience and after-effects of suffering from physical and sexual abuse. Violence is more than just its physical effects. Violence works on the body *and* the mind, on the mind-and-body whole that is a human being.

Works by those who have endured violence repeatedly emphasize its impact on the whole self, in contrast to popular and pornographic depictions of violence that *dehumanize* their victims, reducing them to mere bodies. 'Hollywood made a movie called *The Accused*,' writes feminist Andrea Dworkin,

> a brilliant, incredible movie in which Jodie Foster, through her artistry, shows us that a woman is a human being. It takes two hours to establish for a mainstream audience that in fact that's true, so at the point when we reach the gang-rape scene, we understand that someone has

been hurt in a way that goes beyond the sum of the physical brutalities that were done to her.[65]

Dworkin's own intensely powerful and distressing novel *Mercy* includes graphic descriptions of rape from the perspective of the woman who is being raped.[66] Among the words that recount her pain and suffering – the embodied experience of violence – two words appear over and over again. They are 'me' and 'death'. Rape is not something that happens *to the body*, it is something that happens *to me*; and the experience feels like a death.

The image of rape as death is also found in philosopher Susan Brison's account of her own rape and attempted murder. While being examined by doctors after her attack, she remembers, 'I felt as if I was experiencing things posthumously.'[67] This experience is common: 'Survivors of trauma frequently remark that they are not the same people they were before they were traumatized.'[68] Brison describes her own experience in the following way:

> I was no longer the same person I was before the assault, and one of the ways in which I seemed changed was that I had a different relationship with my body. My body was now perceived as an enemy . . . and as a site of increased vulnerability. But rejecting the body and returning to the life of the mind was not an option, since body and mind had become nearly indistinguishable . . . The intermingling of mind and body is also apparent in traumatic memories that remain in the body, in each of the senses, in the heart that races and the skin that crawls whenever something resurrects the only slightly buried treasure.[69]

The literature on trauma and violence demonstrates that the body is not a mere object or tool that can be damaged or altered, whose damage or alteration we might regard in the same way as we regard a chip in our car's paintwork, the breaking of a favourite mug, or a pleasing restoration of an artwork. *The body is us*. What happens to our bodies *happens to us*. And so valuing our bodies, just as they are, amounts to valuing us, just as we are.

The underlying ethical value of the body cannot be separated from the underlying ethical value of the self.[70] Attacks on the body are attacks on the self, whether those attacks are direct physical interventions, psychological pressures, or political acts of domination and discrimination. This makes the body morally privileged in the same way as the self is morally privileged. This moral privilege is appropriately described as a *baseline* because it is not possible to go any deeper: it is a claim about moral value that underpins everything else.

These observations help us to deal with the profoundly difficult case of Ashley, whose parents sought treatment that would keep her permanently small and pre-pubescent. Ashley, it is assumed, is not capable of autonomy and perhaps also has no sense of self. What, then, is the justification for regarding her as having bodily integrity in the way I have proposed, where bodily integrity acts as a default against modification?

Ashley cannot consent to her treatment. Of course, she cannot consent to anything that happens to her. But this fact is not reason to disregard her lack of consent. It is reason not to do anything to her that is not *very clearly* in her interests, because we cannot justify our actions by appealing to consent.

Similarly, we assume that Ashley does not have an open future: she will never be autonomous. But this fact is not reason to intervene regardless. It is reason to recognize that we cannot justify intervening in her body by appealing to her right to an open future (as perhaps we might do in the case of Ethan), and so we may not be able to justify intervening at all.

In other words, the right way of thinking about the case of Ashley is not that we have *no* reason to *refrain* from intervention, but that we *lack* the strong reasons necessary *for* intervention. All we have is a claim about what is in her best interests, but this is not decisive in hard cases like Ashley's precisely because we *don't know* whether intervention is in her interests or not. In unknowable, controversial cases like this, the principle of bodily integrity says that we should *not* intervene. Ashley might experience her treatment as an act of violence against her, as an act that causes her suffering, invades her bodily integrity and denies her sense of self. We cannot be sure whether body modification will do these things; it may not. But if we cannot be sure, then we shouldn't modify her body. It is worse to err by intervention than by non-intervention in difficult cases, because the harms of wrongful intervention are of the most ethically serious kind.

Modifying others' bodies without their consent requires greater certainty than we are justified in having in cases like Ashley's, because wrongful modification of others is a very serious sort of wrong. The stakes are very high. As philosopher Andrea Sangiovanni puts it:

> It takes no great imagination to see that children, the mentally ill, and those with severe cognitive disability are, as a result, very vulnerable not only to social cruelty but also to other forms of, for example, physical cruelty. This is in part due to their inability to understand the physical and social world adequately to coordinate their responses to it in coherent and consistent ways, and especially their inability to resist maltreatment. But it is also in part because they lack the shield of consent.[71]

The intense vulnerability that comes from this lack of a shield means that we must create an alternative shield for them, in the form of a tie-breaking principle of bodily integrity.

And of course, if we are considering authorizing body modification for someone other than ourselves, they will have to undergo the physical and mental stress of the procedures. As Partridge puts it, in a passage aimed at patients facing facial surgery:

> Your willingness to go back for more operations may well flag, as you gradually rehabilitate yourself outside and as you increasingly balance the extra facial benefits to be derived from the next operation against the costs ... You are the one who must make the ultimate decision whether to go ahead or not. You are the one who will suffer the discomfort and pain – and, despite analgesia and sensitive nursing, these are ever present. You are the one who has to face the anticipation and fear of needles and operations ... You are the one who has to endure hospitalization, the loss of freedom and privacy, and you are the one who could be choosing to spend your time in many more enjoyable ways than in an operating theatre.[72]

When decisions are being made for others, we must remember that we are not the ones facing the interventions, and act with restraint.

SOCIAL CONSIDERATIONS

Finally, consider social reasons why it makes sense to think of the unmodified body as morally privileged compared to the modified body. These considerations don't have the same weighty moral status as the previous argument. But they are extra evidence that the ethical principle of bodily integrity as non-modification should be taken very seriously.

First, ruling in favour of the unmodified body in hard cases gives clear guidance, whereas a principle of favouring modification would be open-ended and indeterminate. The unmodified body is comparatively stable when compared to the alternative of the modified body. Of course, the unmodified body is in a state of constant flux. Our bodies change throughout our lives, gaining and losing hair, mobility, weight, skin tone and wrinkles, muscle, height. We can't find some authentic, true body amid all that inevitable change. But it's fairly easy to distinguish the unmodified body from the modified one in the context of medical or cosmetic intervention. The unmodified body is what we have if we leave things alone. It's what we have if we do nothing.

The modified body, in contrast, is a mysterious beast. There is in principle no end to the ways in which we can be modified, no settled content to the practice of intervention. And so if we broke ties in favour of modification we'd still need to answer the question of which modification to do, or of where modification ends. Does Rosie need clitoral surgery, or vaginal surgery, or both? Should Ashley just take growth-limiting hormones, or should she also have the mastectomy and hysterectomy? What about other procedures we haven't thought of yet? If we're piercing baby Priscilla's ears, should we also give her cosmetic surgery? If the morally privileged baseline were the modified body as opposed to the unmodified one we would be locked into a duty to seek constant modification, constant enhancement, unending surgery or self-improvement or technological advance. There would be no principled end.

Second, the unmodified body has a claim to moral privilege because the unmodified body is diverse. The unmodified body is sensitive to human individuality and uniqueness. If modification were considered morally privileged that would suggest that there is some objective standard to which we should all conform, some process by which we should all become the same. We should all be striving to some vision of perfection. In contrast, privileging the unmodified body protects us as we are, in all our physical diversity.

We already know that standards of beauty, ideals of perfection and trends of body modification pressure us towards a homogeneity that reflects and strengthens existing axes of oppression. It pushes us to iron out differences of race, sex, gender and dis/ability, aspiring to an ideal that recreates and reifies structural inequality. The dominant-body ideal is the idea of the body that dominates. Insisting on the moral privilege of the unmodified body allows us to resist those forces. It defends diversity. It values the under-valued.

The fundamental claim of *Intact* – the political principle that *your body is good enough just as it is* – is a principle of equality. Insisting on the moral privilege of the unmodified body allows us to insist that the impaired body is not defective, to reject gendered beauty standards and cultural practices that demean and injure us, to resist tropes that liken people with facial disfigurements to villains, to fight standards of 'professionalism' and uniformity that act as vehicles for racism. And an insistence on the moral privilege of the unmodified body allows us to insist on the humanity, the dignity and respect owed to the people who inhabit all kinds of bodies – which means *all people*.

Coda

All the other women should love their bodies
But I wanna lose five pounds!
Rachel Lark, 'I Wanna Lose Five Pounds' (2017)[1]

By allowing the focus to rest on the 'body positivity' move-
ment, we are allowing wealthy companies to cash in on a fight
that has been fought by fat activists since the 1960s. Fat activ-
ism is very rarely about the individual's struggle with their
self-esteem or feelings about their stretch marks. It is about
changing the anti-fat bias, particularly the way it affects fat
people politically.

Sofie Hagen, *Happy Fat* (2019)[2]

We're not promoting obesity, or telling people to be fat, we're
just saying, if you're fat you don't have to hate yourself.
Stephanie Yeboah (2018)[3]

The body positivity movement urges us to reject the constant feeling of dissatisfaction in favour of loving ourselves, seeing ourselves as beautiful regardless of how our bodies are. That's a good thing. But it suggests that the problem is primarily one of individual self-esteem: that it is up to us to choose to be beautiful, to choose to feel good about ourselves. It obscures the political and economic structures that set us up to feel bad. In privatizing a political problem, it offers another way to fail. Now you can feel bad about your body, and you can feel bad about failing to love it.

The body positivity movement is not all bad, not at all. Deliberate measures to cultivate good body image can work, to an extent. One study exposed young women to one of three curated Instagram feeds. The first contained appearance-neutral images of home interiors without any people in them. The second featured 'fitspiration' images, a term coined from 'fit' and 'inspiration' that encourages users to push themselves to new heights of athleticism and fitness. The fitspiration feed contained images of women actively engaging in physical activity or posing in workout gear. The third stream featured self-compassion images, usually featuring a quote inspiring self-love or positive thinking and a picture or pattern with no people. The study found that viewing the self-compassion quotes for just five minutes improved women's mood and body image.[4]

But the body positivity movement is not without its problems. It has been used, ironically, by major beauty brands. Most prominent among them is Dove, which describes itself as 'the home of real beauty'.[5] Dove has commandeered the use of body positivity as a marketing tool. Some of its work is evidence-based, in partnership with respected academic experts on body image. For example, the Dove Self-Esteem Project provides resources on improving body image that can be used by schools, youth leaders and parents – and also gets the Dove brand name into the classroom. But some of Dove's forays into body positivity perpetuate the problem they claim to solve.

In 2015 Dove ran a 'Choose Beautiful' campaign in five cities around the world.[6] Large signs reading either 'Beautiful' or 'Average' were placed above entrances to major public buildings, so that anyone entering the building had to choose between them. Dove released a video showing women making their choices and discussing them afterwards.

'I went through the Average door,' says one woman. 'Really?!' says her friend. 'Yeah, I didn't even hesitate,' the first replies. Another woman describes her decision straight to camera. 'Every day I go through the Average door. But yesterday was a unique day. So I chose to go through the Beautiful one.' She looks elated. Several parts of the video show one woman pushing another through the Beautiful door, including a mother and daughter and a woman literally being pushed in a wheelchair. The video closes with women and girls triumphantly choosing the Beautiful door and the hashtag #ChooseBeautiful.

The video is meant as a celebration of individuality, of body positivity, of the choice to call oneself beautiful. But in reality it replicates the same old tropes. All the people depicted making the choice are women. None of them are fat. No men are shown confronting how they appear to the outside world, forced to make and display a choice about whether they are beautiful. Despite its supposedly empowering aim, the choice between 'Beautiful' and 'Average' forces women to rank themselves against each other. And, of course, not everyone can be beautiful if beautiful means not-average. This nonsensical choice replicates the beauty ideal: every woman should be beautiful, but universal beauty is impossible. If every woman is beautiful then 'beautiful' and 'average' are the same anyway.

My favourite part of the video passes without commentary or explanation. A woman arrives outside the building, looks at the signs, frowns, turns and walks away.

Choice is important, but choice is not everything.

We do not choose the bodies we are born with.

We do not choose our social context.

We do not choose how our bodies will be racialized.

We do not choose how gender is understood and enforced.

We do not choose the content of the beauty ideal.

We do not choose to be on the receiving end of an endless barrage of images of the 'perfect' body.

We do not choose the judgement, the appraisal, the comments on our appearance and the assumptions made about our identity.

We do not choose to live in a world where we are constantly receiving the message that how we look is one of, if not the most important things about us.

We live in a society that is becoming ever more visual, ever more focused on how we look. Our appearance becomes a measure of our value. Our bodies become an indication of our character. There is no flaw that cannot be fixed, no limit to the project of self-improvement, *no body that is good enough*.

It is time to say *STOP*. It is time to allow our bodies to be good enough. It is time to recognize that, when virtually everyone feels bad about their bodies, the bodies are not the problem. It is time to reclaim the value of the unmodified body. It is time to let our bodies, our selves, be whole, intact.

Acknowledgements

I wrote this book under extraordinary circumstances, as the Covid-19 pandemic changed lives and bodies all around the world. Most of the book was researched and written in my office at Jesus College, Cambridge, where I was sustained by the beautiful gardens and architecture, delicious food and fellowship. But for large periods of time I was working at the kitchen table while my children sat next to me in online school, or in a bedroom when it was my partner's turn to be teaching assistant, or in the garden hiding behind the washing line. I am so grateful to my family for their forbearance and support.

My children, Harley and Caspar, coped incredibly with the changing circumstances. They are a constant source of joy, love, inspiration, engaging conversation and challenging questions on the topic of this book (and much else). Phil Parvin has been my partner in all things for twenty years. He and I have debated the issues discussed here over and over again; we agree often, but not always, and the disagreement is always illuminating. I rely on his insight, his encouragement and all the practical and emotional ways he supports my work.

Two other people have contributed so much to the writing of this book that their names appear frequently in these acknowledgements. Both are immensely supportive friends, deeply impressive philosophers and repeat readers of various drafts.

Heather Widdows has been an inspiration. She has convinced me of her views many times; often, no convincing was necessary. Heather's work is a model for how to combine philosophy and policy concerns, and Heather herself is a model for how to be and support women in philosophy. My heartfelt thanks to Heather for always checking in.

Lori Watson is a steadfast friend, challenging critic and constant support. Over phallic cocktails, drafts read by return email and video calls she has saved me many times. Whether debating the finer points of Rawlsian theory or the fundamental principles of feminism, I always want to know Lori's point of view. She doesn't just have an immense ability to point out problems – the *raison d'être* of any philosopher – she also has the much rarer capacity and generosity to help solve them.

The pandemic also meant that opportunities to present drafts of the book have been more limited than usual. Before Covid, I was fortunate that Simon Caney offered the opportunity of an in-person workshop on some very early drafts at the University of Warwick. I learned a lot from all the participants, particularly the assigned commentators: Kimberley Brownlee, Simon Caney, Ida Lubben, Andrew Mason, Katy Wells and Heather Widdows.

While Covid restrictions were still in place, I was very graciously hosted for a virtual manuscript workshop by Andrew I. Cohen at the Jean Beer Blumenfeld Center for Ethics at Georgia State University. It is a huge commitment to dedicate the time necessary to read an entire draft manuscript closely and prepare comments, and the participants in this workshop did not even have the incentive of being wined and dined in reward. I could not have asked for better feedback, and I am so grateful to all the participants: the official commentators Kimberley Brownlee, Brian Earp, Christie Hartley, Cressida Heyes, Suzie Love, Lori Watson and Heather Widdows; and the other participants and observers, some of whom sent written comments: Andrew I. Cohen, Bill Edmundson, Connor Kianpour, George Rainbolt and Cynthia Stark.

I shared drafts of individual chapters with audiences at University College London, the University of Cambridge and the University of York, and have had additional valuable conversations, email exchanges and reading suggestions from Jessica Berenbeim, Sophia Connell, Elaine Gadd, Fiona Green, Ronja Griep, Dominique Hawksley, Robert Newman, Phil Parvin, Nichola Rumsey, Andrea Sangiovanni, Findlay Stark and others already mentioned. Brian Earp has long been an inspiration in the field of genital cutting, and it has been an honour to work with him on other projects at the same time as writing this book. Jon Howell and Clara Swinson have supported me over a quarter of a century of friendship, and also gave very welcome material support by giving me the use of Vista Point, their beautiful holiday house, to allow me to finish the first draft of the manuscript in the final days before the second England lockdown.

I learned a great deal about the ethics of body modification from working with colleagues on the Nuffield Council on Bioethics Working Party on Cosmetic Procedures: Sharron Brown, Alex Clarke, Jeanette Edwards, Kate Harvey, Mark Henley, Jane O'Brien, James Partridge, Nichola Rumsey, Tom Shakespeare, Shirley Tate, Michael Thomson, Heather Widdows and Katherine Wright. Many of them have since become friends, and their work has been crucial to many of my arguments here.

Nikhil Krishnan inspired me to look beyond traditional academic publishing and introduced me to my superb agent, Sophie Scard. Sophie supported the book from the outset and shepherded the proposal through a series of revisions and rejections with good humour and encouragement. Casiana Ionita, my editor at Allen Lane, saw what the book could be and allowed me to make it so. Casiana gave invaluable advice and insight along the way, too. It has been an honour to work with these two wonderful women.

Research for this book was generously funded by the Leverhulme Trust, who awarded me a three-year Major Research Fellowship for the purpose. I am extremely grateful to the Trust for the grant: the teaching and administrative workloads of academics are so high that most of us rely on external funding to provide the time and intellectual space to engage in extended research like this. I should also like to give particular thanks to Cécile Fabre, Anne Phillips and Heather Widdows for their advice and support of my grant application.

Finally, I want to record my heartfelt thanks to those people who have spoken to me about their personal experiences. Some of these stories have made it directly into the book, anonymously or under pseudonyms, others have informed my thinking or changed my mind. It is not easy to disclose personal information about struggles with one's body: these stories are intimate, personal and often infused with shame. Telling them publicly, as Tom Rosenthal does in his show 'Manhood' (a show I was privileged to preview at the Future Choices conference), or allowing them to be told anonymously, as 'Hannah' does in Chapter 7, is an act of bravery and selflessness. Many thanks to

Hannah for her story and determination, to Tom, David Smith, and the other men who have spoken to me about their circumcision, to Hibo Wardere and the other women who have spoken about their experiences of FGM and labiaplasty, to cosmetic surgeons who have told me their stories and ethical dilemmas, to the men who have discussed their own practice of bodybuilding, to the many women who have shared their anxieties about their weight, shape, hair and face or told their menstruation and menopause stories, to 'Owen' for his openness about living with an abdominal apron, and to the people who have shared their struggles with gender identity or their experiences of disability. We all have our own stories to tell about our bodies: our anxiety, our shame, our pride, our defiance. We must carry on telling these stories, and we must carry on learning from the stories of others.

Bibliography and Sources

15 Square at https://15square.org.uk

Adams, Richard, *Watership Down* (Rex Collings, 1972)

Adjmi, David, 'I had the best body I'd ever had – so why did I feel so much shame?', *Guardian*, 20 October 2020, https://www.theguardian.com/us-news/2020/oct/20/leaving-my-perfect-male-body-in-the-past?CMP=soc_567&fbclid=iwAR3Tpi3IoyyDDmpqyipZVhsnwDqd-52r_ZVozFWroIjgzxWsNLjTSUBDmLo

Affinity Magazine staff, 'Why you should be careful with using the term "Dreads"', *Affinity*, 14 January 2017, http://affinitymagazine.us/2017/01/14/why-you-should-be-careful-saying-dreads/

Alahmad, Ghiath and Dekkers, Wim, 'Bodily integrity and male circumcision: an Islamic perspective', *Journal of the Islamic Medical Association of North America*, 44, 2012

Alexander, Harriet, 'Women worry about their bodies 252 times a week', *Daily Telegraph*, 23 November 2009, https://www.telegraph.co.uk/news/uknews/6634686/Women-worry-about-their-bodies-252-times-a-week.html

Ali, Nimko, *What We're Told Not to Talk About (But We're Going to Anyway): Women's Voices From East London to Ethiopia* (Viking, 2019)

Allen, David, 'Moving the needle on recovery from breast cancer', *Journal of the American Medical Association*, 317 (7), 2017

American Academy of Pediatrics, 'Baby helmet therapy: parent FAQs', https://www.healthychildren.org/English/health-issues/conditions/Cleft-Craniofacial/Pages/Baby-Helmet-Therapy-Parent-FAQs.aspx

American Academy of Pediatrics, 'Newborn male circumcision', https://www.aap.org/en-us/about-the-aap/aap-press-room/pages/newborn-male-circumcision.aspx

Amnesty International, 'The World's Worst Places to be a Woman', https://www.amnestyusa.org/the-worlds-worst-places-to-be-a-woman/

Amundson, Ron, 'Against normal function', *Studies in History and Philosophy of Biological and Biomedical Sciences*, 31 (1), 2000

Archard, David, *Children: Rights and Childhood* (Routledge, 2014)

Archard, David and Macleod, Colin (eds.), *The Moral and Political Status of Children: New Essays* (Oxford University Press, 2002)

BAAPS, 'Cosmetic surgery stats: number of surgeries remains stable amid calls for greater regulation of quick fix solutions', 20 May 2019, https://baaps.org.uk/media/press_releases/1708/cosmetic_surgery_stats_number_of_surgeries_remains_stable_amid_calls_for_greater_regulation_of_quick_fix_solutions

Badham,Van, 'Female genital mutilation is alive in Australia. It's just called labiaplasty', *Guardian*, 26 August 2015, https://www.theguardian.com/commentisfree/2015/aug/26/female-genital-mutilation-is-alive-in-australia-its-just-called-labiaplasty

Bailenson, Jeremy N., 'Nonverbal overload: a theoretical argument for the causes of Zoom fatigue', *Technology, Mind, and Behavior*, 2 (1), 2021

Banyard, Kat et al., 'Cosmetic surgery ads should be banned', *Guardian* Letters page, 14 March 2012, https://www.theguardian.com/lifeandstyle/2012/mar/14/cosmetic-surgery-advertising-ban

Barnes, Elizabeth, *The Minority Body: A Theory of Disability* (Oxford University Press, 2016)

Barnes, Julian, *Letters from London 1990–1995* (Vintage, 1995)

Baron-Cohen, Simon, *The Essential Difference: Men, Women and the Extreme Male Brain* (Penguin/Basic Books, 2003)

Bartky, Sandra Lee, 'Foucault, femininity, and the modernization of patriarchal power', in Diana Tietjens Meyers (ed.), *Feminist Social Thought: A Reader* (Routledge, 1997)

Bartky, Sandra Lee, *Femininity and Domination: Studies in the Phenomenology of Oppression* (Routledge, 1990)

Bateman, Oliver Lee, 'Death by muscle', *Mel* magazine, https://melmagazine.com/en-us/story/death-by-muscle-2

BBC News, 'Angelina Jolie has double mastectomy due to cancer gene', 14 May 2013, https://www.bbc.co.uk/news/world-us-canada-22520720

BBC Radio 4, 'Being a girl is ace, Mia', in *The Archers*, 22 March 2019, https://www.bbc.co.uk/sounds/play/p074bb8q

Bearak, Jonathan et al., 'Global, regional, and subregional trends in unintended pregnancy and its outcomes from 1990 to 2014: estimates from a Bayesian hierarchical model', *The Lancet Global Health*, 6, 2018

Beauvoir, Simone de, *The Second Sex* (Virago, 1997)

Beethoven, Ludwig van, 'Letter to my brothers Carl and Johann Beethoven', 6 October 1802, in *The Project Gutenberg EBook of Beethoven's Letters 1790–1826* (ed. Lady Wallace), https://www.gutenberg.org/files/13065/13065-h/13065-h.htm#let26

Beethoven, Ludwig van, letter to Karl Amanda at http://www.lvbeethoven.com/Bio/BiographyDeafness.html

Belly Bandit, http://www.bellybandit.co.uk

Benatar, David, 'Introduction: the ethics of contested surgeries', in David Benatar (ed.), *Cutting to the Core: Exploring the Ethics of Contested Surgeries* (Rowman & Littlefield, 2006)

Benatar, Michael and Benatar, David, 'Between prophylaxis and child abuse: the ethics of neonatal male circumcision', in David Benatar (ed.), *Cutting to the Core: Exploring the Ethics of Contested Surgeries* (Rowman & Littlefield, 2006)

Benenson, Joyce F., 'Sex on the brain', *Nature*, 424, 2003

Berer, Marge, 'Labia reduction for non-therapeutic purposes vs. female genital mutilation: contradictions in law and practice in Britain', *Reproductive Health Matters*, 18 (35), 2010

Bettcher, Talia Mae, 'Trans women and the meaning of "woman"', in Nicholas Power, Raja Halwani and Alan Soble (eds.), *The Philosophy of Sex: Contemporary Readings* (Rowman & Littlefield, 2012)

Bickenbach, Jerome, 'Disability, health, and difference', in Adam Cureton and David Wasserman (eds.), *The Oxford Handbook of Philosophy and Disability* (Oxford University Press, 2018)

Blackledge, Catherine, *The Story of V: Opening Pandora's Box* (Orion Books, 2003)

Bliss, Cass, 'Here's what it's like to get your period when you're not a woman', *Huffpost Personal*, 20 August 2018, https://www.huffpost.com/entry/nonbinary-period-menstruation_n_5b75ac1fe4b0182d49b1c2ed?guccounter=1&guce_referrer=aHR0cHM6Ly93d3cuZ29vZ2xlLmNvbS8&guce_referrer_sig=AQAAAJItD6n2q_ugQqoxgq-NAljpSEegR8wBBeFwXEfpTfyJTYxsyARct1jcfkYBPS1zXxEMK_zEyd9bYBdwwz1UbhfdsIFvxdCSudJ6XXbq9cWfXlmM6qFqx4NeQT7GYEilx6Pi-xVW1JOI_okWyQ9grl5IRUqodTNK36UXhaW3zBkR

Blossom, Priscilla, '9 things white families don't understand about piercing a baby's ears', *Romper*, 19 June 2017, https://www.romper.com/p/9-things-white-families-dont-understand-about-piercing-a-babys-ears-64446

Bodybuilding.com, 'Arnold Schwarzenegger Pro Bodybuilding Profile', https://www.bodybuilding.com/content/bodybuilders-arnold.html

Bodybuilding.com forum, https://forum.bodybuilding.com/

Boorse, Christopher, 'Health as a theoretical concept', *Philosophy of Science*, 44 (4), 1977

Boorse, Christopher, 'On the distinction between disease and illness', *Philosophy & Public Affairs*, 5, 1975

Bordo, Susan, *Unbearable Weight: Feminism, Western Culture, and the Body* (University of California Press, 2003)

Bornstein, Kate, *Gender Outlaw: On Men, Women, and the Rest of Us* (Routledge, 1994)

Bourdieu, Pierre, *Masculine Domination* (Polity Press, 2001)

Bourdieu, Pierre, *The Logic of Practice* (Polity Press, 1990)

Bovet, Jeanne, 'Evolutionary theories and men's preferences for women's waist-to-hip ratio: which hypotheses remain? A systematic review', *Frontiers in Psychology*, 4 June 2019

Brison, Susan, *Aftermath: Violence and the Remaking of a Self* (Princeton University Press, 2002)

British Association of Teachers of the Deaf, 'Ethan Mount-Jones by his mother', in 'Personal Experiences – Cochlear Implants', https://www.batod.org.uk/information/personal-experiences-cochlear-implants/

British Natural Bodybuilding Federation, 'Banned Substances', https://www.bnbf.co.uk/banned-subtances/

British Natural Bodybuilding Federation, 'Criteria Explained – Women's Criteria', https://www.bnbf.co.uk/events/criteria-explained/womens-criteria/

Brown, Amy, 'Research into pregnancy, birth, and infant care are historically underfunded – and women are paying the price', *The Conversation*, 19 November 2019, http://theconversation.com/research-into-pregnancy-birth-and-infant-care-are-historically-underfunded-and-women-are-paying-the-price-126629?utm_source=twitter&utm_medium=twitterbutton

Brown, Paul, Perera, Shyama and Wainwright, Martin, 'Protest by CND stretches 14 miles', *Guardian*, 2 April 1983, https://www.theguardian.com/fromthearchive/story/0,,1866956,00.html

Browne, Kingsley, *Divided Labours: An Evolutionary View of Women at Work* (Yale University Press, 1999)

Burns, Katelyn 'What the battle over a 7-year-old trans girl could mean for families nationwide', *Vox*, 11 November 2019, https://www.vox.com/identities/2019/11/11/20955059/luna-younger-transgender-child-custody

Butler, Judith, *Gender Trouble: Feminism and the Subversion of Identity* (Routledge, 1999)

Byrd, Rudolph P., Cole, Johnnetta Betsch and Guy-Sheftall, Beverly (eds.), *I am Your Sister: Collected and Unpublished Writings of Audre Lorde* (Oxford University Press, 2009)

Califia, Patrick, *Sex Changes* (Cleis Press, 2nd edn, 2003)

Cannold, Leslie, 'The ethics of neonatal male circumcision', in David Benatar (ed.), *Cutting to the Core: Exploring the Ethics of Contested Surgeries* (Rowman & Littlefield, 2006)

Centre for Appearance Research, https://www.uwe.ac.uk/research/centres-and-groups/appearance

Chambers, Clare, 'Choice and female genital cosmetic surgery', in Sarah Creighton and Lih-Mei Liao (eds.), *Female Genital Cosmetic Surgery: Solution to What Problem?* (Cambridge University Press, 2019)

Chambers, Clare, 'Blending in and standing out: comfort and visibility in beauty practices', Beauty Demands blog, 10 December 2018, http://beautydemands.blogspot.com/2018/12/blending-in-and-standing-out-comfort.html

Chambers, Clare, 'Reasonable disagreement and the neutralist dilemma: abortion and circumcision in Matthew Kramer's *Liberalism with Excellence*', *American Journal of Jurisprudence*, May, 2018

Chambers, Clare, *Against Marriage: An Egalitarian Defence of the Marriage-Free State* (Oxford University Press, 2017)

Chambers, Clare, 'Judging women: twenty-five years further *Toward a Feminist Theory of the State*', *Feminist Philosophy Quarterly*, 3 (2), 2017

Chambers, Clare, 'Review of Anne Phillips, *Our Bodies, Whose Property?* (Princeton University Press, 2012)', *Political Theory*, 43 (1), 2015

Chambers, Clare, *Sex, Culture, and Justice: The Limits of Choice* (Penn State University Press, 2008)

Chambers, Clare, 'Are breast implants better than female genital mutilation? Autonomy, gender equality and Nussbaum's political liberalism', *Critical Review of International Social and Political Philosophy*, 7 (3), 2004

Chappell, Sophie-Grace, 'An open letter to JK Rowling's blog post on sex and gender', *Crooked Timber*, 14 June 2020, https://crookedtimber.org/2020/06/14/guest-post-an-open-letter-to-jk-rowling-blog-post-on-sex-and-gender-by-sophie-grace-chappell/

Clare, Eli, *Exile and Pride: Disability, Queerness, and Liberation* (Duke University Press, 2015)

CNN, 'Bullied kids receive free plastic surgery', 27 July 2012, https://www.youtube.com/watch?v=5BdL9GEbplo

Coleman, Patrick A., 'When can you pierce a baby's ears?', *Fatherly*, 18 May 2020, https://www.fatherly.com/health-science/when-to-pierce-a-babys-ears/

Collins, Patricia Hill, *Black Feminist Thought* (Routledge, 2000)

Colucci, Chris, 'Big dead bodybuilders: the ultimate price of pro bodybuilding?', *TNation*, 28 October 2016, https://www.t-nation.com/pharma/big-dead-bodybuilders

Combahee River Collective, 'A Black feminist statement (1977)', in Cherrie Moraga and Glora Anzaldua (eds.), *This Bridge Called My Back: Writings by Radical Women of Color* (Kitchen Table/Women of Color Press, 1981)

Commanding Hands, 'Adding facial expressions to signs in British Sign Language', https://www.youtube.com/watch?v=Q25hzuU4lOk

Connell, R. W., *Masculinities* (Polity Press, 1995)

Cooper, Edward, 'Will steroids shrink my balls?', *Men's Health*, 19 February 2018, https://www.menshealth.com/uk/building-muscle/a758780/will-steroids-shrink-my-balls/

Creighton, Sarah, 'Surgery for intersex', *Journal of the Royal Society of Medicine*, 94 (2001)

Crenshaw, Kimberlé, 'Mapping the margins: intersectionality, identity politics, and violence against women of color', *Stanford Law Review*, 43, 1993

Crenshaw, Kimberlé, 'Demarginalizing the intersection of race and sex: a Black feminist critique of antidiscrimination doctrine, feminist theory and anti-racist politics', *University of Chicago Legal Forum*, 1989

Criado Perez, Caroline, *Invisible Women: Exposing Data Bias in a World Designed by Men* (Chatto & Windus, 2019)

Cystic Fibrosis Trust, 'Physiotherapy FAQs', https://www.cysticfibrosis.org.uk/what-is-cystic-fibrosis/cystic-fibrosis-care/physiotherapy/physiotherapy-faqs

Dabiri, Emma, *Don't Touch My Hair* (Allen Lane, 2019)

Dahlqvist, Anna, *It's Only Blood* (Zed Books, 2018)

Darby, Robert, 'Moral hypocrisy or intellectual inconsistency? A historical perspective on our habit of placing male and female genital cutting in separate ethical boxes', *Kennedy Institute of Ethics Journal*, 26 (2), 2016

Darby, Robert, 'The masturbation taboo and the rise of routine male circumcision: a review of the historiography', *Journal of Social History*, 36 (3), 2003

Darby, Robert J. L., 'The child's right to an open future: is the principle applicable to non-therapeutic circumcision?', *Journal of Medical Ethics*, 39, 2013

Davis, Bill, 'How to Get Brutally Huge'; 'Brutally Huge: The Body Parts'; and 'The Best of the Rest of Brutally Huge', https://brutallyhuge.com

Dewan, P. A., Tieu, H. C. and Cheing, B. S., 'Phimosis: is circumcision necessary?', *Journal of Paediatrics and Child Health*, 32 (4), 1996.

Diabetes Daily Grind, https://www.diabetesdailygrind.com/

Diary of a Fit Mommy, https://diaryofafitmommy.com/how-i-got-my-body-back-after-baby-2/

Direkvand-Moghadam, A. et al., 'Epidemiology of premenstrual syndrome (PMS) – a systematic review and meta-analysis study', in *Journal of Clinical and Diagnostic Research*, 8 (2), 2014

Dodsworth, Laura, *Manhood: The Bare Reality* (Pinter & Martin, 2017)

Donaghy, Kathy, 'Life after Katie', *Independent.ie*, 2 September 2000, https://www.independent.ie/irish-news/life-after-katie-26108190.html

Douglas, Gillian, 'The retreat from Gillick', *Modern Law Review*, 55 (4), 1992

Dove, https://www.dove.com/uk/home.html

Dove, 'Beautiful or Average', https://www.youtube.com/watch?v=aocx88vuLzE

Dreger, Alice, *Galileo's Middle Finger: Heretics, Activists, and One Scholar's Search for Justice* (Penguin, 2015)

Dreger, Alice Domurat, *One of Us: Conjoined Twins and the Future of Normal* (Harvard University Press, 2004)

Drescher, Jack, 'Gender identity diagnoses: history and controversies', in P. Baudewijntje, C. Kreukels, Thomas D. Steensma and Annelou L. C. de Vries (eds.), *Gender Dysphoria and Disorders of Sex Development: Progress in Care and Knowledge* (Springer, 2013)

Duncan, Maxim, 'Brazilian family cross extra fingers for sixth world cup', Reuters, 21 June 2014, https://uk.reuters.com/article/uk-soccer-world-bra-fingers/brazilian-family-cross-extra-fingers-for-sixth-world-cup-idUKKBN0EW06R20140621

Durkin, Erin, 'New York to ban hairstyle policies that discriminate against black people', *Guardian*, 18 February 2019, https://www.theguardian.com/us-news/2019/feb/18/new-york-hairstyle-discrimination-ban-african-american?CMP=Share_iOSApp_Other

Dustin, Moira, 'Female genital mutilation/cutting in the UK', *European Journal of Women's Studies*, 17 (1), 2010

Duteille, Franck, Perrot, Pierre, Bacheley, Marie-Hélène and Stewart, Sharon, 'Eight-year safety data for round and anatomical silicone gel breast implants', *Aesthetic Surgery Journal*, 38 (2), 2018

Dworkin, Andrea, *Life and Death: Unapologetic Writings on the Continuing War against Women* (Virago, 1997)

Dworkin, Andrea, *Mercy* (Arrow Books, 1992)

Dworkin, Andrea, *Letters from a War Zone* (Martin Secker & Warburg, 1988)

Dworkin, Andrea, *Woman Hating* (E. P. Dutton, 1974)

Dworkin, Shari L., ' "Holding back": negotiating a glass ceiling on women's muscular strength', in Rose Weitz (ed.), *The Politics of Women's Bodies: Sexuality, Appearance, and Behavior* (Oxford University Press, 2003)

Dyer, Clare, 'High Court rules that 14 year old Jehovah's Witness should have blood transfusions', *BMJ*, 2019, https://www.bmj.com/content/367/bmj.l6513

Earp, Brian D., 'The child's right to bodily integrity', in David Edmonds (ed.), *Ethics and the Contemporary World* (Routledge, 2019)

Earp, Brian D., 'Between moral relativism and moral hypocrisy: reframing the debate on "FGM"', *Kennedy Institute of Ethics Journal*, 26 (2), 2016

Earp, Brian D., 'Female genital mutilation and male circumcision: toward an autonomy-based ethical framework', *Medicolegal and Bioethics*, 5, 2015

Earp, Brian D., 'Female genital mutilation (FGM) and male circumcision: should there be a separate ethical discourse?', *Practical Ethics*, 18 February 2014, https://www.academia.edu/8817976/Female_genital_mutilation_FGM_and_male_circumcision_Should_there_be_a_separate_ethical_discourse

Earp, Brian D. and Darby, Robert, 'Circumcision, sexual experience, and harm', *University of Pennsylvania Journal of International Law*, 3 (2), 2017

Eliot, Lise, *Pink Brain, Blue Brain: How Small Differences Grow into Troublesome Gaps – And What We Can Do About It* (Oneworld Publications, 2012)

Emanuel, Daniella, 'Raising an intersex child: "This is your body . . . There's nothing to be ashamed of"', CNN, 15 April 2019, https://edition.cnn.com/2019/04/13/health/intersex-child-parenting-eprise/index.html

Engelhardt, Jr, H. T., 'The concepts of health and disease', in H. T. Engelhardt, Jr and S. F. Spicker (eds.), *Evaluation and Explanation in Biomedical Sciences* (D. Reidel, 1975)

Everyday Lookism, https://everydaylookism.bham.ac.uk

Evolution of Bodybuilding staff, 'Natural bodybuilding supplements: essentials for building muscle growth', 14 August 2018, https://www.evolutionofbodybuilding.net/natural-bodybuilding-supplements/

Fair, John D., *Mr. America: The Tragic History of a Bodybuilding Icon* (University of Texas Press, 2015)

Feagin, Joe and Bennefield, Zennobia, 'Systemic racism and U.S. health care', in *Social Science & Medicine*, 103, 2014

Feinberg, Joel, 'The child's right to an open future', in Randall Curren (ed.), *Philosophy of Education: An Anthology* (Blackwell Publishing, 2007)

Fine, Cordelia, *Delusions of Gender: How Our Minds, Society, and Neurosexism Create Difference* (Norton, 2010)

Fish, Max, Shahvisi, Arianne, Gwaambuka, Tatenda, Tangwa, Godfrey B., Ncaylyana, Daniel and Earp, Brian D., 'A new Tuskegee? Unethical human experimentation and Western neocolonialism in the mass circumcision of African men', *Developing World Bioethics*, 2020

Fletcher, Gem, '"Instead of a scar, I had a piece of art": women on their post-mastectomy tattoos', *Guardian*, 22 September 2018, https://www.

theguardian.com/lifeandstyle/2018/sep/22/instead-scar-piece-art-women-mastectomy-tattoos

Fonda, Jane, *Jane Fonda's Workout* videotape (1982)

Foucault, Michel, *Discipline and Punish* (Penguin, 1991)

Fox, Marie and Thomson, Michael, 'Embodied integrity, embodiment, and the regulation of parental choice', *Journal of Law and Society*, 44, 2017

Freeman, Michael, 'Rethinking Gillick', *International Journal of Children's Rights*, 13 (1–2), 2005

Friend, David, 'How the Brazilian bikini wax conquered the 90s', *Vanity Fair*, 12 September 2017, https://www.vanityfair.com/style/2017/09/secret-history-of-the-brazilian-wax-the-naughty-nineties

Fuss, Diana, *Essentially Speaking: Feminism, Nature and Difference* (Routledge, 1989)

Gabbara, Princess, 'The history of dreadlocks', *Ebony*, 18 October 2016, https://www.ebony.com/style/history-dreadlocks/

Germanotta, Stefani and Laursen, Jeppe, 'Born This Way' (2010)

Gheaus, Anca, Calder, Gideon and de Wispeleare, Jurgen (eds.), *Routledge Handbook of the Philosophy of Childhood and Children* (Routledge, 2019)

Gillick v. West Norfolk and Wisbech AHA, http://www.bailii.org/uk/cases/UKHL/1985/7.html

Gimlin, Debra, *Body Work: Beauty and Self-Image in American Culture* (University of California Press, 2002)

Girlguiding UK, 'Girls' Attitudes Survey 2019', https://www.girlguiding.org.uk/globalassets/docs-and-resources/research-and-campaigns/girls-attitudes-survey-2019.pdf

Girlguiding UK, Written Evidence to UK Parliament Women & Equalities Select Committee, https://committees.parliament.uk/writtenevidence/9367/pdf/

Glick, Leonard B., *Marked in Your Flesh: Circumcision from Ancient Judea to Modern America* (Oxford University Press, 2005)

Glover, Jonathan, *Choosing Children: Genes, Disability, and Design* (Oxford University Press, 2006)

Goodman, Ruth, *How to be a Tudor: A Dawn-to-Dusk Guide to Tudor Life* (Liveright Publishing Corporation, 2015)

Goosens, William K., 'Values, health, and medicine', *Philosophy of Science*, 47, 1980

Grandi, Giovanni et al., 'Prevalence of menstrual pain in young women: what is dysmenorrhea?', *Journal of Pain Research*, 5, 2012

Gray, Jeremy, 'Are you swole, jacked, or yoked?', *Muscle & Strength*, https://www.muscleandstrength.com/articles/swole-jacked-yoked-lingo

Greatest Physiques, 'Steve Reeves', https://www.greatestphysiques.com/male-physiques/steve-reeves/

Green Beauty Channel, 'Locks in the Military (ARMY)', featured in Christopher Mele, 'Army lifts ban on dreadlocks, and Black servicewomen rejoice', *New York Times*, 10 February 2017, https://www.nytimes.com/2017/02/10/us/army-ban-on-dreadlocks-black-servicewomen.html

Greenham: A Common Inheritance, 'Embrace the Base', http://www.greenham-common.org.uk/ixbin/hixclient.exe?a=query&p=greenham&f=generic_largerimage_postsearch.htm&_IXFIRST_=914&_IXMAXHITS_=1&m=quick_sform&tc1=i&partner=greenham&tc2=e&s=dH_78s4Naaq

Greer, Germaine, *The Female Eunuch* (Flamingo, 1993)

Grew, Tony, 'Inquiry into surge in gender treatment ordered by Penny Mordaunt', *The Times*, 16 September 2018, https://www.thetimes.co.uk/article/inquiry-into-surge-in-gender-treatment-ordered-by-penny-mordaunt-b2ftz9hfn?wgu=270525_54264_16058053857606_5be24942c4&wgexpiry=1613581385&utm_source=planit&utm_medium=affiliate&utm_content=22278

Griffith, Richard, 'What is Gillick competence?', *Human Vaccines and Immunotherapeutics*, 12, 2016

Guinness World Records, 'Largest natural breasts', https://www.guinnessworldrecords.com/world-records/largest-natural-breasts?fb_comment_id=680689828716187_703832239735279

Hagen, Sofie, *Happy Fat: Taking Up Space in a World That Wants to Shrink You* (Fourth Estate, 2019)

Halberstam, Jack, *Trans*: A Quick and Quirky Account of Gender Variability* (University of California Press, 2018)

Halberstam, Judith, *Female Masculinity* (Duke University Press, 1998)

Halkitis, Perry N., 'Masculinity in the age of AIDS: HIV-seropositive gay men and the "buff agenda"', in Peter Nardi (ed.), *Gay Masculinities* (Sage Publications, 2000)

Haller, John S. Jr., *Outcasts from Evolution: Scientific Attitudes of Racial Inferiority 1859–1900* (Southern Illinois University Press, 1995)

Haraway, Donna J., *Simians, Cyborgs, and Women: The Reinvention of Nature* (Free Association Books, 1991)

Harrison, Diana, 'I need a bra that fits me, not the male gaze', *the f word*, 31 October 2018, https://thefword.org.uk/2018/10/i-need-a-bra-that-fits-me-not-the-male-gaze/

Haslanger, Sally, *Resisting Reality: Social Construction and Social Critique* (Oxford University Press, 2012)

Hausman, Bernice L., 'Body, technology, and gender in transsexual autobiographies', in Susan Stryker and Stephen Whittle (eds.), *The Transgender Studies Reader* (Routledge, 2006)

HealthyChildren.org, 'Should the baby be circumcised?', https://www.healthy children.org/English/ages-stages/prenatal/decisions-to-make/Pages/ Should-the-Baby-be-Circumcised.aspx

Heffernan, Conor, 'Bodybuilders who passed away too young', *Physical Culture Study*, 27 October 2018, https://physicalculturestudy.com/2018/10/27/ bodybuilders-who-passed-away-too-young/

Heffernan, Conor, 'How Britain became the birthplace of modern bodybuilding', 7 November 2016, https://www.playingpasts.co.uk/articles/ physical-culture/how-britain-became-the-birthplace-of-modern-bodybuilding/

Heist Studios, https://www.heist-studios.com/?utm_source=google&utm_ medium=cpc&utm_campaign=Shapewear-UK-Search-Generic&utm_ term=shapewear&utm_content=314429620529&gclid=EAIaIQobChMI 57q6ocyA5wIVh63tCho59gjkEAAYASAAEgJ9_fD_BwE

Hern, Alex, 'Heroin for middle-class nerds: how Warhammer conquered gaming', *Guardian*, 21 January 2019, https://www.theguardian.com/life andstyle/2019/jan/21/heroin-for-middle-class-nerds-how-warhammer-took-over-gaming-games-workshop

Herring, John and Wall, Jesse, 'The nature and significance of the right to bodily integrity', *The Cambridge Law Journal*, 76 (3), 2017

Higgins, S. and Wysong, A., 'Cosmetic surgery and body dysmorphic disorder – an update', *International Journal of Women's Dermatology*, 4 (1), 2017

Hill, Pamela D., Wilhelm, Patricia A., Aldag, Jean C. and Chatterton, Robert T. Jr, 'Breast augmentation and lactation outcome: a case report', *American Journal of Maternal Child Nursing*, 29 (4), 2004

History of Corsetry, http://tahliamckellartextiles.weebly.com/corset-timeline. html

Hobbes, Thomas, *Leviathan* (Hackett, 1994)

Hodges, Frederick M., 'The ideal prepuce in Ancient Greece and Rome: male genital aesthetics and their relation to *lipodermos*, circumcision, foreskin restoration, and the *kynodesme*', *Bulletin of the History of Medicine*, 75, 2001

Hoffmann, Diane E. and Tarzian, Anita J., 'The girl who cried pain: a bias against women in the treatment of pain', *Journal of Law, Medicine & Ethics*, 29, 2001

House of Commons Women & Equalities Select Committee, 'Changing the Perfect Picture: An Enquiry into Body Image', 2021, https://committees.parliament.uk/publications/5357/documents/53751/default/

Howland, Genevieve, 'Labor interventions: how to avoid them (and why you'd want to)', Mama Natural, 24 May 2019, https://www.mamanatural.com/labor-interventions/

Human Rights Watch, '"I want to be like nature made me": medically unnecessary surgeries on intersex children in the US', 25 July 2017, https://www.hrw.org/report/2017/07/25/i-want-be-nature-made-me/medically-unnecessary-surgeries-intersex-children-us

Hume, David, *An Enquiry Concerning the Principles of Morals* (1777)

Hurst, Nancy, 'Lactation after augmentation mammoplasty', *Obstetrics & Gynecology*, 87 (1), 1996

Huszar, Stephanie, 'How to do natural makeup', *Real Simple*, 5 January 2018, https://www.realsimple.com/beauty-fashion/makeup/makeup-face/barely-there-makeup?

IPSOS, 'More Americans have tattoos today than seven years ago', 29 August 2019, https://www.ipsos.com/en-us/news-polls/more-americans-have-tattoos-today

Jeffreys, Sheila, *Beauty and Misogyny* (Routledge, 2005)

Jeffries, Stuart, 'Orlan's art of sex and surgery', *Guardian*, 1 July 2009, https://www.theguardian.com/artanddesign/2009/jul/01/orlan-performance-artist-carnal-art

Jenkins, Katharine, 'Amelioration and inclusion: gender identity and the concept of *woman*', *Ethics*, 126 (2), 2016

Jones, Paul Anthony, 'When Arthur Conan Doyle judged a bodybuilding contest', http://mentalfloss.com/article/63418/when-arthur-conan-doyle-judged-bodybuilding-contest

Jones, Richard, '8 tips on how to bulk up for 2018, from a Mr. Olympia finalist', *Daily Telegraph*, 31 January 2018, https://www.telegraph.co.uk/health-fitness/body/8-tips-bulk-2018-Mr.-olympia-finalist/

Jowett, Victoria, 'Nine ways to ensure your makeup always looks natural', *Cosmopolitan*, 2 November 2018, https://www.cosmopolitan.com/uk/beauty-hair/makeup/g18192402/natural-makeup-look/

Ju, H., Jones, M. and Mishra, G., 'The prevalence and risk factors of dysmenorrhea', *Epidemiologic Reviews*, 36, 2014

Junor, Beth, *Greenham Common Women's Peace Camp: A History of Non-Violent Resistance 1984–1995* (Working Press, 1995)

Kasprzak, Emma, 'Why are black mothers at more risk of dying?', BBC News, 12 April 2019, https://www.bbc.co.uk/news/uk-england-47115305

Kelly, B. and Foster, C., 'Should female genital cosmetic surgery and genital piercing be regarded ethically and legally as female genital mutilation?', *BJOG: An International Journal of Obstetrics & Gynaecology*, 119, 2012

Kessel, Anna, 'The rise of the body neutrality movement', *Guardian*, 23 July 2018

Kessen, William, 'Rousseau's children', *Daedalus*, 107 (3), 1978

Kittay, Eva Feder, 'Forever small: the strange case of Ashley X', *Hypatia*, 26 (3), 2011

Knitted Knockers, https://www.knittedknockers.org

Knitted Knockers UK, https://www.kkukciowix.com/

Kruz, Norma I. and Korchin, Leo, 'Breastfeeding after augmentation mammaplasty with saline implants', *Annals of Plastic Surgery*, 64 (5), 2010

Kymlicka, Will, *Multicultural Citizenship: A Liberal Theory of Minority Rights* (Oxford University Press, 1995)

Kymlicka, Will, *Liberalism, Community, and Culture* (Oxford University Press, 1989)

Lancôme, 'New Year nude makeup look with Chinutay', https://www.lancome.co.uk/discover-lancome/simple-natural-makeup-look/

Lark, Rachel & The Damaged Goods, 'I Wanna Lose Five Pounds', https://www.youtube.com/watch?v=iZNRriHkJsI

Lester, C. N., *Trans Like Me: A Journey for All of Us* (Virago, 2017)

Liao, Lih-Meh and Creighton, Sarah, 'Requests for cosmetic genitoplasty: how should healthcare providers respond?', and 'Responses', *BMJ*, 334 (7603), 2007, http://www.bmj.com/content/334/7603/1090

Lightfoot-Klein, Hanny, *Prisoners of Ritual: An Odyssey into Female Genital Circumcision in Africa* (Harrington Park Press, 1989)

Linguistic Society of America, 'FAQ: Bilingualism', https://www.linguisticsociety.org/resource/faq-what-bilingualism

Liszewski, Walter, Kream, Elizabeth, Helland, Sarah, Cavigli, Amy, Lavin, Bridget C. and Murina, Andrea, 'The demographics and rates of tattoo complications, regret, and unsafe tattooing practices', *Dermatologic Surgery*, 41 (11), 2015

Lloyd, Moya, *Beyond Identity Politics: Feminism, Power, and Politics* (Sage Publications, 2005)

Locke, John, *Two Treatises of Government* (Cambridge University Press, 1994)

MacCormick, Tom, 'Tip: cutting phase 101', *TNation*, 28 October 2017, https://www.t-nation.com/diet-fat-loss/tip-cutting-phase-101

McDonald, Laura, 'A trainer explains: top 13 ways I get back in shape', MindBodyGreen, https://www.mindbodygreen.com/0-7611/a-trainer-explains-top-13-ways-i-get-back-in-shape.html

Mackenzie, Macaela, 'American women spend 6 full days a year doing their hair',https://www.shape.com/lifestyle/beauty-style/time-saving-hair-styling-tips

MacKinnon, Catharine, *Women's Lives, Men's Laws* (Harvard University Press, 2005)

MacKinnon, Catharine, *Toward a Feminist Theory of the State* (Harvard University Press, 1989)

McLean Clinic, 'FTM top surgery', https://www.mcleanclinic.com/surgical-procedures/breast/ftm-top-surgery/

McNish, Hollie, *Nobody Told Me: Poetry and Parenthood* (Blackfriars, 2016)

McTavish, Lianne, *Feminist Figure Girl: Look Hot While You Fight the Patriarchy* (State University of New York Press, 2015)

Martin, Karin A., *Puberty, Sexuality, and the Self: Boys and Girls at Adolescence* (Routledge, 1996)

Maximuscle, '4 week bulking transformation diet', https://www.maxinutrition.com/sports/bodybuilding/4-Week-Bulking-Transformation-Diet/

Mayo Clinic, 'Otoplasty', https://www.mayoclinic.org/tests-procedures/otoplasty/about/pac-20394822

Mazor, Joseph, 'On the strength of children's right to bodily integrity: when is the right infringed?', *Journal of Applied Philosophy*, 36 (1), 2019

Meierhands, Jennifer, 'Make-up on the train: what's the problem?', BBC News, 4 September 2018, https://www.bbc.co.uk/news/uk-england-45343836

Mellor, Mary, *Feminism & Ecology* (Polity Press, 1997)

Melzer, Scott, *Manhood Impossible: Men's Struggle to Control and Transform Their Bodies and Work* (Rutgers University Press, 2018)

Mermaids, 'Do you still use the phrase "Born in the wrong body?"', 25 September 2020, https://mermaidsuk.org.uk/news/do-you-still-use-the-phrase-born-in-the-wrong-body/

Meyerowitz, Joanne, 'A "fierce and demanding" drive', in Susan Stryker and Stephen Whittle (eds.), *The Transgender Studies Reader* (Routledge, 2006)

Michalopoulos, K., 'The effects of breast augmentation surgery on future ability to lactate', *The Breast Journal*, 13, 2007

Mill, John Stuart, *On Liberty* (1859) in *Utilitarianism, On Liberty,* and *Considerations on Representative Government* (Everyman, 1993)

Mill, John Stuart, *The Subjection of Women* in *On Liberty* and *The Subjection of Women* (Wordsworth, 1996)

Mills & Reeve, 'Briefing: The Female Genital Mutilation Act and its relation to female genital cosmetic surgery', October 2013, http://www.mills-reeve.

com/files/Publication/e023b495-a726–4241-b4dc-5d607f22d2f4/Presentation/PublicationAttachment/efa6e8e7–14e1–498d-9496–5fc0bde49384/FGMA_Oct13.pdf

Mills, Claudia, 'The child's right to an open future?', *Journal of Social Philosophy*, 34 (4), 2003

Mitchell, Bea, 'Chest binding is an integral part of the transitioning process for lots of trans men – here's how it works', *Pink News*, 30 April 2018, https://www.pinknews.co.uk/2018/04/30/chest-binding-transgender-transitioning/

Moore, Jo, https://twitter.com/JoMoore_/status/1194676687381905408

Moore, Suzanne, Khaleeli, Homa, Sarner, Moya, Harper, Leah and McCurry, Justin, 'How the Greenham Common protest changed lives: "We danced on top of the nuclear silos"', *Guardian*, 20 March 2017, https://www.theguardian.com/uk-news/2017/mar/20/greenham-common-nuclear-silos-women-protest-peace-camp

Morrison, Toni, *The Bluest Eye* (Vintage, 1999)

Morton, Deana, 'Putting my baby in a helmet was the toughest decision of my life', *Today's Parent*, 20 September 2018, https://www.todaysparent.com/baby/baby-health/putting-my-baby-in-a-helmet-was-the-toughest-decision-of-my-life/

Muscle Memory, 'Measurements of later Mr. America winners', https://www.musclememory.com/articles/Mr.Asizes.html

Museum of Classical Archaeology, 'Why casts?', https://www.classics.cam.ac.uk/museum/about-us/why-casts

National Health Service (NHS), 'Plagiocephaly and brachycephaly (flat head syndrome)', https://www.nhs.uk/conditions/plagiocephaly-brachycephaly/

Neifert, M., DeMarzo, S., Seacat, J., Young, D., Leff, M. and Orleans, M., 'The influence of breast surgery, breast appearance, and pregnancy-induced breast changes on lactation sufficiency as measured by infant weight gain', *Birth*, 17, 1990

Nelson, Maggie, *The Argonauts* (Melville House UK, 2016)

New Look Holiday, https://www.newlookholiday.co.uk/combined-procedures-abroad/

NHS Choices, 'Birthmarks', https://www.nhs.uk/conditions/birthmarks/treatment/

NHS Choices, 'Braces and orthodontics', https://www.nhs.uk/live-well/healthy-body/braces-and-orthodontics/

NHS Choices, 'Circumcision in boys', http://www.nhs.uk/conditions/Circumcision-in-children/Pages/Introduction.aspx

NHS Choices, 'Ear correction surgery, including ear pinning', https://www.nhs.uk/conditions/cosmetic-procedures/ear-correction-surgery/

NHS Choices, 'Gender dysphoria', https://www.nhs.uk/conditions/gender-dysphoria/treatment/

NHS Choices, 'Is cosmetic surgery available on the NHS?', http://www.nhs.uk/Conditions/cosmetic-treatments-guide/Pages/is-cosmetic-surgery-available-on-the-NHS.aspx

NHS Choices, 'Your guide to cosmetic procedures: labiaplasty (vulval surgery)', https://www.nhs.uk/conditions/cosmetic-treatments/labiaplasty/

NHS Great Ormond Street Hospital for Children, 'Additional little fingers', https://www.gosh.nhs.uk/conditions-and-treatments/conditions-we-treat/additional-little-fingers

NHS Great Ormond Street Hospital for Children, 'Syndactyly', https://www.gosh.nhs.uk/conditions-and-treatments/conditions-we-treat/syndactyly

Nordberg, Jenny, *The Underground Girls of Kabul: The Hidden Lives of Afghan Girls Disguised as Boys* (Virago, 2014)

Nuffield Council on Bioethics, 'Cosmetic procedures: ethical issues', 2017, http://nuffieldbioethics.org/wp-content/uploads/Cosmetic-procedures-full-report.pdf

Nuffield Council on Bioethics, 'Online questionnaire: summary', 2017, https://www.nuffieldbioethics.org/assets/pdfs/CP-Survey-Monkey-Questionnaire-analysis.pdf

O'Brien, Michelle, 'Tracing this body: transsexuality, pharmaceuticals, and capitalism', in Susan Stryker and Aren Z. Aizura (eds.), *The Transgender Studies Reader* 2 (Routledge, 2013)

Okin, Susan Moller, *Justice, Gender, and the Family* (Basic Books, 1989)

Okin, Susan Moller, *Women in Western Political Thought* (Princeton University Press, 1979)

Oliver, Michael, 'Medicine and disability: steps in the wrong direction', *International Journal of Medical Engineering and Technology*, 2 (3), 1978

Orbach, Susie, *Fat Is A Feminist Issue* (Random House, 2010)

ORLAN, 'Manifesto of Carnal Art' (1989), reproduced at https://www.slow-words.com/carnal-art-manifesto/

Partridge, James, *Face It: Facial Disfigurement and My Fight for Facial Equality* (Whitefox Publishing, 2020)

Partridge, James, *Changing Faces: The Challenge of Facial Disfigurement* (Changing Faces Publication, 2012)

Peitzmeier, Sarah, Gardner, Ivy, Weinand, Jamie, Corbet, Alexandra and Acevedo, Kimberlynn, 'Health impact of chest binding among transgender adults: a community-engaged, cross-sectional study', *Culture, Health, and Sexuality*, 19 (1), 2017, https://doi.org/10.1080/13691058.2016.1191675

Penney, Tarra L. and Kirk, Sara F. L., 'The health at every size paradigm and obesity: missing empirical evidence may help push the reframing obesity debate forward', *American Journal of Public Health*, 105, 2015

Perkins, Sabrina, 'How often should you wash your hair?', Naturally Curly, https://www.naturallycurly.com/curlreading/wavy-hair-type-2/curlies-how-often-should-you-wash-your-hair

Pool, Hannah, 'Dare to dread', *Guardian*, 23 August 2003, https://www.theguardian.com/lifeandstyle/2003/aug/23/features.weekend

PRASIS, 'Code of Practice', 2017, https://www.prasis.co.uk/support_guidance/best_practice/prasis_code_of_practice_2017.aspx

Prosser, Jay, *Second Skins: The Body Narratives of Transsexuality* (Columbia University Press, 1998)

Pumping Iron (1977), dirs. George Butler and Robert Fiore

R (on the application of) Quincy Bell and A v. Tavistock and Portman NHS Trust and others [2020] EWHC 3274

Red magazine staff, 'Sex education', *Red* magazine, July 2019

Reuters, 'A man covered his face with tattoos and turned his eyes black. He says it cost him his kindergarten teaching job', CNN News, 28 September 2020, https://edition.cnn.com/2020/09/28/europe/sylvain-helaine-tattoo-teaching-job-scli-intl/index.html

Rich, Adrienne, *Of Woman Born: Motherhood as Experience and Institution* (W. Norton & Company, 1976)

Richards, Christopher, Maxwell, Julie and McClune, Noel, 'Use of puberty blockers for gender dysphoria: a momentous step in the dark', *Archives of Disease in Childhood*, 17 January 2019, https://adc.bmj.com/content/archdischild/early/2019/01/17/archdischild-2018-315881.full.pdf

RNID, 'Cochlear implants', https://rnid.org.uk/information-and-support/hearing-loss/hearing-implants/cochlear-implants/

Roeder, Amy, 'America is failing its Black mothers', *Harvard Public Health*, Winter 2019, https://www.hsph.harvard.edu/magazine/magazine_article/america-is-failing-its-black-mothers/

Rose, Marla Matza, *Muscle Beach: Where the Best Bodies in the World Started a Fitness Revolution* (LA Weekly Books, 2001)

Rosengren, Annika and Lissner, Lauren, 'The sociology of obesity', in M. Korbonits (ed.), *Obesity and Metabolism* (Karger, 2008)

Rosenthal, Tom, 'Manhood', comedy show, 2019

Rousseau, Jean-Jacques, *Émile* or *On Education*, trans. Allan Bloom (Basic Books, 1979)

Royal College of Obstetricians and Gynaecologists, 'Ethical Opinion Paper: Ethical considerations in relation to female genital cosmetic surgery (FGCS)', https://www.rcog.org.uk/globalassets/documents/guidelines/ethics-issues-and-resources/rcog-fgcs-ethical-opinion-paper.pdf

Royal College of Surgeons, 'Statistics', https://www.rcseng.ac.uk/careers-in-surgery/women-in-surgery/statistics/

Rumsey, Nichola and Harcourt, Diana (eds.), *The Oxford Handbook of the Psychology of Appearance* (Oxford University Press, 2012)

Sanghani, Radhika, 'Outlawing "designer vaginas": have MPs gone mad?', *Daily Telegraph*, 16 March 2015, http://www.telegraph.co.uk/women/womens-health/11475276/Designer-vaginas-to-be-made-illegal-Have-MPs-gone-mad.html

Sangiovanni, Andrea, *Humanity without Dignity: Moral Equality, Respect, and Human Rights* (Harvard University Press, 2017)

Schwarzenegger, Arnold, 'Arnold Schwarzenegger 2018 – The speech that broke the internet – Most Inspiring ever', https://www.youtube.com/watch?v=u_ktRTWMX3M

Schwarzenegger, Arnold, speaking at Arnold Classic 2015, available at https://igniteperformancehealthfitness.wordpress.com/tag/classic-vs-modern-bodybuilding-physiques/

Scott, Ellen, 'Around half of all young women in the UK are entirely removing their pubic hair', *Cosmopolitan*, 21 March 2016, https://www.cosmopolitan.com/uk/body/news/a42147/half-young-women-uk-removing-all-pubic-hair/

Searing, Linda, 'The big number: 45 million Americans go on a diet each year', *Washington Post*, 1 January 2018, https://www.washingtonpost.com/national/health-science/the-big-number-45-million-americans-go-on-a-diet-each-year/2017/12/29/04089aec-ebdd-11e7-b698–91d4e35920a3_story.html

Sex and the City, Season 3, Episode 14, 'Sex and Another City' (2000), dir. John David Coles, https://www.imdb.com/title/tt0698662/

Shadow Pro, 'How natural is natural bodybuilding?', *TNation*, 23 July 2014, https://www.t-nation.com/training/how-natural-is-natural-bodybuilding

Shahvisi, Ariane and Earp, Brian D., 'The law and ethics of female genital cutting', in Sarah Creighton and Lih-Mei Liao (eds.), *Female Genital Cosmetic Surgery: Solution to What Problem?* (Cambridge University Press, 2019)

Shakespeare, Tom, 'A short story', in Charles Fernyhough (ed.), *Others: Writers on the Power of Words to Help Us See Beyond Ourselves* (Unbound, 2019)

Shakespeare, Tom, *Disability Rights and Wrongs Revisited* (Routledge, 2014)

Sharma, Ashish, Madaan, Vishaal and Petty, Frederick D., 'Exercise for mental health', *The Primary Care Companion to the Journal of Clinical Psychiatry*, 8 (2), 2006

Shrier, Abigail, *Irreversible Damage: The Transgender Craze Seducing Our Daughters* (Regnery Publishing, 2020)

Shweder, Richard A., 'What about "female genital mutilation"? And why understanding culture matters in the first place', *Daedalus*, 129 (4), 2000

Singleton, Jenny L. and Tittle, Matthew D., 'Deaf parents and their hearing children', *Journal of Deaf Studies and Deaf Education*, 5 (3), 2000

Sinicki, Adam, 'Why do bodybuilders have large guts?', https://www.health guidance.org/entry/17668/1/why-do-bodybuilders-have-large-guts.html

Slater, Amy, evidence given to the UK Parliament Women & Equalities Select Committee, https://committees.parliament.uk/oralevidence/928/pdf/

Slater, Amy, Varsani, Neesha and Diedrichs, Phillippa C., '#fitspo or #love-yourself? The impact of fitspiration and self-compassion Instagram images on women's body image, self-compassion, and mood', *Body Image*, 22, 2017, https://doi.org/10.1016/j.bodyim.2017.06.004

Smith, Courtney, 'Who defines "mutilation"? Challenging imperialism in the discourse of female genital cutting', *Feminist Formations*, 23 (1), 2011

Snicket, Lemony, *The Carnivorous Carnival* (HarperCollins, 2002)

Solmi, Francesca, evidence given to the UK Parliament Women & Equalities Select Committee, https://committees.parliament.uk/oralevidence/928/pdf/

Solomon, Andrew, *Far From The Tree: Parents, Children and the Search for Identity* (Vintage, 2014)

Spade, Dean, 'Mutilating gender', in Susan Stryker and Stephen Whittle (eds.), *The Transgender Studies Reader* (Routledge, 2006)

Sparrow, Robert, 'Defending Deaf culture: the case of cochlear implants', *Journal of Political Philosophy*, 13 (2), 2005

Spelman, Elizabeth V., *Inessential Woman: Problems of Exclusion in Feminist Thought* (Women's Press, 1990)

Stamp, Rebecca, 'Average person will try 126 fad diets in their lifetime, poll shows', *Independent*, 8 January 2020, https://www.independent.co.uk/life-style/diet-weight-loss-food-unhealthy-eating-habits-a9274676.html

Steinem, Gloria, *Outrageous Acts and Everyday Rebellions* (Flamingo, 1985)

Stokes, Penelope, *The Common Good: The History of Greenham Common* (Greenham Trust, 2017)

Stoltenberg, John, *The End of Manhood: A Book for Men of Conscience* (Penguin, 1993)

Stone, Sandy, 'The Empire Strikes Back: a posttranssexual manifesto', in Susan Stryker and Stephen Whittle (eds.), *The Transgender Studies Reader* (Routledge, 2006)

Stump, Patrick, 'Who's the (Bat)Man?', from *The Lego Batman Movie* (2017), dir. Chris McKay

Tasca, C., Rapetti, M., Carta, M. G. and Fadda, B., 'Women and hysteria in the history of mental health', *Clinical Practice and Epidemiology in Mental Health*, 8, 2012

Tate, Shirley, 'Black beauty: shade, hair, and anti-racist aesthetics', *Ethnic and Racial Studies*, 30 (2), 2007

Tate, Shirley Anne, 'Not all the women want to be white: decolonizing beauty studies', in Encarnacion Gutierrez Rodriguez, Manuela Boatcă, and Sérgio Costa (eds.), *Decolonizing European Sociology: Transdisciplinary Approaches* (Routledge, 2010)

Taylor, Paul C., 'Malcolm's conk and Danto's colors; or, four logical petitions concerning race, beauty, and aesthetics', in Peg Zeglin Brand (ed.), *Beauty Matters* (Indiana University Press, 2000)

The Female Lead Society, 'Body positivity vs. body neutrality', 19 June 2020, https://www.thefemaleleadsociety.com/body-positivity-vs-body-neutrality

The Hospital Group, https://www.thehospitalgroup.org

The Lancet Infectious Diseases Editorial, 'Should we vaccinate children against SARS-CoV-2?', 10 June 2021, https://www.thelancet.com/journals/laninf/article/PIIS1473-3099(21)00339-X/fulltext

The National Archives, 'Records of Greenham Women's Peace Camp', https://discovery.nationalarchives.gov.uk/details/r/d625b55a-e807-4729-9d8c-087c918dbaff

The Walt Disney Company, *Disney Look*, 2021, https://disneycasting.net/downloads/wdpr/Disney_Look_Book.pdf

Thomsen, Michael, 'Braces: pointless and essential', *Atlantic*, 9 July 2015, https://www.theatlantic.com/health/archive/2015/07/braces-dentures-history/397934/

Thornhill, Randy and Palmer, Craig T., *A Natural History of Rape: Biological Bases of Sexual Coercion* (MIT Press, 2000)

TLC UK, 'Strange attractions: largest NATURAL breasts in the world!', https://www.youtube.com/watch?v=LDJb1gdqZsA

Transform cosmetic surgery, www.transforminglives.com

Turner, Ellie and Winter, Lottie, 'Conference call coverage: here's how to keep your makeup natural but profesh', *Glamour* magazine, 24 March 2020

UK Female Genital Mutilation Act 2003, http://www.cps.gov.uk/legal/d_to_g/female_genital_mutilation/#a01

UK Female Genital Mutilation Act 2003, Explanatory Note, http://www.legislation.gov.uk/ukpga/2003/31/contents

UNICEF, 'Nine things you didn't know about menstruation', 25 May 2018, https://www.unicef.org/press-releases/fast-facts-nine-things-you-didnt-know-about-menstruation

USA Declaration of Independence, http://www.ushistory.org/declaration/document/

Uskul, Ayse K., 'Women's menarche stories from a multicultural sample', *Social Science and Medicine*, 59, 2004

Wardere, Hibo, *Cut: One Woman's Fight against FGM in Britain Today* (Simon & Schuster, 2016)

WebMD, 'Get your body back after pregnancy', https://www.webmd.com/parenting/baby/features/get-your-body-back-after-pregnancy#1

Whiteman, Honor, 'Helmet therapy for infant positional skull deformation "should be discouraged"', *Medical News Today*, 2 May 2014, https://www.medicalnewstoday.com/articles/276281

Widdows, Heather, *Perfect Me: Beauty as an Ethical Ideal* (Princeton University Press, 2018)

Williams, Brett, 'Cut, ripped, jacked, or swole? Where do your favourite celebs fall on the continuum – and what are you?', *Men's Health*, 7 November 2018, https://www.menshealth.com/fitness/a24079330/muscular-definition-guide/

Williamson, Marvel L. and Williamson, Paul S., 'Women's preferences for penile circumcision in sexual partners', *Journal of Sex Education and Therapy*, 14 (2), 1988

Wolf, Naomi, *The Beauty Myth* (Chatto & Windus, 1990)

Wollstonecraft, Mary, *A Vindication of the Rights of Woman* and *A Vindication of the Rights of Men* (Oxford University Press, 2008)

Wootton, David, *Bad Medicine* (Oxford University Press, 2006)

World Bank, 'Population, female', https://data.worldbank.org/indicator/SP.POP.TOTL.FE.ZS

World Health Organization, 'Maternal mortality', 15 February 2018, https://www.who.int/news-room/fact-sheets/detail/maternal-mortality

Yang, Sarah, 'The natural look is in – here's how to achieve it', *Real Simple*, 4 August 2016, https://www.realsimple.com/beauty-fashion/natural-makeup-look

Yates, Danielle, '21 mastectomy tattoos you have to see', *Headcovers Unlimited*, 24 October 2018, https://www.headcovers.com/blog/mastectomy-tattoos/

Young, Iris Marion, *On Female Body Experience: 'Throwing Like a Girl' and Other Essays* (Oxford University Press, 2005)

Zimmerman, Nigel, 'Gillick competence: an unnecessary burden', *The New Bioethics*, 25 (1), 2019

Zuckerman, Diana and Abraham, Anisha, 'Teenagers and cosmetic surgery: focus on breast augmentation and liposuction', *Journal of Adolescent Health*, 43 (4), 2008

Notes

INTRODUCTION

1. CNN, 'Bullied kids receive free plastic surgery', 27 July 2012, https://www.youtube.com/watch?v=5BdL9GEbplo.
2. Not all cosmetic surgeons are members of BAAPS, so these figures significantly under-report the total number of procedures; a national register of cosmetic surgery procedures is sorely needed. The number of procedures fell more recently as the Covid-19 pandemic limited non-essential surgery. BAAPS, 'Cosmetic surgery stats: number of surgeries remains stable amid calls for greater regulation of quick fix solutions', 20 May 2019, https://baaps.org.uk/media/press_releases/1708/cosmetic_surgery_stats_number_of_surgeries_remains_stable_amid_calls_for_greater_regulation_of_quick_fix_solutions.
3. https://twitter.com/JoMoore_/status/1194676687381905408.
4. Laura McDonald, 'A trainer explains: top 13 ways I get back in shape', MindBodyGreen, https://www.mindbodygreen.com/0-7611/a-trainer-explains-top-13-ways-i-get-back-in-shape.html.
5. WebMD, 'Get your body back after pregnancy', https://www.webmd.com/parenting/baby/features/get-your-body-back-after-pregnancy#1.
6. Diary of a Fit Mommy, https://diaryofafitmommy.com/how-i-got-my-body-back-after-baby-2/.
7. Amy Slater, evidence to the UK Parliament Women & Equalities Select Committee, https://committees.parliament.uk/oralevidence/928/pdf/.
8. https://www.feabie.com/Home/FAQ.
9. David Hume, *An Enquiry Concerning the Principles of Morals* (1777), Section VIII, https://www.gutenberg.org/files/4320/4320-h/4320-h.htm.
10. Sabrina Perkins, 'How often should you wash your hair?', Naturally Curly, https://www.naturallycurly.com/curlreading/wavy-hair-type-2/curlies-how-often-should-you-wash-your-hair.

11. Macaela Mackenzie, 'American women spend 6 full days a year doing their hair', https://www.shape.com/lifestyle/beauty-style/time-saving-hair-styling-tips.

12. A Google search for 'how to go to bed with natural hair' returns 322 million results, with the top hits including pages like 'How to protect natural hair at night', '9 ways to sleep with natural hair without totally ruining it', '9 ways to sleep with curls', and 'How to sleep with your natural hair'.

13. Emma Dabiri, *Don't Touch My Hair* (Allen Lane, 2019), p. 61.

14. Cystic Fibrosis Trust, 'Physiotherapy FAQs', https://www.cysticfibrosis.org.uk/what-is-cystic-fibrosis/cystic-fibrosis-care/physiotherapy/physiotherapy-faqs.

15. https://www.diabetesdailygrind.com/.

16. Heather Widdows, *Perfect Me: Beauty as an Ethical Ideal* (Princeton University Press, 2018), p. 108.

17. *Sex and the City,* Season 3, Episode 14, 'Sex and Another City', https://www.imdb.com/title/tt0698662/.

18. David Friend, 'How the Brazilian bikini wax conquered the 90s', *Vanity Fair*, 12 September 2017, https://www.vanityfair.com/style/2017/09/secret-history-of-the-brazilian-wax-the-naughty-nineties.

19. A survey reported in *Cosmopolitan* found that half of women under the age of 35 remove their pubic hair completely. Ellen Scott, 'Around half of all young women in the UK are entirely removing their pubic hair', *Cosmopolitan*, 21 March 2016, https://www.cosmopolitan.com/uk/body/news/a42147/half-young-women-uk-removing-all-pubic-hair/.

20. Although historian Ruth Goodman reports that this regime is surprisingly effective at keeping odours at bay in her *How to be a Tudor: A Dawn-to-Dusk Guide to Tudor Life* (Liveright Publishing Corporation, 2015).

21. History of Corsetry, http://tahliamckellartextiles.weebly.com/corset-timeline.html.

22. See evidence given by Francesca Solmi to the UK Parliament Women & Equalities Select Committee, https://committees.parliament.uk/oralevidence/928/pdf/.

23. Susie Orbach, *Fat Is A Feminist Issue* (first published 1978; page numbers from rev. edn Random House, 2010), p. 9.

24. Patricia Hill Collins, *Black Feminist Thought* (Routledge, 2000), pp. 98ff.; Audre Lorde, *Your Silence Will Not Protect You* (Silver Press, 2017); Toni Morrison, *The Bluest Eye* (Vintage, 1999).

25. Nichola Rumsey and Diana Harcourt, 'Introduction' to their (eds.), *Oxford Handbook of the Psychology of Appearance* (Oxford University Press, 2012), p. 1.

26. Ibid.

27. Girlguiding UK, 'Girls' attitudes survey 2019', https://www.girlguiding.org.uk/globalassets/docs-and-resources/research-and-campaigns/girls-attitudes-survey-2019.pdf, p. 17.

28. Sophie-Grace Chappell, 'An open letter to JK Rowling's blog post on sex and gender', Crooked Timber, 14 June 2020, https://crookedtimber.org/2020/06/14/guest-post-an-open-letter-to-jk-rowling-blog-post-on-sex-and-gender-by-sophie-grace-chappell/.

29. Debra Gimlin, *Body Work: Beauty and Self-Image in American Culture* (University of California Press, 2002), p. 9.

30. Ibid., p. 38.

31. Widdows, *Perfect Me*.

32. Gimlin, *Body Work*, p. 96.

33. Combahee River Collective, 'A Black feminist statement (1977)', in Cherrie Moraga and Glora Anzaldua (eds.), *This Bridge Called My Back: Writings by Radical Women of Color* (Kitchen Table/Women of Color Press, 1981); Kimberlé Crenshaw, 'Demarginalizing the intersection of race and sex: a Black feminist critique of antidiscrimination doctrine, feminist theory and antiracist politics', *University of Chicago Legal Forum*, 1989; Kimberlé Crenshaw, 'Mapping the margins: intersectionality, identity politics, and violence against women of color', *Stanford Law Review*, 43, 1993; Elizabeth V. Spelman, *Inessential Woman: Problems of Exclusion in Feminist Thought* (Women's Press, 1990); Patricia Hill Collins, *Black Feminist Thought* (Routledge, 2009).

34. For example, since it was published just as this book was being edited, I have not been able to engage with the variety of diverse perspectives explored in Maxine Leeds Craig (ed.), *The Routledge Companion to Beauty Politics* (Routledge, 2021).

PART ONE

1. For a critique of the gendered assumptions of canonical philosophers, see Susan Moller Okin, *Women in Western Political Thought* (Princeton University Press, 1979), and the works in the *Re-Reading the Canon* series published by Penn State University Press, http://www.psupress.org/books/series/book_SeriesReReading.html.

2. 'Largest natural breasts', on the Guinness World Records website, https://www.guinnessworldrecords.com/world-records/largest-natural-breasts?fb_comment_id=680689828716187_703832239735279.

3. TLC UK, 'Strange attractions: largest NATURAL breasts in the world!', https://www.youtube.com/watch?v=LDJb1gdqZsA.

I. KEEPING THINGS NATURAL

1. Alex Hern, 'Heroin for middle-class nerds: how Warhammer conquered gaming', *Guardian*, 21 January 2019, https://www.theguardian.com/lifeandstyle/2019/jan/21/heroin-for-middle-class-nerds-how-warhammer-took-over-gaming-games-workshop.

2. 'Who's the manliest man? BATMAN! With the buns of steel? BATMAN! Who could choke-hold a bear? BATMAN! Who never skips leg day? BATMAN! Who always pays his taxes? NOT BATMAN!', Patrick Stump, 'Who's the (Bat)Man?', from *The Lego Batman Movie* (2017).

3. See, for example, the photo of Art Livingston at https://sites.psu.edu/strongman/.

4. Paul Anthony Jones, 'When Arthur Conan Doyle judged a bodybuilding contest', http://mentalfloss.com/article/63418/when-arthur-conan-doyle-judged-bodybuilding-contest.

5. Conor Heffernan, 'How Britain became the birthplace of modern bodybuilding', 7 November 2016, https://www.playingpasts.co.uk/articles/physical-culture/how-britain-became-the-birthplace-of-modern-bodybuilding/.

6. John D. Fair, *Mr. America: The Tragic History of a Bodybuilding Icon* (University of Texas Press, 2015), p. 45.

7. Museum of Classical Archaeology, 'Why Casts?', https://www.classics.cam.ac.uk/museum/about-us/why-casts.

8. Ibid.

9. Fair, *Mr. America*, pp. 76–7.

10. Poster for the 1939 Mr. America contest, as reproduced ibid., p. 70.

11. Bob Hoffman, quoted in Fair, *Mr. America*, pp. 72–3.

12. Marla Matza Rose, *Muscle Beach: Where the Best Bodies in the World Started a Fitness Revolution* (LA Weekly Books, 2001), p. 26.

13. Bob Hoffman, quoted in Fair, *Mr. America*, p. 80.

14. Ibid., p. 105.

15. Ibid., p. 126.

16. Ibid., pp. 239–40, 362–4.

17. Museum of Classical Archaeology, 'Why Casts?'

18. Greatest Physiques, 'Steve Reeves', https://www.greatestphysiques.com/male-physiques/steve-reeves/.

19. Bodybuilding.com, 'Arnold Schwarzenegger pro bodybuilding profile', https://www.bodybuilding.com/content/bodybuilders-arnold.html.

20. *Pumping Iron* (1977), excerpt available at https://www.youtube.com/watch?v=keIghFgeh4A.

21. Fair, *Mr. America*, p. 228.

22. Muscle Memory, 'Measurements of later Mr. America winners', https://www.musclememory.com/articles/Mr.Asizes.html.

23. Fair, *Mr. America*, p. 259.

24. Arnold Schwarzenegger speaking at Arnold Classic 2015, available at https://igniteperformancehealthfitness.wordpress.com/tag/classic-vs-modern-bodybuilding-physiques/.

25. Richard Jones, '8 tips on how to bulk up for 2018, from a Mr. Olympia finalist', *Daily Telegraph*, 31 January 2018, https://www.telegraph.co.uk/health-fitness/body/8-tips-bulk-2018-Mr.-olympia-finalist/.

26. Maximuscle, '4 week bulking transformation diet', https://www.maxi-nutrition.com/sports/bodybuilding/4-Week-Bulking-Transformation-Diet/.

27. Tom MacCormick, 'Tip: cutting phase 101', *TNation*, 28 October 2017, https://www.t-nation.com/diet-fat-loss/tip-cutting-phase-101.

28. Schwarzenegger, quoted in Fair, *Mr. America*, pp. 260–61.

29. Fair, *Mr. America*, p. 355.

30. Adam Sinicki, 'Why do bodybuilders have large guts?', https://www.healthguidance.org/entry/17668/1/why-do-bodybuilders-have-large-guts.html.

31. Evolution of Bodybuilding, 'Natural bodybuilding supplements: essentials for building muscle growth', 14 August 2018, https://www.evolutionofbodybuilding.net/natural-bodybuilding-supplements/.

32. British Natural Bodybuilding Federation, 'Banned Substances', https://www.bnbf.co.uk/banned-subtances/.

33. Jeff Everson, quoted in Fair, *Mr. America*, p. 303.

34. Fair, *Mr. America*, p. 365.

35. Ibid., p. 356.

36. Brett Williams, 'Cut, ripped, jacked, or swole? Where do your favourite celebs fall on the continuum – and what are you?', *Men's Health*, 7 November 2018, https://www.menshealth.com/fitness/a24079330/muscular-definition-guide/.

37. Jeremy Gray, 'Are you swole, jacked, or yoked?', *Muscle & Strength*, https://www.muscleandstrength.com/articles/swole-jacked-yoked-lingo.

38. Greg Zulak, quoted in Fair, *Mr. America*, p. 298.

39. Edward Cooper, 'Will steroids shrink my balls?', *Men's Health*, 19 February 2018, https://www.menshealth.com/uk/building-muscle/a758780/will-steroids-shrink-my-balls/.

40. See, for example, Bill Davis, 'How to Get Brutally Huge'; 'Brutally Huge: The Body Parts'; and 'The Best of the Rest of Brutally Huge' at https://brutallyhuge.com.

41. Scott Melzer, *Manhood Impossible: Men's Struggle to Control and Transform Their Bodies and Work* (Rutgers University Press, 2018), p. 19.

42. Ibid., pp. 227–8.

43. John Stoltenberg, *The End of Manhood: A Book for Men of Conscience* (Penguin, 1993).

44. Mike Katz, in *Pumping Iron*.

45. Ibid.

46. Melzer, *Manhood Impossible*, p. 11.

47. On the heteronormativity of the masculinity ideal see R. W. Connell, *Masculinities* (Polity Press, 1995), pp. 103–6, 143.

48. There is controversy about whether drag subverts and redefines gender ideals and norms, or whether it reinforces traditional gender norms or even exhibits misogyny. For discussion on this point see Moya Lloyd, *Beyond Identity Politics: Feminism, Power, and Politics* (Sage Publications, 2005).

49. Perry N. Halkitis, 'Masculinity in the age of AIDS: HIV-seropositive gay men and the "buff agenda"', in Peter Nardi (ed.), *Gay Masculinities* (Sage Publications, 2000), p. 131.

50. Ibid., p. 132.

51. Ibid., p. 149.

52. Melzer, *Manhood Impossible*, p. 113.

53. Ibid.

54. Fair, *Mr. America*, p. 338.

55. Conor Heffernan, 'Bodybuilders who passed away too young', *Physical Culture Study*, 27 October 2018, https://physicalculturestudy.com/2018/10/27/bodybuilders-who-passed-away-too-young/.

56. Oliver Lee Bateman, 'Death by muscle', *Mel* magazine, https://melmagazine.com/en-us/story/death-by-muscle-2.

57. Chris Colucci, 'Big dead bodybuilders: the ultimate price of pro bodybuilding?', *TNation*, 28 October 2016, https://www.t-nation.com/pharma/big-dead-bodybuilders.

58. Ibid.

59. Fair, *Mr. America*, p. 355.

60. Shadow Pro, 'How natural is natural bodybuilding?', *TNation*, 23 July 2014, https://www.t-nation.com/training/how-natural-is-natural-body building. See also Fair, *Mr. America*, pp. 315ff.

61. Fair, *Mr. America*, p. 343.

62. Rachel McLish, quoted ibid., p. 282.

63. Shari L. Dworkin describes how many gym-going women fear looking like a female bodybuilder, an image that they see as unfeminine and that causes them to limit their weightlifting, in her '"Holding back": negotiating a glass ceiling on women's muscular strength', in Rose Weitz (ed.), *The Politics of Women's Bodies: Sexuality, Appearance, and Behavior* (Oxford University Press, 2003).

64. British Natural Bodybuilding Federation, 'Criteria explained – women's criteria', https://www.bnbf.co.uk/events/criteria-explained/womens-criteria/.

65. Ibid.

66. Lianne McTavish, *Feminist Figure Girl: Look Hot While You Fight the Patriarchy* (State University of New York Press, 2015) pp. 100–102.

2. NATURE, YOUR FRENEMY

1. Anna Dahlqvist, *It's Only Blood* (Zed Books, 2018), p. 18.

2. Emma Dabiri, *Don't Touch My Hair* (Allen Lane, 2019), p. 177.

3. Sarah Yang, 'The natural look is in – here's how to achieve it', *Real Simple*, 4 August 2016, https://www.realsimple.com/beauty-fashion/natural-makeup-look.

4. World Health Organization, 'Maternal mortality', 15 February 2018, https://www.who.int/news-room/fact-sheets/detail/maternal-mortality.

5. Giovanni Grandi et al., 'Prevalence of menstrual pain in young women: what is dysmenorrhea?', *Journal of Pain Research*, 5, 2012; H. Ju, M. Jones and G. Mishra, 'The prevalence and risk factors of dysmenorrhea', *Epidemiologic Reviews*, 36, 2014; A. Direkvand-Moghadam et al., 'Epidemiology of premenstrual syndrome (PMS) – a systematic review and meta-analysis study', *Journal of Clinical and Diagnostic Research*, 8 (2), 2014.

6. Jonathan Bearak et al., 'Global, regional, and subregional trends in unintended pregnancy and its outcomes from 1990 to 2014: estimates from a Bayesian hierarchical model', *The Lancet Global Health*, 6, 2018.

7. Emma Kasprzak, 'Why are black mothers at more risk of dying?', BBC News, 12 April 2019, https://www.bbc.co.uk/news/uk-england-47115 305; Amy Roeder, 'America is failing its Black mothers', *Harvard Public*

Health, Winter 2019, https://www.hsph.harvard.edu/magazine/maga-zine_article/america-is-failing-its-black-mothers/.

8. One disparity is that, as Amy Brown puts it, 'five times more research is conducted into erectile dysfunction – a condition that affects 19% of men – compared with premenstrual syndrome, which affects 90% of women'. See Amy Brown, 'Research into pregnancy, birth, and infant care are historically underfunded – and women are paying the price', *The Conversation*, 19 November 2019, http://theconversation.com/ research-into-pregnancy-birth-and-infant-care-are-historically-underfunded-and-women-are-paying-the-price-126629?utm_source=twitter&utm_medium=twitterbutton.

9. The global population is currently 7.7 billion, and UNICEF reports that 26% of the global population is of menstruating age. The figure of 500 million is a rough estimate, based on the fact that the average period lasts between 2 and 7 days each month. See UNICEF, 'Nine things you didn't know about menstruation', 25 May 2018, https://www.unicef. org/press-releases/fast-facts-nine-things-you-didnt-know-about-menstruation.

10. Sandra Lee Bartky, *Femininity and Domination: Studies in the Phenomenology of Oppression* (Routledge, 1990), p. 87.

11. Ibid., p. 95.

12. Nimko Ali, *What We're Told Not to Talk About (But We're Going to Anyway): Women's Voices from East London to Ethiopia* (Viking, 2019).

13. BBC Radio 4, 'Being a girl is ace, Mia', *The Archers*, 22 March 2019, https://www.bbc.co.uk/sounds/play/p074bb8q.

14. Ibid.

15. Dahlqvist, *It's Only Blood*, pp. 79–82.

16. Ibid., p. 54.

17. Ibid., pp. 96–9.

18. Ibid., pp. 183–5.

19. Julian Barnes, *Letters from London 1990–1995* (Vintage, 1995), pp. 162–3. Barnes should have referred to her as Dr Greer even then; three years later she would become Professor Greer.

20. Quoted in Dahlqvist, *It's Only Blood*, p. 180.

21. Ibid., p. 176.

22. Audre Lorde, 'Eye to Eye: Black Women, Hatred, and Anger' (1983), in *Your Silence Will Not Protect You* (Silver Press, 2017), p. 138.

23. Shirley Tate, 'Black beauty: shade, hair, and anti-racist aesthetics', *Ethnic and Racial Studies*, 30 (2), 2007, p. 306.

24. Paul C. Taylor, 'Malcolm's conk and Danto's colors; or, four logical petitions concerning race, beauty, and aesthetics', in Peg Zeglin Brand (ed.), *Beauty Matters* (Indiana University Press, 2000), pp. 57–8.

25. John S. Haller, Jr, *Outcasts from Evolution: Scientific Attitudes of Racial Inferiority 1859–1900* (Southern Illinois University Press, 1995).

26. Taylor, 'Malcolm's conk and Danto's colors', p. 58.

27. Tate, 'Black beauty', p. 302.

28. Ibid.

29. This style is often called 'dreadlocks' or 'dreads', but these terms are considered offensive by some, who point to the term 'dreadlocks' being used by white people to describe Rastafarian hair in particular, and Afro hair in general, as dreadful and disgusting. Others disagree with the etymology, and proudly use the term to describe both the hairstyle and their own hair – the Bob Marley song 'Natty Dread' is perhaps the most famous example. I am not Black, and so I have chosen to use the term 'locks' to avoid repeating the history of white people denigrating Black hair. 'Locks' is often spelled 'locs'; I have chosen 'locks' because this is the spelling used in the campaign video I discuss shortly. See *Affinity* Magazine staff, 'Why you should be careful with using the term "dreads"', *Affinity*, 14 January 2017, http://affinitymagazine.us/2017/01/14/why-you-should-be-careful-saying-dreads/; Princess Gabbara, 'The history of dreadlocks', *Ebony*, 18 October 2016, https://www.ebony.com/style/history-dreadlocks/; Hannah Pool, 'Dare to dread', *Guardian*, 23 August 2003, https://www.theguardian.com/lifeandstyle/2003/aug/23/features.weekend.

30. Dabiri, *Don't Touch My Hair*, p. 92.

31. Ibid., pp. 137–8.

32. Ibid., p. 8.

33. Tate, 'Black beauty', p. 303.

34. Shirley Anne Tate, 'Not all the women want to be white: decolonizing beauty studies', in Encarnacion Gutierrez Rodriguez, Manuela Boatcă and Sérgio Costa (eds.), *Decolonizing European Sociology: Transdisciplinary Approaches* (Routledge, 2010).

35. Tate, 'Black beauty', p. 311.

36. Ibid.

37. Erin Durkin, 'New York to ban hairstyle policies that discriminate against black people', *Guardian*, 18 February 2019, https://www.theguardian.com/us-news/2019/feb/18/new-york-hairstyle-discrimination-ban-african-american?CMP=Share_iOSApp_Other.

38. Green Beauty Channel, 'Locks in the Military (ARMY)', as featured in Christopher Mele, 'Army lifts ban on dreadlocks, and Black servicewomen

rejoice', *New York Times*, 10 February 2017, https://www.nytimes.com/2017/02/10/us/army-ban-on-dreadlocks-black-servicewomen.html.

39. This section is based on Clare Chambers, 'Blending in and standing out: comfort and visibility in beauty practices', Beauty Demands blog, 10 December 2018, http://beautydemands.blogspot.com/2018/12/blending-in-and-standing-out-comfort.html.

40. https://www.facebook.com/VivoreeEOfficialpage34534/videos/402720503726208/.

41. This article was originally titled 'Here's every single trick we know for "I woke up like this" natural looking makeup' in *Glamour* magazine, 16 November 2018, found at https://www.glamourmagazine.co.uk/article/natural-makeup-look. Now, the same link points to a very similar article, complete with 9-step process: Ellie Turner and Lottie Winter, 'Conference call coverage: here's how to keep your makeup natural but profesh', *Glamour* magazine, 24 March 2020.

42. Victoria Jowett, 'Nine ways to ensure your makeup always looks natural', *Cosmopolitan*, 2 November 2018, https://www.cosmopolitan.com/uk/beauty-hair/makeup/g18192402/natural-makeup-look/.

43. Lancôme, 'New Year nude makeup look with Chinutay', https://www.lancome.co.uk/discover-lancome/simple-natural-makeup-look/.

44. Stephanie Huszar, 'How to do natural makeup', *Real Simple*, 5 January 2018, https://www.realsimple.com/beauty-fashion/makeup/makeup-face/barely-there-makeup?

45. 'How to look youthful & rested!', https://www.beautyandtheboutique.tv/younger/.

46. Nuffield Council on Bioethics, 'Cosmetic Procedures: Ethical Issues', 2017, p. 10.

47. Ibid., pp. 10–11.

48. Sandra Lee Bartky, 'Foucault, femininity, and the modernization of patriarchal power', in Diana Tietjens Meyers (ed.), *Feminist Social Thought: A Reader* (Routledge, 1997), p. 95.

49. Jennifer Meierhands, 'Make-up on the train: what's the problem?', BBC News, 4 September 2018, https://www.bbc.co.uk/news/uk-england-45343836.

50. Jeremy N. Bailenson, 'Nonverbal overload: a theoretical argument for the causes of Zoom fatigue', *Technology, Mind, and Behavior*, 2 (1), 2021.

51. Genevieve Howland, 'Labor interventions: how to avoid them (and why you'd want to)', Mama Natural, 24 May 2019, https://www.mamanatural.com/labor-interventions/.

3. KILLING THE ENEMY

1. Jean-Jacques Rousseau, *Émile or On Education*, trans. Allan Bloom (Basic Books, 1979), p. 363.

2. Andrea Dworkin, 'Feminism: An Agenda' (1983), in her *Letters from a War Zone* (Secker & Warburg, 1988), p. 151.

3. The analysis in this and the following paragraph comes from Amnesty International, 'The world's worst places to be a woman', https://www.amnestyusa.org/the-worlds-worst-places-to-be-a-woman/.

4. Jenny Nordberg, *The Underground Girls of Kabul: The Hidden Lives of Afghan Girls Disguised as Boys* (Virago, 2014), p. 42.

5. Ibid.

6. I am following Nordberg in referring to a *bacha posh* as a girl and using feminine pronouns.

7. Nordberg, *The Underground Girls of Kabul*, p. 170.

8. Michel Foucault, *Discipline and Punish* (Penguin, 1991).

9. Pierre Bourdieu, *Masculine Domination* (Polity Press, 2001) and *The Logic of Practice* (Polity Press, 1990).

10. Iris Marion Young, 'Throwing like a girl: a phenomenology of feminine body comportment, motility, and spatiality' (1977), in her *On Female Body Experience: 'Throwing Like a Girl' and Other Essays* (Oxford University Press, 2005), p. 43.

11. Ibid., p. 45.

12. Nordberg, *The Underground Girls of Kabul*, p. 178.

13. Hobbes's proposed method for taming nature was the Leviathan or *government*: an all-powerful ruler who could constrain human aggression. See Thomas Hobbes, *Leviathan* (Hackett, 1994).

14. John Locke, *Two Treatises of Government* (Cambridge University Press, 1994), p. 271.

15. USA Declaration of Independence, http://www.ushistory.org/declaration/document/.

16. Locke, *Two Treatises of Government*, p. 320.

17. Ibid.

18. Rousseau, *Émile*, p. 363.

19. Ibid., p. 361. Rousseau argued that one of the chief lessons that nature teaches us about the morality of sex is that women must, above all else, be faithful. His thinking was this: men have no way of knowing whether a child is theirs other than by the word and fidelity of the child's mother. Infidelity thus means tricking a man into supporting a child who may not be his. Infidelity, for Rousseau, is not wrong merely on human terms.

20. William Kessen, 'Rousseau's children', *Daedalus*, 107 (3), 1978.

21. Rousseau, *Émile*, p. 365.

22. Ibid.

23. Ibid., p. 367.

24. Ibid.

25. Mary Wollstonecraft, *A Vindication of the Rights of Woman* and *A Vindication of the Rights of Men* (Oxford University Press, 2008), p. 95.

26. John Stuart Mill, *The Subjection of Women* in *On Liberty* and *The Subjection of Women* (Wordsworth, 1996), p. 128.

27. Wollstonecraft, *A Vindication of the Rights of Woman*, p. 72.

28. Ibid., p. 110.

29. Mill, *The Subjection of Women*, p. 128.

30. Ibid., pp. 136–7.

31. Simone de Beauvoir, *The Second Sex* (Virago, 1997), p. 13.

32. Ibid., p. 295.

33. Ibid., p. 61.

34. Ibid., p. 65.

35. Ibid., pp. 18–19.

36. Ibid., p. 67.

37. Ibid., p. 56.

38. Catharine MacKinnon, *Toward a Feminist Theory of the State* (Harvard University Press, 1989), p. 54.

39. This section is based on Clare Chambers, 'Judging women: twenty-five years further *Toward a Feminist Theory of the State*', *Feminist Philosophy Quarterly*, 3 (2), 2017.

40. MacKinnon, *Toward a Feminist Theory of the State*, p. 54.

41. Ibid.

42. Ibid., p. 55.

43. Ibid., p. 56.

44. Catherine Blackledge, *The Story of V: Opening Pandora's Box* (Orion Books, 2003), pp. 190–94.

45. I am paraphrasing Dworkin's speech to the Midwest Regional Conference of the National Organization for Changing Men: 'I came here today because I don't believe that rape is inevitable or natural. If I did, I would have no reason to be here. If I did, my political practice would be different than it is. Have you ever wondered why we are not just in armed combat against you? It's not because there's a shortage of kitchen knives in this country.' (Dworkin, *Letters from a War Zone*, pp. 169–70.)

46. MacKinnon, *Toward a Feminist Theory of the State*, p. 218.

47. Cass Bliss, 'Here's what it's like to get your period when you're not a woman', *Huffpost Personal*, 20 August 2018, https://www.huffpost.com/

entry/nonbinary-period-menstruation_n_5b75ac1fe4b0182d49b1c2ed?
ncid=engmodushpmgooooooo6UbhfdsIFvxdCSudJ6XXbq9cWfXlmM6
qFqx4NeQT7GYE1lx6Pi-xVW1JOI_okWyQ9grl5IRUqodTNK36UXh
aW3zBkR.

48. Donna J. Haraway, 'The Contest for Primate Nature: Daughters of Man-
the-Hunter in the Field 1960–80', first published in 1983, reprinted in
her *Simians, Cyborgs, and Women: The Reinvention of Nature* (Free
Association Books, 1991), p. 106.

49. Haraway, *Simians, Cyborgs, and Women*, p. 96.

50. Ibid.

51. Ibid., p. 42.

52. Ibid., p. 72.

53. Judith Butler, *Gender Trouble: Feminism and the Subversion of Identity*
(Routledge, 1999), p. 11.

54. Ibid., p. xxvii.

55. Ibid., p. 10.

56. Ibid., p. 144.

57. Ibid., p. 168.

58. Talia Mae Bettcher, 'Trans women and the meaning of "woman"', in
Nicholas Power, Raja Halwani and Alan Soble (eds.), *The Philosophy of
Sex: Contemporary Readings* (Rowman & Littlefield, 2012), p. 241.

59. Sally Haslanger, *Resisting Reality: Social Construction and Social Critique* (Oxford University Press, 2012), p. 230.

60. Caroline Criado Perez, *Invisible Women: Exposing Data Bias in a World
Designed by Men* (Chatto & Windus, 2019).

61. Katharine Jenkins, 'Amelioration and inclusion: gender identity and the
concept of *woman*', *Ethics*, 126 (2), 2016, p. 394.

62. Ibid., p. 396.

63. Ibid., p. 404. Emphasis added.

64. Lori Watson, 'The woman question', *Transgender Studies Quarterly*, 3
(1–2), 2016.

65. Jenkins's account is but one among many defences of using self-identification
to define gender. Matthew Salett Andler argues that even this is insufficiently trans-inclusive, in his 'Gender identity and exclusion: a reply to
Jenkins', *Ethics*, 127 (4), 2017.

66. Nordberg, *The Underground Girls of Kabul*, p. 126.

67. See, for example, Gloria Steinem, 'If men could menstruate', in her *Outrageous Acts and Everyday Rebellions* (Flamingo, 1985).

4. WEAVING, BINDING, SPINNING

1. Catharine MacKinnon, 'Keeping it Real: On Anti-"Essentialism"' (1997), in her *Women's Lives, Men's Laws* (Harvard University Press, 2005), p. 89.

2. Diana Fuss, *Essentially Speaking: Feminism, Nature and Difference* (Routledge, 1989), p. 51.

3. 'Anal can be pleasurable' instructs *Red* magazine, aimed at women. 'Many people are turned off by anal due to the association with discomfort and pain,' the magazine notes. I'd say being turned off by something you associate with discomfort and pain is a pretty good sign you should exclude it from your sex life, but apparently not. Sex therapist Chris Donague (a man) recommends that women try it – after working hard to suppress their instincts. 'Get used to the experience of [your anus] being touched and associated with pleasure,' he says. 'If you are stressed or anxious, your entire body will tense. Practice, relaxation and breathing are important prerequisites.' ('Sex education', *Red* magazine, July 2019, p. 55.) 'Practice, relaxation and breathing' is hardly a recipe for sexual autonomy. It's instructions on how to submit to someone else's idea of how sex should be. 'Getting out of your comfort zone is key to enjoying a long-lasting and fulfilling sex life,' *Red* instructs. But why? Why isn't *comfort* vital?

4. On this point see Susan Moller Okin's work, particularly *Women in Western Political Thought* (Princeton University Press, 1979) and *Justice, Gender, and the Family* (Basic Books, 1989).

5. Beauty thus becomes a moral imperative, as Heather Widdows shows in *Perfect Me: Beauty as an Ethical Ideal* (Princeton University Press, 2018).

6. Widdows, *Perfect Me,* pp. 152–4.

7. Emma Dabiri, *Don't Touch My Hair* (Allen Lane, 2019), ch. 2.

8. Of course, each person's right to a full and free sex life is limited by the equal rights of others.

9. Kimberlé Crenshaw, 'Demarginalizing the intersection of race and sex: a Black feminist critique of antidiscrimination doctrine, feminist theory and antiracist politics', *University of Chicago Legal Forum*, 1989, and Kimberlé Crenshaw, 'Mapping the margins: intersectionality, identity politics, and violence against women of color', *Stanford Law Review*, 43, 1993.

10. Audre Lorde, quoted in Rudolph P. Byrd, Johnetta Betsch Cole and Beverly Guy-Sheftall (eds.), *I am Your Sister: Collected and Unpublished Writings of Audre Lorde* (Oxford University Press, 2009), p. 26.

11. Adrienne Rich, *Of Woman Born: Motherhood as Experience and Institution* (W. Norton & Company, 1976), p. 40.

12. I undertake a sustained critical analysis of the concept of choice in Clare Chambers, *Sex, Culture, and Justice: The Limits of Choice* (Penn State University Press, 2008).

13. Suzanne Moore, Homa Khaleeli, Moya Sarner, Leah Harper and Justin McCurry, 'How the Greenham Common protest changed lives: "We danced on top of the nuclear silos"', *Guardian*, 20 March 2017, https://www.theguardian.com/uk-news/2017/mar/20/greenham-common-nuclear-silos-women-protest-peace-camp.

14. Ibid.

15. Ibid.

16. Richard Adams, *Watership Down* (Rex Collings, 1972).

17. Penelope Stokes, *The Common Good: The History of Greenham Common* (Greenham Trust, 2017).

18. The National Archives, 'Records of Greenham Women's Peace Camp', https://discovery.nationalarchives.gov.uk/details/r/d625b55a-e807–4729–9d8c-087c918dbaff.

19. Paul Brown, Shyama Perera and Martin Wainwright, 'Protest by CND stretches 14 miles', *Guardian*, 2 April 1983, https://www.theguardian.com/fromthearchive/story/0,,1866956,00.html.

20. Greenham: A Common Inheritance, 'Embrace the Base', http://www.greenham-common.org.uk/ixbin/hixclient.exe?a=query&p=greenham&f=generic_largerimage_postsearch.htm&_IXFIRST_=914&_IXMAXHITS_=1&m=quick_sform&tc1=i&partner=greenham&tc2=e&s=dH_78s4Naaq.

21. Moore et al., 'How the Greenham Common protest changed lives'.

22. Beth Junor, *Greenham Common Women's Peace Camp: A History of Non-Violent Resistance 1984–1995* (Working Press, 1995), p. xi.

23. Stokes, *The Common Good*, p. 54.

24. Moore et al., 'How the Greenham Common protest changed lives'.

25. Ibid.

26. Stokes, *The Common Good*, p. 58.

27. Mary Mellor, *Feminism & Ecology* (Polity Press, 1997), p. 44.

28. Rich, *Of Woman Born*, p. 280.

29. Ibid., p. 216.

30. Ibid., p. 251.

31. Ibid., p. 252.

32. Ibid., p. 212.

33. Hollie McNish, 'post partum', in *Nobody Told Me: Poetry and Parenthood* (Blackfriars, 2016). Posted on Twitter, 13 November 2019, https://twitter.com/holliepoetry/status/1194672505425936384.

34. Rich, *Of Woman Born*, p. 13.

35. Ibid., p. 40.

36. Ibid., p. 103.

37. Ibid., p. 129.

38. Ibid., p. 285.

39. Mellor, *Feminism & Ecology*, p. 60

40. Ibid., pp. 68–9.

41. Ibid., p. 71.

42. Ynestra King, 'Toward an ecological feminism and feminist ecology', quoted in Mellor, *Feminism & Ecology*, p. 62.

43. Rich, *Of Woman Born*, p. 284.

44. Andrea Dworkin, *Woman Hating* (E. P. Dutton, 1974), pp. 110–12.

45. Belly Bandit, 'How it works', https://www.bellybandit.co.uk/pages/how-it-works.

46. Belly Bandit, 'About us', https://www.bellybandit.co.uk/pages/about-us.

47. Belly Bandit, 'Get sized', https://www.bellybandit.co.uk/pages/get-sized.

48. Belly Bandit, 'About us'.

49. The strapline is found on the Google description for this page: http://uk.triumph.com/shapewear?gclid=EAIaIQobChMI57q6ocyA5wIVh63tCho59gjkEAAYAiAAEgLhavD_BwE.

50. Heist Studios at https://www.heist-studios.com/?utm_source=google&utm_medium=cpc&utm_campaign=Shapewear-UK-Search-Generic&utm_term=shapewear&utm_content=314429620529&gclid=EAIaIQobChMI57q6ocyA5wIVh63tCho59gjkEAAYASAAEgJ9_fD_BwE.

51. Susie Orbach, *Fat Is A Feminist Issue* (Random House, 2010), p. 9.

52. Bea Mitchell, 'Chest binding is an integral part of the transitioning process for lots of trans men – here's how it works', *Pink News*, 30 April 2018, https://www.pinknews.co.uk/2018/04/30/chest-binding-transgender-transitioning/.

53. Sarah Peitzmeier, Ivy Gardner, Jamie Weinand, Alexandra Corbet and Kimberlynn Acevedo, 'Health impact of chest binding among transgender adults: a community-engaged, cross-sectional study', *Culture, Health, and Sexuality*, 19 (1), 2017, https://doi.org/10.1080/13691058.2016.1191675.

54. Maggie Nelson, *The Argonauts* (Melville House UK, 2016).

55. Orbach, *Fat Is A Feminist Issue*, p. 10.

56. Ibid.

57. C. N. Lester, *Trans Like Me: A Journey for All of Us* (Virago, 2017), p. 34.

58. Orbach, *Fat Is A Feminist Issue*, p. 46.

59. Ibid., p. 145.

60. Karin A. Martin, *Puberty, Sexuality, and the Self: Boys and Girls at Adolescence* (Routledge, 1996), p. 27.

61. Sofie Hagen, *Happy Fat: Taking Up Space in a World That Wants to Shrink You* (Fourth Estate, 2019), p. 35.

62. Martin, *Puberty, Sexuality, and the Self*, p. 32.

63. Ibid., p. 20.

64. Ibid., p. 25.

65. Ultimately, of course, diets don't work, which traps girls into a cycle of shame. As Martin puts it, 'girls' dislike of their bodies often becomes a dislike of the self when the diet fails.' (Martin, *Puberty, Sexuality, and the Self*, p. 38.)

66. The UK Parliament's Women & Equalities Select Committee has recently begun this work. See House of Commons Women & Equalities Select Committee, 'Changing the Perfect Picture: An Enquiry into Body Image', 2021, https://committees.parliament.uk/publications/5357/documents/53751/default/.

67. See, for example, the Everyday Lookism campaign at https://everyday-lookism.bham.ac.uk.

68. Dworkin, *Woman Hating*, p. 116.

69. Andrea Dworkin, 'Biological Superiority: The World's Most Dangerous and Deadly Idea' (1977), in *Letters from a War Zone* (Secker & Warburg, 1988).

70. Dworkin, *Woman Hating*, p. 186.

71. Ibid.

72. Ibid., p. 187.

73. Ibid., pp. 156–7.

74. Chambers, *Sex, Culture, and Justice*, p. 49.

75. For a discussion of various versions of this claim see Jeanne Bovet, 'Evolutionary theories and men's preferences for women's waist-to-hip ratio: which hypotheses remain? A systematic review', *Frontiers in Psychology*, 4 June 2019.

76. Randy Thornhill and Craig T. Palmer, *A Natural History of Rape: Biological Bases of Sexual Coercion* (MIT Press, 2000).

77. Joyce F. Benenson, 'Sex on the brain', *Nature* 424, 2003, pp. 132–3, reviewing Simon Baron-Cohen, *The Essential Difference: Men, Women and the Extreme Male Brain* (Penguin/Basic Books, 2003).

78. http://www.lse.ac.uk/cpnss/research/archive/darwin-at-lse/publications/darwinism-today.

79. Publisher's webpage for Kingsley Browne, *Divided Labours: An Evolutionary View of Women at Work* (Yale University Press, 1999), https://yalebooks.yale.edu/book/9780300080261/divided-labours.

80. One feminist who makes that case to great effect is psychologist Cordelia Fine. Fine points out the flaws in a range of scientific accounts and emphasizes – as Mill did 200 years before – the vast weight of social gendering that we heap upon our 'natural' brains and bodies. Cordelia Fine, *Delusions of Gender: How Our Minds, Society, and Neurosexism Create Difference* (Norton, 2010). See also Lise Eliot, *Pink Brain, Blue Brain: How Small Differences Grow into Troublesome Gaps – And What We Can Do About It* (Oneworld Publications, 2012).

PART TWO

1. James Partridge, *Face It: Facial Disfigurement and My Fight for Facial Equality* (Whitefox Publishing, 2020), p. 32.

2. The connection between fatness and ill-health is widely assumed but is controversial. See Tarra L. Penney and Sara F. L. Kirk, 'The health at every size paradigm and obesity: missing empirical evidence may help push the reframing obesity debate forward', *American Journal of Public Health*, 105, 2015.

3. Sofie Hagen, *Happy Fat: Taking Up Space in a World That Wants to Shrink You* (Fourth Estate, 2019), p. 36.

5. THE NORMAL BODY

1. The most prominent naturalist is Christopher Boorse, for example in his 'On the distinction between disease and illness', *Philosophy & Public Affairs*, 5, 1975.

2. Normativist works include William K. Goosens, 'Values, health, and medicine', *Philosophy of Science*, 47, 1980; Ron Amundson, 'Against normal function', *Studies in History and Philosophy of Biological and Biomedical Sciences*, 31 (1), 2000; and H. T. Engelhardt, Jr, 'The concepts of health and disease', in H. T. Engelhardt, Jr and S. F. Spicker (eds.), *Evaluation and Explanation in Biomedical Sciences* (D. Reidel, 1975).

3. C. Tasca, M. Rapetti, M. G. Carta and B. Fadda, 'Women and hysteria in the history of mental health', *Clinical Practice and Epidemiology in Mental Health*, 8, 2012.

4. Robert Darby, 'The masturbation taboo and the rise of routine male circumcision: a review of the historiography', *Journal of Social History*, 36 (3), 2003.

5. The World Bank, 'Population, female', https://data.worldbank.org/indicator/SP.POP.TOTL.FE.ZS.

6. Christopher Boorse, 'Health as a theoretical concept', *Philosophy of Science*, 44 (4), 1977.

7. Jerome Bickenbach, 'Disability, health, and difference', in Adam Cureton and David Wasserman (eds.), *The Oxford Handbook of Philosophy and Disability* (Oxford University Press, 2018), p. 5.

8. David Wootton, *Bad Medicine* (Oxford University Press, 2006), p. 2.

9. See Clare Chambers, 'Choice and female genital cosmetic surgery', in S. Creighton and L.-M. Liao (eds.), *Female Genital Cosmetic Surgery: Solution to What Problem?* (Cambridge University Press, 2019).

10. This practice is referred to by various names, including 'female circumcision', 'female genital cutting' and 'female genital mutilation'. Each term has something to recommend it. 'Female circumcision' is the term used by many cultures that practise it, and highlights similarities with male circumcision. 'Female genital cutting' is a more neutral term that leaves normative questions open to debate. I have chosen 'female genital mutilation' for two reasons: first, it is the term used in the legislation and dominant narratives of the Western cultures on which I focus in this book; and second, it is the term used by many critics who have themselves undergone the practice, such as British campaigners Nimko Ali, Leila Hussein and Hibo Wardere.

11. For an overview of practices of genital cutting around the world see Ariane Shahvisi and Brian D. Earp, 'The law and ethics of female genital cutting', in S. Creighton and L.-M. Liao (eds.), *Female Genital Cosmetic Surgery: Solution to What Problem?* (Cambridge University Press, 2019) and Brian D. Earp, 'Female genital mutilation and male circumcision: toward an autonomy-based ethical framework', *Medicolegal and Bioethics*, 5, 2015.

12. UK Female Genital Mutilation Act 2003, http://www.cps.gov.uk/legal/d_to_g/female_genital_mutilation/#a01.

13. Alice Dreger, *Galileo's Middle Finger: Heretics, Activists, and One Scholar's Search for Justice* (Penguin Books, 2015); Human Rights Watch, '"I

want to be like nature made me": medically unnecessary surgeries on intersex children in the US', 25 July 2017, https://www.hrw.org/report/2017/07/25/i-want-be-nature-made-me/medically-unnecessary-surgeries-intersex-children-us.

14. Legal firm Mills & Reeve refers to female genital cosmetic surgery as 'technically unlawful'. See Mills & Reeve, 'Briefing: The Female Genital Mutilation Act and its relation to female genital cosmetic surgery', October 2013, p. 1, http://www.mills-reeve.com/files/Publication/e023b495-a726-4241-b4dc-5d607f22d2f4/Presentation/PublicationAttachment/efa6e8e7-14e1-498d-9496-5fcobde49384/FGMA_Oct13.pdf. Marge Berer notes that, in the UK, 'there is a law against female genital mutilation (FGM) which describes it in the very same terms as the procedure described by the Department of Health as labia reduction.' See Marge Berer, 'Labia reduction for non-therapeutic purposes vs. female genital mutilation: contradictions in law and practice in Britain', *Reproductive Health Matters*, 18 (35), 2010.

15. Mills & Reeve, 'Briefing', p. 2.

16. Explanatory Note to Female Genital Mutilation Act 2003, http://www.legislation.gov.uk/ukpga/2003/31/contents.

17. NHS Choices, 'Your guide to cosmetic procedures: labiaplasty (vulval surgery)', https://www.nhs.uk/conditions/cosmetic-treatments/labiaplasty/.

18. For discussion of the similarities and differences between FGM and female genital cosmetic surgery, see Royal College of Obstetricians and Gynaecologists, 'Ethical Opinion Paper: Ethical considerations in relation to female genital cosmetic surgery (FGCS)', https://www.rcog.org.uk/globalassets/documents/guidelines/ethics-issues-and-resources/rcog-fgcs-ethical-opinion-paper.pdf; Radhika Sanghani, 'Outlawing "designer vaginas": have MPs gone mad?', *Daily Telegraph*, 16 March 2015, http://www.telegraph.co.uk/women/womens-health/11475276/Designer-vaginas-to-be-made-illegal-Have-MPs-gone-mad.html; Van Badham, 'Female genital mutilation is alive in Australia. It's just called labiaplasty', *Guardian*, 26 August 2015, https://www.theguardian.com/commentisfree/2015/aug/26/female-genital-mutilation-is-alive-in-australia-its-just-called-labiaplasty; Lih-Meh Liao and Sarah Creighton, 'Requests for cosmetic genitoplasty: how should healthcare providers respond?', and Responses, *BMJ*, 334 (7603), 2007, http://www.bmj.com/content/334/7603/1090; Moira Dustin, 'Female genital mutilation/cutting in the UK', *European Journal of Women's Studies*, 17 (1), 2010; B. Kelly and C. Foster, 'Should female genital cosmetic surgery and genital piercing be regarded ethically and legally as female genital mutilation?', *BJOG: An International Journal of Obstetrics & Gynaecology*, 119, 2012.

19. Heather Widdows, *Perfect Me: Beauty as an Ethical Ideal* (Princeton University Press, 2018).

20. Clare Chambers, *Sex, Culture, and Justice: The Limits of Choice* (Penn State University Press, 2018); Naomi Wolf, *The Beauty Myth* (Chatto & Windus, 1990); Sheila Jeffreys, *Beauty and Misogyny* (Routledge, 2005).

21. For a graphic account of one woman's experience of FGM as a child, including her account of asking for FGM without understanding what was entailed, see Hibo Wardere, *Cut: One Woman's Fight against FGM in Britain Today* (Simon & Schuster, 2016).

22. For discussion of breast implants in children see Chambers, *Sex, Culture, and Justice*; Diana Zuckerman and Anisha Abraham, 'Teenagers and cosmetic surgery: focus on breast augmentation and liposuction', *Journal of Adolescent Health*, 43 (4), 2008.

23. Clare Chambers, 'Are breast implants better than female genital mutilation? Autonomy, gender equality and Nussbaum's political liberalism', *Critical Review of International Social and Political Philosophy*, 7 (3), 2004; Chambers, *Sex, Culture, and Justice*.

24. Courtney Smith, 'Who defines "mutilation"? Challenging imperialism in the discourse of female genital cutting', in *Feminist Formations*, 23 (1), 2011, p. 36.

25. Nancy Hurst, 'Lactation after augmentation mammoplasty', *Obstetrics & Gynecology*, 87 (1), 1996; M. Neifert, S. DeMarzo, J. Seacat, D. Young, M. Leff and M. Orleans, 'The influence of breast surgery, breast appearance, and pregnancy-induced breast changes on lactation sufficiency as measured by infant weight gain', *Birth*, 17, 1990; Norma I. Kruz and Leo Korchin, 'Breastfeeding after augmentation mammaplasty with saline implants', *Annals of Plastic Surgery*, 64 (5), 2010; Pamela D. Hill, Patricia A. Wilhelm, Jean C. Aldag and Robert T. Chatterton, Jr, 'Breast augmentation and lactation outcome: a case report', *American Journal of Maternal Child Nursing*, 29 (4), 2004; K. Michalopoulos, 'The effects of breast augmentation surgery on future ability to lactate', *The Breast Journal*, 13, 2007.

26. Michalopoulous found that many women were not fully informed about the consequences for breastfeeding, or did not take them into account, at the time of consenting to breast implants, in 'The effects of breast augmentation surgery'.

27. Smith, 'Who defines "mutilation"?', p. 35.

28. Leonard B. Glick, *Marked in Your Flesh: Circumcision from Ancient Judea to Modern America* (Oxford University Press, 2005); Ghiath Alahmad and Wim Dekkers, 'Bodily integrity and male circumcision: an

Islamic perspective', *Journal of the Islamic Medical Association of North America*, 44, 2012.

29. For an overview of the justifications given for FGM in Sudan and Africa, see Hanny Lightfoot-Klein, *Prisoners of Ritual: An Odyssey into Female Genital Circumcision in Africa* (Harrington Park Press, 1989).

30. Richard A. Shweder, 'What about "female genital mutilation"? And why understanding culture matters in the first place', *Daedalus*, 129 (4), 2000, pp. 216, 218–19; Brian D. Earp, 'Between moral relativism and moral hypocrisy: reframing the debate on "FGM"', *Kennedy Institute of Ethics Journal*, 26 (2), 2016, pp. 116–17. This judgement is by no means universal among women who have undergone FGM. Wardere describes how she was unable to look at her own vulva for over a decade after she underwent FGM, and managed to do so only by taking photographs and mustering the courage to look at them. When she did, 'there was only one word for it: devastating . . . [T]here were no fleshy labia like other women had, no protection, no beauty.' Wardere, *Cut*, p. 113. For other accounts of women who do not find their post-FGM genitals to be beautiful, see Earp, 'Between moral relativism and moral hypocrisy', p. 141.

31. Marvel L. Williamson and Paul S. Williamson, 'Women's preferences for penile circumcision in sexual partners', *Journal of Sex Education and Therapy*, 14 (2), 1988, found that most American women preferred circumcised penises aesthetically, and that this preference influenced their decision to circumcise their sons. This finding is reflected in popular culture, with the judgement that uncircumcised penises are unattractive featuring in TV shows such as *Seinfeld* and *Sex and the City*, as well as various novels and jokes. See Glick, *Marked in Your Flesh*, for discussion.

32. Frederick M. Hodges, 'The ideal prepuce in Ancient Greece and Rome: male genital aesthetics and their relation to *lipodermos*, circumcision, foreskin restoration, and the *kynodesme*', *The Bulletin of the History of Medicine*, 75, 2001.

33. NHS Choices, 'Is cosmetic surgery available on the NHS?', http://www.nhs.uk/Conditions/cosmetic-treatments-guide/Pages/is-cosmetic-surgery-available-on-the-NHS.aspx.

34. P. A. Dewan, H. C. Tieu and B. S. Chieng, 'Phimosis: is circumcision necessary?', *Journal of Paediatrics and Child Health*, 32 (4), 1996, http://www.cirp.org/library/treatment/phimosis/dewan/.

35. NHS Choices, 'Circumcision in boys', http://www.nhs.uk/conditions/Circumcision-in-children/Pages/Introduction.aspx (accessed May 2018).

36. Glick, *Marked in Your Flesh*, p. 9.

37. Max Fish, Arianne Shahvisi, Tatenda Gwaambuka, Godfrey B. Tangwa, Daniel Ncaylyana and Brian D. Earp, 'A new Tuskegee? Unethical human experimentation and Western neocolonialism in the mass circumcision of African men', *Developing World Bioethics*, 2020.

38. American Academy of Pediatrics, 'Newborn male circumcision', https://www.aap.org/en-us/about-the-aap/aap-press-room/pages/newborn-male-circumcision.aspx (accessed May 2018).

39. HealthyChildren.org, 'Should the baby be circumcised?', https://www.healthychildren.org/English/ages-stages/prenatal/decisions-to-make/Pages/Should-the-Baby-be-Circumcised.aspx (accessed May 2018).

40. Ibid.

41. Ibid. As Brian Earp notes, there is a significant double standard concerning the prevention of UTIs, which can be summed up as 'washing the genitals for girls, foreskin amputation for boys'. See Brian D. Earp, 'Female genital mutilation (FGM) and male circumcision: should there be a separate ethical discourse?', *Practical Ethics*, 18 February 2014, p. 7, https://www.academia.edu/8817976/Female_genital_mutilation_FGM_and_male_circumcision_Should_there_be_a_separate_ethical_discourse. And, as Robert Darby points out, the WHO funds research into both male circumcision and FGM, but 'In neither case is the research open-ended: in relation to women the search is for damage, in relation to men it is for benefit; and since the initial assumptions influence the outcomes, these results are duly found.' See Robert Darby, 'Moral hypocrisy or intellectual inconsistency? A historical perspective on our habit of placing male and female genital cutting in separate ethical boxes', *Kennedy Institute of Ethics Journal*, 26 (2), 2016, p. 157.

42. Dewan, Tieu and Cheing, 'Phimosis: is circumcision necessary?'

43. As Earp notes, 'Western societies don't seem to think that "health benefits" are particularly relevant to the question of whether we should be cutting off parts of the external genitalia of healthy girls.' Earp, who opposes both FGM and routine circumcision, is particularly concerned that even engaging with the question of whether circumcision brings health benefits opens the door to similar discussions around FGM. Earp, 'Female genital mutilation (FGM) and male circumcision', p. 7.

44. Similarly, the idea of what counts as a *medical* reason is cultural, as the normativists in philosophy of medicine argue. In the 19th century in Anglophone countries masturbation was seen as the cause of many diseases, and male circumcision was seen as the appropriate cure for masturbation and thus for disease. According to medical discourse at the time, then, male circumcision would have counted as a clinical procedure

rather than a cultural one. And yet that aim, of lessening sexual desire and activity, is very similar to the discourse surrounding FGM in many communities today. From a contemporary Western perspective, sexual desire and activity, including masturbation, is normal and healthy. So, from a contemporary Western perspective, genital surgery aimed at reducing desire, such as FGM, is cultural not clinical. But that judgement depends on the cultural and historical perspective from which it emanates, so the judgement is itself already a matter of culture.

45. Evidence given to the Nuffield Council on Bioethics Working Party on Cosmetic Procedures. See the report, 'Cosmetic Procedures: Ethical Issues', http://nuffieldbioethics.org/wp-content/uploads/Cosmetic-procedures-full-report.pdf.

46. This is an account of a real man's experience, as told to me in person, but his name has been changed.

47. Annika Rosengren and Lauren Lissner, 'The sociology of obesity', in M. Korbonits (ed.), *Obesity and Metabolism* (Karger, 2008).

48. NHS Great Ormond Street Hospital for Children, 'Conditions we treat: additional little fingers', https://www.gosh.nhs.uk/conditions-and-treat ments/conditions-we-treat/additional-little-fingers (accessed May 2018).

49. See, for example, the Da Silva family: 14 family members have additional fingers and toes. Maxim Duncan, 'Brazilian family cross extra fingers for sixth world cup', Reuters, 21 June 2014, https://uk.reuters.com/article/uk-soccer-world-bra-fingers/brazilian-family-cross-extra-fingers-for-sixth-world-cup-idUKKBN0EW06R20140621.

50. HealthyChildren.org, 'Should the baby be circumcised?'

51. Jack Drescher, 'Gender identity diagnoses: history and controversies', in Baudewijntje P. C. Kreukels, Thomas D. Steensma and Annelou L. C. de Vries (eds.), *Gender Dysphoria and Disorders of Sex Development: Progress in Care and Knowledge* (Springer, 2013).

52. See Robert Sparrow, 'Defending Deaf culture: the case of cochlear implants', *Journal of Political Philosophy*, 13 (2), 2005. Sparrow directly compares sex and deafness, asking 'if critics want to insist that deaf people are disabled because they do not have the full range of normal human capacities, it is appropriate to ask whether they think that it is men or women who are disabled? If they insist that both men and women have normal human bodies despite the fact that they have different bodily capacities, then the question arises as to why they are not prepared to admit that this range might include deaf persons as well?' (p. 139).

6. DISABILITY, IMPAIRMENT, IDENTITY

1. Ludwig van Beethoven, 'Letter to my brothers Carl and Johann Beethoven', 6 October 1802, in *The Project Gutenberg EBook of Beethoven's Letters 1790–1826* (ed. Lady Wallace), https://www.gutenberg.org/files/13065/13065-h/13065-h.htm#let26.

2. Elizabeth Barnes, *The Minority Body: A Theory of Disability* (Oxford University Press, 2016), p. 1.

3. Ludwig van Beethoven, letter to Karl Amanda, http://www.lvbeethoven.com/Bio/BiographyDeafness.html.

4. Sharron Ridgeway, quoted in Jonathan Glover, *Choosing Children: Genes, Disability, and Design* (Oxford University Press, 2006), p. 5.

5. For a demonstration see Commanding Hands, 'Adding facial expressions to signs in British Sign Language', https://www.youtube.com/watch?v=Q25hzuU4lOk.

6. Andrew Solomon, *Far From The Tree: Parents, Children and the Search for Identity* (Vintage, 2014), p. 80.

7. Linguistic Society of America, 'FAQ: Bilingualism', https://www.linguisticsociety.org/resource/faq-what-bilingualism.

8. Solomon, *Far From The Tree*, p. 92.

9. Ibid., p. 98.

10. Ibid.

11. Ibid.

12. Common practice is to use 'deaf' in lower case to describe the impairment, and 'Deaf' to describe Deaf culture.

13. Jenny L. Singleton and Matthew D. Tittle, 'Deaf parents and their hearing children', *Journal of Deaf Studies and Deaf Education*, 5 (3), 2000, p. 225.

14. Ibid., p. 223.

15. Solomon, *Far From The Tree*, p. 96.

16. Ibid., p. 108.

17. Ibid., p. 87.

18. RNID, 'Cochlear implants', https://rnid.org.uk/information-and-support/hearing-loss/hearing-implants/cochlear-implants/.

19. Solomon, *Far From The Tree*, p. 87.

20. Ibid., p. 88.

21. Ibid., p. 89.

22. Ibid.

23. Will Kymlicka, *Liberalism, Community, and Culture* (Oxford University Press, 1989) and *Multicultural Citizenship: A Liberal Theory of Minority Rights* (Oxford University Press, 1995).

24. Singleton and Tittle, 'Deaf parents and their hearing children', p. 222.

25. British Association of Teachers of the Deaf, 'Ethan Mount-Jones by his mother', Personal Experiences – Cochlear Implants, https://www.batod.org.uk/information/personal-experiences-cochlear-implants/.

26. Ibid.

27. Michael Oliver, 'Medicine and disability: steps in the wrong direction', *International Journal of Medical Engineering and Technology*, 2 (3), 1978, p. 137.

28. Eli Clare, *Exile and Pride: Disability, Queerness, and Liberation* (Duke University Press, 2015), p. 122.

29. Ibid.

30. Caroline Criado Perez, *Invisible Women: Exposing Data Bias in a World Designed by Men* (Chatto & Windus, 2019).

31. Lemony Snicket, *The Carnivorous Carnival* (HarperCollins, 2002), p. 79.

32. Tom Shakespeare, *Disability Rights and Wrongs Revisited* (Routledge, 2014), p. 12.

33. Clare, *Exile and Pride*, p. 130.

34. Of course, it's not just gender and disability that intersect in this way: further refraction and filtering is done by class, race, age, sexuality, and so on.

35. Shakespeare, *Disability Rights and Wrongs Revisited*, p. 13.

36. Clare, *Exile and Pride*, pp. 109–10.

37. Shakespeare, *Disability Rights and Wrongs Revisited*, pp. 32–3.

38. Clare, *Exile and Pride*, p. 7.

39. Ibid., p. 8.

40. Shakespeare, *Disability Rights and Wrongs Revisited*, p. 101.

41. Ibid., pp. 140ff.

42. Ibid., p. 141.

43. Ibid., p. 142.

44. Ibid., p. 141.

45. Barnes, *The Minority Body*, p. 71.

46. Ibid., p. 54.

47. Ibid., p. 96.

48. Ibid., p. 111.

49. Dostoevsky, quoted ibid., p. 91.

50. Barnes, *The Minority Body*, p. 112.

51. Diane E. Hoffmann and Anita J. Tarzian, 'The girl who cried pain: a bias against women in the treatment of pain', *The Journal of Law, Medicine & Ethics*, 29, 2001; Criado Perez, *Invisible Women*; Joe Feagin and Zennobia Bennefield, 'Systemic racism and U.S. health care', *Social*

Science & Medicine, 103, 2014; Debra Gimlin, *Body Work: Beauty and Self-Image in American Culture* (University of California Press, 2002), pp. 129–30.

7. CHOOSING TO BE NORMAL

1. Nuffield Council on Bioethics, 'Online questionnaire: summary', June 2017, p. 8, https://www.nuffieldbioethics.org/assets/pdfs/CP-Survey-Monkey-Questionnaire-analysis.pdf.

2. Diana Harrison, 'I need a bra that fits me, not the male gaze', *the f word*, 31 October 2018, https://thefword.org.uk/2018/10/i-need-a-bra-that-fits-me-not-the-male-gaze/.

3. Hannah's story is the true story of one woman's experience, as told to me in person, but her name has been changed.

4. BBC News, 'Angelina Jolie has double mastectomy due to cancer gene', 14 May 2013, https://www.bbc.co.uk/news/world-us-canada-22520720.

5. NHS Choices, 'Braces and orthodontics', https://www.nhs.uk/live-well/healthy-body/braces-and-orthodontics/.

6. Michael Thomsen, 'Braces: pointless and essential', *The Atlantic*, 9 July 2015, https://www.theatlantic.com/health/archive/2015/07/braces-dentures-history/397934/.

7. NHS Choices, 'Braces and orthodontics'.

8. NHS Choices, 'Ear correction surgery, including ear pinning', https://www.nhs.uk/conditions/cosmetic-procedures/ear-correction-surgery/.

9. Mayo Clinic, 'Otoplasty', https://www.mayoclinic.org/tests-procedures/otoplasty/about/pac-20394822.

10. NHS Great Ormond Street Hospital for Children suggest that the operation is best performed on children under three months old, 'Additional little fingers', https://www.gosh.nhs.uk/conditions-and-treatments/conditions-we-treat/additional-little-fingers.

11. NHS Great Ormond Street Hospital for Children, 'Syndactyly', https://www.gosh.nhs.uk/conditions-and-treatments/conditions-we-treat/syndactyly.

12. 'Laser treatment often works better in younger children': NHS Choices, 'Birthmarks', https://www.nhs.uk/conditions/birthmarks/treatment/.

13. See Chapter 5.

14. Sarah Creighton, 'Surgery for intersex', *Journal of the Royal Society of Medicine*, 94, 2001.

15. *Gillick v. West Norfolk and Wisbech AHA*, http://www.bailii.org/uk/cases/UKHL/1985/7.html.

16. Richard Griffith, 'What is Gillick competence?', *Human Vaccines and Immunotherapeutics*, 12, 2016.

17. Where a surgeon's name has been withheld, she or he made the relevant remarks in conversation with me, and I have quoted or paraphrased them as closely as possible.

18. Nichola Rumsey, in conference presentations and in conversation. Some of that body of evidence is found in Nichola Rumsey and Diana Harcourt (eds.), *The Oxford Handbook of the Psychology of Appearance* (Oxford University Press, 2012).

19. Nuffield Council on Bioethics, 'Cosmetic Procedures: Ethical Issues', 2017, http://nuffieldbioethics.org/wp-content/uploads/Cosmetic-procedures-full-report.pdf, pp. 117–18.

20. S. Higgins and A. Wysong, 'Cosmetic surgery and body dysmorphic disorder – an update', *International Journal of Women's Dermatology*, 4 (1), 2017.

21. Royal College of Surgeons, 'Statistics', https://www.rcseng.ac.uk/careers-in-surgery/women-in-surgery/statistics/ (accessed July 2019).

22. Kat Banyard et al., 'Cosmetic surgery ads should be banned', *Guardian* Letters page, 14 March 2012, https://www.theguardian.com/lifeand-style/2012/mar/14/cosmetic-surgery-advertising-ban.

23. In July 2019, before the Covid-19 pandemic, New Look Holiday: Plastic Surgery Abroad were offering discounted combined surgery procedures, with a 10% discount for each additional procedure ('The best example for ideal and the most common package is Tummy tuck procedure combined with liposuction, where there is not just discounted price, but also more effective result after the surgery. Tummy tuck together with liposuction will achieve better contouring of the body and will save you over 20% of the price'), along with a €150 discount if clients refer a friend; Transform cosmetic surgery and The Hospital Group were offering 0% finance. See www.transforminglives.com; https://www.the hospitalgroup.org;https://www.newlookholiday.co.uk/combined-procedures-abroad/.

24. PRASIS 'Code of Practice', 2017, https://www.prasis.co.uk/support_guidance/best_practice/prasis_code_of_practice_2017.aspx.

25. Nuffield Council on Bioethics, 'Cosmetic Procedures: Ethical Issues', p. 41.

26. Discussion at Royal Society of Medicine event 'Changing the Image of Cosmetic Surgery: Patients Before Profit' in October 2017.

27. Harriet Alexander, 'Women worry about their bodies 252 times a week', *Daily Telegraph*, 23 November 2009, https://www.telegraph.co.uk/

news/uknews/6634686/Women-worry-about-their-bodies-252-times-a-week.html.

28. Debra Gimlin, *Body Work: Beauty and Self-Image in American Culture* (University of California Press, 2002), p. 11.

29. Jameela Jamil, actor, model and advocate of body neutrality, said, 'I'm not advocating body positivity. I'm trying to spread body neutrality where I can sit here and not think about what my body is looking like.' The Female Lead Society, 'Body positivity vs. body neutrality', 19 June 2020, https://www.thefemaleleadsociety.com/body-positivity-vs-body-neutrality.

30. Ayse K. Uskul, 'Women's menarche stories from a multicultural sample', *Social Science & Medicine*, 59, 2004, p. 671.

31. Karin A. Martin, *Puberty, Sexuality, and the Self: Boys and Girls at Adolescence* (Routledge, 1996), p. 32.

32. Ibid.

33. Ibid., p. 36.

34. Ibid., p. 23.

35. Tom Shakespeare, 'A short story', in Charles Fernyhough (ed.), *Others: Writers on the Power of Words to Help Us See Beyond Ourselves* (Unbound, 2019), p. 137.

36. Shakespeare, 'A short story', p. 140.

37. James Partridge, *Changing Faces: The Challenge of Facial Disfigurement* (Changing Faces Publication, 2012), p. 12.

38. James Partridge, *Face It: Facial Disfigurement and My Fight for Face Equality* (Whitefox Publishing, 2020), p. 31.

39. Partridge, *Changing Faces*, p. 4.

40. Partridge details the various forms of professional help, support groups and social interactions that aid the process of coming to terms with facial disfigurement, and notes time as a significant factor. 'The transition from first realizing what you have done to your "old" face to the moment when you really feel happy with your "new" one is likely to be long and drawn out, maybe taking five to ten years, or more.' Partridge, *Changing Faces*, p. 4.

41. Martin, *Puberty, Sexuality, and the Self*, p. 122.

42. Evidence given by Amy Slater to UK Parliament Women & Equalities Select Committee, https://committees.parliament.uk/oralevidence/928/pdf/.

43. Amy Slater is based at the Centre for Appearance Research at the University of the West of England, which is the leading centre for research into the impact of body image and appearance. You can see their work

at https://www.uwe.ac.uk/research/centres-and-groups/appearance. The UK Parliament Women & Equalities Select Committee report 'Changing the Perfect Picture' includes a range of policy recommendations, some of which echo recommendations made by the Nuffield Council on Bioethics in their report 'Cosmetic Procedures: Ethical Issues'.

44. Partridge, *Changing Faces*, p. 50.
45. Ibid., pp. 39, 65.
46. Franck Duteille, Pierre Perrot, Marie-Hélène Bacheley and Sharon Stewart, 'Eight-year safety data for round and anatomical silicone gel breast implants', *Aesthetic Surgery Journal*, 38 (2), 2018, p. 151.
47. Various charities exist providing knitted prostheses for post-mastectomy women, including Knitted Knockers UK, https://www.kkukciowix.com/ and Knitted Knockers, https://www.knittedknockers.org.

PART THREE

1. This is the position laid out in John Stuart Mill's canonical text *On Liberty*. While not without its flaws, which are the subject of an enormous philosophical literature and innumerable undergraduate essays, his account is highly plausible and adequate for my purposes here.
2. We are at liberty to *seek* to modify our bodies because we might legitimately be constrained by many things: technological limits, fair resource distribution, and others' right to refuse to perform a procedure.

8. DECIDING TO MODIFY

1. John Stuart Mill, *On Liberty* (1859), in *Utilitarianism, On Liberty,* and *Considerations on Representative Government* (Everyman, 1993), p. 78.
2. Stefani Germanotta (Lady Gaga) and Jeppe Laursen, 'Born This Way' (2010).
3. The Walt Disney Company, *Disney Look*, 2021, https://disneycasting.net/downloads/wdpr/Disney_Look_Book.pdf.
4. Ibid.
5. There are still restrictions on the sorts of tattoos that are allowed. Tattoos must not be 'on the face, head or neck' and 'must be no larger than the Cast Member's hand when fully extended with the fingers held together ... Tattoos that depict nudity, offensive or inappropriate language or images, or violate Company policies ... are not permitted.' The Walt Disney Company, *Disney Look*, p. 7.

6. IPSOS, 'More Americans have tattoos today than seven years ago', 29 August 2019, https://www.ipsos.com/en-us/news-polls/more-americans-have-tattoos-today.

7. Studies find highly variable rates of regret; a reasonable estimate is that a fifth of people regret at least one of their tattoos. See Walter Liszewski, Elizabeth Kream, Sarah Helland, Amy Cavigli, Bridget C. Lavin and Andrea Murina, 'The demographics and rates of tattoo complications, regret, and unsafe tattooing practices', *Dermatologic Surgery*, 41 (11), 2015.

8. David Allen, 'Moving the needle on recovery from breast cancer', *Journal of the American Medical Association*, 317 (7), 2017; Danielle Yates, '21 mastectomy tattoos you have to see', *Headcovers Unlimited*, 24 October 2018, https://www.headcovers.com/blog/mastectomy-tattoos/.

9. Diane, in Gem Fletcher, '"Instead of a scar, I had a piece of art": women on their post-mastectomy tattoos', *Guardian*, 22 September 2018, https://www.theguardian.com/lifeandstyle/2018/sep/22/instead-scar-piece-art-women-mastectomy-tattoos.

10. Kerry, quoted ibid.

11. Elaine, quoted ibid.

12. Sarah G., quoted ibid.

13. Juanita, quoted ibid.

14. Eli Clare, *Exile and Pride: Disability, Queerness, and Liberation* (Duke University Press, 2015), p. 150.

15. I leave it open that other principles might be used to deny even evidence-based treatments: for example, principles of distributive justice and the allocation of scarce resources.

16. Francesca Solmi, Evidence to UK Parliament Women & Equalities Select Committee, 23 September 2020, https://committees.parliament.uk/oralevidence/928/pdf/.

17. Audre Lorde, 'A Burst of Light: Living with Cancer', entry from 1 December 1986, in Rudolph P. Byrd, Johnetta Betsch Cole and Beverly Guy-Sheftall (eds.), *I am Your Sister: Collected and Unpublished Writings of Audre Lorde* (Oxford University Press, 2009), p. 147.

18. Emma Dabiri, *Don't Touch My Hair* (Allen Lane, 2019), p. 83.

19. Jane Fonda, *Jane Fonda's Workout* videotape (1982).

20. Heather Widdows, *Perfect Me: Beauty as an Ethical Ideal* (Princeton University Press, 2018), p. 191.

21. Arnold Schwarzenegger, 'Arnold Schwarzenegger 2018 – The speech that broke the internet – Most inspiring ever', https://www.youtube.com/watch?v=u_ktRTWMX3M.

22. Girlguiding UK, Written evidence to UK Parliament Women & Equalities Select Committee, https://committees.parliament.uk/writtenevidence/9367/pdf/.

23. Rebecca Stamp, 'Average person will try 126 fad diets in their lifetime, poll shows', *Independent*, 8 January 2020, https://www.independent.co.uk/life-style/diet-weight-loss-food-unhealthy-eating-habits-a9274676.html.

24. Linda Searing, 'The big number: 45 million Americans go on a diet each year', *Washington Post*, 1 January 2018, https://www.washingtonpost.com/national/health-science/the-big-number-45-million-americans-go-on-a-diet-each-year/2017/12/29/04089aec-ebdd-11e7-b698-91d4e35920a3_story.html.

25. Ibid.

26. Evidence given by Amy Slater to UK Parliament Women & Equalities Select Committee, https://committees.parliament.uk/oralevidence/928/pdf/.

27. Evidence given by Amy Slater and Francesca Solmi to UK Parliament Women & Equalities Select Committee.

28. Evidence given by Amy Slater to UK Parliament Women & Equalities Select Committee.

29. Bodybuilding.com forum, https://forum.bodybuilding.com/forumdisplay.php?f=29.

30. https://forum.bodybuilding.com/showthread.php?t=179125541.

31. Dabiri, *Don't Touch My Hair*, pp. 84–5.

32. Ibid., p. 85.

33. Widdows, *Perfect Me*, p. 152.

34. Ashish Sharma, Vishaal Madaan and Frederick D. Petty, 'Exercise for mental health', *The Primary Care Companion to the Journal of Clinical Psychiatry*, 8 (2), 2006.

35. Arnold Schwarzenegger in *Pumping Iron* (1977), excerpt available https://www.youtube.com/watch?v=7nZ1v96-veM; Lianne McTavish also compares orgasm and exercise in *Feminist Figure Girl* (State University of New York Press, 2015), pp. 42–3.

36. Jan Morris, *Conundrum* (1974), quoted in Bernice L. Hausman, 'Body, technology, and gender in transsexual autobiographies', in Susan Stryker and Stephen Whittle (eds.), *The Transgender Studies Reader* (Routledge, 2006), p. 350.

37. C. N. Lester, *Trans Like Me: A Journey for All of Us* (Virago, 2017), p. 71.

38. Judith Halberstam, *Female Masculinity* (Duke University Press, 1998), p. 87.

39. Nancy Hunt, quoted in Hausman, 'Body, technology, and gender in transsexual autobiographies', p. 348.

40. Joanne Meyerowitz, 'A "fierce and demanding"' drive', in Stryker and Whittle (eds.), *The Transgender Studies Reader*, p. 362.

41. Ibid.

42. Lester, *Trans Like Me*, p. 51.

43. Ibid., p. 52.

44. Ibid., p. 56.

45. Michelle O'Brien, 'Tracing this body: transsexuality, pharmaceuticals, and capitalism', in Susan Stryker and Aren Z. Aizura (eds.), *The Transgender Studies Reader 2* (Routledge, 2013), pp. 56–7.

46. Jay Prosser, *Second Skins: The Body Narratives of Transsexuality* (Columbia University Press, 1998), p. 69.

47. Lester, *Trans Like Me*, p. 56.

48. Ibid., p. 71.

49. Meyerowitz, 'A "fierce and demanding" drive', p. 362.

50. Prosser, *Second Skins*, p. 83.

51. Mermaids, 'Do you still use the phrase "Born in the wrong body?"', 25 September 2020, https://mermaidsuk.org.uk/news/do-you-still-use-the-phrase-born-in-the-wrong-body/.

52. Ibid.

53. Ibid.

54. See, for example, Meyerowitz, 'A "fierce and demanding" drive'; Hausman, 'Body, technology, and gender in transsexual autobiographies'; Dean Spade, 'Mutilating gender', in Stryker and Whittle (eds.), *The Transgender Studies Reader*.

55. Tony Grew, 'Inquiry into surge in gender treatment ordered by Penny Mordaunt', *The Times*, 16 September 2018, https://www.thetimes.co.uk/article/inquiry-into-surge-in-gender-treatment-ordered-by-penny-mord aunt-b2ftz9hfn?wgu=270525_54264_16058053857606_5be24942c4 &wgexpiry=1613581385&utm_source=planit&utm_medium=affiliate&utm_content=22278.

56. David Adjmi, 'I had the best body I'd ever had – so why did I feel so much shame?', *Guardian*, 20 October 2020, https://www.theguardian.com/us-news/2020/oct/20/leaving-my-perfect-male-body-in-the-past?CMP=soc_567&fbclid=IwAR3Tpi3IoyyDDmpqyipZVhsnwDqd-52r_ZVozFWroIjgzxWsNLjTSUBDmLo.

57. Sandy Stone, 'The Empire Strikes Back: a posttranssexual manifesto', in Stryker and Whittle (eds.), *The Transgender Studies Reader* p. 231.

58. Kate Bornstein, *Gender Outlaw: On Men, Women, and the Rest of Us* (Routledge, 1994), p. 24.

59. Ibid., p. 47.

60. Ibid., p. 30.

61. Ibid., p. 50.

62. ORLAN, 'Manifesto of Carnal Art' (1989), reproduced at https://www.slow-words.com/carnal-art-manifesto/.

63. Stuart Jeffries, 'Orlan's art of sex and surgery', *Guardian*, 1 July 2009, https://www.theguardian.com/artanddesign/2009/jul/01/orlan-performance-artist-carnal-art.

64. Reuters, 'A man covered his face with tattoos and turned his eyes black. He says it cost him his kindergarten teaching job', CNN News, 28 September 2020, https://edition.cnn.com/2020/09/28/europe/sylvain-helaine-tattoo-teaching-job-scli-intl/index.html.

65. For the maths of hairstyling, see Dabiri, *Don't Touch My Hair.*

66. Spade, 'Mutilating gender', p. 319.

67. Jack Halberstam, *Trans*: A Quick and Quirky Account of Gender Variability* (University of California Press, 2018), pp. 23–4.

68. McLean Clinic, 'FTM top surgery', https://www.mcleanclinic.com/surgical-procedures/breast/ftm-top-surgery/.

69. Quoted in Abigail Shrier, *Irreversible Damage: The Transgender Craze Seducing Our Daughters* (Regnery Publishing, 2020), p. 175.

70. Halberstam, *Trans**, p. 34.

71. I suspect Halberstam would be happy to exclude children from those eligible to use hormones and surgery as part of their creative self-expression. 'New modes of parenting among white middle-class "designer" parents have shifted the coordinates of belonging such that the trans* child that might previously have been viewed as disruptive might now be displayed as a trophy, a mark of the family's flexibility, a sign of the liberal family's capacious borders,' he writes. 'The trans* child is also placed by their parents within an ever-expanding and dizzying array of disabilities that the parents claim for their children and then seek to cure, ameliorate, or medicalize.' Halberstam, *Trans**, p. 60.

72. Patrick Califia, *Sex Changes* (Cleis Press, 2nd edn, 2003), p. 5.

9. BODILY INTEGRITY, INTERVENTION AND RESISTANCE

1. See the accounts of Ashley X in Andrew Solomon, *Far From The Tree: Parents, Children and the Search for Identity* (Vintage, 2014), pp. 383ff., and in Eva Feder Kittay, 'Forever small: the strange case of Ashley X', *Hypatia*, 26 (3), 2011.

2. 'Charlie' is the name I have invented for the baby in the case described in Deana Morton, 'Putting my baby in a helmet was the toughest decision of my life', *Today's Parent*, 20 September 2018, https://www.todaysparent.com/baby/baby-health/putting-my-baby-in-a-helmet-was-the-toughest-decision-of-my-life/.

3. This is the case of *An NHS Trust v. C NHS Trust and others* [2019] EWHC 3033 (Fam), as reported in Clare Dyer, 'High Court rules that 14 year old Jehovah's Witness should have blood transfusions', *BMJ*, 2019, https://www.bmj.com/content/367/bmj.l6513.

4. This is the true story of Eilish and Katie Holton, as told in Alice Domurat Dreger, *One of Us: Conjoined Twins and the Future of Normal* (Harvard University Press, 2004), and Kathy Donaghy, 'Life after Katie', *Independent.ie*, 2 September 2000, https://www.independent.ie/irish-news/life-after-katie-26108190.html.

5. This is the case of Ethan Mount-Jones discussed in Chapter 6 and recounted at British Association of Teachers of the Deaf, 'Ethan Mount-Jones by his mother', 'Personal Experiences – Cochlear Implants', https://www.batod.org.uk/information/personal-experiences-cochlear-implants/.

6. This is the case of Luna Younger as described in Katelyn Burns, 'What the battle over a 7-year-old trans girl could mean for families nationwide', *Vox*, 11 November 2019, https://www.vox.com/identities/2019/11/11/20955059/luna-younger-transgender-child-custody.

7. Priscilla Blossom, '9 things white families don't understand about piercing a baby's ears', *Romper*, 19 June 2017, https://www.romper.com/p/9-things-white-families-dont-understand-about-piercing-a-babys-ears-64446; Patrick A. Coleman, 'When can you pierce a baby's ears?', *Fatherly*, 18 May 2020, https://www.fatherly.com/health-science/when-to-pierce-a-babys-ears/.

8. This is the case of Rosie Lohman, as described in Daniella Emanuel, 'Raising an intersex child: "This is your body . . . There's nothing to be ashamed of"', CNN, 15 April 2019, https://edition.cnn.com/2019/04/13/health/intersex-child-parenting-eprise/index.html.

9. This is the autobiographical account given by comedian Tom Rosenthal in his show 'Manhood' (2019).

10. David Benatar, 'Introduction: the ethics of contested surgeries', in David Benatar (ed.), *Cutting to the Core: Exploring the Ethics of Contested Surgeries* (Rowman & Littlefield, 2006), p. 1.

11. The second part of this sentence conceals a vast amount of complexity, not least concerning what counts as genuine consent. I critique the idea

that choice, consent and autonomy are synonymous in Clare Chambers, *Sex, Culture, and Justice: The Limits of Choice* (Penn State University Press, 2008).

12. As we'll see, there may be many reasons why parents and doctors wish to withhold interventions requested by their child, and not all of them are related to bodily integrity. Parents and doctors may have religious, moral, or ethical objections to intervention; or evidence-based objections; or reason to believe that the child's preferences will not be stable; or resource limitations, to take just some examples.

13. Laura Dodsworth, *Manhood: The Bare Reality* (Pinter & Martin, 2017), p. 36.

14. As legal theorists John Herring and Jesse Wall put it, 'When a person infringes upon the bodily integrity of another, the infringement amounts to a disrespect that is broader than disrespect for the person's capacity to live life according to reasons and motivations that one takes as one's own (their autonomy).' John Herring and Jesse Wall, 'The nature and significance of the right to bodily integrity', *The Cambridge Law Journal*, 76 (3), 2017, p. 577.

15. Joel Feinberg, 'The child's right to an open future', in Randall Curren (ed.), *Philosophy of Education: An Anthology* (Blackwell Publishing, 2007), p. 118.

16. Claudia Mills, 'The child's right to an open future?', *Journal of Social Philosophy*, 34 (4), 2003.

17. For an excellent account of how and why to apply the child's right to an open future to the case of circumcision, see Robert J. L. Darby, 'The child's right to an open future: is the principle applicable to non-therapeutic circumcision?', *Journal of Medical Ethics*, 39, 2013.

18. For example, see Gillian Douglas, 'The retreat from Gillick', *The Modern Law Review*, 55 (4), 1992; David Archard and Colin Macleod (eds.), *The Moral and Political Status of Children: New Essays* (Oxford University Press, 2002); Michael Freeman, 'Rethinking Gillick', *The International Journal of Children's Rights*, 13 (1–2), 2005; David Archard, *Children: Rights and Childhood* (Routledge, 2014); Nigel Zimmerman, 'Gillick competence: an unnecessary burden', *The New Bioethics*, 25 (1), 2019; Anca Gheaus, Gideon Calder and Jurgen de Wispeleare (eds.), *Routledge Handbook of the Philosophy of Childhood and Children* (Routledge, 2019).

19. Michael Benatar and David Benatar, 'Between prophylaxis and child abuse: the ethics of neonatal male circumcision', in Benatar (ed.), *Cutting to the Core*, p. 26.

20. As Leslie Cannold puts it, 'most newborns will one day acquire the competency necessary to make autonomous decisions about circumcision and other medical and life issues.' Leslie Cannold, 'The ethics of neonatal male circumcision', in Benatar (ed.), *Cutting to the Core*, p. 50.

21. Dodsworth, *Manhood*, p. 34.

22. Ibid., pp. 158–9. Second and third ellipses in the original.

23. Ibid., p. 194.

24. Ibid., p. 249.

25. Brian D. Earp and Robert Darby, 'Circumcision, sexual experience, and harm', *University of Pennsylvania Journal of International Law*, 3 (2), 2017.

26. Much more complex issues arise in 'sacrifice surgeries', when both twins will die if left conjoined but one has a chance of life if separated. Discussing the principles involved in these cases would distract from my argument. They are discussed with care and sensitivity in Dreger, *One of Us*.

27. American Academy of Pediatrics (AAP), 'Baby helmet therapy: parent FAQs', https://www.healthychildren.org/English/health-issues/conditions/Cleft-Craniofacial/Pages/Baby-Helmet-Therapy-Parent-FAQs. aspx; National Health Service (NHS), 'Plagiocephaly and brachycephaly (flat head syndrome)', https://www.nhs.uk/conditions/plagiocephaly-brachycephaly/.

28. Honor Whiteman, 'Helmet therapy for infant positional skull deformation "should be discouraged"', *Medical News Today*, 2 May 2014, https://www.medicalnewstoday.com/articles/276281.

29. Morton, 'Putting my baby in a helmet was the toughest decision of my life'.

30. In a recent case the High Court of England and Wales concluded: 'There will be enormous difficulties in a child under 16 understanding and weighing up this information and deciding whether to consent to the use of puberty blocking medication. It is highly unlikely that a child aged 13 or under would be competent to give consent to the administration of puberty blockers. It is doubtful that a child aged 14 or 15 could understand and weigh the long-term risks and consequences of the administration of puberty blockers.' *R (on the application of) Quincy Bell and A v. Tavistock and Portman NHS Trust and others* [2020] EWHC 3274, para. 151.

31. Abigail Shrier, *Irreversible Damage: The Transgender Craze Seducing Our Daughters* (Regnery Publishing, 2020) p. 82; *R (on the application of) Quincy Bell and A v. Tavistock and Portman NHS Trust and others* [2020] EWHC 3274 para. 56.

32. NHS Choices, 'Gender dysphoria', https://www.nhs.uk/conditions/gender-dysphoria/treatment/.

33. Christopher Richards, Julie Maxwell and Noel McClune, 'Use of puberty blockers for gender dysphoria: a momentous step in the dark', *Archives of Disease in Childhood*, 17 January 2019, https://adc.bmj.com/content/archdischild/early/2019/01/17/archdischild-2018–315881.full.pdf.

34. This was the position of Keira Bell, one of the claimants in *R (on the application of) Quincy Bell and A v. Tavistock and Portman NHS Trust and others* [2020] EWHC 3274. Bell had received puberty blockers at the age of 16, followed by cross-sex hormones and surgery (mastectomy) as part of her transition into a man. In her early twenties she came to the conclusion that the procedures were a mistake and that she was and always had been a woman; however, she was left with facial hair, a deep voice, no breasts and doubts about her fertility.

35. Some treatments aimed at restoring the foreskin do exist; however, they are painful or effortful and have only limited effectiveness, and can, in any case, only stretch the remaining skin of the penis and not restore a functioning foreskin. For information on these procedures and support for men unhappy with their circumcision, see the charity 15 Square at https://15square.org.uk.

36. Dodsworth, *Manhood*, p. 34.

37. Ibid., pp. 124–5.

38. Ibid., p. 186.

39. Ibid., p. 249.

40. Ibid., p. 23.

41. One question that arises at this point is 'What counts as a person?' This enormously important and difficult question arises in many ethical discussions, raising profound questions about matters such as abortion, euthanasia, the treatment of people who are 'brain dead' or in a vegetative state, and the ethical difference between humans and other animals. This book is not the place to go into those discussions, not least because they have to be solved whatever your view of the ethics of bodily interventions and body modifications, and because my account does not depend on having a specific answer to them.

42. Joseph Mazor, 'On the strength of children's right to bodily integrity: when is the right infringed?', *Journal of Applied Philosophy*, 36 (1), 2019.

43. Chambers, *Sex, Culture, and Justice*, pp. 35–6.

44. Partridge uses the term 'facial disfigurement' and so I've used it here when discussing his account; some people prefer the term 'visible difference'.

45. James Partridge, *Face It: Facial Disfigurement and My Fight for Facial Equality* (Whitefox Publishing, 2020), p. 224.

46. Ibid., p. 250.

47. Ibid., p. 184.

48. James Partridge, *Changing Faces: The Challenge of Facial Disfigurement* (Changing Faces Publications, 2012), p. 89.

49. Ibid., p. 95.

50. Ibid., p. 48.

51. Partridge, *Face It*, p. 189.

52. For an extended discussion of the issue of reasonable disagreement as applied to circumcision, see Clare Chambers, 'Reasonable disagreement and the neutralist dilemma: abortion and circumcision in Matthew Kramer's *Liberalism with Excellence*', *American Journal of Jurisprudence*, May 2018.

53. Brian D. Earp, 'The child's right to bodily integrity', in David Edmonds (ed.), *Ethics and the Contemporary World* (Routledge, 2019), p. 227.

54. While it is in principle possible for a conjoined twin to be the parent of conjoined twins, I know of no such cases.

55. The first case in which adult conjoined twins asked to be separated was the case of Ladan and Laleh Bijani, who opted to be separated in 2003 at the age of 29. Tragically, both died 50 hours into the surgery. See Dreger, *One of Us*, pp. 41–2.

56. Ibid., p. 43.

57. Ibid., p. 46.

58. Kittay, 'Forever small', p. 615.

59. Ibid.

60. Ibid., p. 622.

61. Many vaccination programmes operate in this way. For example, at the time of writing, the case for vaccinating children against Covid-19 rests on the benefits to adults rather than to children, since children are understood to be relatively safe from the virus. See *The Lancet* Infectious Diseases Editorial, 'Should we vaccinate children against SARS-CoV-2?', 10 June 2021, https://www.thelancet.com/journals/laninf/article/PIIS 1473-3099(21)00339-X/fulltext.

62. I discuss the balance between religious freedom and other values, particularly bodily integrity and equality, in several places. See Chambers, *Sex, Culture, and Justice*; Clare Chambers, *Against Marriage: An Egalitarian Defence of the Marriage-Free State* (Oxford University Press, 2017), ch. 6; and Chambers, 'Reasonable disagreement and the neutralist dilemma'.

63. To borrow a term from Mazor, 'On the strength of children's right to bodily integrity'.

64. Sandy Stone, 'The Empire Strikes Back: a posttranssexual manifesto', in Susan Stryker and Stephen Whittle (eds.), *The Transgender Studies Reader* (Routledge, 2006), p. 231.

65. Andrea Dworkin, 'Terror, Torture, and Resistance', in *Life and Death: Unapologetic Writings on the Continuing War against Women* (Virago, 1997), p. 116.

66. Andrea Dworkin, *Mercy* (Arrow Books, 1992).

67. Susan Brison, *Aftermath: Violence and the Remaking of a Self* (Princeton University Press, 2002), p. 8.

68. Ibid., p. 38.

69. Ibid., p. 44

70. Legal theorists Michael Thomson and Marie Fox express this idea when they argue that the concept of bodily integrity should be replaced with what they call 'embodied integrity', an idea that recognizes bodies as 'a constitutive part of human identity', as part of 'who we are'. (Marie Fox and Michael Thomson, 'Embodied integrity, embodiment, and the regulation of parental choice', *The Journal of Law and Society*, 44, 2017, p. 521.) We come to experience ourselves only through our bodies, and how we use and inhabit our bodies is part-and-parcel of who we are. Children must be allowed to develop their sense of self, to come to terms with their own embodiment, by being given final authority over their own bodily experiences and private enjoyment of their developing embodied identities. According to Thomson and Fox, 'our analysis helps deepen a child's right to an open future. It emphasizes the significance of embodied integrity in the processes of self-determination that enable the individuated self, and contrasts sharply with the static, propertied, and bounded notion often envisioned in legal discussions of conventional integrity.' (Fox and Thomson, 'Embodied integrity, embodiment, and the regulation of parental choice', p. 529.)

71. Andrea Sangiovanni, *Humanity without Dignity: Moral Equality, Respect, and Human Rights* (Harvard University Press, 2017), p. 107.

72. Partridge, *Changing Faces*, p. 55.

CODA

1. Rachel Lark & The Damaged Goods, 'I Wanna Lose Five Pounds', https://www.youtube.com/watch?v=iZNRriHkJsI.

2. Sofie Hagen, *Happy Fat: Taking Up Space in a World That Wants to Shrink You* (Fourth Estate, 2019), p. 9.

3. Stephanie Yeboah, quoted in Anna Kessel, 'The rise of the body neutrality movement', *Guardian*, 23 July 2018.

4. Amy Slater, Neesha Varsani and Phillippa C. Diedrichs, '#fitspo or #loveyourself? The impact of fitspiration and self-compassion Instagram images on women's body image, self-compassion, and mood', *Body Image*, 22, 2017.

5. Dove, https://www.dove.com/uk/home.html.

6. Dove, 'Beautiful or Average', https://www.youtube.com/watch?v=aocx88vuLzE.

Index

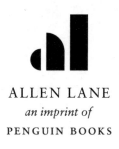

ALLEN LANE
an imprint of
PENGUIN BOOKS

Also Published

Ian Kershaw, *Personality and Power: Builders and Destroyers of Modern Europe*

Alison Bashford, *An Intimate History of Evolution: The Story of the Huxley Family*

Lawrence Freedman, *Command: The Politics of Military Operations from Korea to Ukraine*

Richard Niven, *Second City: Birmingham and the Forging of Modern Britain*

Hakim Adi, *African and Caribbean People in Britain: A History*

Jordan Peterson, *24 Rules For Life: The Box Set*

Gaia Vince, *Nomad Century: How to Survive the Climate Upheaval*

Keith Fisher, *A Pipeline Runs Through It: The Story of Oil from Ancient Times to the First World War*

Christoph Keller, *Every Cripple a Superhero*

Roberto Calasso, *The Tablet of Destinies*

Jennifer Jacquet, *The Playbook: How to Deny Science, Sell Lies, and Make a Killing in the Corporate World*

Frank Close, *Elusive: How Peter Higgs Solved the Mystery of Mass*

Edward Chancellor, *The Price of Time: The Real Story of Interest*

Antonio Padilla, *Fantastic Numbers and Where to Find Them: A Cosmic Quest from Zero to Infinity*

Henry Kissinger, *Leadership: Six Studies in World Strategy*

Chris Patten, *The Hong Kong Diaries*

Lindsey Fitzharris, *The Facemaker: One Surgeon's Battle to Mend the Disfigured Soldiers of World War 1*

George Monbiot, *Regenesis: Feeding the World without Devouring the Planet*

Caroline Knowles, *Serious Money: Walking Plutocratic London*

Serhii Plokhy, *Atoms and Ashes: From Bikini Atoll to Fukushima*

Dominic Lieven, *In the Shadow of the Gods: The Emperor in World History*

Scott Hershovitz, *Nasty, Brutish, and Short: Adventures in Philosophy with Kids*

Bill Gates, *How to Prevent the Next Pandemic*

Emma Smith, *Portable Magic: A History of Books and their Readers*

Kris Manjapra, *Black Ghost of Empire: The Long Death of Slavery and the Failure of Emancipation*

Andrew Scull, *Desperate Remedies: Psychiatry and the Mysteries of Mental Illness*

James Bridle, *Ways of Being: Beyond Human Intelligence*

Eugene Linden, *Fire and Flood: A People's History of Climate Change, from 1979 to the Present*

Cathy O'Neil, *The Shame Machine: Who Profits in the New Age of Humiliation*

Peter Hennessy, *A Duty of Care: Britain Before and After Covid*

Gerd Gigerenzer, *How to Stay Smart in a Smart World: Why Human Intelligence Still Beats Algorithms*

Halik Kochanski, *Resistance: The Undergroud War in Europe, 1939-1945*

Joseph Sassoon, *The Global Merchants: The Enterprise and Extravagance of the Sassoon Dynasty*

Clare Chambers, *Intact: A Defence of the Unmodified Body*

Nina Power, *What Do Men Want?: Masculinity and Its Discontents*

Ivan Jablonka, *A History of Masculinity: From Patriarchy to Gender Justice*

Thomas Halliday, *Otherlands: A World in the Making*

Sofi Thanhauser, *Worn: A People's History of Clothing*

Sebastian Mallaby, *The Power Law: Venture Capital and the Art of Disruption*

David J. Chalmers, *Reality+: Virtual Worlds and the Problems of Philosophy*

Jing Tsu, *Kingdom of Characters: A Tale of Language, Obsession and Genius in Modern China*

Lewis R. Gordon, *Fear of Black Consciousness*

Leonard Mlodinow, *Emotional: The New Thinking About Feelings*

Kevin Birmingham, *The Sinner and the Saint: Dostoevsky, a Crime and Its Punishment*

Roberto Calasso, *The Book of All Books*

Marit Kapla, *Osebol: Voices from a Swedish Village*

Malcolm Gaskill, *The Ruin of All Witches: Life and Death in the New World*

Mark Mazower, *The Greek Revolution: 1821 and the Making of Modern Europe*

Paul McCartney, *The Lyrics: 1956 to the Present*

Brendan Simms and Charlie Laderman, *Hitler's American Gamble: Pearl Harbor and the German March to Global War*

Lea Ypi, *Free: Coming of Age at the End of History*

David Graeber and David Wengrow, *The Dawn of Everything: A New History of Humanity*

Rupa Marya and Raj Patel, *Inflamed: Deep Medicine and the Anatomy of Injustice*

Richard Zenith, *Pessoa: An Experimental Life*

Michael Pollan, *This Is Your Mind On Plants: Opium—Caffeine—Mescaline*

Amartya Sen, *Home in the World: A Memoir*

Jan-Werner Müller, *Democracy Rules*

Robin DiAngelo, *Nice Racism: How Progressive White People Perpetuate Racial Harm*

Rosemary Hill, *Time's Witness: History in the Age of Romanticism*

Lawrence Wright, *The Plague Year: America in the Time of Covid*

Adrian Wooldridge, *The Aristocracy of Talent: How Meritocracy Made the Modern World*

Julian Hoppit, *The Dreadful Monster and its Poor Relations: Taxing, Spending and the United Kingdom, 1707-2021*

Jordan Ellenberg, *Shape: The Hidden Geometry of Absolutely Everything*

Duncan Campbell-Smith, *Crossing Continents: A History of Standard Chartered Bank*

Jemma Wadham, *Ice Rivers*

Niall Ferguson, *Doom: The Politics of Catastrophe*

Michael Lewis, *The Premonition: A Pandemic Story*

Chiara Marletto, *The Science of Can and Can't: A Physicist's Journey Through the Land of Counterfactuals*

Suzanne Simard, *Finding the Mother Tree: Uncovering the Wisdom and Intelligence of the Forest*

Giles Fraser, *Chosen: Lost and Found between Christianity and Judaism*

Malcolm Gladwell, *The Bomber Mafia: A Story Set in War*

Kate Darling, *The New Breed: How to Think About Robots*

Serhii Plokhy, *Nuclear Folly: A New History of the Cuban Missile Crisis*

Sean McMeekin, *Stalin's War*

Michio Kaku, *The God Equation: The Quest for a Theory of Everything*

Michael Barber, *Accomplishment: How to Achieve Ambitious and Challenging Things*

Charles Townshend, *The Partition: Ireland Divided, 1885-1925*

Hanif Abdurraqib, *A Little Devil in America: In Priase of Black Performance*

Carlo Rovelli, *Helgoland*

Herman Pontzer, *Burn: The Misunderstood Science of Metabolism*

Jordan B. Peterson, *Beyond Order: 12 More Rules for Life*

Bill Gates, *How to Avoid a Climate Disaster: The Solutions We Have and the Breakthroughs We Need*

Kehinde Andrews, *The New Age of Empire: How Racism and Colonialism Still Rule the World*

Veronica O'Keane, *The Rag and Bone Shop: How We Make Memories and Memories Make Us*

Robert Tombs, *This Sovereign Isle: Britain In and Out of Europe*

Mariana Mazzucato, *Mission Economy: A Moonshot Guide to Changing Capitalism*

Frank Wilczek, *Fundamentals: Ten Keys to Reality*

Milo Beckman, *Math Without Numbers*

John Sellars, *The Fourfold Remedy: Epicurus and the Art of Happiness*

T. G. Otte, *Statesman of Europe: A Life of Sir Edward Grey*

Alex Kerr, *Finding the Heart Sutra: Guided by a Magician, an Art Collector and Buddhist Sages from Tibet to Japan*

Edwin Gale, *The Species That Changed Itself: How Prosperity Reshaped Humanity*

Simon Baron-Cohen, *The Pattern Seekers: A New Theory of Human Invention*

Christopher Harding, *The Japanese: A History of Twenty Lives*

Carlo Rovelli, *There Are Places in the World Where Rules Are Less Important Than Kindness*

Ritchie Robertson, *The Enlightenment: The Pursuit of Happiness 1680-1790*

Ivan Krastev, *Is It Tomorrow Yet?: Paradoxes of the Pandemic*

Tim Harper, *Underground Asia: Global Revolutionaries and the Assault on Empire*

John Gray, *Feline Philosophy: Cats and the Meaning of Life*

Priya Satia, *Time's Monster: History, Conscience and Britain's Empire*

Fareed Zakaria, *Ten Lessons for a Post-Pandemic World*

David Sumpter, *The Ten Equations that Rule the World: And How You Can Use Them Too*

Richard J. Evans, *The Hitler Conspiracies: The Third Reich and the Paranoid Imagination*

Fernando Cervantes, *Conquistadores*

John Darwin, *Unlocking the World: Port Cities and Globalization in the Age of Steam, 1830-1930*

Michael Strevens, *The Knowledge Machine: How an Unreasonable Idea Created Modern Science*

Owen Jones, *This Land: The Story of a Movement*

Seb Falk, *The Light Ages: A Medieval Journey of Discovery*

Daniel Yergin, *The New Map: Energy, Climate, and the Clash of Nations*

Michael J. Sandel, *The Tyranny of Merit: What's Become of the Common Good?*

Joseph Henrich, *The Weirdest People in the World: How the West Became Psychologically Peculiar and Particularly Prosperous*

Leonard Mlodinow, *Stephen Hawking: A Memoir of Friendship and Physics*

David Goodhart, *Head Hand Heart: The Struggle for Dignity and Status in the 21st Century*

Claudia Rankine, *Just Us: An American Conversation*

James Rebanks, *English Pastoral: An Inheritance*

Robin Lane Fox, *The Invention of Medicine: From Homer to Hippocrates*

Daniel Lieberman, *Exercised: The Science of Physical Activity, Rest and Health*

Sudhir Hazareesingh, *Black Spartacus: The Epic Life of Touissaint Louverture*

Judith Herrin, *Ravenna: Capital of Empire, Crucible of Europe*

Samantha Cristoforetti, *Diary of an Apprentice Astronaut*

Neil Price, *The Children of Ash and Elm: A History of the Vikings*

George Dyson, *Analogia: The Entangled Destinies of Nature, Human Beings and Machines*

Wolfram Eilenberger, *Time of the Magicians: The Invention of Modern Thought, 1919-1929*

Kate Manne, *Entitled: How Male Privilege Hurts Women*

Christopher de Hamel, *The Book in the Cathedral: The Last Relic of Thomas Becket*

Isabel Wilkerson, *Caste: The International Bestseller*

Bradley Garrett, *Bunker: Building for the End Times*

Katie Mack, *The End of Everything: (Astrophysically Speaking)*

Jonathan C. Slaght, *Owls of the Eastern Ice: The Quest to Find and Save the World's Largest Owl*

Carl T. Bergstrom and Jevin D. West, *Calling Bullshit: The Art of Scepticism in a Data-Driven World*

Paul Collier and John Kay, *Greed Is Dead: Politics After Individualism*

Anne Applebaum, *Twilight of Democracy: The Failure of Politics and the Parting of Friends*

Sarah Stewart Johnson, *The Sirens of Mars: Searching for Life on Another World*

Martyn Rady, *The Habsburgs: The Rise and Fall of a World Power*

John Gooch, *Mussolini's War: Fascist Italy from Triumph to Collapse, 1935-1943*

Roger Scruton, *Wagner's Parsifal: The Music of Redemption*

Roberto Calasso, *The Celestial Hunter*

Benjamin R. Teitelbaum, *War for Eternity: The Return of Traditionalism and the Rise of the Populist Right*

Laurence C. Smith, *Rivers of Power: How a Natural Force Raised Kingdoms, Destroyed Civilizations, and Shapes Our World*

Sharon Moalem, *The Better Half: On the Genetic Superiority of Women*

Augustine Sedgwick, *Coffeeland: A History*

Daniel Todman, *Britain's War: A New World, 1942-1947*

Anatol Lieven, *Climate Change and the Nation State: The Realist Case*

Blake Gopnik, *Warhol: A Life as Art*

Malena and Beata Ernman, Svante and Greta Thunberg, *Our House is on Fire: Scenes of a Family and a Planet in Crisis*

Paolo Zellini, *The Mathematics of the Gods and the Algorithms of Men: A Cultural History*

Bari Weiss, *How to Fight Anti-Semitism*

Lucy Jones, *Losing Eden: Why Our Minds Need the Wild*

Brian Greene, *Until the End of Time: Mind, Matter, and Our Search for Meaning in an Evolving Universe*

Anastasia Nesvetailova and Ronen Palan, *Sabotage: The Business of Finance*

Albert Costa, *The Bilingual Brain: And What It Tells Us about the Science of Language*

Stanislas Dehaene, *How We Learn: The New Science of Education and the Brain*

Daniel Susskind, *A World Without Work: Technology, Automation and How We Should Respond*

John Tierney and Roy F. Baumeister, *The Power of Bad: And How to Overcome It*

Greta Thunberg, *No One Is Too Small to Make a Difference: Illustrated Edition*

Glenn Simpson and Peter Fritsch, *Crime in Progress: The Secret History of the Trump-Russia Investigation*

Abhijit V. Banerjee and Esther Duflo, *Good Economics for Hard Times: Better Answers to Our Biggest Problems*

Gaia Vince, *Transcendence: How Humans Evolved through Fire, Language, Beauty and Time*

Roderick Floud, *An Economic History of the English Garden*

Rana Foroohar, *Don't Be Evil: The Case Against Big Tech*

Ivan Krastev and Stephen Holmes, *The Light that Failed: A Reckoning*

Andrew Roberts, *Leadership in War: Lessons from Those Who Made History*

Alexander Watson, *The Fortress: The Great Siege of Przemysl*

Stuart Russell, *Human Compatible: AI and the Problem of Control*

Serhii Plokhy, *Forgotten Bastards of the Eastern Front: An Untold Story of World War II*

Dominic Sandbrook, *Who Dares Wins: Britain, 1979-1982*

Charles Moore, *Margaret Thatcher: The Authorized Biography, Volume Three: Herself Alone*

Thomas Penn, *The Brothers York: An English Tragedy*

David Abulafia, *The Boundless Sea: A Human History of the Oceans*

Anthony Aguirre, *Cosmological Koans: A Journey to the Heart of Physics*

Orlando Figes, *The Europeans: Three Lives and the Making of a Cosmopolitan Culture*

Naomi Klein, *On Fire: The Burning Case for a Green New Deal*

Anne Boyer, *The Undying: A Meditation on Modern Illness*

Benjamin Moser, *Sontag: Her Life*

Daniel Markovits, *The Meritocracy Trap*

Malcolm Gladwell, *Talking to Strangers: What We Should Know about the People We Don't Know*

Peter Hennessy, *Winds of Change: Britain in the Early Sixties*

John Sellars, *Lessons in Stoicism: What Ancient Philosophers Teach Us about How to Live*

Brendan Simms, *Hitler: Only the World Was Enough*

Hassan Damluji, *The Responsible Globalist: What Citizens of the World Can Learn from Nationalism*

Peter Gatrell, *The Unsettling of Europe: The Great Migration, 1945 to the Present*

Justin Marozzi, *Islamic Empires: Fifteen Cities that Define a Civilization*

Bruce Hood, *Possessed: Why We Want More Than We Need*

Susan Neiman, *Learning from the Germans: Confronting Race and the Memory of Evil*